Lívia De Souza Lima, Edith Otero Quezada, Julia Roth (eds.)
Feminisms in Movement

Gender Studies

Lívia De Souza Lima is a PhD candidate in InterAmerican Studies at Universität Bielefeld and a fellow at the Rosa Luxemburg Foundation. Her main research focus lies in the intersection of gender and political representation, in which she works with Black and decolonial feminist perspectives.

Edith Otero Quezada is a PhD candidate in InterAmerican Studies and a member of the research training group "Experiencing Gender" at the Interdisciplinary Center for Gender Studies at Universität Bielefeld. Her research interests are postcolonial and decolonial feminist epistemologies, political subjectivity, (post)memory, guerrillas, and social movements, especially in Latin America and Central America.

Julia Roth is a professor of American studies with a focus on gender studies and director of the Center for InterAmerican Studies (CIAS) at Universität Bielefeld, where she is also PI of the graduate school "Experiencing Gender". Her research interests are gender approaches, intersectionality theorizing, gender and citizenship, right-wing populism and gender, migrant knowledges and new feminist movements.

Lívia De Souza Lima, Edith Otero Quezada, Julia Roth (eds.)
Feminisms in Movement
Theories and Practices from the Americas

[transcript]

The publication of this volume was made possible thanks to the the generous support of the Bielefeld University Library and the DFG Graduate School "Experiencing Gender. Constitution and Transformation of Being in the World."

Bibliographic information published by the Deutsche Nationalbibliothek
The Deutsche Nationalbibliothek lists this publication in the Deutsche Nationalbibliografie; detailed bibliographic data are available in the Internet at http://https://dnb.dnb.de/

This work is licensed under the Creative Commons Attribution-NonCommercial-NoDerivatives 4.0 (BY-NC-ND) which means that the text may be used for non-commercial purposes, provided credit is given to the author.
https://creativecommons.org/licenses/by-nc-nd/4.0/
To create an adaptation, translation, or derivative of the original work and for commercial use, further permission is required and can be obtained by contacting rights@transcript-publishing.com
Creative Commons license terms for re-use do not apply to any content (such as graphs, figures, photos, excerpts, etc.) not original to the Open Access publication and further permission may be required from the rights holder. The obligation to research and clear permission lies solely with the party re-using the material.

First published in 2024 by transcript Verlag, Bielefeld
© Lívia De Souza Lima, Edith Otero Quezada, Julia Roth (eds.)

Cover layout: Kordula Röckenhaus, Bielefeld
Printed by: Majuskel Medienproduktion GmbH, Wetzlar
https://doi.org/10.14361/9783839461020
Print-ISBN: 978-3-8376-6102-6
PDF-ISBN: 978-3-8394-6102-0
ISSN of series: 2625-0128
eISSN of series: 2703-0482

Printed on permanent acid-free text paper.

Contents

Introduction
Julia Roth, Edith Otero Quezada and Lívia de Souza Lima 9

Part I
Theorizations and Epistemic Dialogues

The Coloniality of Gender
María Lugones 35

Coloniality and Modern Patriarchy
Expansion of the State Front, Modernization, and the Lives of Women
Rita Laura Segato 59

A Decolonial Critique of Feminist Epistemology Critique
Yuderkys Espinosa-Miñoso 79

From the Center to the Margins, (Re)Politicizing Intersectionality
Mara Viveros Vigoya 91

The Feminist and Decolonial Pedagogy of Lélia Gonzalez and Sueli Carneiro
Lívia de Souza Lima 107

Gender-Based Political Violence as a Global Phenomenon
Latin-American Pioneerism, the Brazilian Exception,
and the Silence of the Global North
Ligia Fabris 117

An Analysis of the 11J Protests in Cuba from a Black Feminist Criminal Abolitionist Perspective
Sandra Heidl 133

Territory Body – Body Territory
Julieta Paredes Carvajal 147

Part II
Embodied Experiences and Knowledge Productions

Ties that Bind
Black Women Candidates and Familial Influence on Political Socialization in the US
Nadia E. Brown and India S. Lenear.. 161

"Vamos destruir esse patriarcado, eu creio!"
Inter-American Networks and Articulations of Feminism on Social Media
Saskia Bante... 173

Intersectional Praxis and Socio-Political Transformation at the Colombian Truth Commission in the Caribbean Region
Audes Jiménez González and Juliana González Villamizar 187

Reconstructing Women's Contemporary Political Struggles across the Central American Region
Edith Otero Quezada and Fátima Elizondo Rodríguez 201

Writing Western Nicaragua's LGBTQ+ History
Tiangues, Indigeneity, and Survivance
Victoria González-Rivera... 215

Conceptual Tensions within a *Cuir* [Queer]-Feminist Sociological Approach to Sexuality in Mexico
César Torres-Cruz and Hortensia Moreno-Esparza 227

"May Our Voice Echo"
Housemaids' Narratives in *Eu, Empregada Doméstica*
Larissa Satico Ribeiro Higa 239

Indigenous Literature and Ecofeminism in Brazil
Anna-Lena Glesinski.. 249

Environmental Knowledges in Resistance
Mobilization, (Re)Production, and the Politics of Place. The Case of the
Cooperativa Mujeres Ecologistas de la Huizachera, Jalisco (Mexico)
Daniela Gloss Nuñez and Itxaso García Chapinal......................................261

Part III
Feminist Conversations

Set Fear on Fire!
A Conversation with the Collective LASTESIS on Aesthetic, Performance and
Feminist Resistant Practices
Edith Otero Quezada and Lívia de Souza Lima 277

Marielle Presente!
Defending the Memory and Legacy of Marielle Franco in Brazil.
An Interview with Anielle Franco
Lívia de Souza Lima, Julia Roth and Edith Otero Quezada........................... 283

Feminist Activism and Constitutional Change in Chile
A Conversation with María José Oyarzún Solís
Nicole Schwabe 291

"Rap is Our Best Feminist Tool"
Interview with the Cuban Hip Hop Duo La Reyna y La Real
Julia Roth.. 295

Memory, Re-Imagination and Commemoration
Bridging Academia and Activism. An Interview with Afua Cooper
Safa Al-Dilaimi 301

Intuitive Feminism
María Galindo 313

Contributors 321

Introduction

Julia Roth, Edith Otero Quezada and Lívia de Souza Lima

Feminist organizing and theorizing from "the Americas" have provided some of the most innovative, visible, and all-encompassing voices of resistance against sexism and sexualized violence, misogyny, racism, homo- and transphobia, coloniality, extractivism, climate change, and neoliberal capitalist exploitation (Butler 2015; Roth 2021). This volume seeks to provide insight into a selection of such perspectives, practices, resistances and reconfigurations of the region, e.g. as Abya Yala[1] or Améfrica Ladina[2].

Albeit in the form of different local experiences, the Americas are marked by a long history of "colonization as en-gendering," that is, of creating hierarchies and naturalizations between the colonizers and the colonized (Boatcă 2014; Roth 2014). Conversely, colonial and post-colonial structures of inequality have been marked by a (racialized/intersectional) gender dimension, while gender itself is embedded in colonial power relations (Lugones 2008). This power asymmetry is effective particularly also on the epistemic level, the level of knowledge and theory (Wynter 1990). Such entanglements produced constellations of differently gendered positions between White women, enslaved women of African descent, and native/indigenous women (see Lugones 2008). Although women shared the experience of patriarchal violence and domination all over the Americas, they did so in very different degrees of intensity and intersectionally diverging ways.

---

1 Abya Yala is a term used to refer to the American continent. Its origin can be traced back to the time before European colonization. It is a word from the Kuna language which means "land in its full maturity" or "land of vital blood". Nowadays, the term is widely used by indigenous movements across the region.

2 *Améfrica Ladina* is a concept coined by Black Brazilian feminist Lélia Gonzalez in 1988, offering an Afro-Latin-American and Amerindian perspective of Latin America. The Latin American Studies Association adopted the term for its 2020 conference (Améfrica Ladina: vinculando mundos y saberes, tejiendo esperanzas).

As a consequence of the founding of the Americas within a patriarchal and enslaving colonial order, feminist activities have also, from the outset, been marked by historically produced, close entanglements of race and gender hierarchies and discourses. Feminist practices and politics have varied from context to context in the Americas, providing a wide spectrum of differing feminist movements and positions. Simultaneously, feminists sought transnational alliances in order to fight for common goals on the international level, as well. Many practiced what feminist philosopher and queer theorist Judith Butler (1992) calls "contingent foundations" in order to fight inequality; and, in a similar vein, postcolonial critic Gayatri Spivak calls for a "strategic essentialism" to fight the patriarchy (Spivak 1989). Both the exclusion of women and the system of enslavement exposed the contradictions implicit in the Declaration of Human Rights. It is hence no coincidence that there have been numerous parallel developments and alliances between abolitionist and feminist struggles (see Roth 2019).

A Long Legacy of Resistance to Colonial and Gendered Oppressions

Feminist practices thus long predate the emergence of the term or the movement of 'feminism'. Women have historically opposed their dehumanization, exploitation, and enslavement and fought the slave trade and plantation slavery both in the West Indies and Latin America (Shepherd 2008a; 2008b). Numerous enslaved women also escaped and lived as *"cimarronas"* in maroon societies or in hiding, as they confronted violent and exploitative masters, held birth strikes, participated in abolitionist groups, or sung protest songs (see Shepherd 2008a).

All over the Americas, the Haitian Revolution of 1793 had a decisive impact on abolitionist thinking, practices, and organizing. While around the same time in Europe, White feminists bemoaned that the newly introduced, allegedly "universal" Human Rights applied only to White male property owners, leaving out women (Olympe de Gouges 1791, Mary Wollstonecraft 1792), formerly enslaved Black abolitionist Sojourner Truth in her 1851 speech and intervention "Ain't I a Woman?" at the Women's Rights Convention Akron, Ohio, questioned the universality of White bourgeois feminism. By pointing out her experience as a Black and formerly enslaved woman, Truth anticipated the problem of differences between women and the entanglement of class, racialization, coloniality, and gender, on which recent intersectional practices and theorizing are built.

Consequently, contemporary movements and epistemologies are building on their long legacy of anti-racist feminist struggles, which offers them a rich repertoire of experiences and resistance strategies to counter the extremist and right-wing populist trend and challenges to women's and gender rights.

In the form of numerous and diverse protests and mobilizations against old and new injustices, feminist movements have recently gained great visibility throughout the Americas. Most prominently, the #NiUnaMenos/#NiUnaMás movement, which had started as a protest against femicides and violence against women in Argentina and Mexico in 2015, has grown into one of the largest protests and also inspired the International Women's Strike, also known as *Paro Internacional de Mujeres* or "8M" (see Bidaseca 2017). Feminist collectives such as *Mujeres Creando* and *Mujeres Creando Comunidad* in Bolivia regularly intervene in public spaces with their performances or practice what is now called Communitarian-Feminism. So do LASTESIS and the different feminist collectives in Chile, where the enormous feminist mobilizations of the last years paved the way for a more inclusive government in Chile in 2021 (14 out of 24 ministers being women). Feminist mobilizations, referred to as the "Green Wave" (*marea verde* in Spanish), urged lawmakers to decriminalize and ensure safe access to abortion in Argentina in 2022. In the same year, the afro-descendant politician Francia Márquez Mina was elected the first vice president of Color in Colombia. Before that, both the inaugurations of Donald Trump as US president in January 2016 and of Jair Bolsonaro in Brazil in 2017 had been accompanied by massive feminist mobilizations.

Many current practices, movements, and theorizations throughout the Americas address and attack, in particular, structural axes of inequality and oppression such as coloniality, capitalism, and neoliberalism. They call attention to the notion of violence against women as a structural phenomenon, the systemic devaluation of care work and reproduction, the need for reparations (for enslavement, etc.), for climate justice and reproductive justice and denounce the fallacy of dependency on debts (see Gago 2014, 2017, 2019; Gago et al. 2018; Gago/Cavalleri 2021a, 2021b). Activists of current movements often dialogue between diverse histories and notions of the political, creating a communal body of feminist resistance. In the form of concepts like body-territory (*cuerpo-territorio*, Cabnal 2010, 2016; Paredes 2009, 2015; Zaragocin/Caretta 2020; Cruz 2016; Colectivo Miradas Críticas al Territorio desde el Feminismo 2017), *mestizaje ch'ixi*³ (Rivera Cusiquanci 2012, 2018, 2023) or "the body as a political tool" (Kilomba 2019), feminists of Color and post- and decolonial feminists have long emphasized the importance of the bodily dimension for decolonial feminist aims and for imagining a new poetics and aesthetics.

Based on the described particular history and plurivocality, feminist politics from the Americas connect the "intersectional" focus on the simultaneously articulated and interrelated axes of inequalities and oppression back to the radical roots from which the concept of intersectionality originated (Roth 2018). The notion of "interlocking axes of oppression" goes back to afro-descendant and often queer activists like Sojourner Truth (1851), and later, the Mulheres Negras in Brazil (1975 qtd. in Caldwell 2007) or the Combahee River Collective in the US (1981 [1977]). Their practices and contributions provide a lens for the overlapping and entangled character of categorizations, positions, and hierarchies. The term intersectionality was coined by African American lawyer and activist Kimberlé Crenshaw for a concrete lawsuit involving racial and gender discrimination in the US in 1989 (Crenshaw 1989). Mara Viveros Vigoya (see her contribution in this volume) observes a recent repolitization of the concept of intersectionality, particularly in the context of anti-racist feminist and non-academic movements in the Americas as well as on the epistemic level. Marisa Belausteguigoitia (2009) stresses that to overcome persisting inequalities on the level of knowledge and the production of theory, a dialogue encompassing all parties requires the critical reflection of (academic) disciplines. Decolonial feminist artists and thinkers have also stressed the close entanglement between racialized, gendered, and classed hierarchies with the global inequalities produced by colonial hierarchies and the legacies of enslavement and persistent "North-South" exploitation (see e.g. Lugones 2010; Wynter 1990, 2003; Millán 2014), promoting instead new forms of living together and connectedness. However, all over the Americas, contributions by Black, Chicana, and indigenous feminists have been continuously and structurally rendered invisible, marginalized, and barely quoted in hegemonic feminist contexts and dominant historiographies.

---

3   ch'ixi is an aymara concept that refers to a color formed by juxtaposed black and white dots. Cusicanqui uses this concept to formulate a decolonial and radical notion of mestizaje and a critique of multicultural politics. "Mestizaje ch'ixi inspires a recognition of the strength emerging from lo indio [the indigenous], by being able to inhabit different worlds at once, to think-feel from a closer connection with nature and others" (Rodríguez 2020: 154).

Such feminist contestations show how movements in many parts of the Americas build alliances of solidarity that denounce entangled forms of oppression towards alternative notions of sociability (see Butler 2015). Through their presence in diversity, they further place the myth of separateness, pureness, and linearity – which often also goes unquestioned in hegemonic feminist discourses – under severe scrutiny. They raise hope for an effective counter-discourse to the current rise and revival of White supremacist and racist, sexist, and homo- and trans'phobic' extremist and right-wing tendencies internationally.

Recently (as of 2023), a number of publications have taken the great variety and potential of feminist practice, knowledge, and theorizing from the Americas into account (Roth 2004; Espinosa Damián 2009, 2011; Tambora Dialogues 2022). Newer studies are placing greater focus on social inequalities such as gender relations as being global in scale, transregionally (and, sometimes, globally) interrelated[4], and decolonial[5]. Furthermore, there has recently also been a considerable number of publications voicing a broad range of feminisms, particularly in Spanish[6] and a few in Portuguese[7] with some first translations into English[8]. This imbalance points to the persistent epistemic asymmetries and epistemic violence in and between the Americas (and globally) with regard to access to knowledge production, circulation and translation. And to the persistent, still widely omnipresent division between center and periphery of "relevant" theory that, in the words of Sylvia Wynter, defines who and where are the "theory-givers/(and the) theory-takers" (Wynter 1990: 359). It also points to the difficulties of translating particular contexts and cosmovisions from one context to another and across power hierarchies (see e.g. Álvarez et.al. 2014; Curiel/Pión 2022).

---

4   See e.g. Álvarez et.al. 2003; Shepherd et al. 1995; Shepherd 2008, 2008b; Rodríguez Aguilera 2018; Poferl/Winkel 2021; Scheele/Roth/Winkel 2022.
5   See e.g. Mohanty 2003; Suárez Návaz/Hernández 2008; Lugones 2010; Bidaseca/Vázquez Laba 2011; Espinosa-Miñoso/Gómez Correal/Ochoa Muñoz 2014; Espinosa-Miñoso 2019; Espinosa-Miñoso/Lugones/Maldonado-Torres 2021; Espinosa-Miñoso/Pión 2022; Vergès 2021; Cabnal 2010, 2016; Antivilo 2022;
6   Rubiera Castillo/Martiatu 2011; Espinosa Damián 2009; Espinosa-Miñoso/Gómez Correal/Ochoa Muñoz 2014.
7   Barrancos 2022; Hollanda 2020.
8   E.g. Rubiera Castillo/Martiatu Terry 2020; Gago 2020; Espinosa-Miñoso/Lugones/Maldonado-Torres 2021.

Our volume seeks to present a selection of positions, reflections, concepts, forms, and formats that neither is, nor aims to be, complete or representative. Rather, our aim is to stir curiosity in, direct attention to, and encourage to be inspired by this broad field of feminist, anti-racist, anti-colonial, decolonial, communitarian, intersectional and queer/*cuir* knowledge production. The contributors bring together various perspectives, ranging from Black and decolonial feminist voices, LGBTQ+/queer perspectives to ecofeminist approaches and indigenous women's mobilizations to inspire future feminist practices and inform social and cohabitation projects.

Reading Feminisms in the Americas: Temporality, Movement, and Embodied Experiences

This volume on feminisms in the Americas suggests reading feminisms in the region along three central axes/concepts to map these diverse dimensions: temporality, movement, and embodied experiences. Based on these axes, we ask ourselves: Why should we talk about feminism in the plural form? How do we dialogue with other forms of feminism and women's struggles without employing a linear time frame, as typically used in conventional historical timelines of feminism? How is the relationship between body-practice-theory built in contemporary social movements and political struggles? And finally, from a more transnational perspective, what tensions and/or (dis)connections exist between feminist and queer/*cuir* movements in the Americas in the different global Norths and Souths?

Thus, we start from an idea of *Temporalidad Mixta* [Mixed Temporality] (see Ansaldi 2000; Quijano 1988), i.e., non-linearity, which allows us to transcend the dichotomies between action-structure, diachronic-synchronic, center-periphery, among others. Rodríguez Aguilera (2018) argues that feminisms must be understood as "historical genealogies and simultaneous geographies, with their multiple contradictions and complexities,"[9] (91) meaning that feminisms, especially in the Americas, cannot be viewed from a geographical and historical North that subsequently descends, transits, and imposes itself on the South, but rather as multiple and entangled histories.

---

9   All translations from Spanish into English are our own. All the quotes from Rodríguez Aguilera 2018, Curiel 2009 and Sayak 2021 were originally in Spanish.

Similarly, Ochy Curiel (2009) explains that even though the history of feminism is commonly reconstructed from the first wave[10] with the suffragist struggle, this temporality often ignores other genealogies of women's history and their resistance to patriarchy, thus reinforcing the "knowledge-power relationship [which] has to do with the birth of the modern world system" (1). To decolonize feminism and make room for multiple genealogies and subjects requires including, recognizing, and dialoging with those women's struggles, communitarian or mixed organizations, which, without calling themselves feminist, produce forms of subversion and resistance to the different systems of oppression and exploitation in their everyday life.

We are aware that there has been a long discussion around the definition of the subject of feminism – especially lately and with the emergence of trans-exclusionary discourses. While the aim of this book and introduction is not to give a final answer to this question, as this would require a much broader and collective exercise, we suggest three insights on the topic. The first insight is the critique of the category "women" by Black and Afro-Caribbean activists and/or scholars. As Audre Lorde (2007[1984]), Yuderkys Espinosa-Miñoso (n.d.), and Ochy Curiel (2009, 2013) argue, White and mainstream feminisms have tried to homogenize this category in the name of an apparent "collective unity". This notion led to the erasure of the diversity of contexts, struggles, sexualities, oppressions, intersections, and bodies that affected women – especially Black and racialized women. The second insight is related to Judith Butler's (2002) critique on the idea of the 'subject' that has been key to thinking feminist politics. As Butler has pointed out, subjects themselves are paradoxically constituted by the linguistic, juridical, and political systems of power from which they wish to emancipate themselves. This paradox has real political effects,

---

10   There has been a long-standing discussion about whether the metaphor of waves is still useful to narrate the history of feminism, because most of the times, there are no clear boundaries where they begin and end, instead there are overlaps which transcend the linear and intergenerational time frame (see also Roth 2004). An interesting read on the topic is Amneris Chaparro's (2022) analysis of the value and limitations of the metaphor of the waves, understanding them as an epistemological tool. Nowadays, it is more common to find other metaphors to talk about feminisms, their historicity, and expressions, for example, the metaphor of the tsunami (Jáuregui 2018, 2021); fire as an element of transmutation used by the Chilean collective LASTESIS (2021, 2023); or the "marea verde" [green wave] to refer to the struggle for the decriminalization of abortion. All these aesthetic and literary expressions make a political call to build new imaginaries.

especially when we think about political representation. Therefore, new feminist politics should question the very stability of gender and identity. Finally, we find suggestive the ideas of the Mexican philosopher Sayak Valencia (2010, 2018, 2021) who points out that transfeminism[11] allows us to expand, repoliticize, and de-essentialize the subjects of feminism and build diverse alliances with other g-local feminist movements without the (re)stigmatization of sexual, gender identities, and racialized bodies. In doing so, we could fight what she described as Necroliberalism or Gore Capitalism, which as Valencia (2021) explains is "the use of necropolitical[12] techniques applied by the neoliberal capitalist regime to generate economic, political or social capital through violence and death" (22).

The second axis/concept around which we suggest reading feminisms is movement; a concept that can be understood in two ways: First, movement can be seen in opposition to all sorts of borders (geographical, corporal, cultural, analytical, epistemological, among others) and constructions of otherness. At the same time, however, transborder spaces enable what Edward W. Soja (1989, 2008) and Homi Bhabha (2004) called "Third Space," from which groups such as Chicanas raise their voices in the US. For example, Gloria Anzaldúa (1987) spoke of "the Borderlands/La Frontera" to describe the concrete physical border between Mexico and the USA, and simultaneously, of persons living between spaces, genders, identities, etc. Our second understanding of movement is related to the variety of feminist and queer/*cuir* movements in the Americas, which, from their political practice, bodily construct what we could call "intersectional politics," or "embodied intersectionality" (Mirza 2013; Roth 2020). #Ni

---

11   On transfeminism from a global perspective, see: Transgender Marxism (2021), edited by Jules Joanne Gleeson and Elle O'Rourke, the first book to critically discuss the possible common ground shared by transgender studies and Marxist theory. For a transnational perspective, see also Feminism for the 99%: A manifesto by Arruzza/Bhattacharya/Fraser (2019), which analyzes the shortcomings of liberal and hegemonic feminism and combines the existing struggles of women in different parts of the world with the demands of workers, environmental, LGQTB+ and indigenous movements, etc. in order to build a more internationalist, inclusive and intersectional feminism.

12   Valencia takes up Achille Mbembe's (2003) concept of necropolitics, understood as a form of politics of death or "contemporary forms of subjection of life to the power of death" (39). However, Valencia explores more deeply how certain markets and economic capitalist systems – e.g. drug trafficking – are built around death. In these processes, the author explains, "the destruction of the body becomes in itself the product or commodity" (2018: 13).

Una Menos in Argentina, Marielle Presente in Brazil, *#Black Lives Matter* in the USA, the communitarian feminists in Abya Yala and Central America's Caravan of Mothers provide further examples of such representations.[13]

The third lens we suggest for contextualizing feminisms in the Americas is embodied experiences. Authors such as Donna Haraway (2004) and Sandra Harding (2004) have argued for a feminist epistemology and the notion of Situated Knowledge, which breaks with the idea of the universality of androcentric theory. Black, Latin American, Caribbean, and indigenous feminist authors such as bell hooks, Yuderkys Espinosa-Miñoso, Julieta Paredes Carvajal, Breny Mendoza and Lélia Gonzalez, from their different intersections, also reflect individually and collectively on the relationship between body, practice, and theory, understanding them as entangled processes. From a regional and global perspective, a new generation of feminist researchers and activists, as we can see in this book, follow a similar path to understand their own reality and break/overcome power relationships between the so-called Global North and Global South.

bell hooks (1991) states that theory should not be conceived as a disembodied and abstract place, but as a deep, critical reflection on our reality. Therefore, the exercise of theorizing is circular and dialogical: It starts from the concrete, the bodily experiences (individual and collective), resulting in a permanent political practice of healing and transformation. Such a practice helps us to rethink what Breny Mendoza (2014) calls "política del cuerpo propia" [our own body politics] (451) that puts the diverse intersections, contexts, affects, and complexities of the region at the center, especially in political and economic terms, something that tends to be absent from Western feminist theories.

Hence, through different formats (poetry, essays, and interviews), the contributions of this book approach and dialogue with this mosaic/kaleidoscope of voices and bodies that we call feminisms in movement. As our brief outline shows, current feminist movements, practices, and epistemologies address a broad range of different axes of oppression in their entanglement and thereby represent, practice, and theorize an "intersectional" politics oriented towards praxis and activism.

13　Due to the great diversity of feminist struggles in the region, it is impossible to name all of them here. We name only a few of them in this introduction to exemplify, not generalize, such resistances.

Feminisms in Dialogue

The contributions of this volume are organized into three main parts: Theorizations and Epistemic Dialogues, Embodied Experiences and Knowledge Productions, and Feminist Conversations. We choose to work with these categories to show the different forms of expression employed in the feminist struggles, to exhibit the persistence of gender inequalities and to showcase how women and queer/*cuir* subjects skilfully project escape routes from intersectional structures of domination.

In this introduction, we present the contributions according to their conceptual clusters, outlining how they intersect and dialogue with each other, instead of announcing the chapters in the sequence they appear in the volume. Herewith, we demonstrate the connections among the feminists and activists writing and acting from different regions and positionalities, illustrating the diversity of the feminist movements, theorizations, and practices as well as the intellectual and political synergy of women and LGBTQ+ activism in the Americas. Feminism, or rather feminisms, integrate and align theory, practice, and reality, bearing a critical perspective on conceptual and structural debates that, even if developed as abstract concepts, serve as powerful tools for understanding material realities from the standpoint of those who are oppressed.

The rich contributions shared in this volume address particular themes and genres but are fundamentally based on four key dimensions: 'Coloniality of Gender', 'Black feminism', 'Intersectionality' and 'Methodologies and Pedagogies of Resistance'. Likewise, we employ these thematic categories in mapping out the chapters that compose this volume.

Coloniality of Gender

We start the volume with the seminal discussion inaugurated by María Lugones, when the author launched the concept of 'coloniality of gender'. In this classic text, originally published in 2007, Lugones uses the concept of intersectionality to enrich Aníbal Quijano's discussion of the colonial matrix of power. In thinking specifically about colonial violence against women of Color, Lugones suggests that the modern colonial system is, in fact, a colonial/modern gender system. In general, the intention here is to understand that gender domination over women's bodies and existence is not only an axis or a perspective under which we can understand the development of the new modern colonial order, but that gender is a cornerstone for understanding the transformations imposed by the colonizers in the colonization process, which introduced gender positions for the colonized that were very different from those of the colonizers, and gender itself as a colonial category. The chapters that engage more closely with the colonial legacies of gender and sexual difference highlight the relations between colonial domination and feminism, sharpening this critical debate, including in their analysis the discussions on the coloniality of knowledge and epistemic erasures of traditions of thought conceived at the margins.

Rita Laura Segato's text dialogues directly with María Lugones and suggests a theoretical turn that introduces gender and domination over women as an integral aspect of the development and consolidation of what she calls the new modern colonial order. Segato, however, makes a critical comment on María Lugones' initial assertions, showing that gender and sexual differences were present already in pre-colonial social relations. For Segato, the new modern colonial order transformed the meanings of the gender difference that already existed in pre-colonial societies. What the colonizing interference changed, according to Segato, is that it introduced the colonial/modern exteriority with its notion of sin and morality, of gender binarism and a public/private divide that did not exist in the territory of the conviviality of native and indigenous communities.

In close intersection with Segato's, Julieta Paredes Carvajal' text underlines the existence of unequal relations between men and women in indigenous and pre-colonial societies. Inserted in the political message of decolonization of feminism, the author talks about the proposal of Abya Yala Communitarian-Feminism [*Feminismo Comunitario* in Spanish] to perform interpretations about patriarchy and the capitalist system that emerge from the experiences of the bodies of impoverished, indigenous, rural women and rural workers. Through these embodied experiences, Julieta Paredes Carvajal draws attention to how the colonial gender system introduces hierarchical differences across lines of race, class, and territory that ultimately make other women complicit in a system of gender domination.

Yuderkys Espinosa-Miñoso assembles a feminist critique emerging from her experience as an anti-racist and decolonial intellectual. Focusing on the aspect of the coloniality of knowledge, Espinosa-Miñoso shows how decolonial feminisms, by recovering critical knowledge from women in counter-hegemonic trajectories, construct a critical revision of White, liberal, bourgeois feminism. Decolonial feminists radicalize the critique of universalism by emphasizing that gender, as a category of domination, never operates in an isolated way and stresses that employing an intersectional perspective is a political urgency to make the differences between women salient.

In a critical dialogue with the concepts of coloniality of gender and knowledge, Daniela Gloss Nuñez and Itxaso García Chapinal discuss the concept of environmental knowledge to defend a non-hierarchical dialogue within the coexistence and acceptance of epistemologies that defy the colonial mode of intellectual production. Reflecting on the case of a cooperative run by women, the Cooperativa de Mujeres Ecologistas de la Huizachera in Mexico, the authors describe and discuss how women in action mobilize knowledge that emerges from their collective experience as a means of intervention in their realities.

The last contribution to criticize the imposition of general concepts for nuanced contexts, is the contribution by César Torres-Cruz and Hortensia Moreno-Esparza which reflects on the difficult applicability of the *queer* concept in the Mexican context. The authors propose the use of *cuir*-feminist sociology of sexuality as a tool to explain how assigned relationships between gender, sexuality, and the body generate frameworks of sociocultural analysis and how power mechanisms define sexuality in the Mexican context.

Black Feminism and Intersectionality

The next major theme that appears in this volume is undoubtedly Black feminism, bringing together contributions that address Black women's political thought and action and the theoretical contributions from Black feminists. Intersectionality appears alongside Black feminism as we understand it as a notion emerging from the reflections and criticisms, brought forward by Black women intellectuals who developed an analytical framework based on the lived experiences of Black women. Feminisms in the Americas have a strong intersectional imprint, a necessity emerging from the highly multiracial composition of these societies marked by processes of colonization and enslavement. The discussions brought up in this volume about Black feminism and intersectionality demonstrate the integration between this feminist niche and intersectionality as a concept and as a possible political tool.

Starting with the consideration of the perverse heritage of enslavement and colonialism, Sandra Heidl critiques Cuba's punitive prison state along the lines of criminalization of poverty, Blackness, non-normative sexual orientations, and political dissent. Departing from an analysis of the 2021 protests in

Cuba, also known as 11J, the author examines how the abolitionist feminist proposal, which builds on paradigms introduced and held high by Black feminists, such as care, offers answers for the emancipation of bodies and for the eradication of systemic violence.

Turning the attention to Brazil, another society still symbolically and materially marked by the enslavement of people of African descent, Lívia de Souza Lima positions the thoughts of Sueli Carneiro and Lélia Gonzalez within a feminist and decolonial pedagogical perspective. Such positioning aims to demonstrate how Black feminism is part of a solidary alliance with decolonial feminism, as both share a tradition of critical and engaged knowledge production. This knowledge is critical because it seeks to contribute to insubordination and resistance, and it is engaged in that it produces knowledge associated with the struggles and activism that occur in the territories.

It is almost impossible to talk about feminist struggles in the Americas and, more specifically in Brazil, without mentioning the name of Marielle Franco, the Black Councillor who was assassinated along with her driver Anderson Silva in 2018, an event followed by massive mobilizations initiated by afro-descendant and intersectional feminists. The editors of this volume led an interview with Anielle Franco, Marielle Franco's sister. In this conversation, Anielle Franco talks about the desire to keep Marielle Franco's legacy alive, which made her and her family transform their pain and grief into a political struggle which aims to keep the memory of Marielle Franco alive to inspire others to keep fighting for their rights.

Mara Viveros Vigoya's contribution continues the discussion of Black feminism(s), stressing that intersectionality emerges within the history of struggles of Black women in various regions of the globe. The author discusses the analytical importance of intersectionality as a tool for understanding how the systems of exclusions and oppressions operate in a coordinated manner with the different subject positions within socio-economic hierarchies. Viveros Vigoya returns to the political origins of the concept by demonstrating how intersectionality has been re-politicized and decolonized as a new language of contestation, the formation of new collective identities, and the creation of feminist and anti-racist solidarity bonds in Améfrica Ladina.

Following up directly from Viveros Vigoya's call for politicizing intersectionality, Audes Jiménez González and Juliana González Villamizar report how they mainstreamed intersectionality in their work in transitional justice procedures in the peace accords in Colombia. In this reflection, the authors deal with intersectionality beyond its analytical value, demonstrating the transformative effects of intersectional practice on social and activist work.

Furthering the concept of intersectionality to explain social and political phenomena, India S. Lenear and Nadia E. Brown discuss how individual family trajectories and histories play a role in the development of Black women's political ambition in the United States. With this discussion, the authors aim to examine the differences that persist among women of Color, demonstrating how the concept of intersectionality can be further expanded beyond the classic trilogy of gender, race, and class.

Methodologies and Pedagogies of Resistance

The next characteristic of feminisms in the Americas is the multidimensional character of their practices of resistance and response to the colonial matrix of domination. The fourth major theme of the volume explores the varied expressions of feminist oppositional methods and strategies.

Working with the cases of Berta Cáceres from Honduras and the Asociación Madres de Abril in Nicaragua, Edith Otero Quezada and Fátima Elizondo Rodríguez seek to bring more visibility to women's struggles in Central America. The authors reconstruct these cases as they demonstrate how these actions of resistance reflect not only their contexts and particular territories but are also connected with political struggles in the region that confront necropolitics, neo-extractivism, and patriarchy.

María José Oyarzún Solís, professor and member of the Chilean constitutive assembly, in a conversation with Nicole Schwabe talks about her feminist activism from a historical perspective, showing how women's demands unfold over time. The challenges of past eras reveal feminist victories, while the consideration of the challenges of the present corroborates the need to be in constant motion. Oyarzún Solís also talks about the importance of taking feminist agendas into the state, elaborating on the challenges of this urgent process in the last constitutional process in Chile. With this, she demonstrates the timeliness of the old feminist debate about the false dichotomy between the public and the private and how this issue continues to be central in the struggle for gender equality.

Ligia Fabris's discussion focuses on women's participation in institutional politics, introducing the dimension of violence and the importance of formulating legislation to address the hostilities targeting women in politics.

In this text, Fabris examines gender violence from a legal perspective, more specifically, discussing the concept of gender-based political violence. The author focuses on the Brazilian case, where attention on the phenomenon of gender political violence was heightened with the assassination of councilwoman Marielle Franco in 2018. Further in the chapter, the author discusses the creation of a specific law to prevent and punish this particular type of violence, explaining its current relevance and pitfalls.

Considering the digital world as an essential platform for disseminating a feminist culture, Saskia Bante conducted a qualitative analysis of 89 feminist Instagram accounts to understand the limits and possibilities of digital culture in activism that is committed to an agenda of transformation and women's emancipation.

Anna-Lena Glesinski and Larissa Satico Ribeiro Higa reflect on the different ways how the written word can be a tool for disseminating concepts, creating solidarities, and discussing sensitive and urgent topics. Glesinski explores the relationship between the literary output of indigenous women in Brazil and the concept of ecofeminism. The author argues that this production is part of a contemporary movement that seeks to reaffirm the very existence of an indigenous literary style and to highlight the importance and strength of these narratives in producing theories and practices that teach about the relationship between women and nature. Ribeiro Higa offers a review of the story collection *"Eu, empregada doméstica – a senzala moderna é o quartinho de empregada"* (Me, a maid – the modern slave quarter is the maid's room), a volume edited by the Brazilian rapper, historian, and former domestic worker Preta-Rara. Ribeiro Higa discusses how sharing stories of oppressions experienced by domestic workers in Brazil reveals the remnants of slavery in contemporary labor conditions. In the chapter, the act of storytelling is described as a feminist practice that sheds light on historically silenced and concealed subjects and experiences.

Remaking narratives is a resource that also emerges in Victoria González-Rivera's contribution. The author argues that anti-indigenous racism, homophobia, and transphobia are part of the totalizing ideology of *mestizaje*, which created a distorted picture of Western Nicaragua's LGBTQ+ history, claiming it has no connections with Indigenous people and history. González-Rivera considers that unraveling these connections and displaying the historical continuities from the past to the present is part of a methodology of indigenous survivance in a track for resistance and humanization.

The use of art, and especially, performance as a political instrument, is also present in Edith Otero Quezada and Lívia de Souza Lima's conversation with the Chilean feminist collective LASTESIS. In the performances of LASTESIS, the body, once a central symbol of the apparatus of domination over women and dissident corporealities, emerges as a weapon, as a means of transmitting transgressive messages against the violence of capitalist and colonial patriarchy. LASTESIS' artistic concepts and practices are centered around re-signifying women's and queer bodies as sites of resistance.

Moving on to another form of feminist artistic intervention, we find an ode to the word and the rhyme in Julia Roth's conversation with Cuban rappers La Reyna y la Real. For the duo, hip hop is a gift and a powerful tool for feminist and anti-racist communication, where women speak to other women, with the potential to create solidarity through a reflective process of mutual recognition. In Safa Al-Dilaimi's dialogue with Jamaican-born Canadian academic, poet, and performer Afua Cooper, the different vocations intertwined in the junction of feminist theory and practice are made apparent. The conversation explores how Afua Cooper's work relates to Black feminism in critiquing White and liberal feminism and showing how art inspires people and motivates emancipatory actions.

We end this volume with María Galindo's provocative contribution synthesizing the various concepts and experiences covered in this volume. María Galindo's powerful poem Intuitive Feminism/*Feminismo intuitivo*, while seeking to name and define a feminism she calls intuitive, questions the need to find an appropriate denomination for the type of feminism she addresses, one that has almost exorcistic properties, expelling all the fragments and residues of patriarchal domination from women's bodies. For Galindo, the urgent call, more important than naming and defining feminism, is learning to understand, recognize, and locate feminism and resistance in the everyday practices and relationships of all types of women.

The range of contributions presented in this volume illustrates how feminism can be located and represented in a variety of forms, denominations, platforms of struggle, and methods of disseminating ideas and struggles for equality and creating solidarity between women and individuals affected by gender norms that transform sexual difference into patterns of domination and hierarchies. Feminisms can be found in a variety of sites where there is a will to resist and struggle for equality and the dissolution of the subordinating tutelage of colonial and racial patriarchy.

References

Álvarez, Sonia E. et al. (2003): "Encountering Latin American and Caribbean Feminisms." In: Signs 28/2, pp. 537–79.

Álvarez, Sonia E. et al. (2014): Translocalities/Translocalidades. Feminist Politics of Translation in the Latin/a Américas, Durham and London: Duke University Press.

Ansaldi, Waldo (2000): "La temporalidad mixta de América Latina. Una expresión de multiculturalismo." In: Héctor Silveira Gorski (Ed.), Identidades comunitarias y democracia, Madrid: Trotta, pp. 167–184.

Anzaldúa, Gloria (1987): Borderlands/La Frontera: The New Mestiza, Austin: Aunt Lute Books.

Arruzza, Cinzia/Bhattacharya, Thiti/Fraser, Nancy (2019): Feminism for the 99%: A Manifesto, London: Verso.

Barrancos, Dora (2022): História dos feminismos na América Latina, Rio de Janeiro: Bazar do Tempo.

Belausteguigoitia, Marisa (2009): Güeras y prietas. Género y raza en la construcción de mundos nuevos, Mexico City: UNAM.

Bhabha, Homi K. (2004): The Location of Culture, Abingdon: Routledge.

Bidaseca, Karina (2017): Ni Una Menos. Vivas nos queremos, Buenos Aires: Milena Caserola.

Bidaseca, Karina/Vazquez Laba, Vanesa (eds.) (2011): Feminismos y poscolonialidad. Descolonizando el feminismo desde América Latina, Buenos Aires: Ediciones Godot.

Boatcă, Manuela (2014): "Inequalities Unbound: Transregional Entanglements and the Creolization of Europe." In: Sabine Broeck/Carsten Junker (eds.), Postcoloniality- Decoloniality-Black Critique: Joints and Fissures, Frankfurt and New York: Campus, pp. 211–230.

Butler, Judith (1992): "Contingent Foundations Feminism and the Question of 'Postmodernism." In: Judith Butler/Joan W. Scott (eds.), Feminists Theorize the Political, Routledge, pp. 3–21.

Butler, Judith (2002): "'Women' as the Subject of Feminism." In: Gender Trouble. Feminism and The Subversion of Identity, New York and London: Taylor & Francis e-Library, pp. 3–9.

Butler, Judith (2015): Notes Toward a Performative Theory of Assembly, Cambridge: Harvard University Press.

Cabnal, Lorena (2010): "Acercamiento a la construcción de la propuesta de pensamiento epistémico de las mujeres indígenas feministas comunitarias de Abya Yala." In: Feminismos diversos: El feminismo comunitario: ACSUR-Las Segovias, pp. 11–25 (https://porunavidavivible.files.wordpress.com/2012/09/feminismos-comunitario-lorena-cabnal.pdf).

Cabnal, Lorena (2016): "De las opresiones a las emancipaciones: Mujeres indígenas en defensa del territorio cuerpo-tierra." In: Bio Diversidad LA, 30 January 2023 (https://www.biodiversidadla.org/Documentos/De_las_opresiones_a_las_emancipaciones_Mujeres_indigenas_en_defensa_del_territorio_cuerpo-tierra).

Caldwell, Kia Lilly (2007): Negras in Brazil. Re-envisioning Black Women, Citizenship, and the Politics of Identity, New Brunswick, New Jersey, and London: Rutgers University Press.

Chaparro, Amneris (2022): "Las olas feministas, ¿una metáfora innecesaria?." In: Korpus 21 II/4, pp. 77–92.

Colectivo Miradas Críticas del Territorio desde el Feminismo (2017): "Mapeando el cuerpo-territorio. Guía metodológica para mujeres que defienden sus territorios", 10 January 2023 (https://miradascriticasdelterritoriodesdeelfeminismo.files.wordpress.com/2017/11/mapeando-el-cuerpo-territorio.pdf).

Combahee River Collective (1981 [1977]): "A Black Feminist Statement." In: Cherrie Moraga/Gloria Anzaldúa (eds.), This Bridge Called My Back: Writings by Radical Women of Color, New York: Kitchen Table, Women of Color Press, pp. 210–218.

Crenshaw, Kimberlé (1989): "Demarginalising the Intersection of Race and Sex: A Black Feminist Critique of Anti-Discrimination Doctrine, Feminist Theory, and Anti-Racist Politics." In: The University of Chicago Legal Forum 1989/1, pp. 139–67.

Cruz, Delmy (2016): "Una mirada muy otra a los territorios-cuerpos femeninos." In: Solar 12/1, pp. 35–46.

Curiel, Ochy (2009): "Descolonizando el feminismo: Una perspectiva desde América Latina y el Caribe", 26 January 2023 (https://feministas.org/IMG/pdf/Ochy_Curiel.pdf).

Curiel, Ochy (2013): La nación heterosexual: Análisis desde el discurso jurídico y al régimen heterosexual desde la antropología de la dominación, Bogotá: Brecha Lésbica y en la frontera.

Curiel, Ochy/Pión, Ruth (2022): "The Contributions of Afro-descendant Women to Feminist Theory and Practice: Deuniversalizing the Subject 'Women'." In: Hypatia, 37/3, pp. 478–492, doi:10.1017/hyp.2022.45.

Draper, Susana (2018a): "Strike as Process: Building the Poetics of a New Feminism." In: The South Atlantic Quarterly 117/3, pp. 682–691. In Spanish: (2018b): "El paro como proceso: construyendo poéticas de un nuevo feminismo." In: Verónica Gago/Raquel Gutiérrez Aguilar/Susana Draper/Mariana Menéndez Montanelli/Suely Rolnik, 8M: Constelación feminista. ¿Cuál es tu huelga? ¿Cuál es tu lucha?, Buenos Aires: Tinta Limón, pp. 49–73.

Espinosa Damián, Gisela (2009): Cuatro vertientes del feminismo en México. Diversidad de rutas y cruces de caminos, Mexico City: Universidad Autónoma Metropolitana.

Espinosa Damián, Gisela (2011): "Feminismo popular. Tensiones e intersecciones entre el género y la clase." In: Gisela Espinosa Damián/Ana Lau Jaiven (eds.), Un fantasma recorre el siglo. Luchas feministas en México 1910–2010, Mexico City: UNAM, pp. 277–308.

Espinosa-Miñoso, Yuderkys (ed.) (2019): Feminismo descolonial: Nuevos aportes teórico-metodológicos a más de una década, Quito: Ediciones Abya-Yala.

Espinosa-Miñoso, Yuderkys (n.d.): "El futuro ya fue. Una crítica a la idea del progreso en las narrativas de liberación sexo-genéricas y queer identitarias en Abya Yala." In: Desde el margen, 26 January 2023 (https://desdeelmargen.net/el-futuro-ya-fue-una-critica-a-la-idea-del-progreso-en-las-narrativas-de-liberacion-sexo-genericas-y-queer-identitarias-en-abya-yala/).

Espinosa-Miñoso, Yuderkys/Gómez Correal, Diana /Ochoa Muñoz, Karina (eds.) (2014): Tejiendo de otro modo: feminismo, epistemología y apuestas descoloniales en Abya Yala, Popayán: Editorial Universidad de la Cauca.

Espinosa-Miñoso, Yuderkys/Lugones, María/Maldonado-Torres, Nelson (eds.) (2021): Decolonial Feminism in Abya Yala: Caribbean, Meso, and South American Contributions and Challenges, London: Rowman & Littlefield,

Espinosa-Miñoso, Yuderkys/Pión, Ruth (2022): "Decolonial Feminism in Latin Américfrica: An Essential Anthology" In: Hypatia 37/special issue 3.

Gago, Verónica (2014): La razón neoliberal. Economías barrocas y pragmática popular, Buenos Aires: Tinta Limón. In English: (2017): Neoliberalism from Below: Popular Pragmatics and Baroque Economies. Translated by Liz Mason-Deese, London and Durham: Duke University Press.

Gago, Verónica (2019): La potencia feminista: O el deseo de cambiarlo todo, Buenos Aires: Tinta Limón. In English: (2020): Feminist International: How to Change Everything. Translated by Liz Mason-Deese, London and New York Verso.

Gago, Verónica et al. (2018): 8M: Constelación Feminista. ¿Cuál es tu huelga? ¿Cuál es tu lucha?, Buenos Aires: Tinta Limón.

Gago, Verónica/Cavallero, Luci (2021a): Una lectura feminista de la deuda, Buenos Aires: Tinta Limón and Rosa Luxemburg Stiftung. In English: (2021b): A Feminist Reading of Debt. Translated by Liz Mason-Deese, London: Pluto Press.

Gleeson, Jules Joanne/O'Rourke, Elle (eds.) (2021): Transgender Marxism, London: Pluto Press.

Gonzalez, Lélia (1988): "A categoria politico-cultural de amefricanidade." In: Tempo Brasileiro 92/93, pp. 69–82

Gouges, Olympe de (2003 [1791]): "Declaration of the Rights of Woman and the Female Citizen." In: Paul Gordon Lauren (ed.), The Evolution of International Human Rights, Philadelphia: University of Pennsylvania Press, pp. 18–20.

Haraway, Donna (2004): "Situated Knowledge: The Science Question in Feminism and the Privilege of Partial Perspective." In: Sandra Harding (ed.), The Feminist Standpoint Theory Reader: Intellectual and Political Controversies, New York and London: Routledge, pp. 81–102.

Harding, Sandra (ed.) (2004): "Introduction: Standpoint Theory as a Site of Political, Philosophical, and Scientific Debate." In: The Feminist Standpoint Theory Reader: Intellectual and Political Controversies, New York and London: Routledge, pp. 1–16.

Hollanda, Heloísa Buarque de (ed.) (2020): Pensamento Feminista Hoje: Perspectivas Decoloniais, Rio de Janeiro: Bazar do Tempo.

hooks, bell (1991): "Theory as Liberatory Practice." In: Yale Journal of Law & Feminism 4/1, pp. 123–35, https://doi.org/10.30578/nomadas.n50a8.

Jáuregui, Gabriela (ed.) (2018): Tsunami. 1st ed., Mexico City: Sexto Piso Realidades.

Jáuregui, Gabriela (ed.) (2021): Tsunami 2. 1st ed., Mexico City: Universidad Autónoma Metropolitana.

Kilomba, Grada (2019): "The Body as Political Tool." In: Kadist, 27 January 2023 (https:// kadist.org/program/the-body-as-a-political-tool/).

LASTESIS (2021): Quemar el miedo. Un manifiesto, Barcelona: Editorial Planeta. In English: (2023): Set Fear on Fire. The Feminist Call That Set the Americas Ablaze: Verso.

Lorde, Audre (2007 [1984]). "The Master's Tools Will Never Dismantle the Master's House." In: Sister Outsider: Essays and Speeches, Berkeley, CA: Crossing Press, pp. 110–114.

Lugones, María (2007): "Heterosexualism and the Colonial/Modern Gender System." In: Hypatia 22/1, pp. 186–209.

Lugones, María (2008): "The Coloniality of Gender." In: Worlds & Knowledges Otherwise, 2.

Lugones, María (2010): "Toward a Decolonial Feminism." In: Hypatia 25/4, pp. 742–759.

Mendoza, Breny (2014): "La (ir)relevancia de las teorías feministas occidentales, poscoloniales y queer para la política de los feminismos latinoamericanos (1999)." In: Ensayos de crítica feminista en nuestra América, Mexico City: Herder, pp. 436–452.

Millá, Margara (ed.) (2014): Más allá de feminismo: Caminos para andar. Mexico City: Red de feminismos decoloniales.

Mirza, Heidi (2013): "'A Second Skin': Embodied Intersectionality, Transnationalism and Narratives of Identity and Belonging among Muslim Women in Britain." In: Women's Studies International Forum 36 (January-February), pp. 5–15.

Mohanty, Chandra Talpade (2003): Feminism without Borders: Decolonizing Theory, Practicing Solidarity, Durham and London: Duke University Press.

Mora, Mariana (2017): Kuxlejal Politics: Indigenous Autonomy, Race, and Decolonizing Research in Zapatista Communities. Austin: University of Texas Press.

Paredes Carvajal, Julieta (2009): Hilando Fino. Desde el feminismo comunitario, La Paz: Comunidad Mujeres Creando Comunidad. In English: Paredes Carvajal, Julieta/Cerullo, Margaret/Carcelen-Estrada, Antonia (2015): Hilando Fino: Perspectives from Communitarian Feminism: Comunidad Mujeres Creando Comunidad.

Quijano, Aníbal (1988): Modernidad, Identidad y Utopía en América Latina, Lima: Sociedades & Política Ediciones.

Rivera Cusicanqui, Silvia (2012): "*Ch'ixinakax utxiwa*: A Reflection on the Practices and Discourses of Decolonization." In: South Atlantic Quarterly 111/1, pp. 95–109.

Rivera Cusicanqui, Silvia (2018): Un mundo ch'ixi es posible. Ensayos desde un presente en crisis, Buenos Aires: Tinta Limón. In English: (2023): A Ch'ixi World is Possible. Essays from a Present in Crisis: Bloomsbury Academic. (forthcoming)

Rodríguez Aguilera, Meztli Yoalli (2018): "Diálogos hemisféricos entre feminismos del norte y sur: Genealogías de feminismos críticos latinoamericanos." In: Realidad: Revista de Ciencias Sociales y Humanidades 151, pp. 89–107, https://doi.org/10.5377/realidad.v0i151.6805.

Rodríguez, Denisse (2020): "On Decolonisation: Praxis and Thinking-Feeling from the South." In: Postcolonial Studies 25/1, pp. 153–155.

Roth, Benita (2004): Separate Roads to Feminism: Black, Chicana and White Feminists in America's Second Wave, Cambridge, UK: Cambridge University Press.

Roth, Julia (2014): Occidental Readings, Decolonial Practices: A Selection on Gender, Genre, and Coloniality in the Americas. Tempe, AZ: Bilingual Press/Editorial Bilingüe.

Roth, Julia (2018): "Feminism Otherwise: Intersectionality beyond Occidentalism." In: InterDisciplines 2, pp. 97–122.

Roth, Julia (2019): "'Manifiesto de solidaridad continental' Alliances and Inequalities: Inter-American Feminist Networks 1840–1948." In: Comparative American Studies 14/3-4, pp. 204–220.

Roth, Julia (2021): Can Feminism Trump Populism? Right-Wing Trends and Intersectional Contestations in the Americas, Bielefeld: WVT/University of New Orleans Press. In Spanish: (2020): ¿Puede el feminismo vencer al populismo? Tendencias de derecha y disputas interseccionales en las Américas, Bielefeld: Kipu Verlag.

Rubiera Castillo, Daisy/Martiatu Terry, Inés María (eds.) (2011): Afrocubanas. Historia, pensamiento y prácticas culturales, Havana: Ciencias Sociales. In English: (2020): Afrocubanas. History, Thought, and Cultural Practices. Translated by Karina Alma, London: Rowman & Littlefield International Ltd.

Scheele, Alexandara/Roth, Julia/Winkel, Heidemarie (2022): Global Contestations of Gender Rights, Bielefeld: Transcript.

Shepherd, Verene (2008a): Engendering Caribbean History: Cross-Cultural Perspectives, Kingston and Miami: Ian Randle Publishers.

Shepherd, Verene (2008b): "Women and the Abolition Campaign in the African Atlantic." In: The Journal of Caribbean History, 42/1, pp. 131–153.

Shepherd, Verene at al. (eds.) (1995): Engendering History: Caribbean Women in Historical Perspective, Kingston: Ian Randle Publishers.

Soja, Edward W. (1989): Postmodern Geographies: The Reassertion of Space in Critical Social Theory, London and New York: Verso.

Soja, Edward W. (2008): "Thirdspace: Toward a New Consciousness of Space and Spatiality." In: Karin Ikas/Gerhard Wagner (eds.), Communicating in the Third Space, 1st ed., New York: Routledge, pp. 63–75.

Spivak, Gayatri Chakravorty (1989): "Can the Subaltern Speak?" In: Gayatri Chakravorty Spivak, Other Worlds. Essays on Cultural Politics, New York and London: Routledge.

Suárez Návaz, Liliana/Hernández, Rosalva Aída (eds.) (2008): Descolonizando el feminismo. Teorías y prácticas desde los márgenes, Madrid: Cátedra.

Tambora Dialogues (2022): "¿Qué puede aprender el norte de las mujeres latinoamericanas? Muchas Cosas!" In: Tambora Dialogues with Erasma Beras-Monticiollo and Julia Roth, 27 January 2023 (https://www.youtube.com/watch?v=BKjDUttnWtU).

Truth, Sojourner (1851[1972]): "'Ain't I A Woman?', Speech to the Women's Rights Convention in Akron, Ohio, 1851." In: Miriam Schneir (ed.), Feminism: The Essential Historical Writings, New York: Vintage Books, pp. 94.

Valencia, Sayak (2010): "En el borde del *border* me llamo filo: capitalismo gore y feminismo(s)." In: Capitalismo gore, Barcelona: Melusina, pp. 173–189. In English: (2018): "At the Brink of *El Bordo*, I Become Blade: Gore Capitalism and Feminism(s)." In: Gore Capitalism, Cambridge, Mass and London: Semiotext(e), pp. 161–177.

Valencia, Sayak (2021): "Transfeminismos, necropolítica y política postmortem en las economías sexuales de la muerte." In: Sayak Valencia/Sonia Herrera Sánchez (eds.), Transfeminismos y política postmortem, Barcelona: Icaria señales, pp. 15–47.

Vergès, Françoise (2021): A Decolonial Feminism, Northampton: Pluto Press.

Viveros Vigoya, Mara (2024): "From the Center to the Margins, (Re) Politicizing Intersectionality." In: Lívia de Souza Lima/Edith Otero Quezada/Julia Roth (eds.), Feminisms in Movement. Theories and Practices from the Americas, Bielefeld: transcript (this volume).

Winkel, Heidemarie/Poferl, Angelika (eds.) (2021): Multiple Gender Cultures, Sociology, and Plural Modernities: Re-Reading Social Constructions of Gender across the Globe in a Decolonial Perspective, London: Routledge.

Wollstonecraft, Mary (2004 [1792]): A Vindication on the Rights of Woman, Harmondsworth: Penguin.

Wynter, Sylvia (1990): "Afterword: Beyond Miranda's Meanings. Un/Silencing the 'Demonic Ground' of Caliban's Women." In: Carole Boyce Davies/Elaine Savory Fido (eds.), Out of the Kumbla: Caribbean Women and Literature, Trenton NJ: African World Press, pp. 355–372.

Wynter, Sylvia (2003): "Unsettling the Coloniality of Being/Power/Truth/Freedom: Towards the Human, After Man, Its Overrepresentation. An Argument." In: CR: The New Centennial Review 3/3, pp. 257–337.

Zaragocin, Sofia/Caretta, Martina Angela (2020): "Cuerpo-Territorio: A Decolonial Feminist Geographical Method for the Study of Embodiment." In: Annals of the American Association of Geographers 0/0, pp. 1–16, https://doi.org/10.1080/24694452.2020.1812370.

Part I
Theorizations and Epistemic Dialogues

The Coloniality of Gender

María Lugones

I am interested in the intersection of race, class, gender and sexuality in a way that enables me to understand the indifference that men, but, more importantly to our struggles, men who have been racialized as inferior, exhibit to the systematic violences inflicted upon women of color. I want to understand the construction of this indifference so as to make it unavoidably recognizable by those claiming to be involved in liberatory struggles. This indifference is insidious since it places tremendous barriers in the path of the struggles of women of color for our own freedom, integrity, and wellbeing and in the path of the correlative struggles towards communal integrity. The latter is crucial for communal struggles towards liberation, since it is their backbone. The indifference is found both at the level of everyday living and at the level of theorizing of both oppression and liberation. The indifference seems to me not just one of not seeing the violence because of the categorial separation of race, gender, class, and sexuality. That is, it does not seem to be only a question of epistemological blinding through categorial separation.

Women of Color feminists have made clear what is revealed in terms of violent domination and exploitation once the epistemological perspective focuses on the intersection of these categories. But that has not seemed sufficient to arouse in those men who have themselves been targets of violent domination and exploitation, any recognition of their complicity or collaboration with the violent domination of women of color. In particular, theorizing global domination continues to proceed as if no betrayals or collaborations of this sort need to be acknowledged and resisted.

In this project I pursue this investigation by placing together two frameworks of analysis that I have not seen sufficiently jointly explored. I am referring, on the one hand, to the important work on gender, race and colonization done, not exclusively, but significantly by Third World and Women of Color feminists, including critical race theorists. This work has emphasized the concept of intersectionality and has exposed the historical and the theoretico-practical exclusion of non-white women from liberatory struggles in the name of "Women". The other framework is the one introduced by Aníbal Quijano and which is at the center of his work, that of the coloniality of power. Placing both of these strands of analysis together permits me to arrive at what I am tentatively calling "the modern/colonial gender system". I think this understanding of gender is implied in both frameworks in large terms, but it is not explicitly articulated, or not articulated in the direction I think necessary to unveil the reach and consequences of complicity with this gender system. I think that articulating this colonial/modern gender system, both in the large strokes, and in all its detailed and lived concreteness will enable us to see what was imposed on us. It will also enable us to see its fundamental destructiveness in both a long and wide sense. The intent of this writing is to make visible the instrumentality of the colonial/modern gender system in subjecting us – both women and men of color – in all domains of existence. But it is also the project's intent to make visible the crucial disruption of bonds of practical solidarity. My intent is to provide a way of understanding, of reading, of perceiving our allegiance to this gender system. We need to place ourselves in a position to call each other to reject this gender system as we perform a transformation of communal relations. In this initial paper, I present Aníbal Quijano's model that I will complicate, but one that gives us – in the logic of structural axes – a good ground from within which to understand the processes of intertwining the production of "race" and "gender".

The Coloniality of Power

Aníbal Quijano thinks the intersection of race and gender in large structural terms. So, to understand that intersection in his terms, it is necessary to understand his model of global, Eurocentered capitalist power. Both "race" and gender find their meanings in this model [patrón]. Quijano understands that all power is structured in relations of domination, exploitation and conflict as social actors fight over control of "the four basic areas of human existence: sex, labor, collective authority and subjectivity/intersubjectivity, their resources and products" (2001–2: 1). What is characteristic of global, Eurocentered, capitalist power is that it is organized around two axes that Quijano terms, "the coloniality of power" and "modernity" (Quijano 2000b: 342). The axes order the disputes over control of each area of existence in such a way that the meaning and forms of domination in each area are thoroughly infused by the coloniality of power and modernity. So, for Quijano, the disputes/struggles over control of "sexual access, its resources and products" define the domain of sex/gender and the disputes, in turn, can be understood as organized around the axes of coloniality and modernity.

This is too narrow an understanding of the oppressive modern/colonial constructions of the scope of gender. Quijano's lenses also assume patriarchal and heterosexual understandings of the disputes over control of sex, its resources, and products. Quijano accepts the global, Eurocentered, capitalist understanding of what gender is about. These features of the framework serve to veil the ways in which non-"white" colonized women were subjected and disempowered. The heterosexual and patriarchal character of the arrangements can themselves be appreciated as oppressive by unveiling the presuppositions of the framework. Gender does not need to organize social arrangements, including social sexual arrangements. But gender arrangements need not be either heterosexual or patriarchal. They need not be, that is, as a matter of history. Understanding these features of the organization of gender in the modern/colonial gender system – the biological dimorphism, the patriarchal and heterosexual organizations of relations – is crucial to an understanding of the differential gender arrangements along "racial" lines. Biological dimorphism, heterosexual patriarchy are all characteristic of what I call the "light" side of the colonial/modern organization of gender. Hegemonically these are written large over the meaning of gender. Quijano seems not to be aware of his accepting this hegemonic meaning of gender. In making these claims I aim to expand and complicate Quijano's approach, preserving his understanding of the coloniality of power, which is at the center of what I am calling the "modern/colonial gender system".

The coloniality of power introduces the basic and universal social classification of the population of the planet in terms of the idea of "race" (Quijano 2001–2:1). The invention of "race" is a pivotal turn as it replaces the relations of superiority and inferiority established through domination. It re-conceives humanity and human relations fictionally, in biological terms. It is important that what Quijano provides is a historical theory of social classification to replace what he terms the "Eurocentric theories of social classes" (Quijano 2000b: 367). This move makes conceptual room for the coloniality of power. It makes conceptual room for the centrality of the classification of the world's population in terms of "races" in the understanding of global capitalism. It also makes conceptual room for understanding the historical disputes over control of labor, sex, collective authority and inter-subjectivity as developing in processes of long duration, rather than understanding each of the elements as pre-existing the relations of power. The elements that constitute the global, Eurocentered, capitalist model of power do not stand in separation from each other and none of them is prior to the processes that constitute the patterns. Indeed, the mythical presentation of these elements as metaphysically prior is an important aspect of the cognitive model of Eurocentered, global capitalism.

In constituting this social classification, coloniality permeates all aspects of social existence and gives rise to new social and geocultural identities (ibid: 342). "America" and "Europe" are among the new geocultural identities. "European," "Indian," "African" are among the "racial" identities. This classification is "the deepest and most enduring expression of colonial domination" (Quijano 2001–2: 1). With the expansion of European colonialism, the classification was imposed on the population of the planet. Since then, it has permeated every area of social existence and it constitutes the most effective form of material and inter-subjective social domination. Thus, "coloniality" does not just refer to "racial" classification. It is an encompassing phenomenon, since it is one of the axes of the system of power and as such it permeates all control of sexual access, collective authority, labor, subjectivity/inter-subjectivity and the production of knowledge from within these inter-subjective relations. Or, alternatively, all control over sex, subjectivity, authority and labor are articulated around it. As I understand the logic of "structural axis" in Quijano's usage, the element that serves as an axis becomes constitutive of and constituted by all the forms that relations of power take with respect to control over that particular domain of human existence. Finally, Quijano also makes clear that, though coloniality is related to colonialism, these are distinct as the latter does not necessarily include racist relations of power. Coloniality's birth and its prolonged and deep extension throughout the planet is tightly related to colonialism (Quijano 2000b: 381).

In Quijano's model of global capitalist Eurocentered power, "capitalism" refers to the structural articulation of all historically known forms of control of labor or exploitation, slavery, servitude, small independent mercantile production, wage labor, and reciprocity under the hegemony of the capital-wage labor relation" (2000b: 349). In this sense, the structuring of the disputes over control of labor are discontinuous: not all labor relations under global, Eurocentered capitalism fall under the capital/wage relation model, though this is the hegemonic model. It is important in beginning to see the reach of the coloniality of power that wage labor has been reserved almost exclusively for white

Europeans. The division of labor is thoroughly "racialized" as well as geographically differentiated. Here we see the coloniality of labor as a thorough meshing of labor and "race".

Quijano understands "modernity", the other axis of global Eurocentered capitalism, as "the fusing of the experiences of colonialism and coloniality with the necessities of capitalism, creating a specific universe of intersubjective relations of domination under a Eurocentered hegemony" (Quijano 2000b: 343). In characterizing modernity, Quijano focuses on the production of a way of knowing, labeled rational, arising from *within this subjective universe* since the XVII century in the main hegemonic centers of this world system of power (Holland and England). This way of knowing is Eurocentered. By "Eurocentrism" Quijano understands the cognitive perspective not of Europeans only, but of the Eurocentered world, of those educated under the hegemony of world capitalism. "Eurocentrism naturalizes the experience of people within this model of power" (ibid.).

The cognitive needs of capitalism and the naturalizing of the identities and relations of coloniality and of the geocultural distribution of world capitalist power have guided the production of this way of knowing. The cognitive needs of capitalism include "measurement, quantification, externalization (or objectification) of what is knowable with respect to the knower so as to control the relations among people and nature and among them with respect to it, in particular the property in means of production". This way of knowing was imposed on the whole of the capitalist world as the only valid rationality and as emblematic of modernity.

Europe was mythologically understood to pre-exist this pattern of power as a world capitalist center that colonized the rest of the world and as such the most advanced moment in the linear, unidirectional, continuous path of the species. A conception of humanity was consolidated according to which the world's population was differentiated in two groups: superior and inferior, rational and irrational, primitive and civilized, traditional and modern. "Primitive" referred to a prior time in the history of the species, in terms of evolutionary time. Europe came to be mythically conceived as preexisting colonial, global, capitalism and as having achieved a very advanced level in the continuous, linear, unidirectional path. Thus, from within this mythical starting point, other human inhabitants of the planet came to be mythically conceived not as dominated through conquest, nor as inferior in terms of wealth or political power, but as an anterior stage in the history of the species, in this unidirectional path. That is the meaning of the qualification "primitive" (ibid: 343–344).

We can see then the structural fit of the elements constituting Eurocentered, global capitalism in Quijano's model (pattern). Modernity and coloniality afford a complex understanding of the organization of labor. They enable us to see the fit between the thorough racialization of the division of labor and the production of knowledge. The pattern allows for heterogeneity and discontinuity. Quijano argues that the structure is not a closed totality (ibid: 355).

We are now in a position to approach the question of the intersectionality of race and gender in Quijano's terms. I think the logic of "structural axes" does more and less than intersectionality. Intersectionality reveals what is not seen when categories such as gender and race are conceptualized as separate from each other. The move to intersect the categories has been motivated by the difficulties in making visible those who are dominated and victimized in terms of both categories. Though everyone in capitalist Eurocentered modernity is both raced and gendered, not everyone is dominated or victimized in terms of them. Crenshaw (1995) and other women of color feminists have argued that the categories have been understood as homogenous and as picking out the dominant in the group as the norm, thus "women" picks out white bourgeois women, "men" picks out white bourgeois men, "Black" picks out Black heterosexual men, and so on. It becomes logically clear then that the logic of categorial separation distorts what exists at the intersection, such as violence against women of color. Given the construction of the categories, the intersection misconstrues women of color. So, once intersectionality shows us what is missing, we have ahead of us the task of reconceptualizing the logic of the "intersection" so as to avoid separability. It is only when we perceive gender and race as intermeshed or fused that we actually see women of color.

The logic of structural axes shows gender as constituted by and constituting the coloniality of power. In that sense, there is no gender/race separability in Quijano's model. I think he has the logic of it right. But the axis of coloniality is not sufficient to pick out all aspects of gender. What aspects of gender are shown depends on how gender is actually conceptualized in the model. In Quijano's model (pattern), gender seems to be contained within the organization of that "basic area of existence" that Quijano calls "sex, its resources, and products". That is, there is an account of gender within the framework that is not itself placed under scrutiny and that is too narrow and overly biologized as it presupposes sexual dimorphism, heterosexuality, patriarchal distribution of power, and so on.

Though I have not found a characterization of gender in what I have read of his work, Quijano seems to me to imply that gender difference is constituted in the disputes over control of sex, its resources, and products. Differences are shaped through the manner in which this control is organized. Sex, he understands, as biological attributes that become elaborated as social categories. He contrasts the biological quality of sex with phenotype, which does not include differential biological attributes. "The color of one's skin, the shape of one's eyes and hair "do not have any relation to the biological structure" (Quijano 2000b: 373). Sex, on the other hand seems unproblematically biological to Quijano. He characterizes the "coloniality of *gender* relations", that is, the ordering of gender relations around the axis of the coloniality of power, as follows:

> 1. In the whole of the colonial world, the norms and formal-ideal patterns of sexual behavior of the genders and consequently the patterns of familial organization of "Europeans" were directly founded on the "racial" classification: the sexual freedom of males and the fidelity of women were, in the whole of the Eurocentered world, the counterpart of the "free" – that is, not paid as in prostitution – access of "white" men to "black" women and "indias" in America, "black" women in Africa, and other "colors" in the rest of the subjected world.
> [*En todo el mundo colonial, las normas y los patrones formal-ideales de comportamiento sexual de los géneros y en consecuencia los patrones de organización familiar de los "europeos" fueron directamente fundados en la clasificación "racial": la libertad sexual de los varones y la fidelidad de las mujeres fue, en todo el mundo eurocentrado, la contrapartida del "libre" – esto es, no pagado como en la prostitución, más antigua en la historia – acceso sexual de los varones "blancos" a las mujeres "negras" e "indias", en América, "negras" en el África, y de los otros "colores" en el resto del mundo sometido.*]

> 2. In Europe, instead, it was the prostitution of women, that was the counterpart of the bourgeois family pattern.
> [*En Europa, en cambio, fue la prostitución de las mujeres la contrapartida del patrón de la familia burguesa.*]

> 3. Familial unity and integration, imposed as the axes of the model of the bourgeois family in the Eurocentered world, were the counterpart of the continued disintegration of the parent-children units in the "non-white" "races", which could be held and distributed as property not just as merchandise but as "animals". This was particularly the case among "black" slaves, since this form of domination over them was more explicit, immediate, and prolonged.

> [*La unidad e integración familiar, impuestas como ejes del patrón de familia burguesa del mundo eurocentrado, fue la contrapartida de la continuada desintegración de las unidades de parentesco padres-hijos en las "razas" no-"blancas," apropriables y distribuibles no solo como mercancías sino directamente como "animales". En particular, entre los esclavos "negros," ya que sobre ellos esa forma de dominación fue la más explícita, inmediata y prolongada.*]
>
> 4. The hypocrisy characteristically underlying the norms and formal-ideal values of the bourgeois family are not, since then, alien to the coloniality of power.
> [*La característica hipocresía subyacente a las normas y valores formal-ideales de la familia burguesa, no es, desde entonces, ajena a la colonialidad del poder.*] (ibid: 378) [my translation].

As we see in this complex and important quote, Quijano's framework restricts gender to the organization of sex, its resources and products and he seems to make a presupposition as to who controls access and who becomes constituted as "resources". Quijano appears to take it for granted that the disputes over control of sex is a dispute among men, about men's control of resources who are thought to be female. Men do not seem understood as the "resources" in sexual encounters. Women are not thought to be disputing for control over sexual access. The differences are thought of in terms of how society reads reproductive biology.

Intersexuality

In "Definitional Dilemmas" Julie Greenberg (2002) tells us that legal institutions have the power to assign individuals to a particular racial or sexual category.

> Sex is still presumed to be binary and easily determinable by an analysis of biological factors. Despite anthropological and medical studies to the contrary, society presumes an unambiguous binary sex paradigm in which all individuals can be classified neatly as male or female (112).

She argues that throughout U.S. history the law has failed to recognize intersexuals, inspite of the fact that 1 to 4 percent of the world's population is intersexed, that is they do not fit neatly into unambiguous sex categories, they have some biological indicators that are *traditionally* associated with males and some biological indicators that are *traditionally* associated with females (my emphasis). The manner in which the law defines the terms *male, female,* and *sex* will have a profound impact on these individuals (ibid: 112).

The assignations reveal that what is understood to be biological sex, is socially constructed. During the late nineteenth century until WWI, reproductive function was considered a woman's essential characteristic. The presence or absence of ovaries was the ultimate criterion of sex (ibid: 113). But there are a large number of factors that can enter in "establishing someone's 'official' sex": chromosomes, gonads, external morphology, internal morphology, hormonal patterns, phenotype, assigned sex, self-identified sex (ibid: 112). At present, chromosomes and genitalia enter into the assignment, but in a manner that reveals biology is thoroughly interpreted and itself surgically constructed.

> XY infants with "inadequate" penises must be turned into girls because society believes the essence of manhood is the ability to penetrate a vagina and urinate while standing. XX infants with "adequate" penises, however, are assigned the females sex because society and many in the medical community believe that the essence of womanhood is the ability to bear children rather than the ability to engage in satisfactory sexual intercourse (ibid: 114).

Intersexed individuals are frequently surgically and hormonally turned into males or females. These factors are taken into account in legal cases involving the right to change the sex designation on official documents, the ability to state a claim for employment discrimination based upon sex, the right to marry (ibid: 115). Greenberg reports the complexities and variety of decisions on sexual assignation in each case. The law does not recognize intersexual status. Though the law permits self-identification of one's sex in certain documents, "for the most part, legal institutions continue to base sex assignment on the traditional assumptions that sex is binary and can be easily determined by analyzing biological factors" (ibid: 119).

Julie Greenberg's work enables me to point out an important assumption in the model that Quijano offers us. This is important because sexual dimorphism has been an important characteristic of what I call "the light side" of the colonial/modern gender system. Those in the "dark side" were not necessarily understood dimorphically. Sexual fears of colonizers led them to imagine the indigenous people of the Americas as hermaphrodites or intersexed, with large penises and breasts with flowing milk. But as Gunn Allen and others make clear, intersexed individuals were recognized in many tribal societies prior to colonization without assimilation to the sexual binary. It is important to consider the changes that colonization brought to understand the scope of the organization of sex and gender under colonialism and in Eurocentered global capitalism. If the latter did only recognize sexual dimorphism for white bourgeois males and females, it certainly does not follow that the sexual division is based on biology. The cosmetic and substantive corrections to biology make very clear that "gender" is antecedent to the "biological" traits and gives them meaning. The naturalizing of sexual differences is another product of the modern use of science that Quijano points out in the case of "race". It is important to see that not all different traditions correct and normalize inter-sexed people. So, as with other assumption characteristics it is important to ask how sexual dimorphism served and serves Eurocentered global capitalist domination/exploitation.

When Egalitarianism Takes a Non-Gendered or a Gynecentric Form

As Eurocentered, global capitalism was constituted through colonization, gender differentials were introduced where there were none. Oyèrónkẹ Oyěwùmí shows us that the oppressive gender system that was imposed on Yoruba society did a lot more than transform the organization of reproduction. Her argument shows us that the scope of the system of gender imposed through colonialism encompasses the subordination of females in every aspect of life. Thus Quijano's understanding of the scope of gendering in Eurocentered, global, capitalism is much too narrow. Paula Gunn Allen argues that many Native American tribes were matriarchal, recognized more than two genders, recognized "third" gendering and homosexuality positively and understood gender in egalitarian terms rather than in the terms of subordination that Eurocentered capitalism imposed on them. She enables us to see that the scope of the gender differentials was much more encompassing and it did not rest on biology. Gunn Allen also shows us a construction of knowledge and an approach to understanding "reality" that is gynecentric and that counters the knowledge production of modernity. Thus she points us in the direction of recognizing the gendered construction of knowledge in modernity, another aspect of the hidden scope of "gender" in Quijano's account of the processes constituting the coloniality of gender.

Non-Gendered Egalitarianism

In her *The Invention of Women*, Oyèrónkẹ Oyěwùmí, raises questions about the validity of patriarchy as a valid transcultural category (1997: 20). She does so, not but contrasting patriarchy and matriarchy, but by arguing that "gender was not an organizing principle in Yoruba society prior to colonization by the West" (ibid: 31). No gender system was in place. Indeed she tells us that gender has "become important in Yoruba studies not as an artifact of Yoruba life but because Yoruba life, past and present, has been translated into English to fit the Western pattern of body-reasoning" (ibid: 30). The assumption that Yoruba society included gender as an organizing principle is another case "of Western dominance in the documentation and interpretation of the world, one that is facilitated by the West's global material dominance (ibid: 32). She tells us that "researchers always find gender when they look for it" (ibid: 31).

> The usual gloss of the Yoruba categories *obinrin* and *okunrin* as "female/woman" and male/man," respectively, is a mistranslation. These categories are neither binarily opposed nor hierarchical (ibid: 32–33).

The prefixes obin and okun specify a variety of anatomy. Oyěwùmí translates the prefixes as referring to the anatomic male and the anatomic female, shortened as anamale and anafemale. It is important to note that she does not understand these categories as binarily opposed.

Oyěwùmí understands gender as introduced by the West as a tool of domination that designates two binarily opposed and hierarchical social categories. Women (the gender term) is not defined through biology, though it is assigned to anafemales. Women are defined in relation to men, the norm. Women are those who do not have a penis; those who do not have power; those who cannot participate in the public arena (ibid: 34). None of this was true of Yoruba anafemales prior to colonization.

> The imposition of the European state system, with its attendant legal and bureaucratic machinery, is the most enduring legacy of European colonial rule in Africa. One tradition that was exported to Africa during this period

> was the exclusion of women from the newly created colonial public sphere [...] (ibid: 123).
> The very process by which females were categorized and reduced to "women" made them ineligible for leadership roles [...] The emergence of women as an identifiable category, defined by their anatomy and subordinated to men in all situations, resulted, in part, from the imposition of a patriarchal colonial state. For females, colonization was a twofold process of racial inferiorization and gender subordination. The creation of "women" as a category was one the very first accomplishments of the colonial state. It is not surprising, therefore, that it was unthinkable for the colonial government to recognize female leaders among the peoples they colonized, such as the Yorùbá (ibid: 124). The transformation of state power to male-gender power was accomplished at one level by the exclusion of women from state structures. This was in sharp contrast to Yorùbá state organization, in which power was not gender-determined (ibid: 125).

Oyěwùmí recognizes two crucial processes in colonization, the imposition of races with the accompanying inferiorization of Africans, and the inferiorization of anafemales. The inferiorization of anafemales extended very widely from exclusion from leadership roles to loss of property over land, and other important economic domains. Oyěwùmí notes that the introduction of the Western gender system was accepted by Yoruba males, who thus colluded with the inferiorization of anafemales. So, when we think of the indifference of non-white men to the violences exercised against non-white women, we can begin to have some sense of the collaboration between anamales and Western colonials against anafemales. Oyěwùmí makes clear that both men and women resisted cultural changes at different levels. Thus while

> In the West the challenge of feminism is how to proceed from the gender-saturated category of "women" to the fullness of an unsexed humanity. For Yoruba obinrin, the challenge is obviously different because at certain levels in the society and in some spheres, the notion of an "unsexed humanity" is neither a dream to aspire to nor a memory to be realized. It exists, albeit in concatenation with the reality of separate and hierarchical sexes imposed during the colonial period (ibid: 156).

We can see then that the scope of the coloniality of gender is much too narrow. Quijano assumes much of the terms of the modern/colonial gender system's hegemonic "light" side in defining the scope of gender. I have gone outside the coloniality of gender so as to think of what it hides, or disallows from consideration, about the very scope of the gender system of Eurocentered global capitalism. So, though I think that the coloniality of gender, as Quijano pointedly describes it, shows us very important aspects of the intersection of "race" and "gender," it follows rather than discloses the erasure of colonized women from most areas of social life. It accommodates rather than disrupt the narrowing of gender domination. Oyěwùmí's rejection of the gender lens in characterizing the inferiorization of anafemales in modern colonization makes clear the extent and scope of the inferiorization. Her understanding of gender, the colonial, Eurocentered, capitalist construction, is much more encompassing than Quijano's. She enables us to see the economic, political, cognitive inferiorization as well as the inferiorization of anafemales regarding reproductive control.

Gynecratric Egalitarianism

> "To assign to this great being the position of 'fertility goddess' is exceedingly demeaning: it trivializes the tribes and it trivializes the power of woman" (Gunn Allen 1986: 14).

As she characterizes many Native American tribes as gynecratic, Paula Gunn Allen emphasizes the centrality of the spiritual in all aspects of Indian life and thus a very different intersubjectivity from within which knowledge is produced than that of the coloniality of knowledge in modernity. Many American Indian tribes "thought that the primary potency in the universe was female, and that understanding authorizes all tribal activities" (ibid:26). Old Spider Woman, Corn Woman, Serpent Woman, Thought Woman are some of the names of powerful creators. For the gynecratic tribes, Woman is at the center and "nothing is sacred without her blessing, her thinking" (ibid: 13).

Replacing this gynecratic spiritual plurality with one supreme male being as Christianity did, was crucial in subduing the tribes. Allen proposes that transforming Indian tribes from egalitarian and gynecratic to hierarchical and patriarchal "requires meeting four objectives":

> 1. "The primacy of female as creator is displaced and replaced by male-gendered creators (generally generic)" (ibid: 41).

2. "Tribal governing institutions and the philosophies that are their foundation are destroyed, as they were among the Iriquois and the Cherokee" (ibid: 41).
3. The people "are pushed off their lands, deprived of their economic livelihood, and forced to curtail or end altogether pursuits on which their ritual system, philosophy, and subsistence depend. Now dependent on white institutions for their survival, tribal systems can ill afford gynocracy when patriarchy – that is, survival – requires male dominance" (ibid: 42).
4. The clan structure "must be replaced in fact if not in theory, by the nuclear family. By this ploy, the women clan heads are replaced by elected male officials and the psychic net that is formed and maintained by the nature of nonauthoritarian gynecentricity grounded in respect for diversity of gods and people is thoroughly rent" (ibid: 42).

Thus, for Allen, the inferiorization of Indian females is thoroughly tied to the domination and transformation of tribal life. The destruction of the gynocracies is crucial to the "decimation of populations through starvation, disease, and disruption of all social, spiritual, and economic structures [...]" (ibid: 42). The program of degynocratization requires impressive "image and information control". Thus

> Recasting archaic tribal versions of tribal history, customs, institutions and the oral tradition increases the likelihood that the patriarchal revisionist versions of tribal life, skewed or simply made up by patriarchal non-Indians and patriarchalized Indians, will be incorporated into the spiritual and popular traditions of the tribes (ibid: 42).

Among the features of the Indian society targeted for destruction were the two-sided complementary social structure; the understanding of gender; the economic distribution which often followed the system of reciprocity. The two sides of the complementary social structure included an internal female chief and an external male chief. The internal chief presided over the band, village, or tribe, maintained harmony and administered domestic affairs. The red, male, chief presided over mediations between the tribe and outsiders (ibid: 18). Gender was not understood primarily in biological terms. Most individuals fit into tribal gender roles "on the basis of proclivity, inclination, and temperament. The Yuma had a tradition of gender designation based on dreams; a female who dreamed of weapons became a male for all practical purposes" (ibid: 196).

Like Oyěwùmí, Gunn Allen is interested in the collaboration between some Indian men and whites in undermining the power of women. It is important for us to think about these collaborations as we think of the question of indifference to the struggles of women in racialized communities against multiple forms of violence against them and the communities. The white colonizer constructed a powerful inside force as colonized men were coopted into patriarchal roles. Gunn Allen details the transformations of the Iroquois and Cherokee gynecracies and the role of Indian men in the passage to patriarchy. The British took Cherokee men to England and gave them an education in the ways of the English. These men participated during the time of the Removal Act.

> In an effort to stave off removal, the Cherokee in the early 1800s under the leadership of men such as Elias Boudinot, Major Ridge, and John Ross, and others, drafted a constitution that disenfranchised women and blacks. Modeled after the Constitution of the United States, whose favor they were attempting to curry, and in conjunction with Christian sympathizers to the Cherokee cause, the new Cherokee constitution relegated women to the position of chattel (ibid: 37).

Cherokee women had had the power to wage war, to decide the fate of captives, to speak to the men's council, they had the right to inclusion in public policy decisions, the right to choose whom and whether to marry, the right to bear arms. The Women's Council was politically and spiritually powerful (ibid: 36–37). Cherokee women lost all these powers and rights, as the Cherokee were removed and patriarchal arrangements were introduced. The Iroquois shifted from a Mother-centered, Mother-right people organized politically under the authority of the Matrons, to a patriarchal society when the Iroquois became a subject people. The feat was accomplished with the collaboration of Handsome Lake and his followers (ibid: 33).

According to Allen, many of the tribes were gynecratic, among them the Susquehanna, Hurons, Iroquois, Cherokee, Pueblo, Navajo, Narragansett, Coastal Algonkians, Montagnais. She also tells us that among the eighty-eight tribes that recognized homosexuality, those who recognized homosexuals in positive terms included the Apache, Navajo, Winnebago, Cheyenne, Pima, Crow, Shoshoni, Paiute, Osage, Acoma, Zuñi, Sioux, Pawnee, Choctaw, Creek, Seminole, Illinois, Mohave, Shasta, Aleut, Sac and Fox, Iowa, Kansas, Yuma, Aztec, Tlingit, Maya, Naskapi, Ponca, Maricopa, Lamath, Quinault,

Yuki, Chilula, Kamia. Twenty of these tribes included specific references to lesbianism.

Michael J. Horswell (2003) comments usefully on the use of the term "third gender". He tells that "third gender" does not mean that there are three genders. It is rather a way of breaking with the sex and gender bipolarity. "The 'third' is emblematic of other possible combinations than the dimorphic. The term "berdache" is sometimes used for "third gender". Horswell tells us that male berdache have been documented in nearly one hundred and fifty North American societies and female berdache in half as many groups (27). He also comments that sodomy, including ritual sodomy, was recorded in Andean societies and many other native societies in the Americas (ibid.) The Nahuas and Mayas also reserved a role for ritualized sodomy (Sigal 2003: 104). It is interesting that Sigal tells us that the Spanish saw sodomy as sinful, but Spanish law condemned the active partner in sodomy to criminal punishment, not the passive. In Spanish popular culture, sodomy was racialized by connecting the practice to the Moors and the passive partner was condemned and seen as equal to a Moor. Spanish soldiers were seen as the active partners to the passive Moors (ibid: 102–104).

Allen's work not only enables us to see how narrow Quijano's conception of gender is in terms of the organization of the economy, and the organization of collective authority, she also enables us to see that the production of knowledge is gendered, the very conception of reality at every level. She also supports the questioning of biology in the construction of gender differences and introduces the important question of gender roles being chosen and dreamt. But importantly, Allen also shows us that the heterosexuality characteristic of the modern/colonial construction of gender relations, is produced, mythically constructed. But heterosexuality is not just biologized in a fictional way, it is also compulsory and it permeates the whole of the coloniality of gender, in the renewed, large sense. In this sense, global Eurocentered capitalism is heterosexualist. I think it is important to see, as we understand the depth and force of violence in the production of both the "light" and the "dark" sides of the colonial/modern gender system, that this heterosexuality has been consistently perverse, violent, demeaning, a turning of people into animals, and the turning of white women into reproducers of "the race" and "the class". Horswell's and Sigal's work complements Allen's, particularly in understanding the presence of sodomy and male homosexuality in colonial and pre-colonial America.

The Colonial/Modern Gender System

Understanding the place of gender in pre-colonial societies is pivotal to understanding the nature and scope of changes in the social structure that the processes constituting colonial/modern Eurocentered capitalism imposed. Those changes were introduced through slow, discontinuous, and heterogenous processes that violently inferiorized colonized women. The gender system introduced was one thoroughly informed through the coloniality of power. Understanding the place of gender in pre-colonial societies is also pivotal in understanding the extent and importance of the gender system in disintegrating communal relations, egalitarian relations, ritual thinking, collective decision making, collective authority, and economies. And thus in understanding the extent to which the imposition of this gender system was as constitutive of the coloniality of power as the coloniality of power was constitutive of it. The logic of the relation between them is of mutual constitution. But it should be clear by now that the colonial, modern, gender system cannot exist without the coloniality of power, since the classification of the population in terms of race is a necessary condition of its possibility.

To think the scope of the gender system of Eurocentered global capitalism it is necessary to understand the extent to which the *very process of narrowing* of the concept of gender to the control of sex, its resources, and products constitutes gender domination. To understand this narrowing and to understand the intermeshing of racialization and gendering, it is important to think whether the social arrangements prior to colonization regarding the "sexes" gave differential meaning to them across all areas of existence. That enables us to see whether control over labor, subjectivity/intersubjectivity, collective authority, sex – Quijano's "areas of existence" – were themselves gendered. Given the coloniality of power, I think we can also say that having a "dark" and a "light side" is characteristic of the co-construction of the coloniality of power and the colonial/modern gender system. Considering critically both biological dimorphism and the position that gender socially constructs biological sex is pivotal to understand the scope, depth, and characteristics of the colonial/modern gender system. The sense is that the reduction of gender to the private, to control over sex and its resources and products is a matter of ideology, of the cognitive production of modernity that understood race as gendered and gender as raced in particularly differential ways for Europeans/ "whites" and colonized/"non-white" peoples. Race is no more mythical and fictional than gender, both powerful fictions.

In the development of twentieth century feminisms, the connection between gender, class, heterosexuality as racialized was not made explicit. That feminism centered its struggle and its ways of knowing and theorizing against a characterization of women as fragile, weak in both body and mind, secluded in the private, and sexually passive. But it did not bring to consciousness that those characteristics only constructed white bourgeois womanhood. Indeed, beginning from that characterization, white bourgeois feminists theorized white womanhood as if all women were white.

It is part of their history that only white bourgeois women have consistently counted as women so described in the West. Females excluded from that description were not just their subordinates. They were also understood to be animals in a sense that went further than the identification of white women with nature, infants, and small animals. They were understood as animals in the deep sense of "without gender," sexually marked as female, but without the characteristics of femininity. Women racialized as inferior were turned from animals into various modified versions of "women" as it fit the processes of Eurocentered global capitalism. Thus heterosexual rape of Indian women, African slave women, coexisted with concubinage, as well as with the imposition of the heterosexual understanding of gender relations among the colonized – when and as it suited Eurocentered, global capitalism, and heterosexual domination of white women. But it is clear from the work of Oyěwùmí and Allen that there was no extension of the status of white women to colonized women even when they were turned into similes of bourgeois white women. Colonized females got the inferior status of gendering as women, without any of the privileges accompanying that status for white bourgeois women. Though, the history presented by Oyěwùmí and Allen should make clear to white bourgeois women that their status is much inferior to that of Native American women and Yoruba women before colonization. Oyěwùmí and Allen also make clear that the egalitarian understanding of the relation between anafemales, anamales, and "third" gender people has not left the imagination nor the practices of Native Americans and Yoruba. But these are matters of resistance to domination.

Erasing any history, including oral history, of the relation of white to non-white women, white feminism wrote white women large. Even though historically and contemporarily white bourgeois women knew perfectly well how to orient themselves in an organization of life that pitted them for very different treatment than non-white or working class women. White feminist struggle became one against the positions, roles, stereotypes, traits, desires imposed on white bourgeois women's subordination. No one else's gender oppression was countenanced. They understood women as inhabiting white bodies but did not bring that racial qualification to articulation or clear awareness. That is, they did not understand themselves in intersectional terms, at the intersection of race, gender, and other forceful marks of subjection or domination. Because they did not perceive these deep differences they did not see a need for creating coalitions. They presumed a sisterhood, a bond given with the subjection of gender.

Historically, the characterization of white European women as fragile and sexually passive opposed them to non-white, colonized women, including women slaves, who were characterized along a gamut of sexual aggression and perversion, and as strong enough to do any sort of labor. The following description of slave women and of slave work in the U.S. South makes clear that African slave females were not considered fragile or weak.

> First came, led by an old driver carrying a whip, forty of the largest and strongest women I ever saw together; they were all in a simple uniform dress of a bluish check stuff, the skirts reaching little below the knee; their legs and feet were bare; they carried themselves loftily, each having a hoe over the shoulder, and walking with a free, powerful swing, like *chasseurs* on the march. Behind came the cavalry, thirty strong, mostly men, but a few of them women, two of whom rode astride on the plow mules. A lean and vigilant white overseer, on a brisk pony, brought up the rear (Takaki 1993: 111).

The hands are required to be in the cotton field as soon as it is light in the morning, and, with the exception of ten or fifteen minutes, which is given to them at noon to swallow their allowance of cold bacon, they are not permitted to be a moment idle until it is too dark to see, and when the moon is full, they often times labor till the middle of the night (ibid.).

Patricia Hill Collins provides a clear sense of the dominant understanding of Black women as sexually aggressive and the genesis of that stereotype in slavery:

> The image of Jezebel originated under slavery when Black women were portrayed as being, to use Jewelle Gomez' words, "sexually aggressive wet nurses" (Clarke et al. 1983, 99). Jezebel's function was to relegate all Black women to the category of sexually aggressive women, thus providing a powerful rationale for the widespread sexual assaults by White men typically reported by Black slave women (Davis 1981; D. White 1985). Jezebel

> served yet another function. If Black slave women could be portrayed as having excessive sexual appetites, then increased fertility should be the expected outcome. By suppressing the nurturing that African-American women might give their own children which would strengthen Black family networks, and by forcing Black women to work in the field, "wet nurse" White children, and emotionally nurture their White owners, slave owners effectively tied the controlling images of Jezebel and mammy to the economic exploitation inherent in the institution of slavery (2000: 82).

But it is not just Black slave women who were placed outside the scope of white bourgeois femininity. In *Imperial Leather*, Anne McClintock (1995) as she tells us of Columbus' depiction of the earth as a woman's breast, evokes the "long tradition of male travel as an erotics of ravishment (22)".

> For centuries, the uncertain continents – Africa, the Americas, Asia – were figured in European lore as libidinously eroticized. Travelers' tales abounded with visions of the monstrous sexuality of far-off lands, where, as legend had it, men sported gigantic penises and women consorted with apes, feminized men's breasts flowed with milk and militarized women lopped theirs off (ibid.).

Within this porno tropic tradition, women figured as the epitome of sexual aberration and excess. Folklore saw them, even more than the men, as given to a lascivious venery so promiscuous as to border on the bestial (ibid.).

McClintock describes the colonial scene depicted in a drawing (ca. 1575) in which Jan van der Straet "portrays the "discovery" of America as an eroticized encounter between a man and a woman" (ibid: 25).

> Roused from her sensual languor by the epic newcomer, the indigenous woman extends an inviting hand, insinuating sex and submission...Vespucci, the godlike arrival, is destined to inseminate her with his male seeds of civilization, fructify the wilderness and quell the riotous scenes of cannibalism in the background [...] The cannibals appear to be female and are spit roasting a human leg (ibid: 26).

In the 19th century, McClinctock tells us "sexual purity emerged as a controlling metaphor for racial, economic and political power" (ibid: 47). With the development of evolutionary theory "anatomical criteria were sought for determining the relative position of races in the human series" (ibid: 50).

The English middle-class male was placed at the pinnacle of evolutionary hierarchy. White English middle class women followed. Domestic workers, female miners and working class prostitutes were stationed on the threshold between the white and black races (ibid: 56).

Yen Le Espiritu (1997) tells us that

> representations of gender and sexuality figure strongly in the articulation of racism. Gender norms in the United States are premised upon the experiences of middle- class men and women of European origin. These Eurocentric-constructed gender norms form a backdrop of expectations for American men and women of color – expectations which racism often precludes meeting. In general, men of color are viewed not as the protector, but rather the aggressor – a threat to white women. And women of color are seen as over sexualized and thus undeserving of the social and sexual protection accorded to white middleclass women. For Asian American men and women, their exclusion from white-based cultural notions of the masculine and the feminine has taken seemingly contrasting forms: Asian men have been cast as both hypermasculine (the "Yellow Peril") and effeminate (the "model minority"); and Asian women have been rendered both superfeminine (the "China Doll") and castrating (the "Dragon Lady") (Espiritu 1997: 135).

This gender system congeals as Europe advances the colonial project(s). It begins to take shape during the Spanish and Portuguese colonial adventures and becomes full blown in late modernity. The gender system has a "light" and a "dark" side. The light side constructs gender and gender relations hegemonically. It only orders the lives of white bourgeois men and women, and it constitutes the modern/colonial meaning of "men" and "women". Sexual purity and passivity are crucial characteristics of the white bourgeois females who reproduce the class, and the colonial, and racial standing of bourgeois, white men. But equally important is the banning of white bourgeois women from the sphere of collective authority, from the production of knowledge, from most of control over the means of production. Weakness of mind and body are important in the reduction and seclusion of white bourgeois women from most domains of life, most areas of human existence. The gender system is heterosexualist, as heterosexuality permeates racialized patriarchal control over production, including knowledge production, and over collective authority. Heterosexuality is both compulsory and perverse among white bourgeois men and women since the arrangement does significant violence to the powers and rights of white bourgeois women and it serves to reproduce control over production. White bourgeois women are inducted into this reduction through bounded sexual access.

The "dark" side of the gender system was and is thoroughly violent. We have begun to see the deep reductions of anamales, anafemales, and "third" genders from their ubiquitous participation in ritual, decision making, economics; their reduction to animality, to forced sex with white colonizers, to such deep labor exploitation that often people died working. Quijano tells us

> The vast Indian genocide of the first decades of colonization was not caused, in the main, by the violence of the conquest, nor by the diseases that the conquerors carried. Rather it [sic] was due to the fact that the Indians were used as throwaway labor, forced to work till death (Quijano, 2000a) [my translation].

I want to mark the connection between the work that I am referencing here as I introduce the modern colonial gender system's "dark" side, and Quijano's coloniality of power. Unlike white feminists who have not focused on colonialism, these theorists very much see the differential construction of gender along racial lines. To some extent these theorists understand "gender" in a wider sense than Quijano, thus they think not only of control over sex, its resources and products, but also of labor as both racialized and gendered. That is, they see an articulation between labor, sex, and the coloniality of power. Oyěwùmí and Allen help us realize the full extent of the reach of the colonial/modern gender system into the construction of collective authority, all aspects of the relation between capital and labor, and the construction of knowledge.

There is important work done and to be done in detailing the dark and light sides of what I am calling the "modern colonial gender system". In introducing these arrangements in very large strokes, I mean to begin a conversation and a project of collaborative, participatory, research and popular education to begin to see in its details the long sense of the processes of the colonial/gender system enmeshed in the coloniality of power into the present, to uncover collaboration, and to call each other to reject it in its various guises as we recommit to communal integrity in a liberatory direction. We need to understand the organization of the social so as to make visible our collaboration with systematic racialized gender violence, so as to come to an inevitable recognition of it in our maps of reality.

References

Collins, Patricia Hill (2000): Black Feminist Thought, New York: Routledge.
Crenshaw, Kimberlé (1995): "Mapping the Margins: Intersectionality, Identity Politics, and Violence Against Women of Color." In: Kimberlé Crenshaw/ Neil Gotanda/Gary Peller/Kendall Thomas (eds.), Critical Race Theory, New York: The New Press.
Espiritu, Yen Le (1997): "Race, Class, and Gender in Asian America." In: Elaine H. Kim/Lilia V. Villanueva/Asian Women United of California (eds.), Making More Waves: New Writing by Asian American Women, Boston: Beacon.
Greenberg, Julie. A. (2002): "Definitional Dilemmas: Male or Female? Black or White? The Law's Failure to Recognize Intersexuals and Multiracials." In: Toni Lester Gender (ed.), Nonconformity, Race, and Sexuality: Charting the Connections, Madison: University of Wisconsin Press, pp. 102–106.
Gunn Allen, Paula (1992 [1986]): The Sacred Hoop. Recovering the Feminine in American Indian Traditions, Boston: Beacon Press.
Horswell, Michael J. (2003): "Toward and Andean Theory of Ritual Same-Sex Sexuality and Third-Gender Subjectivity." In: Pete Sigal (ed.), Infamous Desire. Male Homosexuality in Colonial Latin America, Chicago and London: The University of Chicago Press, pp. 25–69.
McClintock, Anne (1995): Imperial Leather. Race, Gender and Sexuality in the Colonial Contest, New York: Routledge.
Oyěwùmí, Oyèrónkẹ (1997): The Invention of Women. Making an African Sense of Western Gender Discourses, Minneapolis: University of Minnesota Press.
Quijano, Aníbal (1991): "Colonialidad, modernidad/racionalidad." In: Perú Indígena 13/29, pp. 11–20.
Quijano, Aníbal (2000a): "Colonialidad del poder, eurocentrismo y América Latina." In: Edgardo Lander (ed.), La colonialidad del saber: eurocentrismo y ciencias sociales. Perspectivas latinoamericanas, Buenos Aires: CLACSO, pp. 201–246.
Quijano, Aníbal (2000b): "Colonialidad del poder y clasificación social." In: Journal of World-Systems Research 6/2, pp. 342–86.
Quijano, Aníbal (2001–2): "Colonialidad del poder, globalización y democracia." In: Revista de Ciencias Sociales de la Universidad Autónoma de Nuevo León 4/7-8, pp. 58–90.
Sigal, Pete (2003): "Gendered Power, the Hybrid Self, and Homosexual Desire in Late Colonial Yucatan." In: Pete Sigal (ed.), Infamous Desire: Male Homo-

sexuality in Colonial Latin America, Chicago and London: The University of Chicago Press, pp. 102–133.

Takaki, Ronald (1993): A Different Mirror, Boston: Little, Brown, and Company.

Coloniality and Modern Patriarchy
Expansion of the State Front, Modernization, and the Lives of Women[1]

Rita Laura Segato

Duality and Binarism-Verisimilitudes between the 'Egalitarian' Gender of Coloniality/Modernity and its Hierarchical Counterpart of the Pre-Intrusion Order

I will refer here to a specific form of infiltration, that of the gender relations of the modern colonial order in the village-world [*mundo-aldea*]. It is of the utmost importance to understand that, in comparing the intrusive process of the colony and, later, of the republican state in the other worlds, with the order of coloniality/modernity and its citizen precept, we not only illuminate the village-world. Also, and above all, we gain access to dimensions of the republic

---

[1] Translated from Spanish by Julia Roth. The full version of this article was republished in 2015 under the title "Género y colonialidad: del patriarcado comunitario de baja intensidad al patriarcado colonial moderno de alta intensidad." In: Rita Laura Segato, La crítica de la colonialidad en ocho ensayos y una antropología por demanda, Buenos Aires: Prometeo, pp. 69–99. This short version is a translation of the 2014 article titled "Colonialidad y patriarcado moderno: expansión del frente estatal, modernización y la vida de las mujeres." In: Yuderkys Espinosa Miñoso/Diana Gómez Correal/Karina Ochoa (eds.), Tejiendo de otro Modo: Feminismo, epistemología y apuestas decoloniales en Abya Yala Muñoz, Popoyán: Editorial Universidad del Cauca, pp. 75–90. Acknowledgments: for another translation of the same excerpt, see Segato, Rita Laura (2021) "Gender and Coloniality: From Low-Intensity Communal Patriarchy to High-Intensity Colonial Modern Patriarchy." Translated by Pedro Monque. In: Hypatia: A Journal of Feminist Philosophy 36, pp. 787–799, reproduced with permission. And Segato, Rita Laura (2022) "Gender and Coloniality. From Communitarian to Colonial Modern Patriarchy." Translated by Ramsey McGlazer. In: The Critique of Coloniality. Eight Essays: Routledge, pp. 57–73.

and of the paths of law that are generally opaque to us. Rendered invisible by the system of beliefs – civic, republican – in which we are immersed, that is, by the civic religiosity of our world. I would also like to note that the analysis of what differentiates the gender of one world from the other reveals with great clarity the contrast between their respective patterns of life in general, in all spheres, and not only in the sphere of gender. This is because gender relations are, despite their typification as a 'particular subject' in sociological and anthropological discourse, a pervasive and omnipresent scene of all life.

I propose, therefore, to read the interface between the pre-intrusion world and colonial modernity based on the transformations of the gender system. That is, it is not merely a matter of introducing gender as one of the themes of decolonial critique, or as one of the aspects of domination in the pattern of coloniality, but to give it a real theoretical and epistemic status by examining it as a central category capable of illuminating all the other aspects of the transformation that are imposed on the lives of communities as they were captured by the new modern colonial order. [2]

---

2 Author's note for this publication: The modelling I present here of the historical process brought about by the transition from what I have called the 'village-world' [*mundo-aldea*] – for lack of a better name to represent the social relations before the colonial intrusion, the world into which the colonial administration intervened, first from overseas and then as a republic – is the result of a ten-year period of observation of the expansion of the 'democratic' state front in the indigenous world of Brazil. The 'democratic' state front to which I refer is that of the post-dictatorships in our countries, which reaches to the indigenous frontier, to the 'village-world', with laws and public policies, companies and NGOs. This front, always colonial, irremediably intrusive and intervening in what remains of the village-world tries to deliver with one hand what it has already withdrawn with the other, it strives to offer antidotes, in the form of rights, to contain the action of the poison it has already inoculated. Due to the constitutive format of the state and the low awareness among its agents of the difference between 'citizenship' as a mass of formally rights-bearing individuals and a communitarian and collectivist organization of life, its actions have an almost inevitably disruptive impact on the web of relationships and system of authority of the village-world and of the memory of its members. I have seen this process unfold, expand, and affect the lives of women, and this is what I speak about in this text. The foundational event of that nearly decade-long period of participation and observation began in 2002, when I was summoned by the Fundación Nacional del Indio – FUNAI – to conduct a seminar-workshop with the aim of creating a lexicon to construct a discourse capable of capturing and transferring the demand for policies of indigenous women to the Brazilian state on the eve of the PT [Brazilian Workers Party] and President Lula's ascension to the presidency of the nation.

This topic, it seems to me, is of course part of a very recent debate, and, in order to situate it, it is appropriate to identify three positions within feminist thought: Eurocentric feminism, which affirms that the problem of gender domination, of patriarchal domination, is universal, with no major differences, justifying under this banner of unity the possibility of transmitting modernity's advances in the field of rights to non-White, indigenous and Black women of the colonized continents. It thus sustains a position of moral superiority of European or Eurocentric women, authorizing them to intervene with their civilizing-colonial/modernizing mission. This position is, in turn, inevitably a-historical and anti-historical, because it encloses history within the very slow, almost stagnant time crystal of patriarchy, and above all occludes the radical twist introduced by the entry of colonial/modern time into the history of gender relations. As I mentioned earlier, both race and gender, despite having been installed by epistemic ruptures that have established new eras – that of coloniality for race, and that of the species for gender – make history within the stability of the episteme from which they originate.

A second position, at the other extreme, is the position of some authors, such as María Lugones and also Oyèrónkẹ Oyěwùmí, who affirm the non-existence of gender in the pre-colonial world (Lugones 2007). I published, in 2003 (2003a), a critical analysis of Oyéronké's 1997 book, in the light of a text of mine from 1986 which expressed the same perplexity about gender in the atmosphere [*atmósfera*] of the Yoruba civilization, but with divergent conclusions.[3]

Indigenous and Afro-American Societies as 'Low-intensity' Patriarchies

And a third position, represented by me here, is supported by a large accumulation of historical evidence and ethnographic accounts that incontrovertibly show the existence of gender nomenclatures in tribal and Afro-American societies. This third strand identifies in indigenous and Afro-American societies a patriarchal organization, albeit different from that of Western gender, which could be described as a low-intensity patriarchy, and does not consider the leadership of Eurocentric feminism to be either effective or opportune. In this

---

3   Segato (1986, 2005 [1986]).

group, we can mention the feminist thinkers linked to the Chiapas process,[4] which constituted a paradigmatic positioning to resolve the tensions arising from women being embedded in the double predicament of indigenous struggles and the internal struggle for better living conditions for their gender.[5]

Women – both indigenous and African American –[6] whose actions and thoughts are divided between, on the one hand, loyalty to their communities and peoples on the external front and, on the other, their internal struggle against the oppression they suffer from within their communities and peoples, have frequently denounced the blackmailing of indigenous authorities, who pressure them to defer their demands as women lest they end up fragmenting the cohesion of their communities, making them more vulnerable to the struggle for resources and rights. This has been contested by the authors I quote.

Documentary, historical, and ethnographic data from the tribal world show the existence of recognizable structures of difference, similar to what we call gender relations in modernity. These contain clear hierarchies of prestige between masculinity and femininity, represented by figures that can be understood as men and women. Despite the recognizable character of gender positions, in this world, there are more frequent openings for transit and circulation between these positions that are forbidden in their modern Western equivalent. As is well known, indigenous peoples, such as the Warao of Venezuela, the Cuna of Panama, the Guayaquís [Aché] of Paraguay, the Trio of Surinam, the Javaés of Brazil, and the pre-Columbian Inca world, among others, as well as a number of Native American peoples in the United States and Canadian First Nations, as well as all African-American religious groups, include transgender languages and contemplate transgender practices, marriages between people whom the West would view as being of the same

---

4   Refers to the 1994 Zapatista (Zapatista Army of National Liberation (Spanish: *Ejército Zapatista de Liberación Nacional*; EZLN)) uprising and ensuing tension between the Mexican state and the indigenous communities and subsistence farmers of the Mexican region of Chiapas from the 1990s to the present day. Negotiations between the government and Zapatistas led to agreements being signed, but were often not complied with in the following years as the peace process stagnated leading to an increasing division between communities with ties to the government and communities that sympathized with the Zapatistas. Note by the translator.
5   See, for example: Gutiérrez/Palomo 1999; Hernández Castillo 2003; and Hernández/Sierra 2005.
6   See, for example: Williams/Pierce 1996.

sex, and other gender transitivities that have been blocked by the absolutely unbending gender system of coloniality/modernity.[7]

Dimensions of constructing masculinity that have accompanied humankind throughout its entire history are also recognizable in the pre-intrusion world, in what I have called "the patriarchal pre-history of humanity" characterized by a very slow temporality, that is to say, of a *longue-durée* that is confused with evolutionary time (Segato 2003b). This masculinity is the construction of a subject obliged to acquire it as a status, going through trials and facing death as in the Hegelian allegory of the lord and his servant. This subject is burdened by the imperative of having to conduct and reconduct himself to it throughout his life under the gaze and evaluation of his peers, proving and reconfirming abilities of resistance, aggressiveness, domination, and the accumulation of what I have called 'feminine tribute' (Segato 2003b), in order to exhibit the package of powers – warlike, political, sexual, intellectual, economic and moral – that will allow him to be recognized and labeled as a masculine subject.

On the one hand, this indicates that gender does exist, albeit in a different form than in modernity. And on the other hand, it shows that when this colonial modernity approaches the gender of the village, it modifies it dangerously. It intervenes in the structure of village relations, capturing them, and reorganizing them from within, maintaining the appearance of continuity, but transforming meanings by introducing an order that is now governed by different rules. That is why I speak of verisimilitude: The nomenclatures remain, but they are reinterpreted in the light of the new modern order.[8] This crossover is truly fatal, because a language that was once hierarchical, in contact with the egalitarian discourse of modernity, is transformed into a super hierarchical and [uprooted] order, due to the factors that I will examine below: the super-inflation of men in the community environment, in their role as intermediaries with the outside world, that is to say, with the emasculation of the men outside of their community in the face of the power of the White administrators; the super-inflation and universalization of the public sphere, ancestrally inhabited by men, with the collapse and privatization of the domestic sphere; and the binarization of duality, resulting from universalizing one of its two terms

---

7   For a list of transgender identities in historical and contemporary societies, see Campuzano (2009a: 76).

8   Author's note for this publication: Something similar has been pointed out by Julieta Paredes (2010) with her idea of the 'Interlocking Patriarchies' [Entroque Patriarcal].

by constituting it as public, in opposition to the other, which is constituted as private.

Totalitarianism of the Public Sphere and the Domesticization of Women

If the village has always been organized by status, divided into well-characterized spaces with their own rules with differential prestige and hierarchical order, inhabited by people destined for them who can be, in a very generic way, recognized from a modern perspective as men and women because of their roles proper to those spaces, and who are marked by this destiny of spatial, labor, ritual distribution; the discourse of coloniality/modernity, although egalitarian, hides within it, as many feminist authors have already pointed out, an abysmal hierarchical hiatus, due to what we could tentatively call the progressive totalization of the public sphere or 'totalitarianism of the public sphere'. It might even be possible to suggest that it is the public sphere that today continues and deepens the colonizing process.[9]

I illustrate this with an example of what happens when we arrive in the villages with the workshops of the Women's Committee of the FUNAI[10] to talk to indigenous women about the growing problems of violence against them, the news of which reaches Brasilia. What is happening, in general, but especially in areas where life that is considered 'traditional' is supposedly more preserved and where autonomy from the state is valued more highly, as in the case of the inhabitants of the Xingu Park, in Mato Grosso, is that the caciques and the men are present and interpose the argument that there is nothing for the state to discuss with their women. They support the argument with the plausible truth that their world "has always been like this": "The control we have over our women is a control we have always had over them". They support this statement, as I anticipated on the previous pages, with a culturalist, and therefore fundamentalist, argument, in that it presupposes that culture had no history.

---

9   Author's note for this publication: If we use the category 'sexual contract' coined by Carole Pateman (1988), we illuminate this idea by affirming that in the village-world, the sexual contract is exposed, while in colonial modernity, the sexual contract is disguised by the language of the citizen contract.

10   Translator's note: FUNAI stands for Fundación Nacional del Indio (National Indian Foundation) which is located in Brazil.

Arlette Gautier calls this historical myopia "the invention of customary law" (Gautier 2005: 697).

The answer, rather complex by the way, that we give them, is: "Partly yes, and partly no". Because, if there was always a hierarchy in the village-world, a prestige differential between men and women, there was also a difference, which is now threatened by the encroachment and colonization of the public republican space, which propagates a discourse of equality and relegates difference to a marginal, problematic position – the problem of the 'other', or relegating the other to a 'problem' status. This inflection, introduced by way of annexation under the aegis, first, of the overseas-based colonial administration, and, later, of the colonial/state administration, as the first of its symptoms, coopts men as the class ancestrally predestined to the tasks and roles of the public space due to characteristics they held pre-intrusion.

Ancestrally, it has been the men's domain to deliberate on the village commons, to go on hunting expeditions, and make contact with other villages, near or far, of their own or other peoples, to parley or go to war with them. This is why, from the perspective of the village, the agencies of the successive colonial administrations are part of this register: with whom one parleys, with whom one fights wars, with whom one negotiates, with whom one makes pacts and, in recent times, from whom one obtains resources and rights (considered as resources) that are claimed in times of identity politics. The ancestral male position, therefore, is now transformed by this relational role with powerful agencies that produce and reproduce coloniality. It is with men that the colonizers fought wars and negotiated, and it is with men that the state of coloniality/modernity does the same things now. For Arlette Gautier, the choice of men as privileged interlocutors was deliberate and functional to the interests of colonization and to the efficacy of its control: "Colonization brings with it a radical loss of women's political power, where it existed, while the colonizers negotiated with certain masculine structures or invented them, in order to gain allies" (2005: 718) and promoted the 'domestication' of women and their greater distance and subjection to facilitate the colonial enterprise (ibid: 690).[11]

The masculine position is thus inflected and promoted to a new and distanced platform that hides behind the preceding nomenclature, now strengthened by privileged access to resources and knowledge about the world of power. It is thus inadvertently dislocated, while the order is being ruptured and reconstituted, maintaining the old names and rituals of gender, but endowing

---

11   Author's note for this publication: On this subject, see also Assis Climaco (2009).

the position with new contents. Men return to the village claiming to be what they have always been but concealing the fact that they are already operating in a new way. We could also speak here of the famous and permanently fertile metaphor of *body-snatching* from the Hollywood classic *The invasion of the body snatchers*; the 'perfect crime' formulated by Baudrillard, because it is effectively hidden in the false analogy, or verisimilitude. We see the gender cast playing out another drama; we see a new grammar applied to its vocabulary.

The Administrative and Pornographic Colonial Gaze

Women and the village itself now became part of an objective externality for the male gaze, infected, by contact and mimesis, of the evil of distance and exteriority which is inherent to the exercise of power in the world of coloniality. The position of men now became simultaneously interior and exterior, with the exteriority and objectifying capacity of the simultaneously administrative and pornographic colonial gaze. In a very synthetic way, on which I cannot expand here, I anticipate that sexuality is transformed, introducing a previously unknown morality, one which reduces women's bodies to objects and, at the same time, inoculates the notion of sin, nefarious crimes, and all that it entails. We must attribute to coloniality/modern exteriority – the exteriority of scientific rationality, administrative exteriority, expurgatory exteriority of the other and of the difference already pointed out by Aníbal Quijano (1992) and by Walter Mignolo (2003 [2000]: 290–291, 424) in their texts – that pornographic character of the colonizing gaze.

It should be noted that, along with this hyperinflation of the male position in the village, they are also being emasculated when they are confronted with the White world, which puts them under stress and shows them the relativity of their masculine position by subjecting them to the sovereign dominion of the colonizer. This process is *violentogenic* [violentogénico], as it oppresses them here while empowering them in the village, forcing them to reproduce and exhibit the capacity of control inherent to the male subject position in the only world that is now possible, to restore damaged virility on the external front. This is true for the entire universe of racialized masculinity, relegated to the condition of non-Whiteness by the order of coloniality.

The hijacking of all politics, that is to say, of all deliberation about the common good, by the nascent and expansive republican public sphere, and the consequent privatization of the domestic space, its *othering* [otrificación], marginalization, and expropriation of everything that was a political task in it, also forms part of this panorama of pre-intrusion gender getting captured by modern gender. The exclusive ties between women, which were geared towards reciprocity and solidarity, both in rituals and in productive and reproductive tasks, are diluted in the process of encapsulating domesticity as 'private life'. For the domestic space and those who inhabit it, this means nothing more and nothing less than a crumbling of their political value and power, that is, of their capacity to participate in the decisions that affect the whole collectivity. The consequences of this rupture of bonds between women – and of the end of the political alliances that these bonds had enabled and encouraged for the women and their causes – were literally fatal for their security. Thus, they became progressively more vulnerable to male violence, in addition to the stress caused by the pressure put on men from the outside world.

The compulsive restriction of the domestic space and of women as its inhabitants to a private refuge has terrible consequences in terms of the violence that victimizes them. It is essential to understand that these consequences are *fully modern and a product of modernity*, remembering that the ever-expanding process *of modernization is also an ongoing process of colonization*. Likewise, the characteristics of the crime of genocide, due to their rationality and systematicity, originated in modern times, and feminicides, as almost machinic practices of extermination of women, are also a modern invention. It is the barbarism of colonial modernity mentioned above. As I have argued elsewhere, its impunity is linked to the privatization of the domestic space as a residual space that is excluded from the sphere of major issues, which are considered to be of general public interest (Segato 2010). With the emergence of the modern universal grid, from which emanate the state, politics, rights, and science, both the domestic sphere and the women who inhabit it are transformed into mere remnants, on the margins of issues considered of universal relevance and neutral perspective.

Gender as a Hierarchical Duality in the *Mallkus*, vs. Modern Binarisms

Although in the public space of the village-world of a large number of Amazonian and Gran Chaco communities, there are precise restrictions on women's participation and speech, and the prerogative of deliberation is reserved for men, it is a well-known practice that these men adjourn their session in the tribal agora at sunset, in many cases in a very ritualized manner, without arriving at any conclusion, in order to hold a consultation in the evening in the domestic space. The parliament only resumes the next day, with the contribution from the women's world, who only speak in the house. Skipping this consultation incurs a severe penalty for men. This is common and occurs in a clearly compartmentalized world where, although there is a public space and a domestic space, politics, as a set of deliberations that lead to decisions that affect collective life, cuts across both spaces. In the Andean world, the authority of the *mallkus*[12], although its internal order is hierarchical, is always dual, involving a male head and a female head. And all community deliberations are accompanied by women, seated next to their husbands, or gathered outside the enclosure where they take place, and they signal their approval or disapproval over the course of the debate. This way, there is no monopoly of politics over the public space and its activities, as in the modern colonial world. On the contrary, the domestic space is endowed with politicization, because it is a space of obligatory consultation and because it is where the women's body corporate is articulated as a political front.

Gender, thus regulated, constitutes a hierarchical duality, in which both terms that compose it, despite their inequality, are ontologically and politically complete. In the world of modernity, there is no duality, there is binarism. While in duality, the relation is one of complementarity, the binary relation is one of supplementarity; one side supplements – and does not complement –the other. When one of these terms becomes 'universal', that is to say, of general representativeness, what was once a hierarchy becomes an abyss, and the second term becomes a mere remnant[13]: This is the binary structure, which is different from the dual.

According to the modern colonial and binary pattern, any element, in order to attain ontological completeness, completeness of being, must be equalized, that is to say, it must be made commensurable based on a frame of reference or universal equivalent. This produces the effect that any manifestation of otherness will constitute a problem, and will only cease to do so when

---

12 *Mallku*: leader in Aymara ("leader", "prince"). The institution of the *Council of Mallkus and Amautas* acts like an upper house of the indigenous parliament of the Andes region. Note by the translator.

13 "*Resto*" in the original: rest, remainder. Note by the translator.

sifted through the equalizing grid, neutralized of particularities, of idiosyncrasies. The other-Indian, the other-non-White, the woman, unless they are either purged of their difference, or their difference is made commensurable as a recognizable identity within the global pattern, do not neatly fit into this neutral, aseptic environment of the universal equivalent that can be generalized and attributed with universal value and interest. In the world of modernity, individual and collective subjects and issues will only acquire politicization and be endowed with political capacity if they can, in some way, be processed, reconverted, transported, and reformulated so as to be expressed in universal terms in the 'neutral' space of the republican subject, where the universal citizen subject speaks. All that is left over in this processing, that which cannot be converted or made commensurable within that grid, is a mere remnant.

However, as other authors have already affirmed, only one native subject can traverse this sphere, this modern agora, naturally because he has emerged from this very space. And this subject, who has formulated the rule of citizenship according to his own image and likeness, because he based it in an exteriority that took shape in this initially belligerent and then immediately ideological process that installed the colonial and modern episteme, has the following characteristics: He is male, White, *pater-familiae* – therefore, at least functionally, heterosexual –, proprietor, and literate. Anyone who wants to mimic his civic capacity will have to reconvert to this profile, by means of politicization – in the sense of 'publicization of identity', since the public is the only thing that has political power in the modern environment.[14]

Gender Dualism vs. Western Individualization and Heteronormativity

'Dualism', as in the case of gender dualism in the indigenous world, as one of the variants of the multiple or the two 'sums-up' [*el dos resume*], epitomizes a multiplicity.[15] Binarism, being proper to coloniality/modernity, results from the episteme of the expurgation and constructed exteriority, of the world of

---

14   For this discussion see Warner (1990); West (2000 [1988]); Benhabib (2006 [1992]); Cornell (2001 [1998]).

15   Author's note for this publication: This multiplicity originated in the transitions between the two poles; the crossings, encounters and crossroads of the many forms of transgenderedness in the worlds in which there was no, or only partial intervention by the structure of coloniality.

the One. The one and the two of indigenous duality are one among many possibilities of the multiple, where the one and the two, though they may function complementarily, are ontologically complete and endowed with politicization, though unequal in value and prestige. The second in this hierarchical duality is not a problem that demands conversion, or being funneled through the grid of a universal equivalent, nor is it a mere remnant of the transposition to the One, but it is fully other, a complete, irreducible other.

By understanding this, we understand that the domestic is a complete space with its own politics, with its own associations, hierarchically inferior to the public, but with the capacity for self-defense and self-transformation. One could say that the gender relationships in this world configure a patriarchy of low intensity, if compared to the patriarchal relations imposed by the colony and stabilized in modern coloniality.

Without going into detail, I draw attention here to the well-known failure of the gender strategies of prestigious international cooperation programs, precisely because they apply a universalist view and start from a Eurocentric definition of 'gender' and the relations it organizes. In other words, the great fragility of collaboration on this matter is due to the fact that it lacks sensitivity to the categories specific to the contexts for which the projects are formulated. In rural communities and indigenous villages, society is dual in terms of gender, and this duality organizes spaces, tasks, and the distribution of rights and duties. This duality defines gender communities or collectives. Therefore, the general community fabric is, in turn, subdivided into two groups, with their internal norms and their own forms of coexistence and association for productive and reproductive tasks as well as ceremonial tasks. In general, the technical cooperation projects and actions of European countries reveal the difficulty of perceiving gender specificity in the community environments in which they operate. As a consequence, projects and actions related to gender and aimed at promoting gender equality are referred to and applied to people, i.e., individual women, or the relationship between women and male individuals, and the result pursued is the direct and unmediated promotion of gender equality conceived as equality of persons and not of spheres. Designed with a focus on individuals, actions to promote gender equity do not take into account that actions sensitive to the community context should be aimed at promoting the domestic sphere and the women's collective as a whole, as opposed to the hierarchy of prestige and power of the public community space and men's collective. Indeed, the goal of the projects should be to promote equality between the men's collectives and the women's collectives within the communities. Only this equality can result, subsequently, in the emergence of outstanding women's personalities who do not distance themselves from their communities of origin, i.e., who permanently return to and practice permanent action together with their group.

In addition to [the aforementioned] individualism inherent in the perspective of the state and state and trans-state programs, the modern world is the world of the 'one', and all forms of otherness in relation to the universal pattern represented by this 'one' constitute a problem. The discipline of anthropology itself is proof of this, for it was born out of the modern conviction that the others have to be explained, translated, made commensurable, processed by the rational operation that incorporates them into the universal grid. Anything that cannot be reduced to it remains as a residue that has no weight in reality, is not ontologically full, is incomplete and irrelevant waste material. Derridean deconstruction, which destabilizes the binary duo, has no place or role to play in the circuit of duality.

With the transformation of dualism, as a variant of the multiple, into the binarism of the 'one' – universal, canonical, 'neutral' – and its other – remnant, residue, anomaly, margin – transitions are closed down, as is the option to circulate between the positions, all of which become colonized by binary logic. Gender is cast, in the Western way, in the heterosexual matrix, and the rights of protection against homophobia and policies to promote equality and sexual freedom, such as same-sex marriage, prohibited in colonial/modern times and accepted in a wide diversity of indigenous peoples of the continent, become necessary.[16]

The pressures imposed by the colonizer on the diverse forms of sexuality that he found in the Inca empire have been reported by Giuseppe Campuzano (2006, 2009, among others) in chronicles and documents of the 16th and 17th centuries. In these texts, the pressure exerted by the norms and the punitive threats introduced to confine those practices to the conquistador's binary heterosexual matrix imposes notions of sin which were foreign to the world encountered here, and propagates its pornographic gaze. This allows us to conclude that many of the moral prejudices that are perceived today as belonging to 'custom' or 'tradition', those that the instrument of human rights tries to combat, are in fact prejudices, customs, and traditions that are already modern, that is, originating from the pattern installed by colonial modernity. In

---

16   I described this difference between the worlds for the Afro-Brazilian religious communities of the Nagô Yoruba of Recife in the article cited above (1986).

other words, the supposedly homophobic 'custom' as well as others, is already modern. And, once again, we find ourselves with the legal antidote that modernity produces to counteract the problems that it itself introduced and continues to propagate.

This rigid casting into positions of identity is also one of the characteristics of racialization, installed by the colonial/modern process, which forces subjects into fixed positions within the binary canon here constituted by the terms White/non-White.[17]

Sadly, the redistribution of the cosmos and the whole earth with all its beings, animate and inanimate, to fit into the binarism of the subject-object relationship of Western science is also part of this process. In the midst of this new situation – new and progressive for many peoples exposed to a permanent and daily process of conquest and colonization –, the struggles for rights and equity-oriented public policies are characteristic of the modern world. And it is not a matter of opposing them, but of understanding to which paradigm they belong and, especially, to understand that to live in a decolonial way is to try to open breaches in a territory totalized by the binary system, which is possibly the most efficient instrument of power.

That is why, when I hold workshops at FUNAI's Working Group on Gender and Generation to present the advances of the *Maria da Penha Law* against Domestic Violence, I tell my indigenous women participants that the state is giving them with one hand what it has already taken from them with the other.

Coloniality as the Depoliticization of the Domestic Space

When the world of the one and the rest, in the binary structure, encounters the world of the multiple, it captures and modifies it from within itself as a consequence of the coloniality of power, which allows for a greater influence of one world over another. It would be more accurate to say that it colonizes it. In this new dominant order, the public space, in turn, comes to capture and monopolize all deliberations and decisions regarding the general common good, and the domestic space as such becomes depoliticized, both because it loses its ancestral forms of intervention in the decisions that were made in the public

---

17   On the co-emergence of colony, modernity, and capitalism with the categories 'Europe', 'America', 'race', 'Indian', 'White', 'Black' see Quijano (1991, 2000) and Quijano/Wallerstein (1992).

space, and also because it is enclosed in the nuclear family and locked in privacy. New imperative forms of conjugality and censorship of the extended ties that once crossed domesticity are becoming the norm (Maia 2010/Abu-Lughod 2002), thus weakening the control exercised by the community gaze, monitoring and judging the community's behavior. The depoliticization of the domestic space makes it vulnerable and fragile, and there are countless testimonies of the degrees and cruel forms of victimization that occur when the protection of the community's gaze on the family world disappears. The authority, value, and prestige of women and their sphere of action crumble.

This critique of the fall of the domestic sphere and of the women's world, from a position of ontological completeness to the level of a remnant or residue of the real, has important gnoseological[18] consequences. Among them is the difficulty we face when, though we do understand the omnipresence of gender relations in social life, we do not manage to view our entire reality from the point of view of gender, giving it a theoretical and epistemic status as a central category capable of illuminating all aspects of social life. In contrast, in the pre-intrusion world, this problem of the gnoseological devaluation of the gender system does not exist, as evidenced by the constant references to duality in all its symbolic fields.

What is most important to note here is that, in this context of change, nomenclatures are preserved and a mirage, a false impression of continuity of the old order occurs, with a system of names, formalities, and rituals that apparently remains, but is now governed by another structure.[19] This passage is subtle, and the lack of clarity about the changes that have occurred causes women to submit without knowing how to answer the men's repeated refrain of "we have always been this way", and their claim to be maintaining a custom that they assume or affirm to be traditional, with the hierarchy of value and prestige that is proper to it. This keeps women in a permanent state of being blackmailed, threatened with the assumption that if they touch and modify this order, it would harm their people's identity, as political capital, and culture, as symbolic capital and reference in the struggles for continuity as a people, thus weakening demands for territories, resources, and rights as resources.

---

18 Gnoseological: Considering the theory of knowledge, note by the translator.
19 I analyzed this in my book of 2007: La Nación y sus otros. Raza, etnicidades y diversidad religiosa en tiempos de Políticas de la Identidad, Buenos Aires: Prometeo.

What has happened, however, and what I have been saying, is that the hierarchical distance and power of those who already had power – elders, chiefs, men in general – has been aggravated internally, within the village space, as a consequence of modern colonization. As I have stated, although one can say that there has always been hierarchy and gender relations as relations of unequal power and prestige, with the colonial state intervention and the entry into the colonial/modern order, this oppressive distance has been aggravated and magnified. A mutation occurs under the mantle of apparent continuity. Therefore, it takes rhetorical skill to convey that the effect of historical depth is an optical illusion to solidify the new forms of authority of men and other hierarchies of the village. For here, we are faced with a perverse culturalism, of which I spoke at the beginning of this essay, which is nothing other than the fundamentalism of the political culture of our times, inaugurated with the Fall of the Berlin Wall and the obsolescence of the Marxist debate, when identities, now politicized, became the language of disputes (Segato 2007).

Ethnic and Communitarian Citizenship: "Unequal *but* Different"

To sum up, and to recapitulate: When we think that we are replacing the hierarchy that used to order the relationship between men and women with an egalitarian relationship, in a gesture that aims at universalizing citizenship, what we are really doing is remedy problems that modernity itself introduced with solutions that are also modern: The state delivers with one hand what it has already withdrawn with the other. Unlike the "different but equal" formula of modern activism, the indigenous world is guided by the formula, difficult for us to access, of "unequal *but* different". That means that it is truly multiple, because the other, which is different, or even inferior, does not represent a problem to be solved. The imperative of commensurability disappears. It is here that the interworld of critical modernity enters taking advantage of pre-intrusion structures for its own benefit, fertilizing the ethnic hierarchy with its discourse of equality, and generating what some are beginning to call ethnic or communitarian citizenship, which can only be adequate if it is based on internal debate and proper jurisdiction, that is, from the debate and deliberation of its members, weaving together the threads of their particular history. I conclude by referring here to the extraordinary film *Mooladé*, by the recently deceased Senegalese director Ousman Sembene, about the struggle of a group of women in a village in Burkina Faso to eradicate the practice of infibulation[20]: From the inside, the internal face of the community, which is, as it has always been, intersected by the surrounding world.

References

Abu-Lughod, Lila (2002 [1998]): Feminismo y modernidad en oriente próximo, Valencia: Cátedra.
Assis Climaco, Danilo (2009): 'Tráfico de mulheres, negócios de homens. Leituras feministas e anticoloniais sobre os homens, as masculinidades e/ou o masculino." Psychology Master Thesis, Florianópolis: Universidade Federal de Santa Catarina.
Benhabib, Seyla (2006 [1992]): El ser y el otro en la ética contemporánea. Feminismo, comunitarismo y posmodernismo, Barcelona: GEDISA.
Campuzano, Giuseppe (2006): "Reclaiming Travesti Histories." In: Sexuality Matters. IDS Bulletin 37/5, pp. 34–39.
Campuzano, Giuseppe (2009a): "Contemporary Travesti Encounters with Gender and Sexuality in Latin America." In: Development 52/1, pp. 75–83.
Campuzano, Giuseppe (2009b): "Andróginos, hombres vestidos de mujer, maricones... el Museo Travesti del Perú." In: Bagoas: Estudos gays: gêneros e sexualidades 3/4, pp. 79–93.
Cornell, Drucilla (2001 [1998]): En el corazón de la libertad. Feminismo, sexo e igualdad, Madrid: Ediciones Cátedra and Universidad de Valencia.
Gautier, Arlette (2005): "Mujeres y colonialismo." In: Marc Ferro (ed.), El libro negro del colonialismo. Siglos XVI al XXI: Del exterminio al arrepentimiento, Madrid: La esfera de los libros, pp. 677–723.
Gutiérrez, Margarita/Palomo, Nellys (1999): "Autonomía con mirada de mujer." In: Cal. Burguete/Aracely Mayor (eds.), México: Experiencias de autonomía indígena, Guatemala and Copenhague: IWGIA, pp. 54–86.
Hernández Castillo, Rosalva Aída (2003): "Re-pensar el multiculturalismo desde el género. Las luchas por el reconocimiento cultural y los feminismos de la diversidad." In: La Ventana. Revista de estudios de género 18, pp. 7–39.
Hernández, Rosalva Aída/Sierra, María Teresa (2005): "Repensar los derechos colectivos desde el género: Aportes de las mujeres indígenas al debate de la autonomía." In: Martha Sánchez (ed.), La doble mirada: Luchas y expe-

---

20 Female Genital Circumcision, note by the translator.

riencias de las mujeres indígenas de América Latina, Mexico City: UNIFEM and ILSB, pp. 105–120.

Lugones, María (2007): "Heterosexualism and the Colonial/Modern Gender System." In: Hypatia 22/1, pp. 186–209.

Maia, Claudia de Jesús (2010): A Invenção da 'Solteirona': Conjugalidade Moderna e Terror Moral – Minas Gerais (1890 – 1948), Florianópolis: Editora das Mulheres.

Mignolo, Walter (2003 [2000]): Histórias locais /Projetos globais, Belo Horizonte: Editora UFMG.

Oyèrónkẹ Oyěwùmí (1997): The Invention of Women. Making an African Sense of Western Gender Discourses, Minneapolis: University of Minnesota Press.

Paredes, Julieta (2010): Hilando fino desde el feminismo comunitario, La Paz: CEDEC and Mujeres Creando Comunidad.

Pateman, Carole (1988): The Sexual Contract, Stanford: Stanford University Press.

Quijano, Aníbal (1991): "La modernidad, el capital y América Latina nacen el mismo día." In: ILLA, Revista del Centro de Educación y Cultura 10, pp. 44–56.

Quijano, Aníbal (1992): "Colonialidad y modernidad-racionalidad." In: Heraclio Bonilla (ed.), Los conquistados. 1492 y la población indígena de las Américas, Quito: Tercer Mundo, Libri Mundi and FLACSO-Ecuador, pp.437-447.

Quijano, Aníbal (2000): "Colonialidad del poder y clasificación social." In: Journal of World-Systems Research. Special Issue: Festschrift for Immanuel Wallerstein – Part I. 6/2, pp. 342–386.

Quijano, Aníbal/Wallerstein, Immanuel (1992): "La americanidad como concepto, o América en el moderno sistema mundial." In: Revista Internacional de Ciencias Sociales 134, pp. 583–591.

Segato, Rita Laura (2003a): "Género, política e hibridismo en la transnacionalización de la cultura Yoruba." In: Revista de Estudios Afro-Asiáticos 2, pp. 333–363.

Segato, Rita Laura (2003b): Las estructuras elementales de la violencia, Buenos Aires: Prometeo.

Segato, Rita Laura (2005 [1986]): "Inventando a Natureza. família, sexo e gênero no Xangô do Recife." In: Rita Laura Segato/Marcelo Carvalho de Oliveira (eds.), Santos e Daimones: o politeísmo afro-brasileiro e a tradição arquetipal, Brasilia: Editora da Universidade de Brasilia, pp. 11–54.

Segato, Rita Laura (2007): La Nación y sus otros. Raza, etnicidades y diversidad religiosa en tiempos de políticas de la identidad, Buenos Aires: Prometeo.

Segato, Rita Laura (2010): "Femi-geno-cidio como crimen en el fuero internacional de los Derechos Humanos: el derecho a nombrar el sufrimiento en el derecho." In: Rosa-Linda Fregoso (ed.), Feminicidio en América Latina, Mexico City: Editora de la UNAM, pp. 249–278.

Segato, Rita Laura (2011). "Género y colonialidad: en busca de claves de lectura y de un vocabulario estratégico descolonial." In: Karina Bidaseca/Vanesa Vazquez Laba (eds.), Feminismos y poscolonialidad: descolonizando el feminismo desde y en América Latina, Buenos Aires: Ediciones Godot, Colección Crítica, pp. 17–48.

Segato, Rita Laura (2014). "Colonialidad y patriarcado moderno: expansión del frente estatal, modernización y la vida de las mujeres." In: Yuderkys Espinosa Miñoso/Diana Gómez Correal/Karina Ochoa Muñoz (eds.), Tejiendo de otro modo: Feminismo, epistemología y apuestas decoloniales en Abya Yala, Popoyán: Editorial Universidad del Cauca, pp. 75–90.

Warner, Michael (1990): The Letters of the Republic: Publication and the Public Sphere in Eighteenth-Century America, Cambridge, Mass.: Harvard University Press.

West, Robin (2000 [1988]): Género y teoría del derecho, Bogotá: Ediciones Uniandes, Instituto Pensar el Siglo del Hombre Editores and Colección Nuevo Pensamiento Jurídico.

Williams, Brackette F./Pierce, Pauline (1996): "And Your Prayers Shall Be Answered through the Womb of a Woman. Insurgent Masculine Redemption and the Nation of Islam." In: Brackette F. Williams (ed.), Women Out of Olace: The Gender of Agency and The Race of Nationality, New York and London: Routledge, pp. 186–215.

A Decolonial Critique of Feminist Epistemology Critique[1]

Yuderkys Espinosa-Miñoso[2]

Abstract: *This essay makes explicit the theoretical production of anti-racist and decolonial feminism as part of the bets to advance in a counter-hegemonic epistemology attentive to Eurocentrism, racism, and coloniality, not only in the production of knowledge in the social and human sciences in general, but concretely within feminist theorizing. The analysis starts by recognizing the previous contributions that nourish the production of theory of decolonial feminism, showing how it radicalizes and doubles the bet in its critique of the theoretical and conceptual frameworks that support the most accepted and popularized truths as the "women's point of view". By means of concrete examples, the contribution shows the type of errors incurred, the operations through which the categories, methodology, and points of view previously criticized are taken up again, without any intention of abandoning them or looking for alternatives to solve the problem.*

In this intervention I intend, from my concrete experience as a decolonial antiracist feminist theorist, in active opposition to the *modern colonial gender system* (Lugones 2008) and heterosexuality as a political regime (Wittig 2006 [1980]), to advance the stakes of decolonial feminism and its epistemological contributions.

---

1 This paper was originally presented under the title "Decolonial Feminism as a counter-hegemonic epistemology" at the round table "¿Cómo construir epistemologías contrahegemónicas? Os desafios da arte, a educação, a tecnologia e a criatividade del Facendo Genero," held on 10 November 2013, Santa Catalina, Brasil. [The Spanish] version was published first under: Espinosa-Miñoso, Yuderkys (2014): "Una crítica descolonial a la epistemología feminista crítica." In: El Cotidiano 184, March-April, pp. 7–12. Available at: https://www.redalyc.org/articulo.oa?id=32530724004
2 Translated from Spanish by Julia Roth.

First of all, I must say that for me, decolonial feminism is first and foremost an epistemic challenge. It is a movement in full growth and maturation "that proclaims itself revisionist of the theory and political proposal of feminism given what it considers its Western, White and bourgeois bias" (Espinosa 2013a). From here, a critique is made of previous feminist epistemologies observing the premises sustaining the great truths that would explain the reason for oppression based on the gender system. Decolonial feminists retrieve the criticisms that have been made of classical feminist thought from the thought produced by marginal and subaltern voices of women and feminism. We begin by recognizing that this classical feminist thought has been produced by a specific group of women, those who have enjoyed epistemic privilege thanks to their class and racial origins. Decolonial feminism elaborates a genealogy of the thinking produced from the margins by feminists, women, lesbians, and racialized people in general; and dialogues with the knowledge generated by intellectuals and activists committed to dismantling the matrix of multiple oppression by assuming a non-Eurocentric point of view.

In agreement with Aníbal Quijano's affirmation that we have reached the moment of an epistemic revolution, I am convinced that this double bet made by decolonial feminism to 1) revise the theoretical-conceptual scaffolding produced by White bourgeois Western feminism, while 2) advancing in the production of new interpretations that explain the performance of power from positions that assume a subaltern point of view, constitutes a fundamental contribution to the production of new epistemologies and conceptual theoretical frameworks that confront the scaffolding of hegemonic truth production imposed by Europe, and later by the United States, by force from the very moment of the conquest and colonization of America. If we agree that oppression is grounded in a system of knowledge and production of the lifeworld, a system of social classification, within which the dominant categories of oppression (gender, race, class) have emerged, a system instituted through the colonizing enterprise, and with imperial reason at its service, the time has come for a broad epistemic disobedience that breaks down the framework of compression of the world as it has been produced and imposed by Western modernity. To discover and abandon *autoethnography* (Pratt 1997) and move, once and for all, to produce and make visible in a broad way our own interpretation of the world, as a priority task for the processes of decolonization. It is a task that must be accompanied by processes of recovery of the traditions of knowledge that have resisted the onslaught of coloniality in Abya Yala, as well as those that from other geographies and from critical positions have contributed to the production of epistemological fractures.

A good example of what I am talking about is how the production of knowledge of decolonial feminism itself embraces the recognition of the knowledge produced by previous counter-hegemonic feminist epistemologies and helps perpetuate their legacy. Decolonial feminist thought recognizes that it is related to the theoretical tradition initiated by Black feminism, feminism of color, and Third World feminism in the United States, and how it helped us think in terms of interweaving forms of oppression (of class, race, gender, sexuality). At the same time, it proposes to recover the critical legacy of afrodescendant and indigenous women and feminists from Latin America who have raised the problem of their own invisibility within their movements and within feminism itself. This prompted an effort to revise their role and importance in the realization and resistance of their communities.

The group also draws on the critical revision of feminism's subject-essentialism and identity politics that began to emerge from lesbian activist writers who stem from color feminism that continues today in an alternative movement to the widespread postulates of post-structuralist feminism and White queer theory. In the same vein, it recovers the legacy of key authors of postcolonial feminism with its critique of epistemic violence, the possibility of a *strategic essentialism* (Spivak 1998 [1988]), the call for a North-South feminist solidarity and the critique of the colonialism of knowledge production of feminist academia based in the North (Mohanty 2008b [2003]). It also includes several of the criticisms of the Latin American autonomous feminist current, of which several of us have been part, incorporating a denunciation of the ideological and economic dependence introduced by developmentalist policies in Third World countries, as well as the process of institutionalization and technocratization of social movements that imposes a global agenda of rights that serves neocolonial interests.

Finally, it has been key for this group to come across the prolific production of the Latin Americanist critical current that is today revisited, and with new vigor, through what has been called the *de(s)colonial turn*, from where an analysis of Western modernity as a product of the process of conquest and colonization of America and its implications for the people of the colonized communities [pueblos colonizados] is carried out.

To continue, I would like to advance some aspects of the issues that antiracist and decolonial feminist theory contributes to the development of *another* epistemology in Abya Yala.

A first effect of developed thinking by decolonial and anti-racist feminists is to radicalize the critique of universalism in the production of theory. Anti-racist decolonial feminists, continuing the legacy begun by Black feminists, feminists of color, and afrodescendant feminists in Latin America, show with their critique of classical theory how these theories do not serve to interpret the reality and oppression of racialized women with origins in colonized territories. While feminist epistemology, with authors such as Evelyn Fox Keller, Donna Haraway, Sandra Harding, just to name a few, has been concerned with analyzing the pretense of objectivity and universality, as well as the androcentrism in the sciences that ended up excluding and hiding the "point of view of women" in the process of knowledge production, the truth is that this critique has shown its limits in its inability to effectively articulate a program of decolonization and disuniversalization of the women subject of feminism. Their contributions to a critique of the scientific method focused almost exclusively on analyzing how the androcentric system of the sciences contributed to silencing the "women" subject – thus thinking universally –, removing it from the production of scientific knowledge.

Although several feminist epistemologists incorporate connections to the debates opened up by Black feminists and feminists of color, this has not led to the dismantling of the basic premises of hegemonic feminist theorizing of gender-based oppression as the dominant category fundamental to explaining women's subordination. While in some analyses, feminist epistemologists acknowledge the effects of racism and colonization on the lives of non-White women, and while several come to recognize the need for an intertwined analysis of race/class/gender/(hetero)sexuality, their overarching theory remains intact.

The classical feminist episteme produced by *White bourgeois* women settled in central countries failed to recognize how its practice reproduced the very problems it criticized about the sciences' way of producing knowledge. While criticizing androcentric universalism, it produced the category of gender and applied it universally to every society and every culture, without even accounting for the way in which the gender system is a construct to explain the oppression of women in modern Western societies and would, therefore, be substantive to this context. White feminist theories and critiques end up producing concepts and explanations oblivious to the historical performance of racism and coloniality as important factors in the oppression of most women while at the same time acknowledging their importance. This problem can be seen in formulations such as the following:

The scientist [male or female] is a subject traversed by determinations from which it is not possible to detach oneself, which must be recognized, and which are linked to a broader social system. Among these determinations, feminists will say, is 'gender' (i.e., the interpretation that each social group makes of sexual differences, the social roles attributed on the basis of this gender, and the relationships culturally established between them). And the challenge is to demonstrate how in the product of the work of this community, a product that has passed the inter-subjective controls that would ensure its neutrality, sexism is installed as a very strong bias. (Maffia 2007:13)[3]

While I would agree with the author's analysis of how the subject producer of scientific knowledge would be "traversed by determinations from which it is not possible to detach oneself" – which would explain why scientific knowledge is not objective –, she then goes on to point out how "feminists" would show that "gender" is one of these determinations. From an anti-racist and decolonial feminist point of view, we can observe and expose the following issue: On the one hand, gender, as pointed out before, would seem to operate as an independent category inherent to women's issues and, therefore, proper to feminist analysis: The feminist critique of epistemology has focused on how belonging to a particular gender affects the production of knowledge and how sexism constitutes a bias. But, if we have already been alerted for some decades to the way in which gender never operates separately. Moreover, if we are attentive to proposals such as that of María Lugones[4] that this category would not adequately explain the way in which the "women" of non-European peoples

---

3   Translator's note: All quotes from Maffia 2007; Lugones 2012, Espinosa 2012, 2013b and Stimpson 1998 were originally in Spanish. All the translations from Spanish into English are my own.

4   María Lugones proposes that "the category of gender corresponds only to the human, that is, to beings of reason whose origin is White European [...] The idea of strength and greater capacity for male reason and the fragility of women could not be applied to non-European peoples, since these people were all equally devoid of reasoning, sublime beauty, and fragility" (Espinosa 2012: 10). "Necessarily, Indians and Blacks could not be men and women, but beings without gender. As beasts they were conceived as sexually dimorphic or ambiguous, sexually aberrant and uncontrolled, capable of any task and suffering, without knowledge, on the side of evil in the dichotomy of good and evil, ridden by the devil. As beasts, they were treated as totally sexually accessible by man and sexually dangerous to woman. 'Woman' then points to bourgeois Europeans, reproducers of race and capital" (Lugones 2012: 130).

have been subjected, we should be willing to accept the inadequacy of a universalist use of the category of gender (the dichotomous division of the world into "women" and "men") or at least always (and not on certain occasions) stick to using it in a way that is unstable and interdependent on other categories such as race, class, and geopolitical location: How does this make the analysis so complex that formulations such as Maffía would no longer be possible?

On the other hand, I am interested in showing aspects of the operation that sustains analytical formulations, such as those illustrated in this paragraph, and that is so common in the analyses to which we are accustomed by epistemologists and Eurocentric feminist theorists. I refer to the way in which feminist researchers and theorists, while criticizing modern scientific thought for hiding its sexist bias, hide their own privileged place of ascription given their class and racial ancestry. Even widely recognized epistemologists, such as Sandra Harding, point out:

> The best feminist analysis [...] insists that the inquirer her/himself be placed in the same critical plane as the overt subject matter, thereby recovering the entire research process for scrutiny in the results of research. That is, the class, race, culture, and gender assumptions, beliefs, and behaviors of the researcher her/himself must be placed within the frame of the picture that she/he attempts to paint (1987: 25).

However, we continue to encounter an epistemological practice that conveniently insists on erasing the privileged place of enunciation of the producers of knowledge about women.

Thus, in the quoted paragraph, Maffía begins by saying that "[...] The scientist (male or female) is a subject traversed by determinations from which it is not possible to detach oneself". The truth is that neither she nor the vast majority of the most eminent feminist epistemologists apply to themselves the critique that they so aptly make of men in the sciences. If they had done so, they would most likely have had to admit their particular and self-interested point of view. The problem has been that they, after admitting that there are important differences between women, immediately return to reassert this much-needed unity of gender, which such differences would deny.

Given that the bias they intend to show is that of "gender" (a category thought of, in addition to being dominant and independent, as binary and dichotomous), their critique ends up producing the very thing they criticized before: According to this analysis, the scientific or knowledge-producing community is separated into two internally homogeneous blocks: that of men and that of women. Each would be producing a particular point of view from the gender position they embody. Since for White-bourgeois feminist theorists, the superior and relevant category is that of gender, they end up assuming that their point of view is the one that represents "women" as a whole. In doing so, they believe themselves exempt from applying to themselves the criticism they have already made of those who, from their point of view, represent a position of power. Relying solely on the analysis of gender as an analytical category that would allow them to explain the subordination of (all) women, feminist theorists have failed to observe and be critical of their own privilege within the group of women and of the race and class bias of the theory they construct. This would be a good example of what I have called *gender racism* [racismo del género]:

> An impossibility of feminist theory to recognize its privileged place of enunciation within the modern colonial gender matrix, an impossibility that stems from its refusal to question and abandon this place at the cost of "sacrificing", diligently invisibilizing, the point of view of "women" on a lower scale of privilege, that is, the racialized impoverished within a heterosexual order (Espinosa 2013b).

The effects of this treatment have been productive of a universalist feminism that claims to establish general knowledge for all women, justifying itself on behalf of all of them; despite simultaneously proclaiming the need for a new epistemology that legitimizes a situated knowledge based on concrete experience. In her work "Nossos feminismos revisatados" [Our Feminisms Revisited], Luiza Bairros explains how the concept of experience, as proposed by feminist epistemology, which was meant to oppose the classical scientific method based on the pretension of objectivity, ended up opening the door to "generalization", that is, to another form of construction of universalisms, given that privileges of race and class allow greater access to the field of ideas to a certain group of women whose experiences and voices end up becoming the parameter of the rest (1995: 459). For Bairros, the point of view of "women" can never be thought of or treated from the presumption of "a unique identity, since the experience of being a woman is socially and historically determined" (1995: 461). The interesting thing is that the more this truth has been declared, the more we come up against the impossibility of feminist theory to overcome this problem.

Thus, the important debate opened by White feminist epistemologists, in spite of their unquestionable contributions, has not been able to solve the problems evidenced by Black, lesbian, and colored feminists, who understood early on the profound interconnection between structures of domination, in particular the relationship between the androcentric gaze, racism, modernity, and coloniality. This misunderstanding prevented and still does not allow feminism, in problematizing the production of knowledge and the criteria to which this production is subjected, to account for the coloniality that permeates all its (own) work.

Detached from the above, there is another particularly important issue that decolonial feminism contributes, among several others: It is about evidencing how lightly and dishonestly hegemonic feminist theorizing treats "differences" among women so that they can always ultimately reconstitute the universality of the premises of a common fundamental oppression and, thus, the idea of women's unity as a particular group beyond the so-named differences. To the extent that afrodescendant, indigenous and non-White feminists in general

> we have been deepening the analysis of the historical conditions that give rise to a social organization that sustains hierarchical structures of oppression and domination that are not only explained by gender; to the extent that we have been approaching a radicalization of our malaise by becoming aware of the way in which these hierarchies are perpetuated even through the movements that have been presented and we have assumed as liberating such as feminism (Espinosa 2012).

We are coming up against fierce resistance on the part of hegemonic feminism against dismantling the mental structures and partialized explanations of this analytical framework that effectively conceals the way in which the web of power operate, thanks to a parallel and homogeneous performance of what are considered dominant categories, but also thanks to the way in which each category is traversed by and depends indistinctly on the others so that relations of power and domination are equally sustained within each of the groups that are considered to be specifically and homogeneously suffering equally from a given oppression – for example, the group of women or racialized people –, or within each group that is considered homogeneously in a position of privilege – for example that of males, or that of White people. When this line of inquiry ends up uncovering the hidden locus of privilege, maintained by a group of women at the expense of the classical interpretation of a sex-gender system, among them many producers of such theories, we can understand that great representatives of feminist theory make great efforts to ignore, minimize and, even more, give a specific treatment to the analyses and contributions of Black, indigenous and feminism of color. With the latter, while making a proclamation of good intentions, it manages to neutralize its effects on the whole of the classical feminist conceptual framework.

Let me illustrate this point with another quotation. This time, my example is Catharine Stimpson's treatment of the question of differences among women in her classic text "¿Qué estoy haciendo cuando hago estudios de mujeres en los noventa?" [What Am I Doing When I Do Women's Studies in the 1990s?] Once she has already expressed that at least six groups of problems have entered women's and gender studies, and in the number six (!!!) she recognized the problem of "deep differences between women themselves", which feminist theory will have to answer, she will express:

> However, I believe that we can also inhabit the problem of studying differences among women in such a way that our experiences of social thought and practice can serve to study differences among all people. In fact, I have called the use of women's studies as a means of *apprehending and living* with human differences "herterogeneity" (ellaterogeneidad) Recognizing diversity and *abhorring the error that erases* it are necessities in and of themselves (Stimpson 1998: 138; italics mine).

The paragraph illustrates the problem we are facing. Much of the feminist theorizing that has made the effort to listen to the critiques of racialized feminists, in addition to the errors we have discussed above, fall into another major trap: diminish the relevance of these differences between women once they have been admitted. This lessened importance consists, on the one hand, in giving a lesser status of conflictivity and relevance to what they consider "other" categories of women's oppression. The problem is twofold, for they continue to think in a compartmentalized way and independently of the oppressions of gender, race, and class, as if race and class were of a different order and acted in parallel, affecting a group of women only in a specific and summative way. In her view, "women" continue to constitute a unity of meaning, beyond the multiplicity of oppression that differentiates them. From their reflexion, we can see how the relevant oppression for feminist studies continues to be that of "oppressing women for being women", a primary oppression that does not allow for any discussion, that makes race and class appear as minor secondary oppressions without any effect on the way we think of the primary oppression. Given this, it is possible to incorporate the study of these variables of difference within the study of women, as particular categories to be taken into account, but they do not define or have general implications for feminist theory as a whole. The treatment of race and class as minor differences among women, that is, among a specific group, tends to naturalize these categories as if they were not produced by structural systems of domination that have ended up defining and organizing the world and social life within which women find themselves. That is why the challenge is not to achieve an idyllic world of recognition and incorporation of difference, since they express systems of domination and exploitation that place women in antagonistic spaces of social life, making their interests irreconcilable.

The epistemological shift, in full transition, that feminists coming from critical and counter-hegemonic trajectories and positions in Abya Yala are experiencing, places us before the challenge of contributing to the development of an analysis of coloniality and racism – no longer as a phenomenon but as an episteme intrinsic to modernity and its liberating projects – and its relationship with the coloniality of gender. The challenge is to abandon and actively question this pretense of unity in oppression among women. To this end, we are willing to feed, articulate, and commit ourselves to the autonomous movements that in the continent carry out processes of decolonization and restitution of lost genealogies that point to the possibility of other significations of interpretation of life and collective life.

References

Bairros, Luiza (1995): "Nossos Feminismos Revisitado." In: Revista Estudos Feministas 3/2, pp. 458–463.

Espinosa-Miñoso, Yuderkys (2012): "¿Por qué es necesario un feminismo descolonial? Diferenciación, dominación co-constitutiva y fin de la política de identidad." Unpublished manuscript presented at the conference of the same name at the Universidad Nacional de Colombia.

Espinosa-Miñoso, Yuderkys (2013a): "Feminismos descoloniales de Abya Yala." In: Béatrice. Didier/Antoinette Fouque/Mireille Calle-Gruber (eds.), Le Dictionnaire des femmes créatrices. À paraître à l'automne, Paris: Des Femmes-Antoinette Fouque Publishing.

Espinosa-Miñoso, Yuderkys (2013b): "Y la una no se mueve sin la otra: descolonialidad, antirracismo y feminismo. Una trieja inseparable para los proceso de cambio." In: Revista Venezolana de Estudios de la Mujer 21/46, pp. 47–64.

Haraway, Donna (1991): Ciencia, cyborgs y mujeres. La reinvención de la naturaleza, Madrid: Cátedra.

Harding, Sandra (1987): "Is There a Feminist Method?" In: Harding, Sandra (ed.), Feminism and Methodology, Bloomington and Indianapolis: Indiana University Press. Spanish version translated by Gloria Elena Bernal, pp. 9–34, 10 August 2013 (https://es.scribd.com/document/362056389/Harding-Sandra-Existe-Un-Metodo-Feminista-1987).

Lugones, María (2008): "Colonialidad y género: Hacia un feminismo descolonial." In: Walter Mignolo (ed.), Género y descolonialidad, Buenos Aires: Ediciones del Signo, pp. 13–42.

Lugones, María (2012): "Subjetividad esclava, colonialidad de género, marginalidad y opresiones múltiples." In: Pensando los feminismos en Bolivia. (Serie Foros 2), La Paz: Conexión Fondo de Emancipación, pp. 129–139.

Maffia, Diana (2007): "Epistemología feminista: La subversión semiótica de las mujeres en la ciencia." In: Revista Venezolana de Estudios de la Mujer 12/28, pp. 63–98.

Mohanty, Chandra Talpade (2008a [1986]): "Bajo los ojos de occidente. Academia feminista y discurso colonial." In: Rosalva Aída Hernández Castillo/Liliana Suárez Navaz (eds.), Descolonizando el feminismo: Teorías y prácticas desde los márgenes, Madrid: Cátedra, pp. 112–161.

Mohanty, Chandra Talpade (2008b [2003]): "De vuelta a *bajo los ojos de occidente*: La solidaridad feminista a través de las luchas anticapitalistas." In: Rosalva Aída Hernández Castillo/Liliana Suárez Navaz (eds.), Descolonizando el feminismo: teorías y prácticas desde los márgenes, Madrid: Cátedra, pp. 404–467.

Pratt, Mary Louise (1997): Ojos imperiales. Literatura de viajes y transculturación. (Ofelia Castillo, trad.), Buenos Aires: Universidad Nacional de Quilmes.

Quijano, Aníbal (2000a): "Colonialidad del poder, eurocentrismo y América Latina." In: Edgardo Lander (ed.), La colonialidad del saber: eurocentrismo y ciencias sociales. Perspectivas latinoamericanas, Buenos Aires: CLACSO, p. 246.

Quijano, Aníbal (2000b): "Colonialidad del poder y clasificación social." In: Journal of World-Systems Research. Special Issue: Festschrift for Immanuel Wallerstein 6/2, pp. 342–386.

Spivak, Gayatri Chakravorty (1998[1988]): "¿Puede hablar el sujeto subalterno?" In: Orbis Tertius 3/6, pp. 1–44.

Stimpson, Catherine R. (1998): "¿Qué estoy haciendo cuando hago estudios de mujeres en los noventa?" In: Marysa Navarro/Catherine R. Stimpson (eds.), ¿Qué son los estudios de mujeres?, Buenos Aires: FCE, pp. 301–307.

Wittig, Monique (2006): "El pensamiento heterosexual." In: El pensamiento heterosexual y otros ensayos, Barcelona: Egales, pp. 45–57.

From the Center to the Margins, (Re)Politicizing Intersectionality

Mara Viveros Vigoya[1]

Introduction

In this paper, I will reflect on the two-way journey that Intersectionality has taken from the margin to the center and from the center to the margin from a theoretical, methodological, and political perspective. I will start from the moment the term was coined in 1991 by Kimberlé Crenshaw, and then trace the academic popularization of the concept following the World Conference against Racism, Racial Discrimination, Xenophobia and Related Intolerance held in South Africa in 2001 up to the present time. With this reflection, I intend to describe and analyze what has happened and intensified in the last decade, in which feminism as a political movement has become more widespread and, at the same time, has redefined the concept of what constitutes the "margin".

I. Genealogies of Intersectional Thought

For some years now, the term Intersectionality has come to designate a theoretical and methodological perspective that seeks to account for the intersecting or overlapping perception of power relations. This approach is not new within feminism, and in fact, there is now agreement that 1) feminist theories had addressed the problem before giving it a name and 2) that the problem of exclusions created by the use of theoretical frameworks that ignore the imbrication of power relations had been existing for a long time in diverse historical and geopolitical contexts.

---

1 Translated from Spanish by Lívia de Souza Lima.

Black women in the United States challenged the nonrecognition of interlocking axes of oppression through organizations that fought for the abolition of slavery, the right to vote for Black people, and against the lynching of Black men and racial segregation. In the last quarter of the 20th century, the Combahee River Collective (1983, 1977), one of the most active groups of Black Feminism in the 1970s, authored a unique formulation of the problem of Intersectionality in their document A Black Feminist Statement. In this document, they define their political action around an active commitment to struggle "against racial, sexual, heterosexual and class oppression" and to "develop an integrated analysis and practice based on the fact that the major systems of oppression are intertwined" (ibid: 15). This notion of 'interlocking' systems of oppression precedes Intersectionality.

Intersectionality matured as a concept at the end of the second half of the 20th century, during a period of immense social change. It recalls the memory of anti-colonial struggles in Africa and Asia as well as anti-imperialist struggles in Latin America; those of the global women's movement; and civil rights movements in multicultural democracies; the end of the Cold War; and the defeat of Apartheid in South Africa. In this context of change, it is worth highlighting the names of certain thinkers such as Angela Davis, Audre Lorde, bell hooks, or June Jordan, who spoke out against the hegemony of "White" feminism in the American academy. They demonstrated that the category of women and the political representation proposed by many feminist theories had been constituted based on the experience of women privileged for reasons of class, race, and sexuality. From this position of privilege, they often ignored the realities of women whose social situation was different, for these same reasons.

At the same time as this debate was going on in North America, Black women's issues in Brazil were raised as topics of political debate within the Brazilian Communist Party (Barroso 1983) as early as the 1960s. Subsequently, in the 1980s, a Black women's movement consolidated, affirming the intersection of race and gender as the center of its political program. Various activists and intellectuals (Thereza Santos, Lélia Gonzalez, Maria Beatriz do Nascimento, Luiza Bairros, Jurema Werneck, and Sueli Carneiro, among others) promoted the theory of the 'race-class-gender' triad of oppressions to articulate the differences between Brazilian women whom the dominant feminist discourse had sought to ignore. These authors were pioneers in pointing out that if feminism wanted to emancipate all women, it had to confront all forms of oppression and not only those based on gender. This is worth underlining because their contribution to the genealogy of Intersectionality is rarely acknowledged.

Together with Black feminists, Uruguayan and Caribbean women, these activists managed, not without difficulty, to raise the need to include the issue of racism in the feminist agenda at the Second Latin American and Caribbean Feminist Meeting held in the city of Lima (Curiel 2007). In Lima, they also set up a regional coordination mechanism among them (Álvarez 1997). Finally, on 19 July 1992, 350 Black women from 32 countries gathered in the Dominican Republic, a country with a long tradition of feminism, to hold the First Meeting of Latin American and Caribbean Black Women. During this meeting, they discussed the agenda for the Fourth World Conference on Women to be held in Beijing in 1995. This meeting made it possible to highlight the ethnic-racial inequalities that characterized the region and the undervaluing of Black women's contributions to shaping Latin American societies. At the same time, it denounced the racist substratum of the new development models and structural adjustment policies and their negative impact on Black women's lives (Galván 1995).

These contributions affirm that, although this reflection is not new, what is unique about Intersectionality is how it has circulated in recent times in different academic and political contexts. It has become one of the critical approaches to contemporary discussions and struggles around "difference," diversity, and plurality, with multiple effects, as we will see in the following.

II. Intersectional Paths from the Margin to the Center

American legal scholar Kimberlé Crenshaw coined the concept of Intersectionality in 1989 as a tool designed to overcome the legal invisibility of the multiple dimensions of oppression experienced by Black women in the labor world. Intersectionality, she wrote, designates "the various ways in which race and gender interact to shape the multiple dimensions of Black women's labor experiences" (Crenshaw 1991: 1244). With this notion, Crenshaw hoped to highlight that Black women in the United States were exposed to violence and discrimination based on both race and gender. Above all, she sought to create concrete legal categories to address discrimination on multiple and varying levels. Referring to the court's rejection of a claim brought by five Black women workers that the General Motors seniority system discriminated against them, Crenshaw argued that the court's refusal to recognize "combined race and sex discrimination" was based on the fact that the boundaries of sex and race discrimination were defined respectively by the experiences of White women and Black men (Crenshaw 1989: 143). The interplay of these boundaries obscured the specific subjective experience of Black women workers.

On numerous occasions, Kimberlé Crenshaw has made clear that her use of Intersectionality has been and continues to be contextual and practical. Her aim was never to create a general theory of oppression, but rather a concept that would allow for analyzing specific legal omissions and inequalities. As she explained:

> Intersectionality, then, was my attempt to make feminism, anti-racist activism, and anti-discrimination law do what I thought they should – highlight the multiple avenues through which racial and gender oppression were experienced so that the problems would be easier to discuss and understand (Crenshaw 2015).

A decade after coining the term, Kimberlé Crenshaw was involved in the preparation of the World Conference against Racism, Racial Discrimination, Xenophobia and Related Intolerance in Durban in 2001. 'Durban' was a turning point in the understanding of the historical functioning of racism in the world and was characterized by the remarkable performance of women. Like the other UN conferences, Durban was also preceded by a series of preparations in different world regions. Their aim was to map the various forms of racism, identify the ethnic and racial groups most exposed to the effects of its manifestation, and propose actions to member states and UN international treaty bodies.

The Third Conference was a special moment of the growing prominence of Black women in the struggle against racism and racial discrimination, both nationally and internationally.

Among the different initiatives developed, the Articulación de Organizaciones de Mujeres Negras Brasileñas Pro-Durban (Articulation of Brazilian Black Women's Organisations Pro-Durban) stands out. The debates, proposed by Black women on their specificities in the systems of production and reproduction, significantly heightened the visibility of problems of racially discriminated women. In this context, Crenshaw gave a seminar on the concept at the Geneva Preparatory Committee in 2000. She pointed out various ways to think about the racial aspects of gender discrimination without losing sight of the gender aspects of racial discrimination. In assessing the limited interpretations of the then-current human rights discourses, Crenshaw outlined a methodology for analyzing intersectional subordination to eliminate the cracks in these discourses through which the rights of women suffering multiple oppressions tend to fall and thus disappear (Bairros 2002). From this moment, the concept of Intersectionality began to be used in such contexts.

At the Durban World Conference, more than ten thousand delegates shared the complexity of their political challenges and life experiences. They adopted the term at the Non-Governmental Organization Forum of this First Conference. Since then, the intersectional perspective, whether under the name "Intersectionality" or other equivalent terms, began to take hold and expand globally (Dell Aquila 2021), as this definition is expressed in the Gender section of the document:

> An intersectional approach to discrimination acknowledges that every person be it man or woman exists in a framework of multiple identities, with [sic.] factors such as race, class, ethnicity, religion, sexual orientation, gender identity, age, disability, citizenship, national identity, geo-political context, health, including HIV/AIDS status and any other status are all determinants in one's experiences of racism, racial discrimination, xenophobia and related intolerances. An intersectional approach highlights the way in which there is a simultaneous interaction of discrimination as a result of multiple identities".[2]

After the World Conference in Durban, Crenshaw's work influenced the drafting of the equality clause in the South African Constitution, became institutionalized in international diplomacy, and gained academic popularity (Crenshaw 2012). Thus, the concept of Intersectionality, born out of a marginalized and contested context, gradually became a broad and widely used concept in these different arenas. In particular, it is worth noting that the UN uses this approach to refer to women's rights as human rights and the diversity of women in very heterogeneous geographical, social, and cultural contexts, such as those of Latin America and the Caribbean.

It is also important to highlight that Intersectionality faced a similar development as the gender approach during the 1990s, the decade of the Great International Conferences of the 20th century. On the one hand, the concept led governmental bodies to make more significant commitments to the fight

---

2   UN WCAR (2001): WCAR NGO Forum Declaration, art. 119, October 26, 2022 (https://www.hurights.or.jp/wcar/E/ngofinaldc.htm).

against multiple discriminations, which has led to substantial advances in the formulation of public policies. Paradoxically, however, its institutionalization has also hollowed and neutralized the concept, often reducing it to a mere rhetorical term, used as a standard academic reference, decontextualized, and separated from its original political imprint. For if our use of Intersectionality leaves the feminist discourse intact, we misunderstand what it is all about. The same holds true if the argument, the analysis, and the intersectional approach consist of applying a new feminist truth "from above" to the understanding of the world of those "below" by pointing out that all inequalities are exacerbated by an additive logic (Espinosa 2020). Intersectionality, on the contrary, orients us towards a new form of interpretation that abandons the gender-centered feminist point of view for a more comprehensive one that seeks to think about and fight sexism, classism, and racism at the same time. The fallacy of the central critical systems of interpretation of the social order – Marxism, feminism, critical race theory – is that each has claimed to offer an understanding of the social world based on what they assume to be the primary axis of inequality from which all others are derived. Moreover, they think that each axis is autonomous, ignoring that their interrelation is constitutive in the configuration of inequalities.

Behind the academic category of Intersectionality lies a rich history of Black women's activism across the globe, and the analytical and political scope of Intersectionality will depend on how the concept is used and for what purposes. On the other hand, the theoretical questions raised by the concept of gender – in the terms introduced by one of its earliest theorists, historian Joan Scott (2010), when she stresses that gender is only helpful as a question and, as such, can only be answered in specific contexts and through thorough research – are also valid for Intersectionality, as I will illustrate in the following.

III. The Uses of Intersectionality as an Analytical Category

The appropriation of Intersectionality as a grid for reading social experiences in their web of multiple oppressions (not as an arithmetical sum) and from their own epistemologies has been slow. It has been challenging to accept that intersectional logic not only works in the daily lives of the people who are our subjects of study, but also in the power relations that are woven within the social and educational organizations that use this approach. Despite the good intentions of those who make up the organizations, gender, class, and educational hierarchies are often perpetuated in these contexts.

Another persistent obstacle to radically embracing an intersectional, race-centered political-theoretical approach is the enduring Latin America narrative of *mestizaje* as the primary guarantor of the absence of racism. This powerful narrative of Latin American national identities, which describes these societies as fundamentally *mestizo* ['mixed'], has hindered the recognition of racism. Furthermore, those who claim that racism exists are subject to moral delegitimization as racists. In Latin America, racism is minimized, denied, or seen as anachronistic or "extraordinary". It is so naturalized that it is mainly unconscious, to the point that the application of this concept is usually limited to practices occurring in other places and times: in the United States, in Nazi Germany, or South Africa, or our region, or earlier historical, colonial, or pre-revolutionary periods. Racism is only perceived as such in case of explicit or violent actions of racial discrimination (Viveros Vigoya 2007).

In this respect, it is very relevant to welcome Lélia Gonzalez's criticism of the founding narrative of Latin American societies that has prioritized Latinidad/Latinity, i.e. the link with Europe, silencing the importance of the historical existence and political agency (past, present, and future) of Black and indigenous peoples. Lélia Gonzalez (1984) named the territory in which we live Améfrica Ladina (Ladino Améfrica), realizing that this America has always been more Amerindian and African than "Latin", and created the political-cultural concept of 'amefricanidade' as a counterpoint to the hegemonic US discourse on Black identity in the Americas.

It is also essential to recognize that most of the studies on Intersectionality that have been developed in the region have focused on the particular positions of those subjects who face forms of oppression and exclusion. In this sense, the privileged subject of analysis has been the oppressed subject, the excluded, the one on whom the logics of domination and inequality fall, and who embodies otherness. Many studies speak of triple and multiple oppression as additive forms of oppression, generating the idea that women are devoid of any possibility of agency and men are endowed with all powers. The problem with this view is that it ignores that women and men can simultaneously occupy different positions, some of the subordinate and some of the dominant ones. Moreover, the most "disadvantaged" position in classist, racist, and sexist societies such as ours is not necessarily that of a poor Black or indigenous woman, when compared, for example, to the situation of young men of the same ethnic and social group, who are more often exposed to certain forms of arbitrariness, such as those associated with police controls. Analyzing particular social configurations can relativize common perceptions of how domination works.

Likewise, an arithmetical understanding of domination and its additive effects does not allow us to understand why, for example, a marriage act, as a status symbol, is not worth the same if it is performed in endogamous contexts in racial terms as if it is performed between interracial couples. In the Colombian case, my previous research has allowed me to identify, for example, that in the marital union between a Black man and a White woman, the White woman loses not only social status, but also prestige as a woman, as she is invested with sexual connotations that are undesirable in a woman of her ethnic-racial status. They also allowed me to understand that marriage, a patriarchal institution that should typically protect a woman against accusations of sexual promiscuity, lost its power when her spouse was racialized as a Black man. I also understood that the relations of gender, class, and race in which marital decisions were embedded could not be analyzed separately, but as simultaneous constructions, produced in a particular historical configuration that gives these relations their significance.

Similarly, my research on masculinities in Colombia has challenged homogenous views of masculinity in Colombia by showing that class and race distribute the rewards and costs associated with gender and race relations unequally, defining differentiated experiences and representations of men's masculinity. Thus, the men who benefit from patriarchal – and racial – dividends and those who suffer most from the costs of the imposition of hegemonic masculinity and White supremacist mandates are not the same. The former generally hold authority in the state and control coercive institutions and are recognized by the media. On the other side of the social spectrum, racialized and impoverished men hold the least skilled, lowest paid, and least recognized jobs and are among the groups most exposed to police control. The intertwining of classism and racism has shaped Latin American institutions from their inception in such a way that today, they show the same brutal face, that of police violence that rages against the bodies of young, racialized, and impoverished men. The connections between police violence, the continuous growth of the prison population, and a long history of humiliation, dehumanization, and terror inflicted on these bodies are undoubtedly some of the social issues that Intersectionality has made visible (Viveros 2018).

Migratory processes bring together different axes of inequalities, so they are also relevant for the theoretical and empirical analysis of Intersectionality. In international migration, the different classifications (gender, class, national origin, race, ethnicity, age, migratory status, etc.) determine migrants' access to rights and opportunities and the situations of privilege or exclusion that derive from these classifications. The complexity and diversity of migrants' experiences depend primarily on the continuous interactions between different hierarchical structures of gender, ethnicity, class, and other axes of inequality at local, national, transnational, and global levels.

Among the Latin American works that have incorporated this perspective in their analyses, it is worth mentioning the pioneering work of Adriana Piscitelli, which focuses on the experiences of Brazilian migrants linked to the sex market. For this author, the experience of Brazilian migrant women (and women travelers) is affected by aspects that cannot be understood based on just one or two categories of differentiation, such as gender and nationality, but by the interweaving notions of sexuality, gender, race, ethnicity, and nationality. The interaction between different axes of inequality is what explains why Brazil has been included in global sex tourism circuits, why Brazilian women have gained visibility in the sex industry in European countries, and why sexist and racist stereotypes about Brazilian women are activated whether or not the women are linked to the sex industry. The assumption that they have a naturally intense predisposition to have sex and a propensity for prostitution, combined with ambiguous notions about their styles of femininity, seen as submissive and simultaneously joyful, tends to affect these migrants indiscriminately in varying proportions according to migratory contexts, social class and, in some cases, skin color. For Piscitelli (2008), the cultural translation of Brazil's subordinate position in transnational relations is one of the main aspects affecting the experiences of these women since this translation is done based on the articulation between the different axes of inequality mentioned above.

Another work worth highlighting is María José Magliano (2015), who explores the labor trajectories of Peruvian migrant women in paid domestic employment in Argentina. Her work brings to the discussion the issue of segmentation and hierarchization of the labor market in ethnic-national and gender terms between native and migrant men and women and within these same groups. The research reconstructs the labor trajectories of Peruvian migrant women from an intersectional perspective that allows it to trace the differences in the labor and migratory experiences of these women based on their class affiliation (linked especially to the labor qualification and level of schooling attained), their migratory status, and their family dynamics. Adopting an intersectional perspective provides tools to understand a migrant and domestic worker's different 'ways of being' according to the specificities of gender, social class, ethnonational origin, and migratory status. In other words, it produces a narrative that goes against the homogenous visions of migrants, showing that the intersections of these social relations configure different possibilities and modalities of labor insertion, vertical and horizontal mobilities, and differentiated access to rights as workers.

Recent research has used the potential of Intersectionality to analyze the effects of socio-political change on the everyday experience of the new indigenous middle classes in Bolivia. In this context of change, Shakow (2022) identifies the dilemmas posed by two competing narratives of social mobility for women who have experienced recent processes of upward social mobility. In the first – which exhorted young Bolivians to stop being indigenous "peasants" and become "professionals" or successful mestizo entrepreneurs – for a Chola, social progress meant getting rid of the pollera and braids, as it was impossible to dress and style one's hair in this way and pretend to have access to higher education. In the second model, promoted by Evo Morales' political project between 2005 and 2019, the emphasis was on changing values, focusing on the affirmation of indigenous cultural pride and women's right to professional and business achievements. This quest for greater equity included appointing ministers of Quechua and peasant origin in order to dissolve the supposed contradiction of claiming to be middle class and dressing as a Chola, affirming a political position instead. The conversion of the Chola into a gendered symbol of the imperatives of these two competing models of social mobility put them in particularly challenging and costly personal dilemmas between different political, community, and family commitments.

This example shows us that the interactions between gender, race, and class always operate in specific social, spatial, and temporal contexts. This way of understanding these relations allows us to escape from visions of femininity, indigeneity, and social ascent as something given, fixed, and immutable. Moreover, the relational foundations of Intersectionality show that the oppression of some groups is continuously interconnected with the opportunity and privilege of other social groups; privilege never exists out of context, but is directly linked to another group's disadvantage.

To conclude, I will no longer refer to the uses of Intersectionality as an analytical category, but to its political dimensions and what is at stake today, as the issue of feminism progressively shifts from its internal borders (the internal composition of the feminist movement) to its external borders and towards the alliances and solidarities that feminism must build with other social movements that defend the interests of other socially minoritized groups (hooks 1984).

IV. Back to the Margins: Decolonizing the Uses of Intersectionality

The last decade in Latin America has seen numerous changes due to political shortcomings and a lack of autonomy of the multicultural state project that had been launched in the 1990s, the regression of social and political processes as well as gains achieved within its framework, and the exacerbation of social and racial inequalities as well as violence linked to the neoliberal project (Hale 2002). Among other things, the failure of the multicultural project stirred renewed public interest throughout Latin America in the issue of racism, with repercussions for the anti-racist work of many social movements, including feminism. In this new conjuncture, Latin American feminist ideas have become more clearly articulated in the critique of racism, not least because of the rapid circulation and growing acceptance of the intersectional perspective (Viveros 2016).

Indeed, in recent years, the socio-political context and some aspects of the dynamic nature of the notion of Intersectionality have brought about a certain re-politicization of the concept. Intersectionality has acquired new meanings. In a certain sense, it has even reinvented itself outside the perimeter of universities; it has done so in the streets and the struggles of social movements. In Argentina and Brazil, the notion of Intersectionality has been used to articulate and connect the movements of indigenous and Black women, rural and metropolitan communities, sexual minorities, and women living in slums without losing sight of their specificity (Mezzadra 2021).

In our Améfrica Ladina, a region characterized by multidimensional heterogeneity – and marked by long historical processes that have generated situations of social exclusion – intersectional political thinking and action has entered into a relationship with other disruptive political thought and action. This means that the use of Intersectionality has not been limited to observing and addressing the multiplicity and complexity of the discriminations that characterize the experience of Ladino-Amefrican women. Rather, it has sought to understand the historical roots to combat the root causes of these discriminations.

This appropriation and these uses of Intersectionality have prompted a re-politicization of the notion, where, to quote Angela Davis, the stakes are "not so much the intersectionality of identities as the intersectionality of struggles" (Davis 2016: 144). Some works, such as that of Afro-Brazilian sociologists Flávia Rios, Olívia Perez and Arlene Ricoldi (2018), point to the emergence of a new generation of Brazilian activism, the bearer of a new language of contestation, which expresses more clearly the articulations between feminism and anti-racism in the public sphere with a view to problematizing the multiple forms of social oppression. Their adoption of Intersectionality as a language goes beyond their understanding of the relevance of this tool for social and political interpretation (Rios/Sotero 2019); the term has become a category of collective political identity, emerging in the context of the transformations of the public sphere and the dynamics of feminist and anti-racist movements, especially among feminists who question the limits of more traditional political activism.

In this sense, it is a different interpretation of the meaning of the term, not only as an analytical category but also as a category that marks the contemporary language of political mobilizations, the forms of naming, and the values that guide the collective actions of those who make the politics of the streets and networks. Thus, the term has ceased to be a noun to adjectivize a new type of feminist belonging and, above all, a new way of conceiving feminism itself. It is thus a reinvention of feminist thought and practice in new forms of solidarity where Intersectionality has become a kind of method to multiply encounters between different social movements and counteract any "hardening" of identity politics. While this has played an influential role in opening up new fields of struggle, it always risks becoming an obstacle to building a more effective basis for struggles against exploitation and oppression.

However, the reinvention of Intersectionality as an "intersectionality of struggles", as Angela Davis has put it, seems to prefigure a new politics of solidarity. One that is not based on vague assumptions of sisterhood or images of complete identification of some women with others, but on political and ethical goals (Mohanty 2020). One that allows for the construction of imagined communities, not around sex or color as inherent or natural characteristics, but around ways of thinking about race, class, and gender.

This return to the margin of intersectional political thought and action means, to paraphrase bell hooks (1989: 23), choosing the margin as a space of radical openness. hooks draws a clear distinction between marginality imposed by oppressive structures and marginality selected as a place of resistance, as a place of radical openness and possibility. This place of resistance is a critical response to domination and a space forged through struggle. We know that the struggle is difficult, challenging, and arduous. But we also know that struggle pleases, delights, and satisfies our desire. With bell hooks, we can imagine the space of intersectional struggles as a radical creative space that affirms and sustains our subjectivity and gives us a new place to articulate our sense of the world.

References

Álvarez, Sonia (1997): "Articulación y transnacionalización de los feminismos latinoamericanos." In: Debates Feministas 15, pp. 146–170 (https://doi.org/https://doi.org/10.22201/cieg.2594066xe.1997.15.379).

Bairros, Luiza (2002): "III Conferência Mundial Contra O Racismo. Dossiê III Conferência Mundial contra o Racismo." In: Revista Estudos Feministas 10/1, pp. 169–170.

Barroso, Carmen (1983): Mulher, mulheres, São Paulo: Cortez.

Combahee River Collective (1983/1977): "The Combahee River Collective Statement." In: Barbara Smith (ed.), Home Girls: A Black Feminist Anthology, New York: Kitchen Table and Women of Colors Press, Inc., pp. 272–282.

Crenshaw, Kimberlé (1989): "Demarginalizing the Intersection of Race and Sex: A Black Feminist Critique of Antidiscrimination Doctrine, Feminist Theory and Antiracist Politics." In: University of Chicago Legal Forum Iss. 1, Article 8, pp. 139–167.

Crenshaw, Kimberlé (1991): "Mapping the Margins: Intersectionality, Identity Politics, and Violence against Women of Color." In: Stanford Law Review 43/6, pp. 1241–1299.

Crenshaw, Kimberlé (2012): A intersecionalidade na discriminação de raça e gênero. In: VV.AA. Cruzamento: raça e gênero, Brasília: Unifem, pp. 7–16, October 26, 2022 (https://static.tumblr.com/7symefv/V6vmj45f5/kimberle-crenshaw.pdf).

Crenshaw, Kimberlé (2015): "Why Intersectionality Can't Wait." In: The Washington Post, October 26, 2022 (https://www.washingtonpost.com/news/in-theory/wp/2015/09/24/why-intersectionality-cant-wait/).

Curiel, Ochy (2007): "Crítica poscolonial desde las prácticas políticas del feminismo antirracista." In: Nómadas 26, pp. 92–101 (https://www.redalyc.org/articulo.oa?id=105115241010).

Davis, Angela (2016): Freedom is a Constant Struggle. Ferguson, Palestine, and the Foundations of a Movement, Chicago: Haymarket Books.

Dell' Aquila, Marta (2021): "Du centre aux marges. Perspectives contre-hégémoniques autour de l'agency." PhD Thesis, Paris: Paris 1 and Institut des sciences juridique et philosophique de la Sorbonne.

Espinosa-Miñoso, Yuderkys (2020). "Interseccionalidad y feminismo descolonial. Volviendo sobre el tema." In: Pikara Magazine (online), January 12, 2021 (https://www.pikaramagazine.com/2020/12/interseccionalidad-y-feminismo-descolonial-volviendo-sobre-el-tema/).

Galván, Sergia (1995): "El mundo étnico-racial dentro del feminismo latinoamericano." In: Fempress, special issue, pp. 34–36.

Gonzalez, Lélia (1984): "Racismo e sexismo na cultura brasileira." In: Revista Ciências Sociais Hoje 2/1, pp. 223–244.

Hale, Charles R. (2002): "Does Multiculturalism Menace? Governance, Cultural Rights and the Politics of Identity in Guatemala." In: Journal of Latin American Studies 34/3, pp. 485–524.

hooks, bell (1984): Feminist Theory: From Margin to Center, Boston: South End Press.

hooks, bell (1989): "Choosing the Margin as a Space of Radical Openness." In: Framework: The Journal of Cinema and Media 36, pp. 15–23.

Magliano, María José (2015): "Interseccionalidad y migraciones: potencialidades y desafíos." In: Revista Estudos Feministas 23, pp. 691–712.

Mezzadra, Sandro (2021): "Intersectionality, Identity, and the Riddle of Class." In: Papeles del CEIC 2021/2, heredada 3, pp. 1–10, http://doi.org/10.1387/pceic.22759.

Mohanty, Chandra. (2020): Feminismo sin fronteras: descolonizar la teoría, practicar la solidaridad, Mexico City: Universidad Nacional Autónoma de México, Centro de Investigaciones y Estudios de Género.

Piscitelli, Adriana (2008): "Interseccionalidades, categorias de articulação e experiências de migrantes brasileiras." In: Sociedade e cultura 11/2, pp. 263–274.

Rios, Flávia/Perez, Olívia /Ricoldi, Arlene (2018): "Interseccionalidade nas mobilizações do Brasil contemporáneo." In: Lutas Sociais 22/40, pp. 36–51.

Rios, Flavia/Sotero, Edilza (2019): "Apresentação: Gênero em perspectiva interseccional." In: PLURAL, Revista do Programa de Pós-Graduação em Sociologia da USP 26/1, pp. 1–10.

Scott, Joan Wallach (2010): "Fantasmes du millénaire: le futur du « genre » au XXIe siècle." In: Clio. Femmes, genre, histoire 32, pp. 89–117.

Shakow, Miriam (2022): "Equality or Hierarchy? Solidarity with Those Above or Below? Dilemmas of Gendered Self-Identification in a New Bolivian

Middle Class." In: Mario Barbosa Cruz/A. Ricardo López-Pedreros/Claudia Stern (eds.), The Middle Classes in Latin America: Subjectivities, Practices, and Genealogies, New York: Routledge, pp. 422–441.

UN WCAR (2001): WCAR NGO Forum Declaration, art. 119, October 26, 2022 (https://www.hurights.or.jp/wcar/E/ngofinaldc.htm).

Viveros Vigoya, Mara (2007): "Discriminación racial, intervención social y subjetividad. Reflexiones a partir de un estudio de caso en Bogotá." In: Revista de estudios sociales 27, pp. 106–121.

Viveros Vigoya, Mara (2016): "La interseccionalidad: una aproximación situada a la dominación." In: Debate feminista 52, pp. 1–17.

Viveros Vigoya, Mara (2018): Les couleurs de la masculinité: expériences intersectionnelles et pratiques de pouvoir en Amérique Latine, Paris: La Découverte.

The Feminist and Decolonial Pedagogy of Lélia Gonzalez and Sueli Carneiro

Lívia de Souza Lima

Lélia Gonzalez and Sueli Carneiro are two Black feminists and intellectuals whose productions are fundamental to understanding gender and racial relations in Brazil and beyond. Lélia Gonzalez, who passed away in 1994, and Sueli Carneiro, who still writes, are fundamental references for Black feminism and activism in Brazil. The scope of their contributions is multifaceted and too ample to be fully covered in the scope of this review. Therefore, I situate Carneiro and Gonzalez' thought as a feminist and decolonial pedagogy reflected through political, methodological, and epistemological practices that guide knowledge production and correspond to an engaged and critical feminist praxis. For this purpose, I resort to the "decolonial feminist pedagogy" framework proposed by Yuderkys Espinosa-Miñoso, Diana Gómez, María Lugones, and Karina Ochoa as a method that refers to a specific type of feminist engaged thinking. This method theorizes and illustrates a feminism that produces knowledge in combination with territories and communities, emerging from political struggles and activism (Spinosa et al. 2013). Moreover, this practice aims to create insubordination tools, effectively transform realities, and develop interpretative approaches to understand the worlds one lives in.

Doing, Thinking, and Engaging in Intersectional Dialogues

To start this reflection, I combine three layers of feminist decolonial pedagogy that highlight: (i) a knowledge emerging from political and social engagement; (ii) the construction of bridges and dialogues among movements; and (iii) the consideration of intersecting and overlapping modes of oppressions. Here, I discuss some of the instances in which these principles reverberate in the intellectual trajectories of Lélia Gonzalez and Sueli Carneiro in an integrated manner.

Firstly, I would like to highlight that Gonzalez and Carneiro are both recognized as activists and intellectuals, vocations which are reflected in their productions and the way they conduct their critiques and analysis. Their life trajectories are marked by active participation in Black and feminist circles, social movements, government bodies, associations of Black cultural resistance and political parties (Perry/Sotero 2019; Santana 2021; Ratts/Rios 2010). Lélia Gonzalez was one of the founders of the *Movimento Negro Unificado* (Unified Black Movement - MNU) and together with other Black women, created the Black women's collective Nzinga in 1983 (Ratts/Rios 2010). Since 1983, Sueli Carneiro was engaged in the construction of spaces for Black women to participate in advisory councils on the condition of women. In 1988, she founded Geledés – *Instituto da Mulher Negra* (Black Women's Institute), an organization in the defense of Black women's rights in Brazil for which she currently serves as director (Santana 2021).

Transcending regional boundaries, both women engaged in building a dialogue between Latin American and Caribbean feminisms, recognizing how the exchange of similar experiences – colonialization and slavery – supports the formation of transnational feminist solidarities. Gonzalez particularly stressed the need for building an Afro-Latin American feminism, arising from the mutual recognition of women who are embedded in similar historical and structural contexts (Gonzalez 1988, 2020a; Perry/Sotero 2019; Rios 2019). In this strategic direction, they propose a break with the hegemony of White feminism in the region and incorporate a Black feminist critique in the constitution of a feminist approach that accounts for the specificities of Latin America (Santana 2021; Ratts/Rios 2010).

Within the Brazilian context, Gonzalez and Carneiro are committed to understanding and exposing the complex realities of Black women and producing political diagnoses about them. What stands out at this point is their critical assessment of the very oppositional movements in which they were active. They sought to understand what is hindering or missing from a political agenda for the emancipation of Black women and consequently of the Black population in Brazil. Carneiro coined the expression "Blackening feminism", which served to demonstrate the White feminist movement's failure to incorporate the issues of Black women into its agenda, and also demanded a feminist critique that accounted for the condition and experiences of the Black woman (Carneiro 2003). At the same time, they perceive the absence of racial debates in the progressive and left circles on the Brazilian political scene. Gonzalez calls this phenomenon "racism by omission", which renders racism secondary and suppresses a qualified discussion over class and racial exploitation, which is essential to grasp the larger nature of structural oppression (Gonzalez 2020b).

Carneiro and Gonzalez' active engagement becomes a method for observing and developing interpretative categories of the social and the political. The chronicles of this engagement demonstrate their capacity to build dialogues and cross borders that open new paths towards thinking and developing collective and intersectional strategies.

Of the Capacity to Act as Historical Subjects

Decolonial feminist pedagogy focuses on those methods of knowledge production that privilege local experiences, especially those emerging from the margins (Spinosa et al. 2013). Gonzalez and Carneiro's work fits into this methodological frame as they make Black women's agency and experience central to understanding and expressing the specificities and particularities of their condition.

The intellectual trajectory of Carneiro and Gonzalez is marked by intense and diverse political participation in which they gain proximity to the lived experiences of Black women. It is noteworthy that both of them share a peripheral and underprivileged origin. However, they shift from a subordinated condition and occupy spaces and positions not necessarily thought or reserved for them in the context of the Brazilian social and racial divide. In the background lies the recognition that their path does not reflect the typical stories of other Black women of similar status. In such a way, a substantive understanding of Black women's condition in Brazilian society requires a (re)approximation towards the women who remained in their territories, women who, unlike them, could not participate in spaces reserved for historically privileged groups (Gonzalez 2020a; Vieira/Almeida/Carneiro 2020; Santana 2021).

This does not mean that their trajectories were not relevant to their propositions; after all, exceptions can be used as a method to comprehend and apprehend the rule. Gonzalez and Carneiro often employed the method of self-referencing, incorporating some of their personal experiences to describe the condition of Black women and the peculiarities and subtle details of racial relations in Brazil. In alluding to anecdotes from their life stories, they demonstrate how ordinary, everyday facts that portray the empirical reality of gender and racial inequalities, are part of experiences shared by other Black women and derived from similar structures of oppression. Notwithstanding, this is a resource frequently used by other Black and decolonial feminists, indicating synergy between non-White feminist projects (Moraga/Anzaldúa 2015; Lugones 2003; Lorde ([1984] 2019).

Constructing and Fomenting a Critical Capacity

This dimension envisages a possible rupture with the colonial discursive order of gender and race that imposes and naturalizes beliefs supporting domination structures. In this instance, decolonial and feminist pedagogy postulates the need for a (de)naturalization of old beliefs and to create alternative ways of representing and interpreting realities (Spinosa et al. 2013: 412). At this stage, this pedagogy questions established knowledges, relating them to oppression systems. Additionally, it underlines the relationship between symbolic and material realities. I highlight here some occasions in which Gonzalez and Carneiro have suggested other ways of telling stories, interrogated established truths, and facilitated the creation of alternative representations to position Black women *vis a vis* a system of racial classification.

In a dialogue with the psychoanalytic field, Gonzalez coined the concept of "Brazilian cultural neurosis", which is characterized by modes of concealment from reality (Gonzalez 2019: 241). In this specific articulation, Gonzalez seeks to review the centrality of Black women to Brazilian identity and, in this way, demonstrates how racism is ignored and dismissed in the most astute manners. For instance, Gonzalez retrieves the figure of the Black Mammy, that is, the Black domestic worker who, in the master's house, was responsible for the household chores and especially for the children. This 'other' mother cared for the children, bathed them, told stories, and played, thus exercising functions traditionally taken as maternal. In exercising these responsibilities, these women transmitted their way of speaking, beliefs, and values, thus influencing the socialization of the master's children. By denouncing the omission of this influence in accounts of social relations and classical sociological interpretations of Brazil's formation, Gonzalez emphasizes how the cover-up of historical facts is a manifestation of racism. Concomitantly, she calls attention to the leading role Black women have had in forming Brazilian society and its sociability (Gonzalez 2019). Thereby, Lélia Gonzalez demonstrates that it is impossible to think about Brazilian culture and identity without acknowledging the profound participation of Black women, which is concrete, symbolic, and affective. For her, the celebration and explicit admission of this heritage are essential in overcoming racism and breaking the cycles of (de)humanization and devaluation of Black women.

Sueli Carneiro also contributed to recalling the existence of structural racism, exposing the myth that Brazil was/is a racial paradise. She pioneered studies containing data about inequalities among women, publishing a cutting-edge article in 1985 that analyzed the socioeconomic condition of Black women in Brazil (Carneiro [1985]2019). This was one way to evidence how racial and sexual inequalities produce discrepant effects on women's material condition, demonstrating the impact of racial differences on the status of women (Cardoso 2016). However, Carneiro was also concerned with relating material vulnerabilities to the demeaning stereotypes associated with Blacks and Black women. In this regard, she turns to African cosmology and the cult of the *Orixás* to rethink and (re)signify the social representations of Black women. The objective here is to demonstrate the varying feminine archetypes existing in this cosmology, which assigns characteristics to Black women that differ from the commonsensical image of the subordinate and suffering body. The female entities in this cosmology are women who do not fit in dichotomous categories, such as good/bad and sacred/profane, but are rather complex beings viewed in their multiplicity. When analyzing cosmologies of African religions, Carneiro contemplates this belief system beyond its notional value, regarding it as a social organization method that seeks to reassemble elements from the life that people in diaspora no longer had access to, a life from which they have been strapped (Carneiro/Cury 2019). Carneiro discusses how African mythical thought brings to the surface another system of social representations and beliefs that repositions the Black woman and releases her from a stereotypical place of subservience and inferiority. The possibility of (re)signifying this woman, in her value, and potency, as a pole of resistance is made possible through the principles of a non-Western thought and epistemic approach.

In different ways, Gonzalez and Carneiro establish a connection between the past, the present, and the future, retelling stories and revisiting Brazilian history from other angles. While doing that, they pave the way for developing alternative narratives and imaginations about Black women to be diffused and incorporated into the public and private spheres.

The Healing Power of this Pedagogy

Spinosa et al. (2013: 416) ascribe a therapeutic and healing function to feminist decolonial pedagogy, besides being a code of resistance. In the engaged thought of Gonzalez and Carneiro, we can identify how making sense of their trajectories yields a (re)interpretation of their individualities, identities, and affections and how this shapes their political activity.

Lélia Gonzalez reports some of the ways in which she was exposed to processes of Whitening and brainwashing while occupying spaces not meant for Blacks, here more specifically in reference to her high educational level and intense participation in intellectual circles. As she moves away from her origins, her insecurity grows, and the 'Whitening' ideology is consequently internalized (Ratts/Rios 2010). In retrieving this piece of her history, Gonzalez recalls having constructed a persona that concealed and erased her Blackness in aesthetical and cultural forms. And it is in the reconnection with her Black and peripheral consciousness that Gonzalez understands the internalization of the Whitening ideology and begins to change her self-presentation to the world. In going back to her roots, she recognizes the importance of her indigenous and illiterate mother for her intellectual development and acknowledges the lived experiences of other Black women as central tools for understanding the complexity of racial and gendered relations. In this same period, Lélia Gonzalez changed her style and fully embodied her African heritage, opting for warmer colors and wearing her hair in its natural form. Gonzalez also adopted a particular way of speaking and writing, a colloquial style that deviated from the more classic patterns of academic writing and is closer to spoken language by employing popular expressions and slang. She coined the term *"pretuguês"* to indicate a Blackened Portuguese that does not obscure its African roots in its linguistic development. Like other traits of the country's culture, Brazilian Portuguese has a profound African influence, and Gonzalez made sure to make that visible and present in her production (Ratts/Rios 2010).

For Sueli Carneiro, this healing and transformative power of decolonization is most evident in the path taken for her political activity, especially in the founding of *Geledés – Instituto da Mulher Negra* (Black Women's Institute). As an organization unplugged from both the White feminist and Black movements, this step can be considered a bold move by Carneiro and her fellow activists. It was a political decision and strategy to form a space where Black women would be positioned as central political subjects and protagonists of their own struggles, a space where issues intersected by racial, gendered, and territorial axis could be confronted, and where a public agenda of organized Black women could be formulated and forwarded to the public sphere. The name *Geledés* also holds a special symbolic meaning, as it was chosen as a reference to traditional *Yorùbá* secret organizations that worship feminine power. Moving away from White, hegemonic, and colonial connections, Carneiro and her partners bridged African culture and ancestrality to an organized Black feminist political association (Vieira/Almeida/Carneiro 2020; Santana 2021: 156). The institutional assimilation of Afro-Brazilian culture might as well symbolize a breach with a system of references that produces demeaning representations of Black women and the African diasporic heritage and memory. Such ruptures with White and Western patterns are instruments of insubordination and acknowledgement of the power within and among Black women, especially when they are assembled. Such appeal to ancestry embodies individual and collective empowerment and sabotages a system that seeks to discipline and limit their agency and creative capacities.

Leaving their positions of subordination and invisibility and refusing the suppression of their own identity and culture are some of the articulations that Sueli Carneiro and Lélia Gonzalez have voiced throughout their careers. These accounts show how these two Black feminists shaped their intellectual production, political activities, and identities to detach themselves from a colonial, racialized, and gendered gaze and reasoning. They rejected the demeaning representations of Black women and refused the burden of misrepresentation. They arrange the ancestry, culture, strength, and value of the Black woman in a visible and honored position in their performances. As anticipated by Spinosa et al. (2013), this demonstrates the political vigor of this feminist pedagogical practice. Indeed, the thought of these two pioneers is a central reference for Critical Race Theories and feminist studies in Brazil, and the celebration of these intellectual and activist trajectories has been a recurrent repertoire for the Black feminism movement and the integrated anti-racist struggle in the country (Paschel 2016; Rios 2019).

Final Remarks

I have composed this text to illustrate the ways in which a decolonial feminist pedagogy manifests itself, offering narratives of the journeys and ideas of Lélia Gonzalez and Sueli Carneiro. Through these tales, we can explore some paths through which knowledge can be weaved and material and symbolic realities can be altered.

The lifeworks of Lélia Gonzalez and Sueli Carneiro are sensitively integrated within a decolonial and feminist pedagogy, forming a knowledge that, anchored in political articulations, intersectional dialogue, and a commitment to the emancipation of Black women, has contributed to fundamental tools for overcoming the oppressive condition of Black women. They demonstrate that it is necessary to occupy various fronts of thought and action to include a Black feminist agenda and a decolonial perspective in the public sphere as part of resistance and democratic strategies. They also show how the relationship between social representations and the discourses that articulate realities have a relevant role in shaping material precariousness and inequality in the distribution of resources.

Demonstrating the similarity between the thought of two historical Black feminists in the Brazilian context and the imaginations proposed by feminists in the Americas uncovers the need to build bridges of mutual recognition. This carries the potential of opening roadways to forge bonds of solidarity between women living and interacting in territories and communities where the coloniality of power has a structural and structuring influence on their existences.

References

Cardoso, Cláudia Pons (2016): "Feminisms from the Perspective of Afro-Brazilian Women." In: Meridians 14/1, pp. 1–29.
Carneiro, Sueli (2003): "Mulheres em Movimento." In: Estudos Avançados 17/49, pp. 117–132.
Carneiro, Sueli ([1985] 2019): "Mulher Negra." In: Suelo Carneiro, Escritos de uma Vida, São Paulo: Editora Jandaíra, pp. 13–59.
Carneiro, Sueli/Cury, Cristiane Abdon (2019): "O Poder Feminino no Culto aos Orixás." In: Sueli Carneiro, Escritos de uma Vida, São Paulo: Editora Jandaíra, pp.60-88.
Gonzalez, Lélia (1988): "A categoria politico-cultural da amefricanidade." In: Tempo Brasileiro 92, pp. 69–82.
Gonzalez, Lélia (2019): "Racismo e Sexismo na Cultura Brasileira." In: Hollanda Cristina Buarque de Holanda (ed.), Pensamento Feminista Brasileiro: formação e contexto, Rio de Janeiro: Bazar do Tempo, pp. 237–256.
Gonzalez, Lélia (2020a): "Mulher Negra." In: Flavia Rios/Márcia Lima (eds.), Por um Feminismo Afro Latino Americano, Rio de Janeiro: Zahar, pp. 95–111.

Gonzalez, Lélia (2020b): "Racismo por Omissão." In: Flavia Rios/Márcia Lima (eds.), Por um Feminismo Afro Latino Americano, Rio de Janeiro: Zahar, pp. 220–221.

Lorde, Audre (2019 [1984]): Sister Outsider, London: Penguin Modern Classics.

Lugones, María (2003): Pilgrimages/Peregrinajes. Theorizing Coalition against Multiple Oppressions, Maryland: Rowman & Littlefield.

Moraga, Cherríe/Anzaldúa, Gloria (2015): This Bridge Called my Back, Albany: State University of New York Press.

Paschel, Tianna (2016): Becoming Black Political Subjects. Movements and Ethno-Racial Rights in Colombia and Brazil, Princeton: Princeton University Press.

Perry, Keisha-Khan Y./Sotero, Edilza (2019): "Amefricanidade: The Black Diaspora Feminism of Lélia Gonzalez." In: Lasa Forum 50/3, pp. 60–64.

Ratts, Alex/Rios, Flávia (2010): Lélia Gonzalez, São Paulo: Selo Negro, 2010.

Rios, Flávia (2019): "Améfrica Ladina: The Conceptual Legacy of Lélia Gonzalez (1935–1994)." Lasa Forum 50/3, pp. 75–79.

Santana, Bianca (2021): Continuo Preta. A Vida de Sueli Carneiro, São Paulo: Companhia das Letras.

Spinosa et al. (2013): "Reflexiones Pedagógicas en torno al feminismo decolonial. Una conversa en cuatro voces." In: Catherine Walsh (ed.), Pedagogías decoloniales. Prácticas insurgentes de rexistir, (re)vivir y (re)vivir. Tomo I, Quito: Ediciones Abya Yala, pp. 403–441.

Vieira, Daniela/Almeida, Mariléa/Carneiro, Sueli (2020): "Between Left and Right, I Remain Black: Interview with Sueli Carneiro." In: Transition 130, pp. 173–189.

Gender-Based Political Violence as a Global Phenomenon
Latin-American Pioneerism, the Brazilian Exception, and the Silence of the Global North

Ligia Fabris

Abstract: *Violence against women in politics is not a new phenomenon. However, naming it, conceptualizing it, and investigating its prevalence is rather recent. Despite its global occurrence (IPU 2016; Krook 2018), the use of the concept, as well as the issuance of legal instruments to define and combat it, was pioneered by Latin American countries. Interestingly, instead of being celebrated as a leading initiative, this Latin American pioneering work seems to have instead given rise to the assessment that the violence experienced is a local problem, typical of "recent" or "not fully solid" democracies in the Global South, and does not merit discussion (as such) in the Global North. Brazil, one of the last Latin American countries to pass a bill to address the problem, has faced increasing gender-based political violence on the one hand, and on the other, has been resisting efforts to advance the sub-continent's instruments to guarantee women more access to the political realm.*

This article joins the literature that assert that gender-based political violence is a phenomenon related to the underrepresentation of women in politics (Freidenberg 2017; Albaine 2017a; Archenti/Albaine 2018; Krook 2017, 2018, 2020; Krook/Sanín, 2016; Sanín 2022; Biroli 2016, 2018; Biroli/Marques 2020: 564; Bardall/Bjarnegård/Piscopo 2019), functioning as a tool of gender inequality to prevent women and LGBTQIA+ people from accessing it worldwide. Based on this background, this article aims to (i) briefly define gender-based political violence (GBPV) and violence against women in politics (VAWIP), addressing the social, political, and legal contexts of its conceptualization; (ii) describe the occurrence of GBPV in Brazil and its new bill to combat it, issued during the Bolsonaro government; (iii) argue, with the help of recent research and data, that the phenomenon is not local, but global, and intertwined with the exclusion of women in politics as constituted by and constituent of gender inequality. As a conclusion, the ubiquity and global scale of aggression against women and gender non-conforming individuals in politics makes it clear that it is time to recognize and combat gender-based political violence worldwide.

Introduction

It is not new that women who defy the gendered separation of public and private and dare to dispute positions of power in the public sphere suffer consequences. Defamation, comments about their family status and sexuality, comments about their appearance (age; clothes; hair; skin tone; body, either as too bad or too good); or temper (too strong or too soft); interrupting, not letting women speak, dismissing their voices as unimportant – to name just a few such practices, is a common part of the life of a woman who dares to be involved in institutional politics.

It is so common that such discriminating and offensive behavior was (and sometimes continues to be) considered a natural part of politics. The Inter-Parliamentary Union has issued reports with anonymized data about the prevalence of violence against women parliamentarians from 39 countries of the five regions of the world, from all age groups: 81.8 per cent of them stated that they had suffered from psychological violence (IPU 2016: 2–3). In Brazil, according to the latest report of the NGOs Terra de Direitos and Justiça Global (2022), the cases of general political and electoral violence increased by 400 per cent between 2018 and 2022 (46 cases in 2018 vs. 266 cases in 2022) (idem: 2). A prior study about political violence against Women of Color in the Brazilian parliament (Lima/Fabris/Goulart 2022) has shown that, considering their intersectionality, Black women are subjected to specific forms of violence, such as a form we have named "misrecognition": the phenomenon that security guards stop and prevent them from entering the legislative house because they do not recognize them as having the characteristics of people who traditionally occupy that position (idem: 60–61). The general message given to all of them is: "That's part of it, if you can't stand it, it is because you are not supposed to be there". And women are not supposed to be there.

Only very recently did this pattern of assaulting women who hold or run for public offices gained a name. In the same way that being battered by one's husband was considered part of marriage, and being sexually harassed by one's boss has, for a long time, been considered part of workplace reality, it was only in the last decade that this has been identified as a specific phenomenon, a particular form of violence, that is, a form of discrimination against women. And that happened because of a brutal case of gender-based political violence: the murder of a councilwoman in Bolivia in 2012.

Conceptualizations: Gender-Based Political Violence and Violence Against Women in Politics

The terms used to refer to the political violence suffered because of gender are mostly variations of "political violence against women" or "gender-based political violence".[1] These different terminologies are sometimes used interchangeably (Krook 2020: 63) but can also connote potential differences in framing and scope. The first is restricted to women (cis- or transgender) and refers to the gender asymmetries between men and women (Archenti/Albaine 2018: 18; Cerva Cerna 2014). It expresses, in a similar way as the studies of violence against women, that this is a violence conducted "on the basis of gender" – that is: a violence a woman suffers *because* she is a woman.

The second concept – gender-based political violence – has a potentially different, less discussed meaning. The use of "gender-based" instead on "women" opens the concept to the possibility of recognizing the violence directed to someone *whose existence defies the heteronorm*. Therefore, *gender-based political violence* can also encompass the violence directed at LGBTQIA+ politicians (Freidenberg 2017; Albaine 2017a; Krook 2017, 2018, 2020; Krook/Sanin, 2016; Biroli 2016, 2018; Biroli/Marques 2020: 564; Bardall/Bjarnegård/Piscopo 2019).

Consequently, although gender-based political violence is not a new phenomenon, it has only recently been named as such and debated in terms of its occurrence and conceptualization. The definition of gender-based political violence does not only encompass extreme forms of violence such as murder, rape, or battering, but also economic and psychological forms of violence.

---

1   Another term – less used – is "gendered political violence". See Bardall, Bjarnegård, Piscopo 2019.

While gender-based political violence is being called a "rising global trend" in its incidence (Krook 2018), the first – and, until now, the only – countries to name it under their domestic legal order are situated in Latin America.

On the international level, several previous instruments paved the way for legal internal frameworks to fight this specific kind of violence. The 1953 Convention on the political rights of women; the 1969 American Convention on Human Rights (Pact of San Jose, Costa Rica), that implemented the Inter-American Human Rights System; the 1979 Convention on the Elimination of All Forms of Discrimination Against Women (CEDAW); 1994 the Inter-American Convention on the Prevention, Punishment, and Eradication of Violence against Women (Convention of Belém do Pará) that created a follow-up mechanism for a continuous and independent evaluation process of its implementation, and the 1995 United Nations' Fourth World Conference on Women in Beijing that stressed the necessity of granting women access to power positions, including politics, and issued a "platform for action". These are instruments created to protect women's political and human rights and were all ratified by Latin-American countries.[2]

The concept of political violence against women first emerged in the late 1990s in Bolivia, but only became a national subject after the emblematic political feminicide[3] of Juana Quispe Apaza, a member of the indigenous and peas-

---

2   Although these mechanisms were mostly held by the UN and the Organization of American States, the United States of America have not ratified neither the American Convention on Human Rights, nor the Convention on the Elimination of All Forms of Discrimination Against Women, and have not signed the Belém do Pará Convention. This can be seen as an "[US-]American exemptionalism, or the hubristic assumption that the United States is being 'above' or an 'exception' to the law" (Schalatek 2019, arguing about the USA not having signed the CEDAW).

3   The initial term used in the English language was "femicide", formulated by Diane Russell (2012, 1) in 1976. She more recently defined it as "the killing of a female because she is a female" (ibid.). In turn, the term "feminicide" was coined in Spanish (*feminicidio*) during Russell's participation on a seminar at the UNAM in 2005 to avoid the idea of a feminization of the word "*homicidio*" (homicide) under a translation into "*femicidio*" (Russell/Radford 1992, 17). Later, Marcela Lagarde added that institutional violence was part of feminicide, leading to impunity (Lagarde 2006, 223). Yet, both terms are often used as synonyms. The term "feminicide" has been established in Latin America and has also been used in English. I use the term "feminicide" because I understand the state to be responsible for the violence against and murder of women. In the case of a killing of a MP or councilwoman, the state is responsible not only for failing to ensure their safety, but also often for not conducting the investigation properly, neither hav-

ant women's movement who was the first female councilwoman elected in Ancoraimes, a municipality in the province of Omasuyos. In April 2010, she won the municipal elections with 70 percent of the votes, and nevertheless was harassed and threatened by the mayor and councilors of the municipality, not only during her campaign but also after being elected (Gil 2019).

On several occasions, the (all-male) councilors changed the council meeting locations without telling her, or ostensibly prevented her from entering the sessions, so they could remove her from office for absenteeism. As a result, Juana Quispe Apaza was removed from her position. She refused to resign and was not reinstated in her position until 2012. Quispe filed a lawsuit and only after 20 months, on 9 February 2012, was she restored to her position (Gil 2019).

A month later, she was found dead with signs of hanging in the city of La Paz. Quispe Apaza was running a project against political gender harassment and violence to combat the constant aggression and pressure that Bolivian women suffer when engaging in politics (Gil 2019). After her political feminicide, the bill that was drafted in the late 1990s following several complaints of violence and presented in 2001 (Freidenberg 2017: 25). It was finally approved on the 28th of May 2012 and became the first law to combat harassment and political violence against women in the world. After that, Costa Rica, Ecuador, Honduras, Mexico and Peru drafted bills (Albaine 2017b: 120, Freidenberg 2017: 25), as well as El Salvador, Argentina, Uruguay and more recently, Brazil.[4] In 2017, the Organization of American States, following the 1994 Convention of Belém do Pará (namely, the Inter-American Convention on the Prevention, Punishment, and Eradication of Violence against Women) published

---

ing the crime resolved, nor holding the perpetrators accountable for it, as in the cases of Juana Quispe (Bolivia) and Marielle Franco (Brazil) (Lima/Fabris/Goulart 2022: 70).

4   Some of those bills came into force. In my free English translation the names of these laws would be: Costa Rica, Act 10235/2022 – Law to prevent, address, punish and eradicate violence against women in politics; Ecuador, Act 157/2018 – Comprehensive Organic Law to Prevent and Eradicate Violence against Women; Mexico – The General Law on Women's Access to a Life Free of Violence, 2007 with political violence against women added in 2013 as art. 20; Peru, Act 31155/2021 – Law that prevents and punishes harassment against women in political life; El Salvador, Decree No. 520/2010 – Special Integral Law for a Life Free of Violence for Women; Argentina, Act 26. 485/2019 – Comprehensive Protection to prevent, punish and eradicate violence against women in the environments in which they develop their interpersonal relationships; Uruguay, Act 19.580/2018 – Gender-based Violence against Women, and Brazil, Act 14.192/2021 – Law to combat political violence against women.

an "Inter-American Model Law on the Prevention, Punishment and Eradication of Violence against Women in Political Life".[5]

In this context, Latin American countries have been pioneers in legislative efforts to define and combat forms of gender-based violence. The Model Law defines it as follows:

> Violence against women in political life shall be understood as any action, conduct, or omission, directly or through third parties, which, on the basis of gender, causes injury or suffering to one or more women, and which has the purpose or effect of impairing or nullifying the recognition, enjoyment, or exercise of their political rights. Violence against women in political life may include, but is not limited to, physical, sexual, psychological, moral, economic, or symbolic violence. (Inter-American Commission of Women 2017: 23).

Violence Against Women in Politics in Brazil: a Political Feminicide, and a New Bill

In the Brazilian public sphere, the subject has gained increasing attention especially after the political feminicide of Marielle Franco in 2018, then the second most voted councilwoman in the municipality of Rio de Janeiro. Marielle Franco was Black, of poor origin, raised in the Favela da Maré in Rio de Janeiro, and openly bi-sexual.

---

5   The relation between the Belém do Pará Convention and the Inter-American Model Law is explained in the document itself: "In 1994, the Inter-American Commission of Women (CIM) promoted the adoption of the Inter-American Convention on the Prevention, Punishment and Eradication of Violence against Women, better known as the Convention of Belém do Pará. The Convention entered into force in 1995 and has been ratified by 32 States to date. In 2004, the States Parties to the Convention agreed on the creation of the Follow-up Mechanism to the Belém do Pará Convention (MESECVI) with the objective of monitoring the implementation of the Convention in the State Parties. Within the framework of its mandate, the MESECVI has recognized the progress of the States in the prevention and punishment of violence against women in the private sphere, however, it has also repeatedly emphasized that 'these actions do not cover all manifestations of violence against women, especially those produced in the public sphere,' and has affirmed the need to make progress in legislation that sanctions violence against women perpetrated in the public sphere" (Inter-American Commission of Women 2017: 5).

She stood up for women's rights, raising topics such as abortion and combating violence against women, and she constantly denounced police abuse in the favelas. On 14 March 2018, as she was leaving an event on Women's Day with young Black women in central Rio, a vehicle pulled up next to Marielle's car and someone fired thirteen shots, killing Marielle Franco and the driver Anderson Pedro Gomes. In 2022, four years after her murder, the case was still under investigation and under political dispute. The police investigation's main hypothesis is that it was a politically motivated execution carried out by paramilitary forces (Phillips 2019). The central question asked by awareness campaigns relating to this crime was: "Who ordered the killing of Marielle Franco?"

Although Marielle Franco has become a symbol against political brutality and feminicide, it was only in 2021, three years after her death, that Brazil passed a law creating the criminal category of "violence against women in politics". And, contrary to all the other extensive laws on the subject by its neighbour countries, this law is very brief and only creates criminal offenses, thus only creating avenues in criminal law to deal with the matter. That means that other legal mechanisms, such as electoral law, torts, administrative law, for instance, which may be more effective in countering the most widespread forms of gender-based political violence, were not considered or addressed in this new Brazilian law. The Act No. 14.192/2021 "establishes norms to prevent, repress and combat political violence against women" and defines in its Art. 3°: "Political violence against women is considered to be all actions, conduct, or omissions with the purpose of preventing, hindering, or restricting women's political rights"[6].

The process of passing this law – under the ultraconservative government of Bolsonaro – was surrounded by disputes. For instance, it was impossible to pass a more comprehensive law, also because the former president and his supporters were often the very entities who attack women, with right-wing congresswomen participating in such defamations. One example is Carla Zambelli, a federal representative of São Paulo State, accused of having committed

---

6   The law adds to the penal code the criminal offense of 'political violence against women', defined as: Art. 326-B – "To harass, coerce, humiliate, persecute or threaten, by any means, a female candidate for elective office or holder of an elective office, using contempt or discrimination against the condition of women or her color, race or ethnicity, with the purpose of preventing or hindering her electoral campaign or the performance of her elective office." (All translations from Portuguese into English by the author).

political violence against Talíria Petrone, Sâmia Bonfim and Manuela D'Ávila, three left-wing women politicians who were called "genocidal leftists" and had their images disfigured with devilish red eyes and horns because they celebrated the passing of the abortion law in Colombia (UOL 2022).

Another reason that made it impossible to speak of "gender-based" political violence is the federal government's ban on using the word gender in any of its official documents, as a sign for its opposition to "gender ideology"[7] and as an attempt to exclude trans women. On a side note: In 2019, it was reported that the Brazilian delegation at the UN opposed the word "gender" – in Portuguese, "*gênero*" –, in all documents, including completely unrelated contexts, such as "foodstuffs" (*gênero alimentício*). In this context, compared to the other Latin American countries, the Brazilian law on gender-based violence turned out to be rather unambitious. Furthermore, it mobilized what is called "penal populism".[8] The terms describes the practice of passing criminal law(s) and advertising it as the solution to social problems that have created public out-

---

[7] On "gender ideology" and its creation by the Catholic Church in the 1990s and its purposes, see Case 2019.

[8] Penal populism can be described as "a process whereby the major political parties compete with each other to be 'tough on crime'. It is generally associated with a public perception that crime is out of control and tends to manifest at general elections when politicians put forward hard-line policies which would remand more offenders into prison prior to sentencing and impose longer sentences. (...) According to a book written by John Pratt (2007), a criminologist and international authority on the subject, penal populism speaks to the way in which criminals and prisoners are thought to have been favored at the expense of crime victims in particular and the law-abiding public in general. It feeds on expressions of anger, disenchantment and disillusionment with the criminal justice establishment. It holds this responsible for what seems to have been the insidious inversion of commonsensical priorities: protecting the well-being and security of law- abiding 'ordinary people', punishing those whose crimes jeopardize this. Pratt wrote that 'as with populism itself, penal populism usually takes the form of 'feelings and intuitions' rather than some more quantifiable indicator: for example, expressions of everyday talk between citizens which revolves around concerns and anxieties about crime and disorder; anger and concern about these matters volubly expressed in the media – not simply the national press or broadcasters; and a variety of new information and media outlets which allow the voices of the general public a much more direct airing – local newspapers and news sheets, talk-back radio and reality television'" (ECPS, available at: https://www.populismstudies.org/Vocabulary/penal-populism/, accessed on 13 October 2022).

cry and scandal; when in fact, critical criminology[9] shows that criminal law is never a (single) solution, since it is of difficult and selective implementation, especially when its intention is to discipline privileged sectors of society, like (male) politicians.

The other Latin-American laws on gender-based political violence represent undeniable advancements, not only in terms of their potential to change their country's reality, but also with regards to the wider debate on women's political rights across the world. This conclusion has not been unanimous, though.

Gender-Based Political Violence: A Global Phenomenon

Internationally, the pioneering spirit of Latin American countries in the field of legislating against gender-based violence has mostly been portrayed as exceptions, inside and outside of the continent. Based on stereotypes of the region rooted in notions of global hierarchy (such as labelling only the Global South as violent, backward and underdeveloped), political contexts in Western countries usually maintain that such a concept would be useless in the Global North, because this kind of violence is believed to only exist in countries with "weak and threatened" democracies.

This, however, is not true. Just as gender-based violence is globally present, so is its occurrence in the political sphere. The aforementioned false arguments punish and invisibilize the continent's protagonism in creating what could be called, following Cho, Crenshaw and McCall (2013: 788), an "analytical tool to

---

9 "... the field of critical criminology is united in its emphasis on addressing power differentials, hierarchies, and inequalities as explanations of crime, as these impact the distribution of crime over time and place, and in relation to definitions of crime and justice and processes of doing justice, as these impact the making and enforcing of laws." (Lynch 2014, available at: https://www.oxfordbibliographies.com/view/document/obo-9780195396607/obo-9780195396607-0064.xml accessed on 13 October 2022). As stated by Alessandro Baratta (2004 [1982]), one of the founders of critical criminology: "The attention of the new criminology, of critical criminology, has been directed above all to the process of criminalization, identifying in it one of the major theoretical and practical knots of the social relations of inequality characteristic of capitalist society, and pursuing, as one of its main objectives, a rigorous expansion of the critique of unequal law to the field of criminal law" (Translated from Spanish into English by the author).

capture and engage contextual dynamics of power", an epistemological frame to name, make visible, and oppose a pervasive phenomenon of subordination. Thus, one overlooks the presence of these acts of violence in countries of the Global North. One example would be the attacks delivered by former president Donald Trump against former candidate Hillary Clinton (Chozick/Parker 2016) or congresswoman Alexandria Ocasio-Cortez and other congresswomen (Pengelly 2019) in the U.S. Or, in Germany, the sexist scrutiny to which Angela Merkel has been subjected (Tagesspiegel 2021a), and the transphobic treatment of MP Tessa Ganserer since she got elected (Tagesspiegel 2021b); and in the UK, the political feminicide of Jo Cox in 2016 (Mondragón/de Cosío 2017: 214).

The first global study on violence against women legislators conducted from the Inter-Parliamentary Union in 39 countries showed that more than 80% of women in politics have experienced psychological violence, understood as "any hostile behavior or act likely to cause psychological harm, suffering and/or fear" (IPU 2016: 3). 65.5 per cent have experienced humiliating sexual or sexist remarks. Almost half, 44.4 per cent have received threats of death, rape, beatings, or abduction. In 2018 another report from the IPU showed alarming levels of sexual abuse and violence in European parliaments (2018: 5).

In addition to leading efforts to recognize gender-based political violence, Latin American countries have recently also made huge advances in increasing women's participation in politics: Of the ten countries with the highest number of women in parliament (ranging in percentages from 42.6 to 61.3 per cent), five are from Latin America: Second in the world is Cuba, with 55.7 per cent; third, Nicaragua, with 51.7 per cent; fourth, Mexico, 50 per cent; eighth, Costa Rica, 47.4 per cent; Bolivia comes now in the eleventh position, with 46.2 per cent (IPU 2023). Thus, violence against women in politics is also a response to the increasing presence of women in the political sphere and their agendas, trying to stop and reverse this tide.

Unlike its neighbors, however, Brazil has faced immense difficulties in advancing on both fields: political violence against women and women's participation in politics. This is even more perplexing as we analyze some data on these phenomena in the country: Brazil is one of the countries with the fewest women in politics in the world: The current figure of 17.5 per cent after 2022's elections is the highest in Brazilian records (n. 131 in the IPU ranking of 187 positions – IPU 2023). The rate of women elected increased by 50 per cent for the first time in history in 2018 compared to the 2014 national elections (it went from about 10 per cent in 2014 to 15 per cent in 2018) and was reached after a Federal Supreme Court decision that granted women candidates access to public campaign resources proportionately to the percentage of candidacies (that is, at least 30 per cent) (Fabris 2019). This landmark decision was issued the day after Marielle Franco's murder. It is important to note that the exclusion rate of Black congresswomen in Brazilian parliament is even greater: Currently, they constitute only 2 per cent of the lower house and only 1 per cent of the senate, while representing 27.8 per cent of the Brazilian population (MND 2023: 7). Additionally, Black congresswomen are more likely to experience political violence, as well as female opposition members, especially Black and trans women MPs, as recent research and episodes have demonstrated (Lima/Fabris/Goulart 2022; Terra de Direitos et al 2022).[10]

The advancement achieved by the Brazilian Supreme Court was followed by political conservative attempts at retrogression: Under the Bolsonaro government, conservative politicians attempted to pass new laws reforming the rules of the Brazilian electoral system, most frequently trying to furtively impede the advancement of women's presence in politics, while also electing some women with a massive number of votes (Araújo/Fabris/Ferreti 2021).

Moreover, Eurocentrically taking Europe and the US as a reference, (conservative) Brazilian politicians have been resisting the adoption of laws and public policies both to increase women's political participation and to comprehensively fight gender-based political violence. Such voices argued that "no civilized country in the world – meaning: in the EU and the USA – has a federal law on a quota or parity for women in politics and on violence against women in politics". With the help of some conservative women MPs, the Parliament

---

10   Benny Briolly, a Black and trans Councilwoman from Niterói and her staff received several death threats, as well as transphobic and racist insults. These facts were denounced to the IPU Committee and the transphobia she suffered from a colleague became the first case to be denounced by the Public Ministry as the conduct of violence against a woman in politics (IACHR & OAS 2022, available at: http://www.oas.org/en/iachr/decisions/mc/2022/res_34-22%20_mc_408-22_br_en.pdf). Also, on the Federal level, the Black and left-wing Congresswoman Talíria Petrone has been a symbol for political violence against (Black) women in Brazil, having her case recently acknowledged as a Human Rights Violation by the IPU Committee on the Human Rights of Parliamentarians, expressing concern on the death threats, acts of intimidation, violation of freedom of opinion and expression, violation of freedom of movement and discrimination she has been suffering, and requesting that state to take measures to protect her (IPU 2022, available at: https://www.ipu.org/sites/default/files/documents/brazil-e_1.pdf).

tried to pass in 2021 a constitutional amendment aiming at ending the 30 per cent quota for women candidates.

Therefore, due to the political, economic, and epistemological global power imbalance, the pioneering role of Latin American countries (actually, of Latin-American women and social movements) in acknowledging and framing this specific form of violence has so far neither been recognized, nor followed by countries of the Global North. On the contrary, this pioneering spirit has been used to rehash the old stereotypical label that the issue is a mere exception pertaining only to violence-ridden and weak democracies.

The omnipresence and global scale of assaults against women and gender-nonconforming individuals makes it clear that it is time for gender-based political violence to be acknowledged: as an attempt to prevent women from entering politics; a response to the ones who made it, so they are unable to do their jobs and represent the interests of women as a group; as an enforcement of gendered division of public and private as hierarchy and inequality per se; as a message for other women who outside of the political realm, all women. Gender-based political violence needs to be recognized as a specific form of discrimination against women and that pervasively occurs on the intersection with other markers of difference and subordination, like racism and LGBTQIA+ phobia. Gender-based political violence forms an integral part of the patriarchy; therefore, it is global and an issue affecting each and every country, not only the Global South. As a consequence, gender-based political violence must, together with Latin America's vanguardism, be acknowledged, as well as addressed and opposed, worldwide.

References

Albaine, Laura (2017a): Contra la violencia política de género en América Latina. Las oportunidades de acción, April 22, 2022 (http://bibliotecadigital.tse.jus.br/xmlui/handle/bdtse/6754).

Albaine, Laura (2017b): "Marcos normativos contra el acoso y/o violencia política en razón de género en América Latina." In: Flavia Freidenberg/Gabriela del Valle Pérez (eds.), Cuando hacer política te cuesta la vida. Estrategias contra la violencia política hacia las mujeres en América Latina, México: Instituto de Investigaciones Jurídicas, Universidad Nacional Autónoma de México, pp. 117–144.

Araújo, Clara/Fabris, Ligia/Ferreti, Michelle (2021): Nota Técnica N° 1: A Reforma Política e os mitos sobre a Participação Política de Mulheres, May

20, 2023 (http://cepia.org.br/wp-content/uploads/2021/06/Nota-Te%CC% 81cnica-1-Forum-Fluminense-Mais-Mulheres-Na-Politica.pdf).

Archenti, Nélida/Albaine, Laura (2018): „O Feminismo na política. Paridade e violência política de gênero na América Latina." In: Cadernos Adenauer XIX/1, pp. 9–24.

Bardall, Gabrielle/Bjarnegård, Elin/Piscopo, Jennifer M. (2020): „How is Political Violence Gendered? Disentangling Motives, Forms, and Impacts." In: Political Studies 68. SAGE Publications, pp. 916–935.

Biroli, Flávia (2016): "Political Violence against Women in Brazil: Expressions and Definitions." In: Revista Direito e Práxis, 7/15, pp. 557–589.

Biroli, Flávia (2018): "Violence against Women and Reactions to Gender Equality in Politics." In: Politics & Gender, 14/4, pp. 681–685.

Biroli, Flávia/Marques, Danusa (2020): "Mulheres e Política: Violência contra as mulheres/de gênero na política." In: Perissinotto, Renato et al. (eds.), Política Comparada: Teoria e Método. Rio de Janeiro: Eduerj, pp. 561–588.

Baratta, Alessandro (2004 [1982]): Criminología crítica y crítica del derecho penal: Introducción a la sociología jurídico penal. (Transl. from italian: Álvaro Búnster), Buenos Aires: Siglo XXI Editores Argentina.

Case, Mary Anne (2019): "Trans Formations in the Vatican's War on 'Gender Ideology'." In: Signs: Journal of Women in Culture and Society 44, Chicago: University of Chicago Press Chicago, pp. 639–664.

Cerva Cerna, Daniela (2014): "Political Participation and Gender Violence in Mexico." In: Revista Mexicana de Ciencias Políticas y Sociales, 59/222, pp. 117–140.

Chozick, Amy/Parker, Ashley (2016): "Donald Trump's Gender-Based Attacks on Hillary Clinton Have Calculated Risk." In: NYT, May 20, 2023 (https://www.nytimes.com/2016/04/29/us/politics/hillary-clinton-donald-trump-women.html).

Cho, Sumi/Crenshaw, Kimberlé Williams/McCall, Leslie (2013): "Toward a Field of Intersectionality Studies: Theory, Applications, and Praxis." In: Signs 38/4, pp. 785–810.

de Souza Lima, Lívia/Fabris, Ligia/Goulart da Silva, Mayra (2022): "Violence against Black Women in Politics: Experiences and Testimonials from Brazil." In: Femina Politica – Zeitschrift für feministische Politikwissenschaft 3/2, pp. 57–71.

European Center for Populism Studies (ECPS) (n.d): "Penal Populism", January 6, 2023 (https://www.populismstudies.org/Vocabulary/penal-populism/).

Fabris, Ligia (2019): "Litígio estratégico para igualdade de gênero: O caso das verbas de campanha para mulheres candidatas." In: Revista Direito e Práxis 10, pp. 593–629.

Freidenberg, Flavia (2017): "La violencia política hacia las mujeres: El problema, los debates y las propuestas para América Latina." In: Flavia Freidenberg/Gabriela del Valle Pérez (eds.), Cuando hacer política te cuesta la vida. Estrategias contra la violencia política hacia las mujeres en América Latina. México: Instituto de Investigaciones Jurídicas, Universidad Nacional Autónoma de México, pp. 4–42.

Gil, Karen (2019): "Juana Quispe, crónica de un asesinato anunciado: Pese al tiempo transcurrido, la muerte de la concejala de Ancoraimes aún no fue esclarecida." In: Correo del Sur, January 6, 2023 (https://correodelsur.com/panorama/20190915_juana-quispe-cronica-de-un-asesinato-anunciado.html).

Inter-American Commission on Human Rights (IACHR) and Organization of American States (OAS) (2022): Inter-American Commission on Human Rights Resolution 34/2022. Precautionary Measure No. 408-22. Benny Briolly Rosa da Silva Santos and members of her work team regarding Brazil, pp. 408–422 (http://www.oas.org/en/iachr/decisions/mc/2022/res_34-22%20_mc_408-22_br_en.pdf).

Inter-Parliamentary Union (2016): Sexism, Harassment and Violence against Women Parliamentarians. Issues Brief, Geneva: IPU, January 6, 2023 (https://www.ipu.org/sites/default/files/documents/brazil-e_1.pdf).

Inter-Parliamentary Union (2018): Sexism, Harassment and Violence against Women in Parliaments in Europe. Issues Brief, Geneva: IPU, January 6, 2023 (https://www.ipu.org/resources/publications/issue-briefs/2018-10/sexism-harassment-and-violence-against-women-in-parliaments-in-europe).

Inter-Parliamentary Union (2022): Brazil Decision Adopted Unanimously by the IPU Governing Council at its 210th Session, Kigali: IPU, January 6, 2023 (https://www.ipu.org/sites/default/files/documents/brazil-e_1.pdf).

Krook, Mona Lena/Sanín, Juliana Restrepo (2016): "Violence against Women in Politics. A Defense of the Concept." In: Política y gobierno 2/2, pp. 459–490.

Krook, Mona Lena (2017): "Violence against Women in Politics." In: Journal of Democracy 28/1, pp. 74–88.

Krook, Mona Lena (2018): "Violence against Women in Politics: A Rising Global Trend." In: Politics & Gender 14/4, pp. 673–675.

Krook, Mona Lena (2020): Violence against Women in Politics, Oxford: Oxford University Press.

Lagarde, Marcela (2006): „Del Femicidio al Feminicidio." In: Desde el Jardin de Freud 6, pp. 216–225.

Lynch, Michael J. (2014): Critical Criminology, January 6, 2023 (https://www.oxfordbibliographies.com/display/document/obo-9780195396607/obo-9780195396607-0064.xml).

Mulheres Negras Decidem (MND) (2023): Por que votar em mulheres Negras: Balanço dos mandatos das parlamentares negras (2019–2023). Report. Brazil, January 6, 2023 (https://mulheresnegrasdecidem.org/balanco-dos-mandatos-das-parlamentares-negras/).

Pengelly, Martin (2019): "'Go Back Home': Trump Aims Racist Attack at Ocasio-Cortez and Other Congresswomen." In: The Guardian, May 20, 2023 (https://www.theguardian.com/us-news/2019/jul/14/trump-squad-tlaib-omar-pressley-ocasio-cortez).

Phillips, Dom (2019): "Brazil: Two Ex-Police Officers Arrested over Murder of Marielle Franco." In: The Guardian, January 6, 2023 (https://www.theguardian.com/world/2019/mar/12/police-officers-arrested-murder-brazilian-politician-marielle-franco).

Radford, Jill/Russell, Diana E. H. (eds.) (2006): Feminicidio: La política del asesinato de las mujeres. (Translation from English: Tlatolli Oílin S.C.), Mexico City: UNAM.

Rodríguez Mondragón, Reyes/Cárdenas González de Cosío, Ana (2017): "Violencia política contra las mujeres y el rol de la justicia electoral." In: Flavia Freidenberg/Gabriela del Valle Pérez (eds.), Cuando hacer política te cuesta la vida. Estrategias contra la violencia política hacia las mujeres en América Latina, México: Instituto de Investigaciones Jurídicas, Universidad Nacional Autónoma de México, pp. 209–229.

Russell, Diana E. H. (2012): Introductory Speech Presented to the United Nations Symposium on Femicide on 11/26/2012. June 9, 2023 (https://www.femicideincanada.ca/sites/default/files/2017-12/RUSSELL%20%282012%29%20DEFINING%20FEMICIDE.pdf)

Sanín, Juliana Restrepo (2022): "Criminalizing Violence against Women in Politics: Innovation, Diffusion, and Transformation." In: Politics & Gender 18, Cambridge University Press, pp. 1–32.

Schalatek, Liane (2019): CEDAW and the USA: When Belief in Exceptionalism Becomes Exceptionalism. May 23, 2023 (https://www.boell.de/en/2019/12/10/cedaw-and-usa-when-belief-exceptionalism-becomes-exemptionalism).

Tagesspiegel (2021a): Sympathisch, aber nicht kompetent: Wie sexistische Klischees den Wahlkampf geprägt haben, May 23, 2023 (https://www.tagesspiegel.de/meinung/sympathisch-aber-nicht-kompetent-wie-sexistische-klischees-den-wahlkampf-gepraegt-haben-256384.html).

Tagesspiegel (2021b): Nyke Slawik und Tessa Ganserer: Trans Frauen beklagen negative Reaktionen nach Wahl in den Bundestag, May 23, 2023 (https://www.tagesspiegel.de/politik/trans-frauen-beklagen-negative-reaktionen-nach-wahl-in-den-bundestag-4282249.html).

Terra de Direitos/Justiça Global (2022): Violência Política e eleitoral no Brasil. Report. Brazil, January 6, 2023 (https://terradedireitos.org.br/violencia-politica-e-eleitoral-no-brasil/index?download=1).

UOL (2022): Zambelli é condenada a indenizar deputadas do PSOL após associá-las a genocídio, January 6, 2023 (https://noticias.uol.com.br/politica/ultimas-noticias/2022/06/29/zambelli-condenada-indenizar-samia-e-taliria-do-psol.htm).

An Analysis of the 11J Protests in Cuba from a Black Feminist Criminal Abolitionist Perspective

Sandra Heidl[1]

Abstract: *Inspired by Black feminist practice, penal abolitionism means overthrowing all institutions that reproduce violence and oppression and abolishing the systems that have historically criminalized and controlled dissident, trans, and Black bodies. It also means eliminating all politics that consider some bodies worthy of living in freedom and not others, and to think of solutions outside the logic of oppressive regimes and prisons. Abolitionist or anti-prison feminists place the community at the center of transformative responses, claiming that alternatives to the criminal justice system must promptly address the historical traumas caused by colonialism and slavery.*

The international debate on punitivism has not yet reached Cuba. The strict dependence on punitive solutions is a reality in the archipelago. The best example, and also the most recent, are the trials and sentencing of participants in the social outburst that took place in the country on 11 and 12 July 2021.[2]

Cuba has a prison state. This encompasses laws, institutions, organizations, and the criminal justice system, as manifested in the state's punitive orientations and actions that criminalize poverty, Blackness, sexual and gender diversity, and political dissidence.

The concept of "carcerality" includes the multiple ways in which the state defines and organizes society through policies of control, surveillance, criminalization, and lack of freedoms. The prison system is not limited only to buildings, i.e. prisons, but encompasses the different ways in which prison logic, technologies, and practices are rooted in our social institutions, impeding the real liberation of those who have been historically marginalized by the state.

---

1   Translation from Spanish and of all original quotes by Julia Roth.
2   Hereinafter, we will refer to these events as 11J.

The Cuban Observatory for Human Rights [Observatorio Cubano de los Derechos Humanos] (n.d.) maintains that there are more than 200 prisons in the country. Although no up-to-date official statistics are available on the racial composition of the incarcerated, officials have indicated that the majority of them are Black and *mestizo* (González 2013).

Prisons, arbitrary detentions, house arrests, confiscation of property, and other tactics of confinement, surveillance, deportations, control, and subjugation are some of the strategies used to preserve and guarantee the reproduction of the status quo, White supremacy, cisheterosexism, and patriarchy in Cuba. The prison state operates through punitive responses to social problems such as poverty, racism, and marginalization, reinforcing and reproducing racial, class, gender, gender identity, religious, and regional inequalities, etc. Likewise, it applies punitive measures to political-ideological dissent, so that thinking differently makes you a criminal and stateless.

Black Feminist Contributions to Penal Abolitionism

Penal abolitionism is both a political vision and a social movement that seeks to eliminate incarceration and policing, pushing for the creation of new systems of care in our communities.

Throughout history, Black populations have led movements to abolish prisons and demand justice. Their struggle has nurtured the abolitionist discourse internationally, identifying not only the dangers of the prison system, but providing transformative models for developing responses and systems to redress the harm. In the long term, the primary goal of the penal abolitionist movement is to create the right conditions for all of us to live in a safe and oppression-free world.

Abolitionist thought has been nourished not only by anti-capitalist currents and critical analysis of "race", but also by feminist thought. It is worth noting that Black feminism has made fundamental contributions to penal abolitionism.

Black feminist abolitionism proposes restorative justice programs, also called healing or restorative, which aim at restitution, community service, and the active participation of those directly involved in the resolution of the negative consequences of their acts. The process would also involve community networks, judicial institutions, and the family, etc. In short, abolitionist or anti-prison feminists place the community at the center of transformative responses, which are also based on care.

Punitivism and the 11J Protests in Cuba

The social outburst of 11J, which took place in more than 60 localities around the country, constitutes an unprecedented event in post-1959 Cuba. These largest social protests in decades arose as an expression of protest against food and medicine shortages during the Covid-19 pandemic. Protestors also addressed the government's Covid measures, the precarious economic situation, and state authoritarianism and human rights abuses. In the context of a deep socioeconomic and health crisis, it has been recognized as the most important political-social-economic demonstration or protest that has taken place in the archipelago since the Cuban Revolution.

Only hours after thousands of people took to the streets, a wave of violent arrests took place with the use of armed military forces, riot gear, police dogs, etc. This display of violence was preceded by President Miguel Mario Díaz-Canel Bermúdez's call to the people to confront the demonstrators. According to the "Justice 11J" working group (n.d.), as a result 1,771 people were arrested within a few days, of which 758 are still in prison and 706 have been tried; 963 are in prison and convicted or pending trial.[3]

The government's response to the social outburst was characterized, roughly speaking, by the following:

- *Internet cuts:* The protests were followed by Internet cuts that made it impossible to immediately locate some of the demonstrators, as well as the conditions in which the arrests took place. Then, after hours and days, the networks were gradually flooded with photos, videos, and testimonies, both of the social outburst and of the repression and detention of the demonstrators.
- *Inhumane treatment, violence, brutality, and police impunity*[4]: police and special troops' actions in the various locations where the demonstrations took

---

[3] The above figures are not official, but the product of a citizens' initiative to collect information, and therefore constitute an underreporting.

[4] As an abolitionist, I start from the premise that every police act is violence, which is experienced on a daily basis in Cuba.

place, as well as during detentions, arrests, and inside prisons (cf. Herrera Fuentes 2021). The arrest of Abel González Lescay (2021), who was taken out of his home naked; as well as that of Joel Daniel Cárdenas Díaz, who was shot in the presence of his two-year-old children (García 2022b), are examples of such violence. The photos of the arrest of young Lázara Karenia González Fernández, which are circulating on the social networks, show the levels of brutality against women participants in the 11J protests. The young Afro-Cuban Diubis Laurencio Tejeda died from a shot fired from the service pistol of officer Yoennis Pelegrín Hernández, who also wounded five other people. As far as we know, the second lieutenant is the only officer who has been tried for his actions so far (Fernández Cuenca 2022).

- *Failure to inform families about the whereabouts of their arrested relatives and failure to notify detainees of the crime with which they have been charged* have been other practices associated with the arrests of the 11J protesters.
- Lack of official public data. On 25 January, 2022, six months after the outbreak of 11J, the portal of the Attorney General's Office published a report with disaggregated information, which was later withdrawn from the site. Later, on 13 June, 2022, another, much shorter report was to be published on the same site, which was also deleted, despite the fact that it was widely quoted by the official media.[5] Thus, at present, it is impossible to access conclusive and official data on the number of detainees, how many people have been released, and how many are still under investigation or in correctional institutions. Nor is it possible to determine how many administrative proceedings have been opened and the exact number of persons who have been criminally prosecuted.
- *Prosecuting for the crime of sedition*[6], which had not been applied in previous episodes of political demonstrations. In fact, during what was called "El Maleconazo", which took place in 1994 and involved locations in the

---

5   However, it has been possible to retrieve some versions of that report. See the following thread, https://twitter.com/justicia11j/status/1537276470657224705?s=21&t=z9uvCxevoK5lDHCnOjgpFg, last access January 20, 2023.

6   "Sedition is a crime regulated in Article 100 of the Cuban Penal Code and establishes penalties of up to 20 years of imprisonment or death for those who 'tumultuously and by express or tacit agreement [....] disturb the socialist order or the holding of elections or referendums, or prevent the fulfillment of any sentence, legal provision or measure issued by the government, or by a civil or military authority in the exercise of their respective functions, or refuse to obey them, or make demands, or resist the fulfillment of their duties.'" (Cañive 2021)

country's capital, convictions of no more than one year were made for the crime of public disorder. Dailfyn Sosa herself, magistrate of the Tribunal Supremo Popular (People's Supreme Court), recognizes the sparse use of this criminal offense in Cuba (Prensa Latina 2022).
- *Prosecuting for the crime of disrespect towards authorities*[7], as documented in the article published in Oncuba, and signed by Julio César Guanche and Harold Bertot Triana (2022). The article explains, among other issues, that this type of criminal offense has been eliminated from the penal code in many countries of the region, as it violates freedom of expression and popular sovereignty.
- *Excessive and disproportionate fines, tax demands, and sanctions*. Fifteen years in prison for people accused of stoning real estate (mainly stores) without taking into account the original oppression experienced by the population when they have to buy in a currency in which they do not earn their salaries. Many of the people fined, detained, tried, and sentenced had no criminal record, they also come from the popular strata and are living the hardships of the economic crisis in Cuba day by day.
- *Civilians tried by military courts*, since part of the events included a network of stores in Cuba that belong to Grupo de Administración Empresarial S.A. GAESA, a military company of the Cuban government in charge of administering state-owned facilities such as stores, hotels, etc. Several people have been accused of acts of violence against these military facilities.
- *The number of persons under 18 years of age, a total of 55* (Fiscalía General de la República 2022), recognized by the United Nations as minors, who participated in the demonstrations and who have been charged with sedition or have had some type of measure taken against them.[8] Some of these younger detainees have been placed in institutions called "centers for minors" belonging to the Ministry of the Interior to be "re-educated".[9]

---

7   The list of the 11J Justice Platform is systematically updated by its creators, Cuban women activists. It keeps a count of people who have been accused of civil disobedience and other crimes. It can be consulted at https://www.justicia11j.org/, last access 19 January, 2023.

8   The Attorney General's Office identifies 55 people between 16 and 18 years of age, of which 28 are kept in precautionary pre-trial detention. Other information speaks of 59 minors.

9   According to the report of the Attorney General's Office, ten minors were placed in comprehensive and behavioral training schools, and 17 are under personalized attention in their regular schools.

- *Conducting summary trials of mothers with infants or school-age children*, the best example being that of young Letis Aile Patterson Rodriguez, who at the time of the protest was 27 years old and in charge of her three infants. She was sentenced to one year in prison. In an interview by Katy Socorro (2022), journalist and activist Marta María Ramírez tells that one of the women of 11J was breastfeeding at the time of the arrest and had to interrupt it. The activist asks herself: "As unjust as it is, why aren't there protocols so that this woman can continue breastfeeding? This is a very clear machista bias of violence".
- *Denial of access to medicines or medical assistance* in cases of various serious pathologies such as psychiatric, arterial hypertension, diabetes mellitus, etc. Disregard for health conditions, such as disabilities or chronic diseases when establishing a sentence (García 2022a).
- *Criminalization of family and friends' complaints.* As a result, several mothers, fathers, siblings, etc., have had police patrols placed in the vicinity of their homes, received summons to police units, suffered harassment by state security, been threatened, placed under police surveillance, and been prevented from exercising rights such as freedom of movement, access to social and medical services, etc.[10]
- *Criminalization of the press and independent activism.* To a large extent, the punitive response of the Cuban government to 11J has been made known through the work of independent journalists and activists who, like their relatives, have been criminalized for it. It is worth noting the silence of the official press about the events.
- *The criminalization and prosecution of everyday activities* such as taking photos, recording video, posting on social networks. One of the best-known cases is that of Yoan de la Cruz, who transmitted a live broadcast of the demonstration in San Antonio de los Baños and has been sentenced to six years in prison.
- *Families with several members in prison.* One of the best-known cases is that of the Taquechel family. The mother, Mayra Taquechel, and her two daughters Katherine Martin, 17 years old and Mariam Martin, 24 years old, who is serving a three-year prison sentence for disobedience, public disorder,

---

10 The case that received the most media attention has been that of Barbara Farrat, mother of (17-year-old) Jonathan Torres Farrat, who is systematically threatened, watched, and besieged, and prevented from leaving the house for daily activities, as Barbara is also a person living with HIV and has her son's baby in her care.

and invitation to commit a crime. Mayra Taquechel, according to the Justice 11 platform (n.d.), was sentenced to eight months imprisonment for public disorder and was not released at the end of her sentence, but was again sentenced to six years imprisonment for the crime of assault.
- *Use of racist and classist profiles* to describe the behavior of protesters (Matienzo Puerto 2021b).
- *Overrepresentation of people living in historically marginalized and criminalized neighborhoods among those investigated.* According to journalist Darci Borrero Batista (15 March 2022), in an article published in the independent media Tremenda Nota, 12 out of every 100 people accused reside in La Güinera, a Havana neighborhood in the municipality of Arroyo Naranjo, one of the most disadvantaged in the capital. To put it another way, of the 489 people in Havana on whom the Prosecutor's Office opened an investigation for participating in the social outburst, 161 reside in La Güinera, of whom 95 have been prosecuted under the crime of sedition (86 men, nine women and one non-binary person).

Community and Feminist Initiatives after the 11J Social Outburst

Community initiatives and feminist activism have played a fundamental role in supporting participants in the social outburst of 11J who have been detained, punished, or imprisoned.

Relatives of prisoners, especially wives and mothers and sisters, have provided important actions to support the accused, detained, and confined people, such as collecting money to pay for legal assistance, buying food, medicine, and hygiene items, with an emphasis on detainees from low-income families. Several campaigns have also been carried out in social networks to denounce the political nature of the trials and reaffirm the peaceful nature of the social outburst.

> [...] [W]omen are playing a fundamental role in sustaining the struggle that began last July [...] It has been the women relatives of prisoners who have organized the most to demand the release of their sons, brothers, or husbands. And it is thousands of women who are now taking on additional tasks to guarantee the well-being of their families: filling plastic bags [*jabas*] with food or medicine for the prisoners; taking care of the chil-

dren of those who are in prison or who had to leave the country (Socorro 2022).

"Help the brave of 11J" is an initiative coordinated by the family of political prisoner and 11J participant Andy García Lorenzo, from the central province of Santa Clara (Gutiérrez Faife 2022). Since November 2021, the project has been raising funds to buy food for the prisoners and thus help their families. With fundamental support from the Cuban diaspora, the initiative began by buying food and supplying it to needy families so they could deliver it to the detainees during visits. At present, after a year of work, they provide financial support to families who actively denounce the situation of their imprisoned family members (Jonathan López 2022, Personal Communication, 17 December 2022). Yanet Rodríguez Sánchez, who supports 13 families in Santiago de Cuba and Holguín, is running a similar, albeit smaller-scale operation in the province of Holguín (El Toque 2022).

The case of Brenda Díaz has been one of the most striking, given that it is an expression of the violence against people of the LGTBQ+ collective. Díaz was one of the trans women and members of the LGTBQ+ collective who participated in the social outburst of 11J.

Brenda Díaz – who lives with HIV and suffers from chronic gastritis and kidney stones – was initially detained together with her brother Luis Manuel Díaz, who was 16 years old at the time. After 18 days, Luis Manuel was released on a provisional court order and with a fine of 1,000 Cuban pesos (Herrera 2022). Brenda is confined in a men's prison, serving a 14-year sentence, accused of public disorder, sabotage of a continuing nature, assault, damage, and burglary with forced entry.

Brenda Díaz has experienced structural transphobia since the beginning of her detention, her gender identity has not been respected; the fact that she is in a men's prison, that her head has been shaved, and that she does not receive the hormone treatment she needs is evidence of how sex-gender-dissident persons are treated in Cuban prisons. She has also received physical violence from one of the prison officials.[11]

---

11 On 3 November 2022, the platform Yo Sí Te Creo en Cuba demanded the protection of Brenda Díaz and the conduct of an investigation based on the complaint of physical violence made by her mother. The link is available at https://twitter.com/YoSiTeCreoCuba/status/1588212515758133248?ref_src=twsrc%5Etfw%7Ctwcamp%5Etweetembed%7Ctwterm%5E1588212515758133248%7Ctwgr%5Edod44aac05e6c182f4b771b366677f9897ca15f1%7Ctwcon%5Es1_&ref_url=https%3A%2F%2Fwww.radiotelevisionmart

Journalists, artists, feminist activists, and people from the LGTBQ+ collective have engaged in social network activity during 2022 to publicize the Brenda Díaz case – undoubtedly one of the most dramatic ones. Since June 2022, journalist and activist Kiana Anandra Pérez has coordinated support for Brenda through her mother Ana María García, collecting money, hygiene material, medicines, food, etc. (Kiana Anandra Pérez 2022, Personal Communication, 16 December 2022).

Another key initiative – initiated as a result of 11J, the working group or platform for the follow-up of the legal actions against the demonstrators – is "Justicia 11J" (Justice 11J, n.d.). It brought together journalists, activists, researchers, mostly feminists, and political dissidents: María Matienzo Puerto, Camila Rodríguez, Salomé García Bacallao, Kirenia Yalit Núñez Pérez, Eylin Lombard, Darcy Borrero, Cynthia de la Cantera, Ivette Leyva and Laritza Diversent (Matienzo Puerto 2021a).

Justicia 11J has documented, to this day, the government's response against the participants of the social outburst. At the same time, according to Camila Rodríguez (2021), one of its managers, it has functioned as a channel to support the relatives of the detained, imprisoned, and prosecuted. "The list" – as the project was initially popularized – emerged as a continuously updated excel database. At present, "Justicia 11J" is a working group whose results can be found on a website that features the list of detainees as well as reports, investigations, a list of repressors, and other relevant information.[12] Justicia 11J works in close collaboration with Cubalex, an organization specialized in law, founded by lawyer Laritza Diversent.

#LibertadParaLosNiñosDel11J (#FreedomForTheChildrenOf11J), more than a hashtag, was an intense campaign developed to draw attention to the minors who participated in the protests and who faced exorbitant sentence requests by prosecutors as well as actual sentences. The fundamental result of these actions, focused on social networks and in which the UN Committees against Torture and for the Rights of the Child participated, was that on 27 May, after appeal, they were released from prison with their sentences commuted to correctional work with and without internment, or with restrictions of liberty, under regular court supervision and police surveillance, and their sentences reduced to five years. Among the minors who were previously sentenced and

---

i.com%2Fa%2Fdenuncian-que-presa-polC3ADtica-trans-fue-atacada-en-la-cC3A1rce l-de-hombres%2F341886.html

12 See https://www.justicia11j.org/.

who benefitted from the commutation are Kendry Miranda Cárdenas, previously sentenced to 19 years in prison, Rowland Jesús Castillo Castro, to 18 years, Lázaro Noel Urgelles Fajardo, to 14 years, and Brandon David Becerra Curbelo, to 13 years. (García 2022)

Conclusion

In general, the sentences requested by public prosecutors for the participants of the social outburst of 11 and 12 July 2021 have been based on factors such as age (in the case of minors or elderly people), profession, gender, etc., that is, appealing to respectability policies that make a difference between political and common prisoners. These policies define categories of people, establishing who deserves to go to jail and who does not. It is also important to note that very few, if any, voices have called attention to this issue. Generally speaking, in Cuban society, even among activists, there is a tacit consensus that people should not go to jail for political issues, but for common crimes. The issue becomes more complicated when the government does not recognize political motives for demonstrating and considers protesters as common criminals.

Penal abolitionism in Cuba implies going beyond freeing the political prisoners of 11J. It implies abolishing all the institutions that reproduce violence and oppression as well as the systems that have historically criminalized and controlled dissident, trans, and Black bodies. It also means eliminating all respectability politics that deem some bodies worthy of living in freedom and not others.

We need to think of solutions outside the logic of oppressive regimes and prisons that have failed to offer us real security. Exploring and investing in alternatives to the criminal justice system is a fundamental part of transformative and restorative justice. Such reparations must promptly address the historical traumas caused by colonialism and slavery, and propose different forms of economic, social, cultural, financial restitution, land redistribution, political self-determination, culturally relevant education programs, recovery of indigenous languages, and so on.

Embracing abolitionism means investing in vital community support systems and developing models that can represent how we want to live in the future. It also includes finding practical responses to remedy the harm which do not perpetuate systemic violence and that bring us progressively closer to that just society, without prisons, without violence.

References

Borrero Batista, Darci (2022): "La Güinera, el barrio de La Habana que pagó más caro las protestas del 11J." In: Tremenda Nora, March 15, 2022 (https://s3.eu-central-1.amazonaws.com/qurium/tremendanota.com/la-guinera-el-barrio-de-la-habana-que-pago-mas-caro-por-las-protestas-del-11j.html).

Cañive, Eloy Viera (2021): "Sedición en Cuba: Nueva cara de la represión política." In: El Toque, April 24, 2022 (https://eltoque.com/sedicion-en-cuba-nueva-cara-de-la-represion-politica).

El Toque (2022): "¡Ayuda a los valientes del 11J!: Solidaridad vs. represión." In: El Toque, August 3, 2022 (https://eltoque.com/ayuda-a-los-valientes-del-11j-solidaridad-vs-represion).

Fernández Cuenca, Waldo (2022): "El policía que mató al joven cubano en La Güinera sigue a la espera de juicio y petición fiscal." In: Diario de Cuba, April 20, 2022 (https://diariodecuba.com/derechos-humanos/1642188264_36814.html).

Fiscalía General de la República (2022): Información sobre los procesos penales derivados de los disturbios del 11 de julio de 2021, January 25, 2022 (https://web.archive.org/web/20220408124546/https://www.fgr.gob.cu/es/informacion-sobre-los-procesos-penales-derivados-de-los-disturbios-del-11-de-julio-de-2021).

Justicia 11J (n.d.): Justicia 11J, January 18, 2023 (https://www.justicia11j.org/).

García, Salomé (2022a): Intervención en el panel "las manifestaciones pacíficas en América Latina: Reflexiones sobre #Cuba a un año del #11J", January 13, 2023 (https://fb.watch/dwX44IGA-U/).

García, Salomé (2022b): "El caso de Daniel Joel Cárdenas. 'Esto no lo pusieron en la televisión'." In: Hypermedia Magazine, April 20, 2022 (https://hypermediamagazine.com/dosieres-hm/los-juicios-del-11j/el-caso-daniel-joel-cardenas/).

González, Ivet (2013): "Cárceles de mujeres cubanas reflejan desventajas de género." In: IPS, April 11, 2013 (https://www.ipscuba.net/genero/carceles-de-mujeres-cubanas-reflejan-desventajas-de-genero/).

González Lescay, Abel (2021): "Testimonios del 11-J: Desnudo en la patrulla." In: Rialta Magazine, August 4, 2021 (https://rialta.org/testimonio-del-11-j-desnudo-en-la-patrulla/?fbclid=IwAR12UQEJRxPWN8IQ7EH8djtWdM4Nd8iRsIXJz_-eYnzaUcmotPpZyLn_-v4&163883707447).

Guanche, Julio César/Triana, Harold Bertor (2022): "El derecho penal y la protesta social en Cuba." In: OnCuba News, April 21, 2022 (https://oncubanews.com/opinion/columnas/la-vida-de-nosotros/el-derecho-penal-y-la-protesta-social-en-cuba/).

Gutiérrez Faife, Yankiel (2022): "En las cárceles cubanas, los presos sobreviven gracias a iniciativas privadas." In: 14yMedio, November 26, 2022 (https://www.14ymedio.com/cuba/carceles-cubanas-sobreviven-iniciativas-privadas_0_3430456927.html).

Herrera, Mel (2022): "«Salir con su vestido la marcó muchísimo»: Las condenas de Brenda, una mujer trans que marchó el 11J." In: Tremenda Nota, May 7, 2022 (https://s3.eu-central-1.amazonaws.com/qurium/tremendanota.com/salir-con-su-vestido-la-marco-muchisimo-las-condenas-de-brenda-una-mujer-trans-que-marcho-el-11j.html).

Herrera Fuentes, Alina (2021): "Protestas, judicialización y salidas legales: 11J en Cuba." In: Oncuba News, April 23, 2022 (https://oncubanews.com/ecos/protestas-judicializacion-y-salidas-legales-11j-en-cuba).

Matienzo Puerto, María (2021a): "11J: La 'Revolución' contra las personas pobres, discapacitadas y las familias." In: Cubanet, September 21, 2021 (https://www.cubanet.org/noticias/11j-la-revolucion-contra-las-personas-pobres-discapacitadas-y-las-familias/).

Matienzo Puerto, María (2021b): "Petición fiscal 143/2021: Un mapa de los barrios pobres de La Habana." In: Cubanet, November 1, 2021 (https://www.cubanet.org/noticias/peticion-fiscal-143-2021-un-mapa-de-los-barrios-pobres-de-la-habana/).

Observatorio Cubano de los Derechos Humanos (n.d.): "Cárceles cubanas", April 19, 2022 (https://observacuba.org/informes-ddhh/carceles-cubanas/).

Prensa Latina (2022): "Delito de sedición no es usual en Cuba, afirma experta." In: Prensa Latina, April 21, 2022 (https://www.prensa-latina.cu/2022/03/26/delito-de-sedicion-no-es-usual-en-cuba-afirma-experta).

Rodríguez, Camila (2021): "De qué hablamos cuando decimos "la lista". Acompañamiento a familiares y construcción de la memoria en Cuba a raíz de los sucesos del 11J." In: Demo Amlat, September 13, 2021 (https://demoamlat.com/de-que-hablamos-cuando-decimos-la-lista-acompanamiento-a-familiares-y-construccion-de-la-memoria-en-cuba-a-raiz-de-los-sucesos-del-11j/).

Socorro, Katy (2022): "11J, Mujeres y Feminismo." In: Alas Tensas, July 25, 2022 (https://alastensas.com/observatorio/especial-11j-11j-mujeres-y-feminismo/).

Audiovisual Material
Tremenda Nota (2021): "Las mujeres trans que se unieron a las protestas en Cuba." YouTube, n.d. (https://www.youtube.com/watch?v=z2j1-q_lMGU&t=127s).

Interviews
Kiana Anandra Pérez: 16 December 2022.
Jonathan López: 17 December 2022.

Territory Body – Body Territory

Julieta Paredes Carvajal[1]

Abya Yala Communitarian-Feminism[2] [Feminismo Comunitario in Spanish] is the organic movement born from the process of change in Bolivia in 2003, which has allowed us not only to challenge the established orders but, above all, to elaborate a methodology, a path, that allow us to produce proposals for solutions for a planet and a life trapped in a world system that is patriarchal, colonialist, and capitalist. The possible solutions undoubtedly present themselves as globally coordinated territorial liberations, which together build the release of humanity and the planet from the current situation of hopelessness and individualism, in which our world and the planet today unfolds in the midst of suffering, bewilderment, agony, and profound struggles of resistance and processes of revolutionary hopes.

It is from our bodies of indigenous women, impoverished rural and urban workers, that we speak of hopes, we speak of and propose solutions from our daily political practices, which are not necessarily theories, but rather political social practices and knowledge; which we have systematized by ourselves and now project, and from which we derive revolutionary proposals. We have developed a path, our own methodology that consists of seeking an explanation of the causes of our conditions and situations, of our pain, but from where we also draw the strength of our dreams, the persistence and historical stub-

---

1   Translated from Spanish by Lívia de Souza Lima and Edith Otero Quezada.
2   Sometimes we write these words together [Communitarian-Feminism/Feminismo Comunitario] to remind that it is a concept created by Julieta Paredes Carvajal within the process of changes of the Bolivian people and it proposes the epistemic autonomy and the decolonization of the struggles of indigenous women from Abya Yala. Abya Yala Communitarian-Feminism is not a current of feminism (Paredes Carvajal 2020).

bornness of continuing to exist as communities [pueblos]³, as women of our communities who dream of a world of Vivir Bien⁴.

Undoubtedly it is not enough to explain; we have to transform and revolutionalize the reality that surrounds us; that is why Bolivia and the Process of Change, as we call it, made a fundamental revolutionary imprint on Abya Yala Communitarian-Feminism, which is to strengthen the hope that another world is possible, that utopia is a word that describes what we are doing and what we can do. We can take care of the planet, take care of our lives, be happy and live well, indulging ourselves the romantic notions we had of revolution, love, happiness, and politics back when we were 18. Today, as we have matured, we still believe it is possible, but only under two preconditions:

- The first is: with, from and for women as half of every community.
- The second is: in the Community of Communities, as a way of cultivating and fostering individuality in a territorial community, not individualism.

1. Decolonizing Bodies from Feminism

Abya Yala Communitarian-Feminism starts from the political, philosophical, and conceptual basis that women are half of everything; it is radically opposed to what has been done so far from the hegemonic spaces of political and philo-

---

3   Translators' note: the notion of "pueblo" is difficult to translate into English because it has multiple meanings. "It can refer to a village or small town, as a descriptor but also as a place related to one's identity, *mi pueblo* (my village, my place of origin); it has a more extensive sense of 'the people' [...] It also has the sense which we have sometimes adopted here of "community" in English, with the amorphous boundaries that word also connotes" (Paredes Carvajal, Julieta/Cerullo, Margaret/Carcelen-Estrada, Antonia 2015: 11).

4   Translators' note: As Paredes Carvajal, Julieta/Cerullo, Margaret/Carcelen-Estrada, Antonia (2015) explain, the notion of "vivir bien" is related to the paradigm of "Buen Vivir", which "is a moral/political paradigm opposed to the developmentalist idea of "living better" – at the expense of others" (36). We would also like to mention the complexity of doing an intercultural translation that grasps all the meanings of the concept of "Buen Vivir" since it also includes the collective, communitarian well-being and the pursuit of a harmonic relationship between the human, the non-human, and nature. This notion and others such as "the Rights of Nature" have been integrated into the political constitutions of countries such as Ecuador and Bolivia.

sophical thought, where women are seen **as a minority**[5] to be tutored, and not as a half that has rights. Euro-centered feminist women are complicit with this reductionism and tutelage, segmenting women into classes a, b, c; third-world women, indigenous women, lesbian, young women, elderly women, women, settlers, etc. An imaginary that naturalizes women's exploitation and creates oppression.

It is the best strategy to reduce and corner us into the conception of a "vulnerable minority", to annul us and take away the political capacity of our demands and therefore dismiss half of the revolutionary force of peoples and organizations.

Women in the world share the same body, forming an existential, biogenetic, historical, spiritual, sexual, and political unit. In other words, our bodies naturally express the varieties of nature, skin tones, size, thickness, and other characteristics of the bodies in the different territories. In nature – where there are no hierarchies of colors or sizes – all are important, unrepeatable, and indispensable. Throughout history, human action has built **conditions and situations** in which hierarchies and dominations have been created as a result of this systemic construction.

Hierarchies among women, then, are not natural, but rather created by political and economic interests; we – Communitarian-Feminists – denaturalize the hierarchies of class and race among women, the relations of power, usufruct, exploitation, discrimination, and oppression among women, to position them in the place of responsibilities and complicities. Women and our bodies are in the midst of power relations in which we participate as accomplices, victims, objects, and subjects. Therefore, certain women can be exploiters and oppressors of other women, men, and nature.

For the most part, Eurocentric feminists in institutions, NGOs, international organizations, and political parties act as accomplices of these colonialist and capitalist hierarchies. It is essential to unveil these relationships between women to better situate both the de-patriarchalizing [*despatriarcalización*] and decolonizing analysis of Abya Yala Communitarian-Feminism, and thus understand what the Community of Communities is claiming and proposing to the world.

European and North American feminists took better advantage of the neoliberal readjustment than we did, to the point that women doctors, sociologists, and engineers from Latin America migrated to those countries to clean

---

5 All emphases and capitalizations in the text are by the author, Julieta Paredes Carvajal.

their toilets and pick up their garbage. Why did they functionalize the women of our peoples to the ambitions of patriarchy, colonialism, and neoliberalism? It would be important to hear an answer.

What we propose from our struggles as Communitarian-Feminists is a political discussion on how to continue fighting against the patriarchal system by those of us who want to continue fighting.

2. Decolonizing Concepts

2.1 What is Patriarchy According to Abya Yala Communitarian-Feminism?

For feminists of different stripes, patriarchy is the relationship of oppression or domination of men towards women, either as a system of oppression or as a relationship of oppression of men towards women, which can be extended to feminized bodies. We, Communitarian-Feminists, understand "patriarchy" as:

> The system of all oppressions and dominations, all exploitations, all violences, and discriminations that humanity (men, women, intersex people) and nature experience. A system of domination, oppression, structural violence and death, historically built on women's biogenetic, historical, spiritual, sexual, and political existential body (Paredes Carvajal 2016: 32).

This conception of the patriarchal system is helpful for our struggles because we affirm that women experience all the forms of oppression that men experience. Still, there is an oppression that is only geared towards our bodies as women, as defined before. In other words, being a woman constitutes, as such, another form of oppression and, at the same time, aggravates the forms of oppression we share with men. In other words, being a woman is the basis on which oppressions are built and invented (Paredes Carvajal 2016).

Women's bodies have been and are the first material basis on which the domination and subordination of history are structured. On it rests the system of all forms of oppression, and even today, it continues to be the base system of domination: The most powerful and enduring system of inequality, in short, is the *system of domination*. It is not the superficiality of pitting all women against all men; our alliances depend on the revolutionary struggles that bind us.

2.2 What is the Ancestral Patriarchy?

It means neither natural nor original, much less original. To our indigenous brothers, the Spanish colonial invasion was what brought and imported *machismo* to our lands, which completely ignores all the data that tells us about the existence of what we call pre-colonial or ancestral patriarchy and that added to the patriarchy of the Spanish invaders, producing Interlocking Phallocentric Patriarchies. In our book *Hilando Fino, desde el feminismo comunitario* [Spinning with Care: Perspectives from Communitarian Feminism], we called it Interlocking Patriarchies [Entroque Patriarcal][6] (Paredes Carvajal 2009: 24). That is to say that, in the colonial event of 1492, although our indigenous grandfathers experienced colonial oppression in their bodies, the indigenous grandmothers experienced it twofold.

To use the term patriarchy exclusively to designate the social structure that invaded our territories, that is, the colony, is to disregard our own forms of domination before the Spanish colonial invasion; not recognizing the power that the Inca had over the women of his empire, managing the *acllas*, also called virgins of the sun, as an instrument of lubrication of the political and economic apparatus of his empire.

Men in the Inca empire felt honored when the Inca paid for their loyalty with women. Male fathers – in this case Aymara, but not only – felt honored when the Inca's emissary chose their child daughter to become an *aclla* and take her to the *aclla wasi*, the house where the *acllas* lived, where this girl would be raised to be used in various ways. Given to Inca warrior chiefs for sexual purposes, killed in sacrifices, or exploited in lifelong servitude for the benefit of the ruling caste (Silverblatt 1996).

And this male father – in this case, Aymara – felt proud when his daughter was taken as yet another of the Inca's wives, that is, as the Inca's mistress. What does this data reveal, if not the coincidence – although in different ways – of using women as sexual booty, practiced by the Spaniards and the indigenous alike? We indigenous people are "neither better nor worse". As any human be-

---

6   Translators' note: As Paredes Carvajal, Julieta/Cerullo, Margaret/Carcelen-Estrada, Antonia (2015) explain, Julieta Paredes Carvajal' concept of "entronque patriarcal" could be translated as "'interlocking patriarchies' [which] is a metaphorical image drawn from the construction of fences by joining tree trunks on top of one another to create a strong – phallicized – structure" (26).

ing, we have made ethical decisions throughout our history, unless we are not considered human.

3. Decolonizing Time

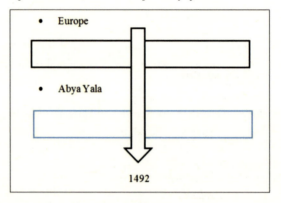

Fig. 1: Parallelisms and contemporaneity of the times

Source: Paredes Carvajal 2020: 37

The colonial view of feminists and Eurocentric thought affirms that the patriarchy in our territories is derived from the European patriarchy, or an underdeveloped, backward form of patriarchy with respect to Europe. We affirm the need to decolonize time and the concept of contemporaneity in order to speak of historical simultaneities that occurred in parallel timelines and were unknown to and ignorant of each other before 1492. It is crucial to decolonize time to understand that our time and our existences were not built based on Europe or that they cannot just be subsumed under Europe's timelines, which claim to define the time of the whole world and, even more arrogantly, situate us in their savage past.

Fig. 2: Europe wanted to eat our time

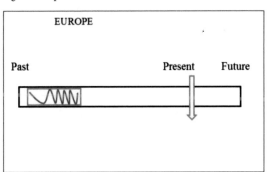

Source: Paredes Carvajal 2020: 37

Despite these two independent timelines, with the colonial fact of 1492 and a reductionist mentality, they try to swallow up or absorb our times, territories, lives, culture, and history and label us as uncivilized, backward savages according to the parameters of their culture. They also maintain the ironic claim to have civilized us, to have driven our development, while "thanks" (or "no thanks") to our "backwardness", "savagery", "lack of civilization", the western world was able to develop, civilize, and technologize. It is essential to decolonize our time, to reclaim our time, our memory, our dignity, and our knowledge.

Europe does not understand who we are; in their ignorance about our world, our people, our lives, and societies, they compress and reduce us according to their concepts and ways of life, interpret us. Having thus diminished our time, lives, and territories, they place us into their own past, compressed and shriveled by their ignorance, to alleviate their existential dread of finding someone who is equal but different, unknown, and unexpected. This is the colonialist form of how Europe understands us to the present day.

Based on this conception of decolonized time, let us compare some contemporaneous realities around 1492 to show the arrogance of western thought.

Table 1: Comparative Charts

Ancestor Patriarchy of Abya Yala	European Colonial Patriarchy
All women owned land	Women in Europe did not have the right to land
Women had knowledge and wisdom and were valued for it. For example, medical knowledge of their bodies and children's bodies.	Women did not have access to knowledge and were persecuted and burned as witches.
Women managed and had access to the rituals of the communities.	Women did not have access to or perform community rituals.; these rites were institutionally controlled by the Catholic Church, managed by men.
Women had command and political power, as can be seen in the indigenous uprising of 1871 in what is now La Paz, Bolivia. Bartolina Sisa had under her command an indigenous army as well as the logistics of the uprising.	Women had no political command; if there were any queens, they were puppets of power struggles between men.

Source: (Paredes Carvajal 2020: 74)

4. Colonial Penetration and Interlocking Patriarchies [Entroque Patriarcal]

As a concept, Colonial Penetration[7] presents penetration as the action of introducing one element into another; penetration evokes a notion of domination with sexual undertones that, although it starts with the bodies, is then projected onto territories and life. I did not choose this word for this concept by chance or exhibitionism. I feel that colonial penetration explains well what we mean when we talk about the colonial invasion of 1492. We can start by saying that it was the violation of our territories, bodies, culture, and life.

The colonial invasion, then, not only penetrated the territories of what is now called Bolivia Abya Yala, the colony invaded the bodies of the women and

---

[7] Title of the Julieta Paredes Carvajal' presentation at the University of Pittsburgh in 2010, published in Cartografías queer (2011): sexualidades y activismo LGBT en América Latina, Pittsburgh: Instituto Internacional de Literatura Iberoamericana, University of Pittsburgh, pp. 217–230.

men who lived in this land, consolidating Interlocking Patriarchies [Entroque Patriarcal] that strengthened the system of oppressions, now corrected and increased, which we call the Patriarchal World System [Sistema Mundo Patriarcal].

Despite all this penetration that tried to annul our strength, here we are today, reinventing ourselves, remaking ourselves, feeling, and filling with meaning our bodies, our desires, pleasures, and proposals for Living Well. They are realities here and now that we build in permanent resistance on the part of our communities [pueblos] and of Communitarian-Feminists. These resistances and rebellions necessarily pass through the de-patriarchalization and decolonization of our women's bodies, of our communities, societies, cultures, and spiritualities. So, what is colonization for women?

The way our indigenous brothers see colonization is partial and complicit since they only see it as power relations exercised by the invading masters. Since our brothers' reflections on decolonization and de-patriarchalization center on the reflection of coloniality, they are only the tip of the iceberg. Therefore, their political actions fundamentally focus on the high places of this power, such as the State, the Government, and its institutions.

This has a dehumanizing and complicit consequence, because it understands us indigenous people as pure, as the good savage, and this is complicity with the colonialist paternalists who exercise their racism from the place of the superior who can protect us. It is complicity with the universalizing and Manichean thinking of evil and good. Indigenous men and women make ethical decisions, just as all humanity does at all times and in all communities around the world, men and women of the Abya Yala indigenous peoples are human beings, we make our own decisions, there is no "a priori purity". The political consequences of this paternalistic purism are that our brothers believe it and are tempted to replace White Eurocentrism with purist and indigenous egocentrism.

What is called coloniality, for us, is essentially Interlocking Patriarchies [Entroque Patriarcal]; it is the systemic form of readjusting patriarchy. When these two patriarchies become intertwined, pacts are created between men that will later mean that the bodies of indigenous women, our grandmothers and those of our brothers, will bear the total weight of the new patriarchy with its violence and violation of women's bodies three- and fourfold. If we do not understand this analysis that we propose from Communitarian-Feminism, it will be impossible for our transformation processes to make even the slightest revolutionary changes, not only for women but all our male brothers, intersex people, and nature.

4.1 Interlocking Patriarchies [Entroque Patriarcal]

The word "entronque" was used in Bolivia in the 1980s to define the incursion of the left into Bolivian nationalism; for us, it meant the betrayal of a particular left to the struggles of the people[8], an alliance to betray the hopes and strengthen the system of oppression with discourses and experiences that we had built in our resistance to the dictatorships. From there, we, the Communitarian-Feminists, seized the right to speak and projected it to our definition of the moment in which another social reality was created, from the colonial invasion of 1492 (Paredes Carvajal 2009).

When we speak of ancestral patriarchy, Euro-Western feminists presume that all patriarchies are modeled on the patriarchy of Europe. What they are really saying is that they believe that by referring to European patriarchy, they have already discovered all forms of domination of women. Marxists follow a similar line of thought, believing that they already know how the system of exploitation works anywhere in the world just from understanding industrial Europe. **Well, no**, we are sorry to disappoint their egocentrism and self-sufficiency, our life patterns do not come from Europe, and neither are we, or have we ever been, backward societies in relation to Europe.

To understand the Interlocking Patriarchies [Entroque Patriarcal], we must start from the fact that these patriarchies had nothing to do with each other until 1492, but then would complement, articulate, and intertwine themselves in the "Entroque Patriarcal" to the great misfortune of the women of our territories, of Abya Yala, creating the Planetary System of Patriarchal domination.

5. The Planetary System of Patriarchal Domination

The *Entroque Patriarcal* presents us with two trunks, the ancestral patriarchy and the colonial-European patriarchy, which are connected, articulated, coordinated, and complementary, but are neither equal nor the same. This is the

---

8   See footnote 4; "pueblo" here can be translated as "people" or "communities".

transcendental historical fact of domination that endures to this day, despite attempts to defeat it.

Our concept of patriarchy (see page 4–5) helps us to analyze the conformation of territorially localized patriarchies in Europe and Abya Yala. The idea of *Entroque Patriarcal* explains the moment when this system of powers and dominations reconfigured to become the monster we face today, which we call the Planetary System of Patriarchal Domination (Paredes Carvajal 2016).

It is against this system that we Communitarian-Feminists fight and call on all of humanity: If we want to end all oppressions of humanity and nature, we must position ourselves with respect to all manifestations and instruments of it. In the *Entroque Patriarcal*, they are reconfigured in a PATRIARCHAL DOMINION SYSTEM, under the hegemonic domination of colonial Europe. Of course, taking into account that to achieve this, it is necessary to "colonize our time". To justify its domination and the mechanisms of its hegemonic imposition, Europe had to, metaphorically speaking, eat us, eat our time, swallow it, and to locate our time in its own past. And thus not to locate its ignorance, limitations, and incapacity as a way of thinking and conception of life.

From then on, patriarchy, as a patriarchal system, has been permanently recycling itself, nourishing itself from the colonized and dominated patriarchies. Learning and rearranging itself from and in the revolutions that humanity undertakes to overthrow them, revolutions that have not necessarily faced or confronted patriarchy as a system of patriarchal domination, yet still have been giving hope to humanity, and still do. However, they are later absorbed by the system itself, for the very reason that we have not fully grasped the system's complexity.

To understand that until today, humanity has been facing the mechanisms of patriarchal domination, such as the imposition of castes or class relations or relations of dependence and colonial usufruct in the territorial or ties of racist domination. Humanity has been confronting these mechanisms but not all simultaneously, and much less with a communitarian strategy of which we women are half. We did not attack them in all their instruments, strategies, and tactics of domination and subjugation.

This is the challenge posed by the Communitarian-Feminist movement of Abya Yala that started from the Bolivian people's process of change; today, in the organic fabrics in territories of Mexico, Chile, Brazil, Peru, and Migrants in Europe, we all call on the indigenous peoples [Pueblos originarios], organizations and social movements, to build the Community of Communities, to fight against all expressions, manifestations, and instruments of the Planetary

System of Patriarchal Domination. We call upon you to define our identities of struggle based on hope and proposals, not from the ANTIS – anti-capitalist, anti-colonial, anti-patriarchal, anti-imperialist – ; for that is purist, hypocritical, and not self-critical, it separates and weakens us, it drives false subjects and revolutionary vanguards. It has not done us any good as revolutionaries to be Manichean and moralistic, putting ourselves in the place of the 'good ones' because nobody is free from this system, and it is not honest to position ourselves as anti-anything. We are communitarian fighters; we are defined by our dreams, our utopia, and our proposal: the **Community of Communities**. We are people who recognize our contradictions and with them, and despite them, we call to build and heal the world, heal the relationships that we are living on this planet and **build the Vivir Bien [Living Well] in the Community of Communities** without borders or classes, or genders, or races.

References

Paredes Carvajal, Julieta (2009): Hilando Fino, desde el feminismo comunitario, La Paz: Comunidad mujeres creando comunidad.

Paredes Carvajal, Julieta (2011): "La penetración colonial." In Daniel Balderston/Arturo Matute Castro (eds.), Cartografías queer: sexualidades y activismo LGBT en América Latina, Pittsburgh: Instituto Internacional de Literatura Iberoamericana and University of Pittsburgh, pp. 217–230.

Paredes Carvajal, Julieta/Cerullo, Margaret/Carcelen-Estrada, Antonia (2015): Hilando Fino: Perspectives from Communitarian Feminism: Comunidad Mujeres Creando Comunidad.

Paredes Carvajal, Julieta (2016): El desafío de la despatriarcalización, La Paz: FECAY (FeminismoComunitario Abya Yala).

Paredes Carvajal, Julieta (2020): Para descolonizar el feminismo, La Paz: FECAY (FeminismoComunitario Abya Yala).

Silverblatt, Irene (1996): Luna, sol y brujas, Cuzco: Centro de estudios regionales andinos Bartolomé de las Casas.

Part II
Embodied Experiences and Knowledge Productions

Ties that Bind
Black Women Candidates and Familial Influence on Political Socialization in the US

Nadia E. Brown and India S. Lenear

Abstract: *Our work helps to dispel the notion that there is a key set of family interactions that lead to political involvement. Family is an important socializing agent because a child's experiences with her immediate authority figures set the stage for their future political beliefs and efficacy. Because parental personality traits are important factors of the political socialization process (Renshon 1975), it is useful to understand how Black women have contextualized personal control and interpersonal trust through the linkages between family and politics. Yet, these studies were mostly conducted with White Americans and males, thus the foundational texts on political socialization did not use an intersectional lens to recognize the importance of a raced/gendered dynamic with the agencies of socialization into politics through the family unit. This analysis broadens the spectrum of feminism(s) in the United States, namely by showcasing how family plays a role in shaping Black women candidate's political ambition via encouraging their political ambition.*

The daughters, granddaughters, and great-granddaughters of the enslaved secured voting rights and pushed for political inclusion. Historian Martha Jones' book *Vanguard* retells the past to examine how Freedwoman and their descendants pushed for universal suffrage at a time when race *or* gender voting rights were being debated (Jones 2020). Instead, courageous Black women like Frances Ellen Watkins Harper were political visionaries who pushed the United States to think more holistically about the intersecting needs manifested by sexism and racism. In doing so, she and others advocated for inalienable rights for Black women who were responding to racial and sexual violence as well as disenfranchisement (Murray/Eastwood 1965).

There is a long lineage of Black women who fought for political rights (Barnett 1993; Brown 2014) although their work has often been invisible in the modern retelling of women's or Black's role in shaping electoral politics (Materson 2009). Yet these women exist. They are the daughters, granddaughters, nieces, cousins, or fictive kin of other Black women who long toiled for freedom and a voice in US politics.

But what role does family play in Black women's political socialization? How do Black women learn about politics and then decide for themselves that they want to enter electoral politics? Our work takes up these questions. Political socialization is defined as the processes through which an individual acquires the beliefs, values, and attitudes of their political system. This concept also refers to the role the individual plays as a citizen within their political system (Greenberg 1970). Political socialization is important because political regimes want to instil a set of behaviors, values, or beliefs into children who will take up these foundational sets of viewpoints in order to maintain the political order. Thus, childhood political learning is instrumental as this lays the foundation for adult political orientations (Van Deth et al. 2011). Indeed, family is an important source of political attitudes and behaviors (Campbell et al. 1960; Berelson/Lazarfeld/McPhee 1954). Yet, how Black families instil (or not) political values in their young female members has yet to be examined from the vantage point of Black women candidates themselves.

In this study, we utilize the narratives of Black women candidates to help to provide a deeper understanding of how their own political socialization through lessons learned by engaging with their family members have led them to seek elected office. Here we uncover how family does (or does not) influence their desire to seek office. By using an intersectional lens, we distinctly analyze the mutually constitutive nature of race and gender on Black women's political socialization and political ambition. Our unique data – interviews with Black women candidates – presents a bird's eye view into their world to learn how family impacts their political calculation. This provides scholars with a more dynamic understanding of how the daughters, granddaughters, and great-granddaughters of the formally enslaved made their way to electoral politics in modern-day America.

Gendered Political Socialization

A vast majority of gendered analyses of candidate emergence considers the way that women candidates' ambitions are stunted due to gender political socialization. Much of this socialization takes place prior to adulthood and stands in direct consequence of a perceived lack of self-esteem, a lack of parental support, a lack of politicized education, and a lack of competitive experiences. Gendered stereotypes emerge from the gendered socialization process, which deters women candidates from even attempting to enter the political arena. In further understanding and grappling with gender-based stereotypes and socialization practices that deter women from running for election, there has to be a consideration of how private roles as mother, wife, sister, and daughter constrain the political activation of women due to traditional gender roles (Sapiro 1983). In particular, the socialization process has instilled a sense of women not being sophisticated or capacious enough to engage with politics. Here a feeling of self-esteem, agency and political knowledge are resources that are not accessible to women, because of their private life ties and traditional gender roles (ibid.). This consistent state of political marginalization is replicated and naturalized for women candidates, obscuring their innate abilities and capacity for politics.

Black Women as Ambitious and Emergent Political Candidates

Black women tend to be more ambitious than White women due to their political socialization, networks, and their raced-gendered identity (Dowe 2020). Indeed, Black women, are participating in electoral politics at an increasing rate; exceeding that of their Black male counterparts (Hardy-Fanta et al. 2016). Simply, Black women do not lack political ambition. Structural barriers prove to be the fundamental cause of Black women candidates' underdeveloped role in the US political arena.

Furthermore, intersectionality-focused literature has taken gender and race gap scholarship further to explain how both race and gender inform the experiences of those who are most marginalized. For example, scholars have found that racial and gender phenotypes of Black women candidates are calculated in voters' evaluations of Black women candidates, in ways that disadvantage candidates who are darker-skinned and have kinky-textured hair (Terkildesen 1993; Lemi/Brown 2020). In sum, an intersectional approach to studying Black women political candidacy makes space for the intricacies and nuances of Black women's political experiences in the US.

Methods and Data

The data for this chapter comes from twenty one-on-one interviews with Black women elected officials and candidates that were conducted between 2011–2021. While data collection for this project has spanned a decade, the narratives of Black women candidates remain rather consistent. These political elites agreed to on-the-record semi-structured interviews with Nadia Brown. The overwhelming majority of these interviews were conducted in person, whereas those that were conducted in 2021 were via Zoom due to the COVID-19 pandemic. Respondents range in age, nativity, social-economic background, previous political experience, and region. There also is great variety in the kinds of positions that these Black women sought. We believe that this variation among the sample provides a unique snapshot of the challenges and opportunities that Black women candidates face and how they navigate this political terrain.

We have given each woman a pseudonym but share accurate details of her political race and other key electoral contexts. We find three themes of the family as influencers in our data: *Supportive Mother; Father as Political Inspiration; No Family Support*. These three categories demonstrate the differences and similarities that Black women candidates find in their family unit as a driving force in their political development.

Family as Influencers

Supportive Mother

Charney Hamilton credits her political activism to her mother. In a March 2012 interview, Delegate Hamilton shared her aspirations for winning a seat in her state's upper chamber. She currently served in the lower chamber and sought to be the first Black woman in her district to earn this position. At the time, Hamilton's Southern state was turning from red to purple. This home of the confederacy was electing more and more Democrats as the population began to shift and new voters of color started to reside in the state. While Charney

Hamilton was ultimately unsuccessful in her bid for the state senate, she was upbeat and optimistic in the interview.

Delegate Hamilton recalled her first political memory as accompanying her mother to Capitol Hill to lobby Members of Congress for healthcare coverage. Her mother was in the military and relied on these benefits to provide for herself and a young Charney after she divorced. Charney Hamilton was 13 when shared with Members of Congress that she and her mother should still have access to military healthcare. "And I remember testifying in front of a committee that Pat Schroeder chaired and talking about my asthma and needing hospital care." When asked about this experience in detail, Delegate Hamilton replied "I think that all the activism, my mom would say that's not me. But yea, it's her. She pushed for things".

Indeed, Delegate Hamilton shared that her mother was her motivating factor in all things- not just politics. "When I was told [that] I shouldn't go to college because we were homeless for a period of time and [my] grades weren't great, my mom said, 'You're gonna apply and you're gonna apply whenever you wanna go." That led Charney Hamilton to apply to Ivy League colleges as well as her local university. "I applied here at home at George Mason. And that's where I got in. Luckily, there was a state program that gave me a summer to prove [that] I could do college-level work. And I got admitted." Because Charney Hamilton's mother believed in her, she also believed in herself. Her mother was influential in developing Delegate Hamilton's outlook as a "go-getter" who was "not bound by external limitations." This belief in herself would be the internal motivation that helped Delegate Charney Hamilton to seek higher office although naysayers advised that her state was not ready for a Black women state senator from her district.

Father as Political Inspiration

Alderwoman Denise Lawrence similarly noted that her father was an inspiration. At the time of the interview on April 11, 2017, Alderwoman Lawrence was serving her first time in office. She was elected to represent her home district in a Midwest city where she grew up and watched her father, Elon Lawrence, engaged in local politics. Elon Lawrence was elected Democratic committeeman for their ward in 1991 and Denise was elected as committeewoman of the same district in 1996. She'd later win a seat on the city council in 2017. Alderwoman Lawrence credits her political orientations to her family's barbershop and not her father's elected position. During our interview, she shared that her father instilled in a young Denise to get a skill. He learned to cut hair after his discharge from the US Army at the conclusion of the Korean War. The Veterans Administration provided the elder Lawrence with job training skills that were proscribed by a segregated society. At the time, Blacks were not allowed to be trained as electricians or carpenters, but they could be trained as barbers. Elon Lawrence later opened a barbershop on the northside of the city, a traditionally Black neighborhood. Denise Lawrence decided that she'd needed to come home from college to care for her mother who was seriously injured in a car accident. While at home, Elon reminded Denise of her need to have a vocation – a skill that she could fall back on. He then enrolled her in barber school. The family barbershop was a political hub. Elon Lawrence cut the hair of the city's most influential politicos, from the president of the National Association for the Advancement of Colored People to the city's mayor. The barbershop was filled with talk about politics. This was Alderwoman Lawrence's introduction to political life.

It was Elon Lawrence's insistence that his daughter learn a trade that helped her to see the value in having a skill. "One of the things my father instilled in me was a work ethic [...] My dad was right. You need a skill because you're not always promised that go to college. He always told me you're not going to succeed unless you go to work. So, I got to work." She credits her father as being foundational in her worldview. She noted "if it wasn't for him, I probably would have missed it. I didn't really get the opportunity at first. This was beneficial for learning." The barbershop was Alderwoman Lawrence's introduction to politics. She recalled that in barber school she was advised to stay away from conversations about "politics, religion, or money. But in our barbershop, we always talked about those things." As an insider in this political hub, Alderwoman Lawrence had the opportunity to openly talk about politics with leaders of the city and in particular, leaders of the Black community in her city.

However, politics did not come naturally to her. She said, "growing up I did not like to be around people, so politics is really something that took me to overcome a lot of things that were challenging to me as a kid [...] I asked God what he wanted me to do and I just felt like it was a calling that I had to answer." During the time when Denise Lawrence was considering running for office, her father was in an elected position. But the mood of the barbershop changed because of Elon Lawrence's political views. The elder Lawrence switched party affiliation and became a Republican because he was unhappy with President Clinton's handling of the Monica Lewinsky situation. "Yeah, he said, 'the president lied to the people.' Well, wouldn't any man lie about that?" So, some of the city politicos stopped coming to the barbershop and the neighborhood started to gentrify. Alderwoman Denise Lawrence reflected on her first campaign and noted that both her father and the barbershop were instrumental to her feelings about politics. She stated "We had voters come to the shop. I was able to campaign in there too. But my dad kind of started turning some people off. And that was kind of hard. And a lot of Caucasians started moving into the neighborhood and we started getting new people, so it was like re-educating. So, about the third of so time that they [political opponents] came after me, they said terrible things in campaigns. I would walk into my campaign office and gag. I just didn't like it. I don't like the competition part of it." While Alderwoman Lawrence expressed disdain for some aspects of politics, she immediately noted that she remains in politics so that she can assist her constituents and the community that surrounds the barbershop. These are her people, and she has an obligation to help them in any way that she can, albeit with a haircut or with public policy.

No Family Support

Conversely, State Senator Jasmine Nealy had no family support. Unlike the other women in the sample, she did not have a supportive nor involved family. Yet, she became an entrepreneur who was known in the community. Her path to politics was "nonconventional, so nonconventional. You know, sometimes people have this fire in their belly, and they have this passion and want to make a difference based on an issue. That wasn't me at all." However, as the conversation unfolded during the interview, it was quickly apparent that State Senator Nealy's upbringing provided the passion and impetus for her political career. She has a passion for helping what society would deem wayward children "because that was me."

During the time of our interview which was held on June 2, 2018, State Senator Nealy was leading a political arm of a Black Lives Matter movement in a midwestern state. She was a community activist who is known for being outspoken on issues of race and racism. But prior to her engagement in electoral politics, Jasmine Nealy was a Black girl who was suffering. "My mother committed suicide [...] And my father came back home from the Vietnam war. And there as a drive-by shooting and he had gotten shot and killed. And my mother was pregnant with me. And I was motherless and fatherless. And once I realized this, I became very angry and bitter. Imagine living in a world motherless and fatherless. So, I was really angry with my parents. I was angry with my condition. Because we had nothing, we were literally in poverty, so I joined a gang. This little girls' gang. And they called me the leader and there were 12 of us and we just go out and wreak havoc." As an orphan, young Jasmine Nealy was in a world of hurt. She joined a gang to have the support that she did not get at home although she lived with her grandmother. Jasmine Nealy seemed to crave family and a connection or bond with others to fill the void left by her parents' death.

When she was not engaged in gang-related activities, Jasmine Nealy would spend time at the local bookstore. She did not like school, but she really enjoyed reading books. The lack of supervision allowed the future state senator to spend the majority of her school day outside of the classroom but inside of the local bookstore. "And I would go to school and my grandmother, bless her heart, she would say 'Go on get out of here. When you go to school wake me up.' And I would get out my book bag and go to school and after lunch would sneak out the side door because I just wasn't into my schoolwork. It just wasn't there. It had gotten so bad that the principal brought me in and said 'You have to go. You are too far behind in your credit and there is no way that you're going to catch up. You just have to get out.' And they literally pushed me out of the system, and they never sent anyone to check on me."

This aspect of State Senator Nealy's early life is harrowing. She later turned this pain into a community resource. She would later open her own bookstore and campaign on a promise to help the indigent children of the city who were pushed out or dropped out of the public school system. Prior to her election as a state senator, Nealy served in her state's House of Representatives. In this capacity she "and members of the clergy within the 60th district me with the interim superintendent at the time. And I said 'look we have approximately 12,000 kids that are on the street or hanging out on their grandmothers' porches. If we do not educate them, we are going to incarcerate them." In response to the indigent children crisis, State Senator Nealy helped to reopen a school that was previously closed just to educate the children that were pushed out or dropped out of school. She made a positive impact on the children in her district by reaching out to them directly. "I knocked on those doors and made phone calls" and contacted the students and or their families directly. This policy priority is personal for State Senator Jasmine Nealy because of her own upbringing. She noted, "I was so geared to do this because it happened to me." In this case, the lack of a stable upbringing and parents who either believed in her or steered her towards politics was precisely the reason why Jasmine Nealy became politically active.

Conclusion

Family shapes how Black women think about politics. The women in our study were absolute in their descriptions of how their familial ties did or did not shape their viewpoints on entering electoral politics. What is important to note, however, is that family plays differing roles for women, and that this is not a universal model for Black women's engagement with family political influencers. For some, family can be either a push or pull factor into electoral politics. But as our data show, it's more complicated than that. The narratives of the Black women in our study demonstrate that family (or the lack thereof) offers unique perspectives on how and why they should enter politics. As a result, these Black women candidates sought different paths and have engaged with the political system in a variety of ways.

Future studies should take this intracategorial approach to revisit traditional topics in political science with an eye towards intersectional analysis. We encourage scholars to deeply investigate differences among provisional groups which we believe will uncover more intersectional knowledge about how minoritized groups engage with US-American politics. Furthermore, we recognize that there may be limitations in our study due to our limited sample size. These women's experiences are unique and cannot be used to generalize to the entirety of Black women candidates. However, our findings are illustrative of the myriad of ways Black women's families help to create their pathways toward electoral politics. In sum, we find that the complexity in which Black women are pushed or pulled into electoral politics by their families is a meaningful one. The nuances that we unearth in this essay demonstrate the importance of family influence for Black women political elites. Even if a candidate does not have a positive experience with family – or lacks concrete and sustained family involvement – the impact of family on setting one's political agenda or desire to run for office is evident. The dynamism between family engagement and nascent political ambition is a factor that should be considered in intersectional conversations about Black women's political activism.

References

Barnett, Bernice McNair (1993): "Invisible Southern Black Women Leaders in the Civil Rights Movement: The Triple Constraints of Gender, Race, and Class." In: Gender & Society 7/2, pp. 162–182.

Berelson, Bernard R./Lazarsfeld, Paul F./McPhee, William N. (1954): Voting, Chicago: University Chicago Press.

Brown, Nadia E. (2014): "Political Participation of Women Color: An Intersectional Analysis." In: Journal of Women, Politics & Policy 35/4, pp. 315–348.

Campbell, Angus/Converse, Philip E./Miller, Warren E./Stokes, Donald E. (1960): The American Voter, New York: Wiley.

Dowe, Pearl K. Ford (2020): "Resisting Marginalization: Black Women's Political Ambition and Agency." In: PS: Political Science & Politics 53/4, pp. 697–702.

Greenberg, Edward (1970): Political Socialization, New York: Transaction Publishers.

Hardy-Fanta, Carol/Lien, Pei-te/Pinderhughes, Dianne M./Sierra, Christine Marie (2016): Contested Transformation: Race, Gender, and Political Leadership in 21st Century America, New York, NY: Cambridge University Press.

Jones, Martha S. (2020): Vanguard: How Black Women Broke Barriers, Won the Vote, and Insisted on Equality for All, New York: Basic Books.

Lemi, Danielle C./Brown, Nadia E. (2020): "The Political Implications of Colorism Are Gendered." In: PS – Political Science and Politics 53/4, pp. 669–673.

Materson, Lisa G. (2009): For the Freedom of Her Race: Black Women and Electoral Politics in Illinois, 1877–1932: University of North Carolina Press.

Murray, Pauli/Eastwood, Mary O. (1965): "Jane Crow and the Law: Sex Discrimination and Title VII." In: George Washington Law Review 34/2, pp.232-256.

Renshon, Stanley A. (1975): "Personality and Family Dynamics in the Political Socialization Process." In: American Journal of Political Science 19/1, pp. 63–80.

Sapiro, Virginia (1983): The Political Integration of Women: Roles, Socialisation, and Politics, Urbana, IL: University of Illinois Press.

Terkildsen, Nayda (1993): "When White Voters Evaluate Black Candidates: The Processing Implications of Candidate Skin Color, Prejudice, and Self-Monitoring." In: American Journal of Political Science 37/4, pp. 1032–1053.

Van Deth, Jan W./Abendschön, Simone/Vollmar, Meike (2011): "Children and Politics: An Empirical Reassessment of Early Political Socialization." In: Political Psychology 32/1, pp. 147–174.

"Vamos destruir esse patriarcado, eu creio!"
Inter-American Networks and Articulations of Feminism on Social Media

Saskia Bante

Introduction

The first two decades of the twenty-first century are marked, among other things, by the rise of social media, which ushered in new ways for people to connect, communicate, and share information, leading to the emergence of new media cultures. In the wake of these developments, social media applications like Facebook, Instagram, or TikTok have become central sites of contemporary feminist media culture and helped boost a new wave of popularity of feminism, especially among young women. Given their size and reach, large feminist accounts have become a major influence in the mediation of feminism and can be considered an integral part of feminist media culture today, as hashtag movements like #MeToo or #NiUnaMenos in Latin America have most prominently shown. Based on these developments, this study aims to contribute to a better understanding of feminist articulations on social media.

For this purpose, 89 Instagram accounts labelled as feminist were analyzed in a qualitative study in terms of their geographical location, popularity, influence within the network, thematic orientation, as well as who speaks and writes on these accounts. Additionally, similarities and differences across regions as well as power imbalances were traced and discussed. The premise of the study was to avoid an analytical framework that intermingles feminist articulations on social media with political activism or views them *a priori* as expressions of a neoliberal or postfeminist culture. Instead, the study was designed as a feminist media and cultural studies project that allowed for a more open-ended approach, viewing feminist articulations on social media as a diverse terrain encompassing a variety of feminist currents, orientations, and modes of engagement with feminism as part of everyday culture.

The overall research design was guided by the idea of mapping and analyzing influential feminist social media accounts from the Americas. In a first step, 89 feminist Instagram accounts from 12[1] countries in the Americas were selected using criterion sampling and snowball sampling. Selection criteria were a minimum of 10,000 followers and an explicit reference to feminism. To avoid violating privacy rights, accounts that were set as private were excluded. After the selection process, a social network analysis (SNA) was carried out, guided by the questions how the accounts are distributed across the Americas, how they are interconnected, and which accounts are most influential within the network. Following the SNA, a forum analysis heuristic, as employed by Jennifer M. Nish (2014) in her dissertation on transnational feminist publics, was adopted and slightly modified. After collecting general information about the accounts and their authors, a thematic analysis was conducted by examining the story highlights section of each account to learn more about the guiding themes and orientations of the accounts, and to discern thematic patterns across regions.

The Landscape of Feminist Instagram Accounts in the Americas

It turned out that the regional distribution of feminist Instagram accounts is highly uneven. Brazil, the USA, and Mexico are the countries with the largest share of feminist accounts within the Americas and with the largest followings. This distribution pattern shows that in certain countries, there already seems to be an extensive network of feminist social media accounts, while in other countries, such networks are either non-existent or much smaller. The SNA also showed that there is a dense network of links within and across national borders, featuring about 70 per cent national and about 30 per cent transnational connections, which means that most of the content circulates nationally. As regards transnational links, distribution turned out to be uneven, as well, as there are a few accounts with a high number of transnational links, while

---

1 The accounts selected for analysis are from Argentina, Bolivia, Brazil, Chile, Colombia, Costa Rica, Colombia, Ecuador, Panama, Peru, Puerto Rico, and the United States. Despite extensive research, it was not possible to locate large feminist accounts that met the selection criteria from other American countries.

the majority of accounts remain within the boundaries of national networks. This is especially true for accounts located in the US, where the distribution of transnational links to Latin American countries is highly centralized, with only 4 out of 19 accounts featuring transnational links. Sharing the same language, Spanish-language Latin American accounts are connected across national borders at a higher degree than Brazilian and US accounts.

For transnational in-degree links, the opposite was true. In comparison, most transnational links lead to US-based accounts, with about 40 percent leading to the overall largest and most influential feminist account within the network. Hence, on a transnational level, US-based accounts appear to have a disproportionately greater influence. However, despite such centralization tendencies, it is important to note that networks on social media are formed simply by one actor following another, with various actors being loosely linked in different orders, and although some accounts are more influential than others, there is no center around which all the actors coalesce, nor is there a common agenda. On the contrary, social media networks are rather characterized by their decentralized structure, with many autonomous actors loosely connected through their participation in online discourses and in the circulation of content.

Who Are the Women Running the Accounts?

The forum analysis showed that most of the accounts are run by individuals or collectives and only a few by organizations, such as NGOs or community organizations. To learn more about the background of the people who run the accounts, data on race, age, and education was collected. Of the accounts that provided such information, about 70 per cent were White women and roughly thirty per cent Women of Color and Black women as well as some Asian American and Chicana women and one trans woman. With few exceptions, nearly all of them have an academic background and are in their twenties.

Most of the women that run the accounts describe themselves as feminists in some way, some of them referring to their geographical location, nationality, cultural, or racial background. Further, there are women who indicate their affiliation to a particular strand of feminism like abolitionist, Marxist, radical, revolutionary, lesbian, or eco-feminism. Among these affiliations, intersectional feminism was one of the most frequently mentioned terms, including descriptions such as antiracist feminism, feminism for all, decolonial, trans-inclusive, or Third World feminism. Perhaps surprisingly, only few women refer to themselves as activists. Instead, terms like blogger or digital creator seem to be used far more often as self-descriptors. What seems noteworthy about these is that these terms are closely linked to professional engagement with social media, such as creating, curating, and sharing content on the platform. However, there are also women who emphasize their struggle, describing themselves as women warriors or *luchadoras* (@luchadoras.mx, n.d.), or who make historical references by referring to themselves as witches, or identifying as descendants of the women who escaped enslavement through maroonage (@redmujeresafrodiasporicas 2020).

As regards the accounts that are run by organizations or collectives, many follow an educational or transformational approach, which is reflected in their self-descriptions such as feminist school, network, transnational articulation, or movement. Furthermore, accounts that are run by organizations are often linked to community projects outside of social media, however, the analysis also showed that with a few exceptions, the history of most accounts is linked to the emergence of social media platforms and does not relate to earlier projects.

Feminist Articulations on Social Media as an Expression of a Democratic Culture

The study is based on an understanding of feminist practices on social media as part of a democratic culture, which legal scholar Jack M. Balkin defines as a "network of people interacting with each other, agreeing and disagreeing, gossiping and shaming, criticizing and parodying, imitating and innovating, supporting and praising [in which] people exercise their freedom" through participation (Balkin 2004: 4). Central to his notion of a democratic culture is the process of meaning-making, which is based on interaction, and which leads to the emergence of new meanings and ideas from old ones. The concept appeared to be particularly useful in the context of the study because it allows for a perspective that does not distinguish between political and non-political expression and what is perceived to be low and high culture, or that asks whether social media feminist practices are aligned with feminist values or a feminist agenda that aims at transformation, but emphasizes the importance of non-political expression, popular culture, individual participation, and individual liberty as integral to the principle of free speech and hence of a democratic culture (ibid: 39).

Feminism in Practice: From Individual Growth to Collective Struggle

The results of the forum and the thematic analysis showed that feminist accounts cover a broad range of topics and approach feminism in diverse ways. Whereas some accounts are run in a rather professional way, using elaborately crafted images, texts, or videos, most accounts feature content that is reposted from other accounts or social media platforms. As the analysis showed, various accounts emphasize empowerment as a primary goal. In this context, the posts are often educational, providing information on feminism-related topics or concepts in an accessible and didactic way, making use of infographics and short sentences, written in an informal and accessible language, or using humor and irony to critically engage with and challenge antifeminist discourses. Some accounts with an educational focus offer workshops or live talks to their followers or provide resources such as e-books or online courses on a range of feminism-related topics.

Feminism as Personal Growth

Much of the analyzed content is aimed at raising awareness and giving advice by explaining, for example, how to recognize a toxic relationship or by providing mental health tips. Often, this type of content is aimed at the individual, with posts containing inspirational quotes or motivational phrases directed at personal growth and building confidence. Such accounts that focus on the individual are primarily concerned with women's bodies and their mental health, frequently using terms like body positivity, self-care, self-love, self-awareness, or healing. There are also a few accounts that intend to provide help for women in need, offering counselling services or providing specific information such as phone numbers and places where women can seek help or find shelter. However, such forms of engagement tend to be the exception.

Feminism as a Collective Struggle

There are also accounts that rather reflect a notion of feminism as a collective struggle and that, for example, locate themselves in a socialist or Marxist tradition, taking an anti-capitalist stance and emphasizing collective action and social justice, drawing attention to the various forms of violence and oppression that women have experienced. The most frequently mentioned terms in this context are patriarchy, *machismo*, masculinity, beauty norms,

White supremacy, colonialism, and capitalism. The account @sororamx is such an example, focusing on posting protest images or messages written on protest banners such as "Nuestra primera soberania territorial son nuestros cuerpos" [Our first territorial sovereignty is our bodies] (@sororamx 2021). In contrast to individualized responses to feminism, such messages can be seen more in the tradition of second wave collective feminist struggles and debates, echoing feminist values like autonomy and social justice. Even more, such messages can also be located in the decolonial discourse of Latin American feminisms through references to sovereignty, territory, and women's bodies. In addition, some accounts particularly focus on or are dedicated to specific communities and their struggles and experiences such as African American or Asian American communities.

From Politics to Trivia

Other accounts rather focus on sharing news items and political content, not always related to feminism. Less frequent were accounts with a commercial focus that promote products or advertise other accounts in exchange for a fee, or accounts with an entertainment focus, which post content on a variety of issues not directly related to feminism but rather concerned with lifestyle, personal tastes, and other random topics.

Guiding Themes and Issues

As regards content and thematic orientation, the analysis showed that protest, feminism, abortion as well as gendered violence and LGBTQ+related topics are particularly prominent. A further group of themes is related to women's bodies, comprising a range of topics related to physical and mental health, sex education, menstruation, and maternity.

Deconstruction as a Feminist Practice

A central term that appears on many accounts is deconstruction, which is presented as a feminist practice aimed at recognizing oppressive social structures, beliefs, and traditions and is linked to an idea of personal growth. It is based on the belief that being or becoming a feminist can be best achieved through (de)constructing oneself and internalized social norms by engaging in a constant process of reflecting, inquiring, and becoming as a feminist, something that Kanai (2020: 31) has described as a "student-like approach" which according to her, has become "entangled in feminist identities" where constant learning is enacted with some kind of rigor and where girls locate themselves within a "trajectory as 'growing' in their feminism" fitting into a neoliberal framework of self-actualization. However, there were also posts in which women critically interrogate and explore the ways in which feminism can or has affected personal development and consciousness-raising, reflecting on how individual and collective processes are intertwined. Further, there were posts that criticized certain types of engagement with feminism or articulations of feminism, echoing postfeminist or neoliberal feminist scholarly debates and differentiating between true and false types of feminism.

Intersectionality

Intersectionality turned out to be another central theme, with various accounts stating that they are rooted in or supportive of intersectional feminism. It does, however, not always become apparent from their content what makes their approach to feminism intersectional. Furthermore, none of the accounts engages critically with the concept itself. One account where an intersectional focus is easily discernible is the overall largest and most influential Instagram account called @feminist, which is described as an "intersectional feminist community made up of a diverse network of change makers from around the [world]", and which almost exclusively shares content from other accounts that fits its notion of intersectionality. The way intersectionality is operationalized on this account suggests that it is something that can be easily achieved by posting a certain type of content. However, the fact that it focuses particularly on a US-context and posts exclusively English-language content raises the question to what extent the content represents or addresses a global community.

In comparison, the account @aafc.nyc, which is linked to a Black and Asian American Feminist Solidarities Project, might actually provide an example of a transversal, dialogic, and intersectional practice, as envisioned in transnational feminist theory (cf. Marshall 2021). As stated on their website, the women who run the project feel "indebted to ways Black feminist thought and Third World feminist movements enable us to think and act critically through our own positionalities to address systems of anti-Black racism, settler colonialism, and xenophobia" (Asian American Feminist Collective 2022).

As can be seen on its Instagram account, @aafc.nyc hosts various joint events with @blackwomenradicals and other community organizations. As stated on their website, they approach feminism as an "ever-evolving practice that seeks to address the multi-dimensional ways Asian/American people confront systems of power at the intersections of race, gender, class, sexuality, religion, disability, migration history and citizenship and immigration status" (ibid.), combining feminist scholarship with political activism. Perhaps unlike most of the other accounts that described themselves as intersectional, the people behind @aafc.nyc and @blackwomenradicals base their thought and action on their own experiences much in the sense as argued by Julia Roth (2019: 333) who has emphasized that "an intersectional perspective always needs to be context-specific and aware of the concrete historical situation in which it is applied and which defines the relevance of the varying social divisions for each context".

Feminist projects like @feminist, on the other hand, are closely tied to and depend on the existence of social media platforms, and despite what might be best intentions, can evoke the impression that their intersectional practice might rather serve as a marker of authenticity, as suggested by Akane Kanai (2020: 25), using it to signal correct behavior and being a 'good' feminist, an approach to feminism that is undergirded by a neoliberal governmentality of self-actualization, leading to an environment in which "the self is re-conceptualized as a 'platform' through which marginalized others are included".

Regional Similarities and Differences

As regards commonalities and differences between regions, it appeared users across the Americas utilize the affordances of social media in largely similar ways. Themes and topics that appear transnationally are empowerment, deconstruction, intersectionality, and LGBTQ+related topics with content related to oppressive social structures as well as content that is directed towards the individual.

Regarding differences, sorority turned out to be a concept that is particularly confined to a Latin-American context, which might be an indicator that is has a distinct cultural meaning, perhaps similar to *comadrismo*, which according to Scholz (2016: 82) can be used to explain a "transnational subjectivity of feminism", which she calls *comadre*, a "politicized subject" that "enacts counterhegemonic agency in transnational communication systems through a relational framework" and that is embedded in a "web of kinship and friendship relations, as well as oppressive asymmetrical global structures" (ibid). Similarly, sorority might be an example for how affect circulates in global cultural flows, providing a conceptual framework for affective relations between women.

Furthermore, protest appears as an overarching theme on Spanish-language accounts. This might be explained by the #NiUnaMenos movement, which sparked an ongoing series of protest marches throughout the region, sometimes referred to as *marea verde* (green tide) due to the widespread use of the *pañuelo verde*, a green bandana scarf which emerged as a symbol for protest against the anti-abortion legislation and which has, according to Larrondo/Ponce (2019: 30), become an identity marker of feminism. Content related to gendered violence and femicides also appeared almost exclusively on Latin American accounts, particularly on Spanish-language accounts. Similarly, one of the topics that turned out to be particularly relevant in a US-American context was #BlackLivesMatter. Immigration and social justice turned out to be further prominent topics on US-American accounts, however, these were not always related to feminism.

Another distinctive feature of Latin American accounts are references to decoloniality as a term that hints at Latin America's colonial past as well as the asymmetrical oppressive global structures, mentioned by Scholz, which it has engendered. As a strand of feminism that emanates from women whose bodies have been racialized and exploited, Nora Garita (2019: 14) has highlighted the centrality of decolonial feminism to Latin American feminism. As she points out, there has been a permanent tension with hegemonial, Eurocentric, or North American feminisms that subscribe to an essentialist version of womanhood, which has led her to distinguish between urban middle-class feminisms and indigenous, communitarian feminisms with their strong links to nature, ancestral practices, as well as *sentipensante* [thinking-feeling] and Cosmovision-related knowledges. In direct comparison, the latter strand seems to be largely absent from the feminist landscape on social media.

Visibility and Representation

The findings of the study showed that although social media applications enable their users to connect across geographical, economic, and cultural borders, existing hegemonic structures and power asymmetries are also (re)produced in these spaces in various ways. Considering that feminist Instagram accounts tend to be run by middle-class women with academic backgrounds and that certain regions and people are only sparsely or not at all represented, the question arises to what extent marginalized standpoints get to circulate in these spaces. It is therefore important to acknowledge that the high number of accounts might not translate into a proportionate wealth of diversity. Thus, when discussing intersectionality in the context of social media, it needs to be considered that many women are left out of the picture, namely the most disadvantaged.

In discussing power asymmetries, it is further necessary to critically examine the role of large and influential accounts that operate by reposting content from other accounts run by individuals whose voices they think should be amplified. Although such accounts afford visibility to certain individuals for a short span of time, they also create dependencies and power structures that may not empower those whose voices the account seeks to amplify, but rather the account itself as well as the people that run it, by affording them the prestige of doing important activist work. Such dynamics, in which large accounts represent those who are perceived in need of representation, likely lead to new regimes of (in)visibility. If the largest and most influential feminist account is a US-American account that purports to cater to a global community, but predominantly features English-speaking individuals from the US, many individuals are left out of the picture. Sarah Jackson and Sonia Banaszczyk came to a similar conclusion in their study on digital feminist counterpublics on Twitter, pointing out that even if it

> works as a space where the historically marginalized standpoints of women can be elevated through virality and collective advocacy, the technological architecture of the platform's trending, retweeting, and mentioning functions, along with the ways mainstream and elite individuals and outlets legitimate the "popular", reproduce the marginalization of intersectional experiences (Jackson/Banaszczyk 2016: 403–404).

It is therefore important to ask whose standpoints tend to be most influential and whose are neglected or even obscured. As the example of @aafc.nyc and @blackwomenradicals has shown that, in the relation to intersectionality, there is a difference between people or groups who use their accounts to draw attention to their projects and those whose intersectionality is solely based on curating content and showcasing individuals that meet their criteria of intersectionality, emphasizing certain people or experiences and neglecting others.

In the former case, the groups' effort to build intersectional and transversal solidarities takes place outside of social media and does not depend on visibility provided by third parties.

Feminist Practices on Social Media as an Ongoing Conversation

Despite such criticisms, it may still be argued that feminist practices on social media offer potential for change. As Caldeira et al. (2020) have argued, it is particularly in the "realm of the everyday and the ordinary that individuals enter into 'conversations' with hegemonic power structures, engaging with them or opposing them, although not always consciously, through their own personal everyday practices", (3) a notion similar to Balkin's concept of a democratic culture. The extent to which this becomes possible, however, is shaped by the platform vernaculars, which according to Caldeira (2021) can be described as a "combination of communicative styles, grammars, and logics that emerge from the relationship between the platform's technological affordances and the practices continuously enacted and negotiated by its users" (7).

Moreover, following Balkin (2004), such potential may also lie in the diversity of feminist articulations on social media that can all be considered integral to maintaining a democratic culture, regardless whether they are accounts that may be interpreted as expressions of neoliberal entanglements with feminism, or accounts that do not fit such framings because their content rather reflects their work on the ground and is aimed at spreading information, announcing events, addressing critical issues like abortion, gendered violence, teen pregnancy, or racism that affect women in their communities. As Tisha Dejmanee (2016: 744) has argued, it might be concluded that

> [u]ser-generated feminism – like popular feminism – is not a perfect expression of feminist politics. The tendency of this movement is to emphasise individual interpretations of feminism, leading to pluralistic and ambivalent outcomes. However, feminist media scholars are also challenged to seek out new ways to analyse the politics of these spaces, given the fact that denouncing individual women for their social media productions has a markedly different valence from campaigning against a media conglomerate's representation of women.

Such a perspective allows for a view of feminist practices on social media as forms of participation in and engagement with the cultural industries and conventions that surround them with all its ambivalences, acknowledging that these practices are not always counterhegemonic, but can sometimes also be complicit with hegemonic structures.

As an outlook, many questions and aspects remain to be discussed in feminist research and theorizing that can provide further insights into (re)articulations of feminism in digital or social media cultural contexts, since a sole recourse to established analytical concepts from feminist media studies or the feminist wave narrative seem to offer little new insight here. Studies that focus on the entanglements in contemporary feminist media cultures, on the role of affect, and the relational frameworks that are at play in feminist social media networks, or that examine the relationship between intersectionality and content creation on social media have already provided new ways of theorizing feminist practices in digital cultures, without falling into the binary of either criticizing contemporary feminism as lacking commitment to a socially transformative feminist agenda, or exaggerating expectations about its capacity to initiate fundamental changes.

References

@feminist (n.d.): Feminist [Instagram profile]. Instagram, November 3, 2021 (https://www.instagram.com/feminist/).
@luchadoras.mx (n.d.): luchadoras.mx. [Instagram profile]. Instagram, November 25, 2021 (https://www.instagram.com/luchadoras.mx/).
@redmujeresafrodiasporicas (2020): "Somos las nietas de las cimarronas que no pudiste esclavizar" [Instagram post]. Instagram, December 28, 2022 (https://www.instagram.com/p/B8IM81xnayp/?hl=de).
@sororamx (29 September 2021): "Nuestra primera soberania territorial son nuestros cuerpos" [Instagram post]. Instagram, January 5, 2022 (https://www.instagram.com/p/CUZIPDiA4UT/).
Asian American Feminist Collective (n.d.): "Who We Are", January 30, 2022 (https://www.asianamfeminism.org/about).
Balkin, Jack M. (2004): "Digital Speech and Democratic Culture: A Theory of Freedom of Expression for the Information Society." In: New York University Law Review 79/1, pp. 1–55.

Caldeira, Sofia P. (2021): "'It's Not Just Instagram Models': Exploring the Gendered Political Potential of Young Women's Instagram Use." In: MaC 9/2, pp. 5–15, https://doi.org/10.17645/mac.v9i2.3731.

Caldeira, Sofia P./De Ridder, Sander/Van Bauwel, Sofie (2020): "Between the Mundane and the Political: Women's Self-Representations on Instagram." In: Social Media + Society 6/3, pp. 1–14, https://doi.org/10.1177/2056305120940802.

Dejmanee, Tisha (2016): "Waves and Popular Feminist Entanglements: Diffraction as a Feminist Media Methodology." In: Feminist Media Studies 16/4, pp. 741–745, https://doi.org/10.1080/14680777.2016.1190046.

Garita, Nora (2019): "Prólogo." In: Marina Larrondo/Camila Ponce (eds.), Activismos feministas jóvenes. Emergencias, actrices y luchas en América Latina, Buenos Aires: CLACSO, pp. 11–20.

Jackson, Sarah J./Banaszczyk, Sonia (2016): "Digital Standpoints." In: Journal of Communication Inquiry 40/4, pp. 391–407, https://doi.org/10.1177/0196859916667731.

Kanai, Akane (2020): "Between the Perfect and the Problematic: Everyday Femininities, Popular Feminism, and the Negotiation of Intersectionality." In: Cultural Studies 34/1, pp. 25–48, https://doi.org/10.1080/09502386.2018.1559869.

Larrondo, Marina/Ponce, Camila (2019): "Activismos feministas jóvenes en América Latina: Dimensiones y perspectivas conceptuales." In: Marina Larrondo/Camila Ponce (eds.), Activismos feministas jóvenes. Emergencias, actrices y luchas en América Latina, Buenos Aires: CLACSO, pp. 21–38.

Marshall, Gul Aldikacti (2021): "Transnational Feminisms." In: Nancy A. Naples (ed.), Companion to Feminist Studies: Wiley-Blackwell, pp. 193–211.

Nish, Jennifer Marie (2014): Transnational Feminist Publics: Digital Contexts for Rhetorical Activism, PhD diss., University of Kansas.

Roth, Julia (2019): "Intersectionality." In: Olaf Kaltmeier/Josef Raab/Michael Stewart/Alice Nash Foley/Stefan Rinke/Mario Rufer (eds.), The Routledge Handbook to the History and Society of the Americas, London and New York: Routledge and Taylor & Francis Group, pp. 330–38.

Scholz, Teresa Maria Linda (2016): "Beyond 'Roaring Like Lions': Comadrismo, Counternarratives, and the Construction of a Latin American Transnational Subjectivity of Feminism. [Abstract]." In: Communication Theory 26/1, pp. 82–101, https://doi.org/10.1111/comt.12059.

Intersectional Praxis and Socio-Political Transformation at the Colombian Truth Commission in the Caribbean Region

Audes Jiménez González and Juliana González Villamizar

1. Introduction

Audes Jiménez González is a Black woman from a popular and peasant background in Colombia. She was born in Chigorodó, Antioquia, but arrived as a child in Barranquilla. In 2020–2022, Jiménez worked as coordinator of the territorial office for Atlántico, the North of Bolívar and San Andrés of the Colombian *Comisión para el Esclarecimiento de la Verdad, la Convivencia y la No Repetición* (CEV; Commission for the Clarification of Truth, Coexistence and Non-Repetition), one of the transitional justice mechanisms established in the peace accords signed between the Colombian government and the FARC-EP guerrilla in 2016.[1]

Juliana González Villamizar is a mestiza, upper-middle class, light-skinned woman from Bogotá. She currently does research on the mainstreaming of intersectionality in the CEV. Her work incorporates participative-action methodologies and aims to build ethical solidarity among activist and knowledge-producing networks.

We share the same dreams and desires to help transform the realities of injustice and inequality in the Colombian Caribbean region, which are, in many

---

1 The Colombian armed conflict began with the formation of the FARC guerrilla in 1964 and extended until the signing of a peace accord with the Colombian government in 2016 in Havana, Cuba. It took place particularly in the rural areas and involved paramilitaries and other guerrilla groups. These armed groups, as well as state forces, are responsible for multiple war crimes and for the victimization of more than nine million people (CEV, 2022). Women, ethnic groups and the peasant population were disproportionately affected by the armed conflict.

ways, interwoven with the violence of the armed conflict.[2] A common concern in our conversations has been how to incorporate an intersectional framework in the work of the CEV, in ways that contribute to transforming the roots of the armed conflict and of socio-political violence in this region. Together with the CEV's work teams in the Caribbean region, we put some of our ideas in practice by co-organizing the 'Women's Agoras' and the 'Marronage Route', two dialogue processes with women and Black, Afro-descendent, Raizal, and Palenquero communities[3] which took place recurrently in 2020 and 2021. This article is the result of our ongoing dialogue and collaborative work around these processes from our different positionalities and enunciation sites.

Women's Agoras brought together Afro-descendent, Indigenous, peasant, lesbian, bisexual, and transgender women leaders from all subregions of the Colombian Caribbean who have suffered sexual and political violence in the armed conflict. The Marronage Route were meetings with female and male representatives of Afro-descendent community councils[4] in the Caribbean region. Both the Women's Agoras and the Marronage Route continued as autonomous mobilization processes after the CEV finalized its work and presented its final report in June 2022. Simultaneously, we carried out a participative study on the possibilities and challenges of mainstreaming intersectionality in the teams' research methodologies.[5] This study involved several in-

---

2   The Colombian armed conflict began with the formation of the FARC guerrilla in 1964 and extended until the signing of a peace accord with the Colombian government in 2016 in Havana, Cuba. It took place particularly in the rural areas and involved paramilitaries and other guerrilla groups. These armed groups, as well as state forces, are responsible for multiple war crimes and for the victimization of more than nine million people (CEV, 2022). Women, ethnic groups and the peasant population were disproportionately affected by the armed conflict.

3   Afro-descendent people in Colombia are divided into subgroups due to internal debates regarding the political value of these categories, as well as the ethnic particularities of Raizal and Palenquero communities, which preserve their ancestral territories and languages.

4   Community councils are Afro-descendent people's legal territorial units, which aim to satisfy their right to self-government and to materialize their cultural traditions according to Law 70 of 1993. Although community councils are a historic achievement of Afro-descendent struggles in Colombia, many have not yet received the collective land properties to which communities are entitled.

5   The German-Colombian Peace Institute (CAPAZ) funded this study, as well as the publication Hilando Resistencias that resulted from the Women's Agoras and the Marronage Route, to which we refer below.

terviews with staff members, including research and social dialogue coordinators, as well as documentors, analysts, and administrative staff, collective dialogue spaces and an online training on intersectionality.

This article includes the voices of three participants in the processes we reflect on. Beatriz Elena Mejía Vizcaína is an Afro-descendent and lesbian woman, practicing attorney, LGBTQ+ human rights defender and currently president of the Diverse and Affirmative Peace Organization in the department of Cesar. Estebana Roa Montoya is an Afro-descendent, peasant woman from a poor family in Acandí, Chocó. She is a women's human rights defender and legal representative of the Victim and Professional Women's Network. Concepción Julio is an Afro-descendant elder woman, social leader, human rights defender of vulnerable populations and victims of the armed conflict, now legal representative of Winds of Peace organization in San Bernardo del Viento, Córdoba. She became the first female councilor of the same municipality.

Based on our and these participants' experience in the context of the CEV's work in the Colombian Caribbean, we aim to shed light on the significance and the transformative effects of an intersectional praxis for the work of transitional justice institutions, as well as for human rights public policy that addresses violence against the body-territories, families, and land of individuals and collectivities. We are interested in transcending perspectives based on the summation of violences, and to identify and contribute to creating the conditions for women and LGBTQ+ people, their families, organizations, and communities to heal and coexist peacefully in their territories in the Colombian Caribbean in the short and medium term.

2. Intersecting Inequality and Conflict Dynamics in the Colombian Caribbean Region

The cultural context of the Caribbean region involves patriarchal practices based on gender and sexuality stereotypes that make women and LGBTQ+ people particularly vulnerable to violence against their bodies and to their exclusion from leadership roles in society. Within this patriarchal culture, armed actors asserted their dominance through weapons and engaged in the massive violation of women's rights, lives, and bodies (Grupo de Memoria Histórica 2011). Mejía's experience evidences, too, that the violence committed by illegal armed groups, as well as by state forces (the military and the police) against people with nonconforming sexual orientations and gender identities was based on prejudices and aimed to preserve a heteropatriarchal order and punish deviant identities and behaviors:

> Once a paramilitary got interested in me and came to my mother's house drunk. He threatened that if I didn't go out with him, he would kill my family. He said I was supposed to be with him. He was very obsessed and I was afraid he would kill me because he couldn't be with me. Men here say, too, that lesbians are unfair competition (Personal Communication, 14 February 2022).

Black communities inhabit large portions of the Colombian Caribbean since the arrival of European colonists in the 16th century as a result of the transatlantic slave trade. Although slavery was officially abolished in Colombia in 1851, Afro-descendent people continued to suffer racial discrimination and to occupy subordinate positions. The agents and dynamics of this violence have changed, but the same colonial logic remains, considering Black people as *others*, inferior, and submissive. The violence exerted by guerrilla groups, paramilitaries, and state forces in many Black territories included the prohibition of social reunions, the exercise of political rights and even funeral ceremonies for the dead. Gender stereotypes aggravated this situation, as Julio's experience shows:

> I had the good and the bad luck to work with 12 councilmen who made my life impossible, due to this idea that women should not participate in politics. Because of my struggles in defense of people's rights and life projects in the countryside, paramilitaries came into my house and threatened to kill my family. I had to move to Bogotá with my kids while they were still little (Personal Communication, 12 February 2022).

Actions such as these have contributed to establishing an extractivist economic model in many Black territories in the Colombian Caribbean. Transnational agroindustrial and mining projects have dried up rivers and swamps, leaving Black people in misery or forcing them to relocate (Jiménez González et al. 2021).

In fact, the most intense period of the armed conflict in the Caribbean region (1997–2005) is also characterized by the expansion of the land tenure by economic and political elites and the massive forced displacement of peasant, racialized populations. Roa's experience shows that sexual violence was employed against rural and racialized women in order to silence them and inhibit their resistance:

> I worked in banana plantations in Apartadó and was part of the labor union. I was handing out flyers with a colleague when four paramilitaries got us off the bus and raped us in a nearby property. The next day, paramilitaries came to my house and I had to leave with my three kids (Personal Communication, 12 February 2022).

Forced displacement affects women severely, as they experience revictimization and a triple discrimination in the urban centers where they arrive, as Roa explains:

> I had to work as a prostitute in Cartagena to support my kids. Once, a bar owner said to me: 'You look good, but we can't hire you because we only hire one Black woman, and we already have one.' I didn't understand then that they were discriminating against me (Personal Communication, 12 February 2022).

3. From Theory to Praxis

Intersectionality is a critical perspective on the simultaneous and inseparable interlocking of various dimensions of inequality based on gender, race, social class, heteronormativity, among others, that also sheds light on the differentiated impact of inequality on people's experiences according to their social positioning. Black feminist legal scholar Kimberlé Crenshaw (1988) developed the concept within the legal field to illustrate the conceptual gaps with regard to discrimination and violence against US women of color.[6] In Latin America and the Caribbean context, feminists aligned with decolonial, critical, and autonomous strands of the movement propose an intersectional framework to critique mainstream feminism for reconducting White patterns and concepts and to acknowledge the interweaving of gender, race, class, and heteronorma-

---

6   The genealogy of intersectionality traces a rich legacy of Black feminist thinkers and activists, such as Sojourner Truth, Ida B. Wells, the Combahee River Collective, Patricia Hill Collins, Barbara Smith, Audre Lorde and Angela Davis, among many others.

tivity in the project of modernity and its colonial legacies.[7] Many of these authors share the conviction, too, that intersectionality is not only a tool for structural analysis, but that it should serve to "construct a social movement that addresses all types of oppression, exclusion and marginalization" (Viveros Vigoya 2016: 13).[8]

The Colombian Truth Commission has the duty to clarify the truth and help recognize victims and the crimes committed, as well as facilitate peaceful-coexistence and non-repetition (Presidency of the Republic 2017). The CEV's methodological guidelines include gender, ethnic, psychosocial, life-course, and territorial approaches to guarantee differentiated attention to specific populations (CEV 2019). Although this framework appeared promising to mainstream intersectionality at first, one of the biggest obstacles to achieving this was that it tended to fragment social struggles instead of interlocking them and focused on the intersectionality of individual identities, rather than the social structures that produce the inequalities (González Villamizar 2021). In the Caribbean region, moreover, the research teams struggled to reflect on gender relations and the impact of the armed conflict on women and men as internally diverse categories. They often analyzed what had happened to peasant or mestiza women and to LGBTQ+ people, but could not explain the violations that occur simultaneously on racialized bodies.

Audes Jiménez González: Juliana arrived at the right moment with her research questions and made us reflect on our methods. Based on her suggestion that we might want to deepen our application of an intersectional framework, many staff members in the CEV research teams in the Caribbean, including myself, began to think that incorporating intersectionality in our work could support the Commission's objectives by explaining the relationship between the armed conflict and "historical continuums of violence that organize power as a gendered and racialized pyramid that have contributed to the persistence of war, even after the signing of the peace accords", as my colleague Eliana Toncel argues (personal Communication, 7 October 2020). We associated intersectionality, thus, with the possibility to intervene in the armed conflict dynamics in ways that help prevent its recurrence.

We considered that facilitating authentic transformation processes at the CEV through an intersectional framework required engaging in a process of "action-reflection-action". This process involves initiating interventions on the

---

7   Cf. Lugones 2014; Gonzalez 2020; Curiel 2020; Espinosa-Miñoso 2016.
8   Cf. Crenshaw 1988; Lorde 1984; Lugones 2000; Curiel 2020.

ground and having many eyes on what we are doing in order to decide which further actions we must engage in. In order to go beyond abstract discourses on the need to transform the world, we need to understand the domination relationships in the context where we act. We hoped this would allow us to construct concepts and confirm relationships among categories based on the work we are doing and, therefore, to propose far more accurate theories. Moreover, I suggested bringing others who are also engaged in advocacy processes on board, as I considered they could be excellent allies. The Women's Agoras and the Marronage Route became our interventions and simultaneously the laboratory to explore our ideas on intersectionality.

Juliana González Villamizar: Engaging in allyship with Audes and her work team, I participated in several meetings to help organize and assess different stages of the Agoras and the Marronage Route. I realized that, throughout this process, Audes was leading us, not only to develop methodologies to analyze intersecting inequalities, but specially to draw upon and utilize an intersectional framework in our activities. She was using intersectionality as a political strategy to build networks of collective action against all forms of oppression. This was evident in the pedagogic work she did with the research teams, as well as in her interest in bringing in allies to the process, including myself. She motivated us to interact with the people on the ground as equals and to recognize and validate their knowledge, if we aimed to produce differentiated analyzes that truly responded to the Caribbean social and political context.

In fact, Audes and many of her co-workers proposed that the Agoras and Marronage Routes should not only aim for recognition, peaceful-coexistence, and non-repetition, as the CEV had stipulated for social dialogue activities, but that they were research activities themselves. The Agoras and the Marronage Route thus became spaces where everyone had the chance to tell their own version of the narrative and to feel they were part of the historical dialogue fostered by the CEV. The publication *Hilando Resistencias*, which reflects these dialogue processes, demonstrates that colonial and racist logics are a pattern in the violence committed against women and ethnic-racial communities in the Caribbean, according to the empirical and analytical bases acquired during the dialogues (Jiménez González et. al 2021). *Hilando Resistencias* also contains the political agendas constructed in the meetings, which engaged local and regional authorities to develop policies that directly address the living conditions of women and Afro-descendent people in the Caribbean.

Jiménez/González: As expressed by Roa:

Thanks to these spaces of articulation and listening, we have published a text that includes our collective experiences. Before, the state had us Black people *enmochilados*[9] in a single bag as victims of the armed conflict. We had never spoken of violence against us as a collectivity. Now, we can make visible the unwritten tragedy endured by the Afro-descendent, Raizal, and Palenquera communities as racialized people (Personal Communication, 19 October 2021).

Our strategy of "action-reflection-action" thereby enacted the transformations an intersectional framework proposes while producing intersectional knowledge of the armed conflict in the Caribbean. In this sense, it produced the synergy between theory and practice that Sirma Bilge and Patricia Hill Collins refer to as they highlight the tensions that lie within intersectionality as a framework oriented to inquiry and political action in interconnected ways (Bilge/Collins 2020). This made us think of our work as 'intersectional praxis' (González Villamizar, n.d.).

4. Healing-Deconstructing the Body-Territory: from the Inside Out and Vice Versa

Jiménez: With the idea in mind that naming the oppressions opens the door to transform them, I ask in which part of the body-territory intersectionality actually takes place and which are its effects.[10] I think: 'I perceive myself as a Black

---

9   Enmochilado in this context means that Black people were classified generally as victims, while their cultural and historical specificity was overlooked.

10 The concept of "body-territory" is very present in the discourses and practices of the peoples of Abya Yala, which is how the territory of Latin America was called by its original inhabitants prior to European colonization. We understand the body-territory as the energetic and spiritual connection of our individual physical bodies with Mother Earth, our ancestors, and our collective memories. Beyond the Cartesian dualism of mind and body that subjects emotions and embodiment to rationality, we recognize the integrality of our lived experience in the physical, psychological, and spiritual dimensions and our interdependence with land. In the ancestral traditions of Indigenous and Afro-descendent peoples in Abya Yala, women sow the navels of the newborn in the earth, signifying this deep connection. Anything that takes place in our bodies and in our minds transcends our physical boundaries and affects the land, and anything that happens to our Mother Earth affects us, because our roots are buried in her.

woman, coming from a peasant background. But this image I have of myself is very similar to the one the oppressors have of people like me!' So I am neither Black, nor woman. These are both social constructs and I need to deconstruct them from within. Our praxis of intersectionality went, therefore, beyond external oppressions and also tackled internal tensions produced by the historic subordination of racialized and gendered beings. As Frantz Fanon duly noted, these tensions involve our tendency to identify ourselves as oppressed people and to appropriate subaltern roles (Fanon 1961: 181).

Jiménez/González: We plead for a concept of democracy that does not only focus on political institutions, but that emphasizes our daily lives as sites of democratic intervention. This requires us to comprehend how our bodies – as our first territories – work and interact with one another. If we do not intervene at this level, we will just go on talking about transformation processes while never actually achieving them. The CEV's official questionnaires asked questions related to the victimizing act and to each identity component (woman, Black, lesbian, poor, etc.). We knew this would not make evident the connections, so we proposed that the dialogue center rather on longer-term and simultaneous layers of the participants' life experiences: Before the victimizing act, which situations made you feel bad, less than, or not entitled? Did these situations produce any complexes or insecurities related to any part of your body or being? Do you know of other women – friends, mothers, grandmothers – who experienced something similar? This way, we aimed to tackle the structural component while allowing the participants to reflect on the similarities and patterns in their experiences.

Mejía's experience shows that this environment and methodology was helpful for the participants to comprehend the inner effects of racial and gender and sexuality constructs and to gain power over them:

> My late grandmother was White. When I was six or seven, she would let all my siblings come inside her house except for me. I would ask her to let me in, but she'd say I have to stay outside because I am dark-skinned, just like my father. Now my family rejects my sexual orientation. Sharing my story at the Agoras and listening to other women's experiences, I began to understand that my family discriminates against me. This knowledge helped me forgive my grandmother and taught me how to speak up to earn my family's respect (Personal Communication, 14 February 2022).

Roa's reflection on the Agoras, on the other hand, demonstrates the positive impact of the experience on her regaining confidence and her sense of self-worth:

> For 24 years after I was raped, I couldn't speak in public. My hands would sweat and I couldn't pronounce a single word. The Agoras helped me because I felt trust with other women who spoke up about everything that has happened to us. I lost my fear because now we all struggle for the women's cause (Personal Communication, 12 February 2022).

Jiménez: Our society is built upon a series of ideals, symbols, and prejudices that don't allow us to live our lives fully. These ideas fill us with insecurities, fear, hatred, and contempt against others, making our minds sick. When we are able to deconstruct these thoughts, we can heal and free ourselves. Whenever leaders undergo this process, it becomes a complete success because their voice then multiplies their individual healing. This is what Mejía was able to do as she forgave her family for their abuses and herself for not winning her family's respect. But also Julio's words demonstrate the gains of this experience from an intersectionality of struggles perspective:

> Ten years ago, I thought it was horrible that a man would like another man. At the Agoras, I listened to the life stories of lesbian, bisexual, and transgender women and began to recognize their value and the fact that we are all on the same path of seeking the truth. I have become a defender of LGBTQ+ people's rights (Personal Communication, 12 February 2022).

Deconstructing the effects of intersectionality in our body-territories means too, therefore, to be able to see ourselves, as well as others, with humanity.

Many Debates, Not Enough Applications?

In the last decades, intersectionality has become a popular framework to analyze social inequalities. People speak either in favor or against intersectionality. "I'm not convinced by intersectionality. It's just another sophism", Ochy Curiel said in a talk in 2020. We agree that there are superficial uses of intersectionality that threaten to instrumentalize the struggles behind it, as happened with other categories, such as gender or human rights. Based on our experience, however, we plead to reinject the notion of intersectionality with transformative content by revitalizing its original contribution as activist knowledge, instead of throwing it away for good. Activist knowledge is practice-based knowledge, as opposed to intellectual and analytic operations that hardly change anything. As Sirma Bilge argues, this use of intersectionality might in fact have caused many 'intersectional' projects to lose sight of any political aspiration (Bilge 2014).

The extended period of violence in Colombia has left a deep wound in our society, which manifests in an inability to trust, to be transparent, and to deal with the enormous pain of the thousands of losses that the conflict has left behind. In order to work through this collective trauma and wake up as a society, we need to transmute such pain through a collective healing process. In contexts such as this, applying intersectionality in transitional justice procedures and human rights programs needs to go way beyond just analyzing structures of inequality. Entire populations have naturalized multiple forms of oppression and cannot even see which transformations are required to live a happy and beautiful life. Fostering collective healing and memory construction with marginalized communities such as Afro-descendent women, LGBTQ+ people, and ethnic communities in the Caribbean may be aided by an intersectional framework if both the inner and outer aspects of our bodies-territories are addressed and we are able to move toward different ways of being, feeling, and acting.

Our intersectional praxis in the context of the Women's Agoras and the Marronage Route in the Colombian Caribbean was key to materialize socio-political transformations by producing counter-hegemonic narratives of the armed conflict that centered around the differentiated experiences of marginalized sectors, while activating healing processes. Rather than mere respondents, the participants in the dialogues became protagonists of this experience and will be forever owners of their truth. We highlight, however, that these transformations are far from sufficient and that transitional justice processes must commit to addressing the economic hardships that very often, as in the case of Colombia, dominate the living conditions of victims. As Roa explains:

> Changes haven't been very big in other areas because of the economic system. Since I barely have a high school diploma and I'm 63 years old, whenever I present my resume, there is immediately some obstacle, and my resume is archived (Personal Communication, 12 February 2022).

References

Bilge, Sirma (2014): "Whitening Intersectionality." In: Wulf. D. Hund/Alana Lentin (eds.), Racism and Sociology, Berlin: Lit, pp. 175–206.

Comisión para el Esclarecimiento de la Verdad, la Convivencia y la No Repetición (CEV) (2019): Lineamientos metodológicos. Escuchar, reconocer y comprender para transformar, November 3, 2022 (https://web.comisiondelaverdad.co/images/zoo/publicaciones/archivos/comision-verdad-lineamientos-metodologicos-22072019.pdf).

Comisión para el Esclarecimiento de la Verdad, la Convivencia y la No Repetición (CEV) (2022): Cifras de la comisión de la verdad presentadas junto con el informe final, December 5, 2022 (https://web.comisiondelaverdad.co/actualidad/noticias/principales-cifras-comision-de-la-verdad-informe-final).

Crenshaw, Kimberlé (1988): "Demarginalizing the Intersection of Race and Sex: A Black Feminist Critique of Antidiscrimination Doctrine, Feminist Theory and Antiracist Politics." In: The University of Chicago Legal Forum 1, pp. 139–167.

Curiel, Ochy (2020): Sobre la interseccionalidad, November 3, 2022 (https://www.youtube.com/watch?v=-bmWZFojH1Q).

Espinosa-Miñoso, Yuderkys (2016): "De por qué es necesario un feminismo decolonial: diferenciación, dominación co-constitutiva de la modernidad occidental y el fin de la política de identidad." In: Solar 12, pp. 141–171.

Fanon, Frantz (1961): The Wretched of the Earth, New York: Grove Press.

González Villamizar, Juliana (2021): "La perspectiva interseccional como herramienta de la memoria en la comisión para el esclarecimiento de la verdad en Colombia." In: Diana Marcela Gómez Correal/Angélica Bernal Olarte/Juliana González Villamizar/Diana María Montealegre/María Mónica Manjarrés (eds.), Comisiones de la verdad y género en países del sur global. Miradas decoloniales, retrospectivas y prospectivas de la justicia transicional, Bogotá: Universidad de los Andes and Instituto CAPAZ.

González Villamizar, Juliana (n.d.): "Feminist Intersectional Praxis in the Colombian Truth Commission: Constructing Counter-Hegemonic Narratives of the Armed Conflict in the Colombian Caribbean." In: Third World Quarterly (forthcoming). doi: 10.1080/01436597.2023.2216647

Gonzalez, Lélia (2020): Por um feminismo afro-latino-americano, Rio Janeiro: Zahar.

Grupo de Memoria Histórica (2011): Mujeres y guerra. Víctimas y resistentes en el caribe colombiano, Bogotá: Taurus, November 3, 2022 (https://centrodememoriahistorica.gov.co/wp-content/uploads/2020/01/Mujeres-y-Guerra.-V%C3%ADctimas-y-Resistentes-en-el-Caribe-Colombiano.pdf).

Hill Collins, Patricia/Bilge, Sirma (2020): Intersectionality, Cambridge: Polity Press.

Jiménez González, Audes/Guerra, Luisa Fernanda/Corena, Edwin/Cubides, Germán Ricardo/González Villamizar, Juliana (2021): Hilando resistencias. Herramienta para la no repetición del conflicto armado y la violencia contra las mujeres y las comunidades negra, afrodescendiente, raizal y palenquera del caribe colombiano, Bogotá: Comisión de la Verdad and Instituto CAPAZ.

Lorde, Audre (1984): Sister Outsider: Essays and Speeches, Berkley: Ten Speed.

Lugones, María (2000): "Multiculturalism and Publicity." In: Hypathia 15, pp. 177–181.

Lugones, María (2014): "Colonialidad y género. Hacia un feminismo decolonial." In: Isabel Jiménez Lucena/María Lugones/Walter Mignolo/Madina Tlostanova (eds.), Género y descolonialidad, Buenos Aires: Ediciones del Signo, pp. 13–42.

Presidency of the Republic (2017): Decreto Ley 588 de 2017. Por el cual se organiza la Comisión para el Esclarecimiento de la Verdad, la Convivencia y la No Repetición, November 3, 2022 (https://www.funcionpublica.gov.co/eva/gestornormativo/norma.php?i=80633).

Viveros Vigoya, Mara (2016): "La interseccionalidad: Una aproximación situada a la dominación." In: Debate Feminista 52, pp. 1–17.

Reconstructing Women's Contemporary Political Struggles across the Central American Region

Edith Otero Quezada and Fátima Elizondo Rodríguez

Introduction

This essay aims at giving more visibility to Central America as a region in this collection of texts on different experiences and perspectives of feminist struggles in the Americas. We voice these reflections from our embodied positionalities as Nicaraguans, Central Americans, migrants, and feminists; positions which also situate us among the silences, tensions, and contradictions of the unresolved political processes in the region. At the same time, we understand the global context in which this region is usually viewed, either as a tourist destination or as territories marked by migration and violence in its multiple expressions.

With this in mind, we reconstruct two emblematic cases, which do not do justice to the complexity of the region, but can, in an exemplary manner, shed light on the contemporary struggles of Central American women and their interconnections as collective bodies in resistance. These cases are (1) the struggles and legacy of the Lenca indigenous leader Berta Cáceres in Honduras, and (2) the work by the Asociación Madres de Abril (April Mothers' Association, AMA) in Nicaragua[1]. Based on these two cases, we ask how the respective actors enunciate their struggles, what positions they assume, and what possible worlds they construct through their political actions and resistances – both individually and collectively[2]. We are also concerned with how these struggles are

---

[1] In both cases, we carried out documentary research. Additionally, in the case of Nicaragua, we conducted an interview with two members of AMA on 11 November 2021.

[2] Regarding positionality, keep in mind that not all women's struggles in the region self-proclaim as feminist, nor is that particularly important to them. However, from their collective actions, they construct political strategies that subvert the traditional gen-

articulated within the respective communities and in relation to other social movements and political struggles in the region.

Our concerns are connected to Diana Taylor's question: "What can we do when apparently nothing can be done, and doing nothing is not an option?" (2020: 2) While there are no easy answers to this question, we center our attention on the contexts, experiences, and *Situated Knowledges* (Haraway 1988) of the region to show some of the political, cultural, or artistic action that is possible in these situations. Fundamentally, we can only approach and understand these questions from the context and the bodies – ergo, the lives – that are directly affected.

"The River Told Me", the Political Struggle of Berta and the COPINH in Honduras

The name of Berta Cáceres, leader of the indigenous Lenca people, resonates in the hearts of many in Central America and other parts of the world. Sadly, her cultural and political significance has become particularly meaningful since her murder in 2016, at the hands of hitmen hired by David Castillo, an official of Honduran Company Desarrollos Energéticos S.A. (COPINH 2022). A slogan (*consigna* in Spanish) better expresses how her seed of struggle and resistance has spread after the fact: "Berta did not die, she multiplied".

Besides raising her voice in defiance of injustices perpetrated against indigenous people in Honduras, Berta actively participated in the struggle for environmental protection through her work as co-founder and coordinator of COPINH (short for the Spanish acronym of the Council of Popular and Indigenous Organizations of Honduras)[3]. When speaking about Berta, it is impor-

---

der order, along with new visions of citizenship, justice – especially political and environmental – , and radical democracy. Moreover, our interest is not to label in which category of feminism we can fit the work of AMA and COPINH, but to explore how they build collective projects from their voices, identities, and actions, which confront the different systems of oppression and exploitation (capitalism, colonialism, and patriarchy) within their communities and beyond.

3 COPINH is a Lenca association founded in 1993. Through its articulations with other indigenous and popular groups inside and outside Honduran borders, it has a strong national impact in Honduras, although the territories of the Lenca communities are located in the southwestern part of the country. See: https://copinh.org/category/english-es/.

tant to underline the efforts that marked her and her family's lives, as an indigenous woman disconnected from the institutionalized political powers and academic circles in Honduras, but deeply involved in political and community organization through COPINH.

Through this organization, which describes itself as "indigenous and popular, anti-patriarchal, anti-imperialist, anti-neoliberal", (COPINH: n.d.)[4] Berta helped coordinate immense participation and mobilization of indigenous communities in Honduras, in direct response to the political and economic system that – still today – means the death of the traditions and ancestral ecosystems of the region. The first major achievement was the ratification of the Indigenous and Tribal Peoples Convention (no. 169) by the Honduran government in 1994, brought about by the pressure exerted by COPINH. This convention binds the governments to guarantee systematic action in order to respect the aspirations of indigenous peoples "to exercise control over their own institutions, ways of life, and economic development and to maintain and develop their identities, languages, and religions, within the framework of the states in which they live" (ILO: n.d.). On their part, COPINH combines constant reporting and complaints, popular education, and practical efforts as part of their permanent criticism of the ideas of democracy and development imposed by the Honduran state.

One of the fruits of a process of deep self-criticism within this organization is the recognition of the fundamental role of indigenous women, who actively participate with "massive presence in the streets and on many fronts of this struggle: in leadership, in political commissions, in international relations, in communication, in security aspects, in the self-defense of the neighborhoods" (Cáceres quoted by Korol 2018: 91). Undoubtedly, recognizing the anti-patriarchal struggle as one of the pillars of COPINH starts with community reflections in which indigenous women participate while putting their communities at the center. Berta said the following about this struggle:

> Patriarchy is not exclusive to the capitalist system, nor to one culture or another. I believe that we have to guarantee that in this process – which is a process to re-found [reinvent] even our very mindsets –, we begin to

---

4   All translations from Spanish into English are our own. All the quotes from COPINH n.d.; Korol 2018; Cáceres 2015a; Pita 2001; AMA 2018, 2022; Rodríguez Aguilera 2018; De Volo 2001; Hilgert/List 2018 and unpublished interviews were originally conducted in Spanish.

dismantle this idea that others have to decide over our bodies; and guarantee that we are the owners and have the right to the autonomy of our bodies. It is a political action, a political proposal (ibid: 105).

Berta's words are not only inspiring, but they always remain critical of patriarchal ways of thinking. This criticism translates, as she puts it, into a political proposal that questions patriarchy even beyond the colonial capitalist system. The work starts in our own bodies and in our communities, a fact that COPNIH put into action by organizing their collective resistance and articulating with other political struggles in the region. The formulation of policies based on the body as territory, on gender, and on the non-human as constitutive of their political commitment is another result of internal community reflections. Likewise, these policies are characteristic of other indigenous struggles in the Americas, albeit in different contexts[5]. Examples are the Zapatista organization in Mexico, the K'iche's peoples in Guatemala, the Aymara between Peru, Bolivia and Chile, or the Mesoamerican Women Territorial Leaders Coordinator (Coordinadora de Mujeres Líderes Territoriales de Mesoamérica, in Spanish). The active participation of women in indigenous organizations seems to respond to Berta's call: "Let's wake up! Let's wake up Humankind! There is no more time. Our consciences will be shaken by the fact that we are only contemplating self-destruction based on capitalist, racist, and patriarchal predation" (Cáceres 2015a)[6].

In the case of Honduras, after the *coup d'état* in 2009 that placed Juan Orlando Hernández in executive power, the government granted multiple concessions for large projects such as industrial sawmills and hydroelectric plants. State officials also began a campaign of criminalizing human rights defenders and environmental activists who opposed these concessions, which were

---

[5] Understandably, the way these social movements see themselves in relation to their bodies – individually and collectively – and to their territories and natural surroundings does not follow Western colonial traditions that see the human and non-human as different, even opposed entities. While this fundamental difference in paradigms is a topic that exceeds the scope of this article, we would like to underline that these challenges and criticisms are alive in the political struggles articulated in these movements.

[6] The entire acceptance speech with English subtitles can be found in: Cáceres, Berta (2015b): "Berta Caceres acceptance speech, 2015 Goldman Prize ceremony." 26 June 2022 (https://www.youtube.com/watch?v=AR1kwx8boms).

issued without consulting the communities that were going to be directly affected (Goldman Environmental Prize n.d.; Reyes/Yaya/Thissen 2015). In this context, the Lenca community achieved a significant victory by preventing the construction of the Agua Zarca dam on the Gualcarque River. As expressed by Berta, this waterway has great spiritual and symbolic value for this community: "We, the Lenca people, are ancestral custodians of the rivers, protected by the spirits of the young girls who teach us that giving our lives in multiple ways to defend the rivers is to give our lives for the good of humanity and this planet" (Cáceres 2015a).

The organized work of COPINH – and the specific struggle of Berta Cáceres – is situated in this context of abuses of institutionalized power in the Honduran state. The persecution of indigenous environmental activists through Honduran military forces and judicial institutions has been recorded in multiple reports by human rights organizations (Global Witness 2017), as it resulted in the assassination of several community leaders, including Berta Cáceres in March 2016. The reactions to Berta's murder have exposed a network of impunity, complicity, and corruption within the Honduran government (Lakhani 2020). Complaints by COPINH and other sister organizations resulted in the sentencing of David Castillo in June 2022 as the mastermind of Berta's murder, although legal efforts to dismantle the criminal network behind the case continue (COPINH 2022). Nonetheless, the lessons of hope and resistance in the face of a system of death, lessons that Berta Cáceres taught by the example of the life she led, are the seeds that continue to germinate in the region.

One of these seeds is the work of Berta Cáceres's own daughter, Laura Zúñiga Cáceres, who started coordinating COPINH after her mother's assassination, as well as the quest for justice she pursues together with her sister Berta, her brother Salvador, and the support of comrades. Berta's legacy is both intergenerational and intersectional, building collective resistance in the Americas as the clamor for justice unifies many sectors and movements: environmental, indigenous, feminists – especially decolonial (Curiel 2020). Her murder is one of many examples of the danger faced by people who defend their territory in Latin America, which, according to reports by the NGO Global Witness (2021), is the region with the most critical conditions for this activity in the world. Finally, Berta's multiple struggles and legacies are also reflected in art, murals, and music that honor her individual and collective memory. In these displays of love and solidarity, among multiple resistances, germinates the seed of shared struggles that bet on "societies capable of coexisting in a just and dignified manner and for life" (Cáceres 2015a).

Mothers of April: Constructing Memories and Politicizing Motherhood

In the contexts of military dictatorships, authoritarian states and their characteristic necropolitics, and forced migrations throughout the continent, it is possible to trace the struggles of different organizations of mothers, grandmothers, and relatives of murdered or disappeared persons. Possibly the best-known organizations in the Americas are the Associations of Mothers and Grandmothers of Plaza de Mayo, both created in 1977 during the period of Jorge Rafael Videla's military dictatorship in Argentina. Here, we approach the contemporary stories of Central American mothers, who represent a turning point in our region on how we understand the political dimension of motherhood, via political and embodied exercises of civil disobedience. In other words, through their struggles, they have reframed how mobilizing notions of "motherhood becomes the key to their entrance into the public sphere" (Pita 2001: 141) and, therefore, to the political struggle.

We will particularly focus on the case of AMA (April Mothers' Association) in Nicaragua, an organization that brings together the mothers and relatives – up to the 3rd degree of kinship – of people who were killed through repressions by the Nicaraguan state, in the course of massive, decentralized protests that began in Nicaragua in April 2018. The circumstantial demands that unleashed the protests, such as the lack of efficient government's response to a forest fire in the Indio Maíz Biological Reserve[7], or reforms to the national social security scheme, grew into larger demands, such as justice, democracy, and the creation of an economic and political model beyond extractivist practices (see Osorio Mercado/Cortez/Sánchez 2018). The intensification of the demands and the massive waves of protests were accompanied by waves of repression by police and paramilitary forces. The result was massive arrests, more than 355 people killed, thousands of reports of people injured, tortured, or sexually abused,

---

7   On April 9, the Nicaraguan government denied aid from the Costa Rican government under the pretext that it was able to manage the crisis with its own resources (see Astorga 2018). Nevertheless, the forest fire continued in the following days without sufficient equipment to control it. The reserve has also suffered the effects of extensive cattle ranching, land invasion and agribusiness, which is promoted or facilitated by the current government and directly affects indigenous communities in that region.

and more than 100,000 people forcibly migrating in the months directly following (Acción Penal et al 2021)[8]. As of February 2023, the state is holding 35 political prisoners (Presas y Presos Políticos Nicaragua 2023)[9].

As Emilia Y. and Tamara M. (both members of AMA) told us in an interview on 17 November 2021, faced with this situation, the mothers of the city of Estelí began to organize in April 2018 to denounce the murders of their children and family members in the media and in judicial spaces. Then, in May, they organized other types of protests: weekly sit-ins in one of the central public roads of the capital, in the Metrocentro roundabout. Even under constant police siege, the mothers congregated there for several weeks and little by little, the organization became stronger. Another germinal moment for this association occurred on Mother's Day that same year (30 May in Nicaragua), when the mothers called for what became known as "the mother of all marches." They called on people to join them in a massive demonstration of mourning for the children and family members killed so far by the state. The popular response was overwhelming. The state's response was also overwhelming, as the central demonstration in Managua culminated in a massacre, with hundreds of people injured and at least 19 killed (Acción Penal et al 2021).

In September of the same year, the April Mothers' Association (AMA) was formally founded, whose acronym in Spanish can also be read as the action form of the verb "love" (Yang Rappaccioli 2022). Starting from the name of the Association, AMA highlights a different circuit of affective and collective action in a hostile political context. In addition, being an association led by family members and mothers enables "the recognition [of their] power, to empower

---

8   Due to the context of political violence and state persecution in the country, there are major difficulties in accessing verifiable information from public state institutions, which in turn deny all these accusations. We take the figures mentioned in this essay from the report presented in 2021 by fifteen Nicaraguan human rights organizations, which systematically condensed the reports documented by national (ANPDH, CENIDH) and international organizations (Office of the United Nations High Commissioner for Human Rights, the IACHR of the OAS through MESENI and the GIEI – which also took on the independent Ayotzinapa case investigations in Mexico –, Amnesty International, Human Rights Watch).

9   Up until February 9th, the number exceeded 245, on which date 222 of those political prisoners were exiled and stripped of their Nicaraguan citizenship through a law reform passed on the same date that classified them as "traitors to the homeland" (Confidencial 2023). See also the monthly report of political prisoners: https://presasypresospoliticosnicaragua.org/lista-mensual-de-personas-presas-politicos/

themselves through the pain, to empower in having an organization in the pursuit of justice and their participation as women" (Tamara M., Personal Communication, 11 November 2021).

It is important to stress that different uses or notions of motherhood were also mobilized within the Nicaraguan political conjuncture. As Hilgert/List (2018) explains, on the one hand, there are strategies to maternalize the political (maternalizar lo político) and strategies to politicize motherhood (politización de la maternidad). The first strategy is used by Vice President Rosario Murillo, as she constructs a discourse in which the state is framed as a family-nation, with Daniel Ortega as the father-president, Murillo as the mother-mediator, and the citizens as the children. In this perspective, any dissident citizenship threatens the peace of the family-nation. Thus, the strategy to maternalize the political is essential "to discredit the opposing political positions, to denigrate the social movements that denounce the current status of this family-nation" (17). Moreover, from this image of the mother-mediator, "peace and reconciliation are pursued, but without considering the issue of social justice" (ibid: 16).

Regarding the second strategy, AMA's activism produces "a political consciousness that enables motherhood to serve as an articulating axis, thus allowing it to enter into the game of hegemony" (ibid: 17). Moreover, this political consciousness manages to articulate the relationship between social movements, justice, and the ethics of love (see hooks 2001: xix) through different strategies. First, by mothers making themselves present and mourning in the public space, where they assert the absence and loss of lives that go unrecognized (see Butler 2016) by the Nicaraguan state. In this way, they challenge the discourse of the family-nation, thus producing a possible emancipatory potential. And second, they make their affective and political practices visible also in their discourses, like in their first public manifesto, where they declare the four pillars of their organization as being: "truth, justice, integral reparation, and the construction of memory" (AMA 2018).

Let us think for a moment about the last pillar, since other mothers' organizations such as the "Committee of Mothers of Heroes and Martyrs" already existed in Nicaragua in the 1980s. However, memory exercises in the country have not only been scarce, but also mostly co-opted and institutionalized by the state. This has created counterproductive effects, as it leads to processes of marginalization of others who do not participate in line with the state's intentions, creating "multiply wounded societies" (Cabrera n.d.: 8). In the case of the 1980s Committee mentioned before, the memories of their relatives were constructed following the images of "heroes and martyrs" of the 1979 Sandinista revolution[10]. This resulted in frames of memories and devices of the gaze in which the only way to remember, name, and mourn lost lives is through heroic death, which in turn is reinforced by the party structures of the FSLN (Sandinista National Liberation Front) and its slogan "Patria libre o morir" (roughly translated to "Free Homeland or Death").

To counterbalance these discourses and the re-victimization operated from the State, the project: "AMA y no olvida: Museo contra la Impunidad" (LOVE and do not forget: Museum against Impunity) was created. This museum follows a participatory, communitarian and transmedia approach, where several actors converge: the members of AMA as central subjects of the process, the Nicaraguan Center for Human Rights (CENIDH), the Academy of Sciences of Nicaragua (ACN), and other people who are independently committed to the struggle of AMA[11]. As project members Tamara and Emilia told us, the museum has sought to provide multiple spaces: a) one of recognition among family members and their stories; b) one of collective mourning, which was denied by the Nicaraguan state by prohibiting masses and demonstrations, disrupting funerals and burials, etc.; and c) one of healing and creation of memories, avoiding discourses of sacrifice and martyrdom to replace them with others that appeal to integral justice for the murder of their relatives.

These exercises of collective memories and actions transcend the museum project itself, which is only one of several activities within the context of the AMA project. Although the main activities are carried out by the mothers, the same dialogue spaces have allowed fathers and young people (especially young

---

10 Although this essay does not conduct an extensive analysis of maternal activism in Nicaragua, it is important to understand the historical and structural context faced by AMA. Thus, as Yang Rappaccioli (2022: 88) explains, quoting De Volo (2001: xvii), the Committee of Mothers of Heroes and Martyrs of Matagalpa in the 1980s functioned as auxiliaries of the Sandinista women's organization, which meant that they had little autonomy to construct their agendas and collective identity. For further analysis, one could ask what other maternal activism and/or notions of motherhood have been historically mobilized in Nicaragua and what possible (dis)connections exist between them. For example, we think of the Committee of Mothers during and after the revolution, as well as mothers of members of the counterrevolution or anti-Sandinistas, and more recently, mothers of political prisoners and mothers and relatives who seek justice without necessarily being formally collectivized, among others.

11 The online museum can be found in the following link: https://www.museodelamemorianicaragua.org/en/home/.

men) to open up about their emotions. In doing so, they are questioning their own masculinities or gender roles, through writing workshops, embroidery, exchanges between family members, or the production of the podcast "Barricadas de la memoria" ("Barricades of Memory")[12]. AMA has also been able to forge ties with other organizations at the regional level, such as, among others, the Mesoamerican women defenders, the Mothers of Plaza de Mayo, the Parents of Ayotzinapa Students, the Casa de la Memoria in Guatemala[13].

Five years after the murders of their loved ones, AMA's struggle continued both through activism from exile and within the country. In the manifesto of 2022, they called for that day to be remembered as a day of national mourning, not a celebration, keeping up their claim: "Ni perdón, ni olvido, ni silencio" [Neither forgiveness, nor forgetting, nor silence] (AMA 2022)[14]. Referring to the organization's strategic use and narratives of motherhood, the final words of the manifesto stand out, highlighting the political action that has been conducted over the years: "Mothers do not give up, they demand justice" (ibid.).

Final Reflections

As we have seen, the described participants in the struggles of women, communities, and bodies-territories do not always declare themselves as feminists. However, they do state their positions as political subjects that seek to articulate resistance to different systems of oppression and exploitation that mark their realities. These systems are sustained by the institutions of the states and their necropolitics, neo-extractivism, and patriarchal practices which has caused the death of many Nicaraguans and indigenous women leaders such as Berta Cáceres. In this sense, Rodríguez Aguilera points out that, although there are feminisms that are communitarian, indigenous, Black, and popular, among others, "it is also important to name those women's struggles in Abya Yala[15], women who from daily and life experience have resisted and

---

12 The Podcast "Barricadas de la memoria" can be found in following link: https://open.spotify.com/show/4Mzova7xlYRxUf76SfyzRg.
13 See website of Casa de la Memoria: https://casadelamemoria.org.gt/.
14 The Mothers and Grandmothers of the Plaza de Mayo used the phrase "Ni olvido, ni perdón" [Neither forgetting, nor forgiveness]. In the case of AMA, they adapted it.
15 Abya Yala is a word of the Kuna/Guna people and refers to one of the ancestral names of the continent, i.e. it emerged in the pre-colonization period. It has been recovered as part of the indigenous struggles for autonomy and self-determination, so it also

continue to resist various forms of violence, without necessarily calling themselves feminists, but simply women who have fought and are still fighting for a dignified life" (2008: 90). Thus, we suggest the struggles presented in this essay should be analyzed in the light of their different intersections, senses of belonging, experiences, bodies, and the voices that they construct daily and collectively.

Mara Viveros Vigoya (2023, in this volume), taking up Angela Davis and bell hooks, speaks of the re-politicization of intersectionality, not only as common identities or oppressions, but also as the articulation of the different struggles, thus building new forms of solidarity. We claim that the described Central American struggles manage to simultaneously articulate both the intersectionality of identities, where collective bodies (of indigenous women, feminists, anti-patriarchal activists, mothers, territorial and affective communities, etc.) converge, and second, the building of alliances with other political struggles, such as the different Central American feminist movements, the EZLN in Chiapas (Mexico), the Mesoamerican Defenders, the Mothers and Grandmothers of Plaza de Mayo, the Parents of Ayotzinapa Students, La Casa Memoria in Guatemala, among others.

Finally, we come back to the question posed by Diana Taylor, on what to do when it *seems* that nothing is possible. We answer it in the same way as Yang Rappaccioli, who asked: "What can we do with this pain? We can collectivize the pain, the love, the hope, and the longing for justice" (2019). This collectivization is what we have seen in the work and political practices of AMA and COPINH, the two exemplary cases reconstructed in this essay.

References

Abate, Marcello/Rosales, Jazmin (2019): Mapeo de grupos y organizaciones indígenas del Occidente de Honduras, Honduras: USAID.

Acción Penal et al. (2021): "Informe de la verdad 'dictadura y represión en Nicaragua: Lucha contra la impunidad'", November 5, 2021 (https://nicaragualucha.org/wp-content/uploads/2021/11/Informe-de-la-Verdad__Dictadura-y-Represion-en-Nicaragua.pdf).

---

works as a way to make visible an anti-colonial political position (See Gallardo 2015: 23; Woons 2014: 15).

AMA (2018): "Manifiesto por la verdad, la justicia y la reparación integral", July 4, 2023 (https://www.facebook.com/media/set/?set=a.256178715254410&type=3).

AMA (2022): "AMA, a 4 Años de la masacre del 30 de mayo de 2018", May 30, 2022 (https://twitter.com/MadresDeAbril/status/1531295967101833217).

Astorga, Lucía (2018): "Nicaragua devolvió a 40 bomberos costarricenses que iban a brindar ayuda para atender el incendio forestal." In: La Nación, June 15, 2022 (https://www.nacion.com/elpais/gobierno/nicaragua-devolvio-a-40-bomberos-costarricenses/BPLXU6UD2NB7BDKPBJTA3R2KL4/story/).

Butler, Judith (2016): Frames of War: When Is Life Grievable?, London and New York: Verso.

Cabrera, Martha (n.d.): "Living and Surviving in a Multiply Wounded Country." In: Medico International, November 5, 2021 (https://www.medico.de/download/report26/ps_cabrera_en.pdf).

Cáceres, Berta (2015a): "Discurso de Berta Cáceres en el Opera House, San Francisco California al recibir el premio ambiental Goldman, el 20 de abril, 2015." In: COPINH, October 20, 2021 (https://copinh.org/2015/04/discurso-de-berta-caceres-en-el-opera-house-san-francisco-california-al-recibir-el-premio-ambiental-goldman-el-20-de-abril-2015/).

Cáceres, Berta (2015b): "Berta Cáceres Acceptance Speech, 2015 Goldman Prize Ceremony", June 26, 2022 (https://www.youtube.com/watch?v=AR1kwx8b oms).

Confidencial (2023): "Despojan de nacionalidad nicaragüense a presos políticos desterrados", February 11, 2023 (https://confidencial.digital/politica/despojan-de-nacionalidad-nicaraguense-a-presos-politicos-desterrados/).

COPINH (n.d.): "¿Quiénes somos?", October 20, 2021 (https://copinh.org/quienes-somos/).

COPINH (2022): "Foro internacional: la sentencia de David Castillo debe ser un paso más hacia la justicia para Berta Cáceres", July 4, 2023 (https://copinh.org/2022/06/foro-internacional-la-sentencia-de-david-castillo-debe-ser-un-paso-mas-hacia-la-justicia-para-berta-caceres/).

Curiel, Ochy (2020): "Berta Cáceres y el feminismo decolonial." In: Lasa Forum, 50/4, pp. 64–70.

De Volo, Lorraine Bayard (2001): Mothers of Heroes and Martyrs: Gender Identity Politics in Nicaragua, 1979–1999, Baltimore: John Hopkins University Press.

Gargallo, Francisca (2014): Feminismos desde Abya Yala. Ideas y proposiciones de las mujeres de 607 pueblos en nuestra América, Mexico City: Corte y Confección, p. 23.

Global Witness (2017): "Honduras: The Deadliest Country in the World for Environmental Activism", November 21, 2021 (https://www.globalwitness.org/en/campaigns/environmental-activists/honduras-deadliest-country-world-environmental-activism/).

Global Witness (2021): "Last Line of Defence", November 21, 2021 (https://www.globalwitness.org/en/campaigns/environmental-activists/last-line-defence/).

Goldman Environmental Prize (n.d.): "2015 Goldman Environmental Prize Winner – Berta Cáceres", October 20, 2021 (https://www.goldmanprize.org/recipient/berta-caceres/).

Haraway, Donna (1988): "Situated Knowledges: The Science Question in Feminism and the Privilege of Partial Perspective." In: Feminist Studies 14/3, pp. 575–99.

Hilgert, Bradley/List, Jared (2018): "Desposición, insurgencia y ciudadanía: maternidades en disputa. Rosario Murillo y la Asociación Madre de Abril en Nicaragua, 2018." In: Istmo. Revista virtual de estudios literarios y culturales centroamericanos 37, pp. 6–29.

hooks, bell (2001): All about Love: New Visions, New York: Harper Perennial.

ILO (n.d.): "C169 – Indigenous and Tribal Peoples Convention, 1989 (No. 169)", January 21, 2021 (https://www.ilo.org/dyn/normlex/en/f?p=NORMLEXPUB:12100:0::NO::P12100_INSTRUMENT_ID,P12100_LANG_CODE:312314,en).

Korol, Claudia (2018): Las revoluciones de Berta, Buenos Aires: América libre.

Lakhani, Nina (2020): Who Killed Berta Cáceres? Dams, Death Squads, and an Indigenous Defender's Battle for the Planet, London and Brooklyn: Verso.

Osorio Mercado, Hloreley/Cortez, Arnín/Sánchez, Mario (2018): "Coyuntura crítica en Nicaragua: Orígenes estructurales y posibles giros de cambio." In: Aleksander Aguiliar Antunes/Esteban de Gori/Carmen Elena Villacorta (eds.), Nicaragua en crisis: Entre la revolución y la sublevación, Buenos Aires: Sans Soleil Ediciones Argentina, pp. 211–253.

Pita, María Victoria (2001): "La construcción de la maternidad como lugar político en las demandas de justicia. Familiares de víctimas de terrorismo de estado y de la violencia institucional en Argentina." In: Arenal. Revista de Historia de Las Mujeres 8/1, pp. 127–154.

Presas y presos políticos de Nicaragua (2023): "Segunda actualización", February 10, 2023 (https://twitter.com/MPresasPresosNi/status/1624158940454871040).

Presas y presos políticos de Nicaragua (2023): "Lista mensual de personas presas políticas", July 4, 2023 (https://presasypresospoliticosnicaragua.org/lista-mensual-de-personas-presas-politicos/).

Reyes, Jimena/Yaya, Natalia/Thissen, Jose Carlos (eds.) (2015): Criminalización de los defensores de derechos humanos en el contexto de proyectos industriales: un fenómeno regional en América Latina, January 30, 2023 (https://www.omct.org/files/2016/02/23630/criminalisationobsangocto2015bassdef.pdf).

Rodríguez Aguilera, Meztli Yoalli (2018): "Diálogos hemisféricos entre feminismos del norte y sur: Genealogías de feminismos críticos latinoamericanos." In: Realidad: Revista de Ciencias Sociales y Humanidades 151, pp. 89–107.

Taylor, Diana (2020): ¡Presente!: The Politics of Presence, Durham and London: Duke University Press.

Viveros Vigoya, Mara (2024): "From the Center to the Margins, (Re) Politicizing Intersectionality." In: Lívia De Souza Lima/Edith Otero Quezada/Julia Roth (eds.), Feminisms in Movement: Theories and Practices from the Americas, Bielefeld: transcript (see this volume).

Woons, Marc (2014): "Introduction: On the Meaning of Restoring Indigenous Self-Determination." In: Marc Woons (ed.), Restoring Indigenous Self-Determination: Theoretical and Practical Approaches, Bristol: E-International Relations, p. 15.

Yang Rappaccioli, Emilia (2019): "About the Museum." In: AMA y no olvida. Museo de la memoria contra la impunidad", November 5, 2021 (https://www.museodelamemorianicaragua.org/en/about-the-museum/).

Yang Rappaccioli, Emilia (2022): "AMA y No Olvida Collectivizing Memory Against Impunity: Transmedia Memory Practices, Modular Visibility, and Activist Participatory Design in Nicaragua." In: International Journal of Communication 16, pp. 309–330.

Yang Rappaccioli, Emilia (2022): "Mujeres, madres y feministas en Nicaragua: resistiendo a través de la construcción de la memoria y la lucha contra la impunidad." In: Velvet Romero García/Aracelí Calderón Cisneros/Ana Gabriela Rincón Rubio (eds.), Feminismos, memoria y resistencia en América Latina, Tuxtla Gutiérrez: Universidad de Ciencias y Artes de Chiapas, pp. 81–109.

Writing Western Nicaragua's LGBTQ+ History
Tiangues, Indigeneity, and Survivance

Victoria González-Rivera

Introduction

Western Nicaragua's LGBTQ+ history is rarely portrayed as Indigenous history. But I argue it is, in significant ways, a history of Indigenous *survivance*, revealing important cultural continuities even in a context like that of Nicaragua's Pacific Coast, where a triumphant nationalist ideology of racial mixing (*mestizaje*) is so hegemonic that very few people are considered Indigenous anymore.[1] Indigenous survivance is the term coined by Anishinaabe scholar Gerald Vizenor to refer to "the union of active [Indigenous] survival and resistance to cultural dominance" (2009: 24).

In this chapter, I argue that anti-Indigenous racism has made it very difficult to document western Nicaragua's history of sexual diversity.[2] And vice-versa, the erasure of western Nicaragua's LGBTQ+ history has facilitated a narrative where Indigenous peoples on the Pacific coast have been homogenized, objectified, dehumanized, compared to animals, and sometimes even declared extinct. In other words, homophobia and transphobia have made it difficult to document fully and accurately Nicaragua's Indigenous history, while racism

---

1 This chapter does not discuss the central or Caribbean regions of Nicaragua. The traditions I discuss are specific to the Pacific region. For a longer discussion on western Nicaragua's LGBTQ+ history, see my co-authored book with Karen Kampwirth (González-Rivera/Kampwirth 2021): Diversidad Sexual en el Pacífico y Centro de Nicaragua. 500 Años de Historia, San Diego: no press.

2 I use the terms LGBTQ+ and sexual diversity interchangeably since they are also used interchangeably in Nicaragua and by Nicaraguans in the diaspora. These umbrella terms include individuals who today identify as non-binary, gender fluid, gender nonconforming, transgender, and gender queer. Among the latter, the term most commonly used in contemporary Nicaragua is transgender (transgénero).

has made it hard to even *see* LGBTQ+ individuals (many of whom were Indigenous) in Nicaragua's past. When Nicaraguan history is seen through the lens of an exultant and totalizing *mestizaje*, we miss Indigenous (and Afro Nicaraguan) history, and we miss Nicaragua's LGBTQ+ history.

Partial and/or inaccurate histories became the standard version of Nicaragua's past and are still commonplace. These narratives are generally considered victimless and harmless by their authors and are part of an elaborate ecosystem that enables *mestizaje* to be continuously normalized as an inevitable *fait accompli*, and for *mestizos* to be considered superior to Nicaraguans who are not of European ancestry. In the following pages, I discuss and disrupt some of those hegemonic narratives, focusing particularly on the writings of three of Nicaragua's most well-known authors: Pablo Antonio Cuadra's essays in *The Nicaraguan (El nicaragüense)* ([1967] 1987), José Coronel Urtecho's *Reflections on the History of Nicaragua (Reflexiones sobre la historia de Nicaragua)* (published originally in 1962 and 1967), and Humberto Belli's overview of Nicaraguan history *Searching for the Promised Land. History of Nicaragua 1492–2019 (Buscando la tierra prometida. Historia de Nicaragua 1492–2019)* (2019).

My discussion builds on earlier arguments I made in *Diversidad Sexual en el Pacífico y Centro de Nicaragua* (González-Rivera/Kampwirth 2021), where I established that some contemporary communities of working-class western Nicaraguan market women who today self-identify as trans have Indigenous precolonial origins. Indeed, I argue that the sale of food and other items in local precolonial Indigenous open-air markets called *tiangues* was a role taken on by cis market women *as well as* individuals who today might identify as trans women, given the link that was made between femininity and local commerce among the Indigenous people in the region *even after* the Spanish conquest in 1492 and Nicaragua's independence from Spain in 1821. Moreover, I argue that throughout the colonial period and the first century after independence, western Nicaraguan elites associated sexual diversity (a term which includes gender diversity, gender non-conformity, gender dissidence, and gender fluidity) with local Indigeneity, until that association was replaced in their imaginary by a link between sexual diversity, first wave feminism, and foreign intervention in the 1920s, during the U.S. military occupation. This history helps explain why discrimination against LGBTQ+ populations in contemporary western Nicaragua is not only homophobic and transphobic, but also profoundly racist, sexist, and classist. What has not been fully explored until now is the role that western Nicaraguan intellectuals have played in crafting the narratives that promote (or allow for) disparaging and even zoomorphic tropes about *all* open-air market women (cis and trans) in elite efforts to foster and uphold a Catholic *mestizo* nationalism.

The Nicaraguan political theorist Juliet Hooker (2005) has documented how the factually incorrect belief that Nicaragua is a *mestizo* nation (a culturally and racially mixed nation of only Indigenous and European ancestry) has negatively impacted non-*mestizo* populations, particularly on Nicaragua's Caribbean coast. The U.S.-American historian Jeffrey L. Gould (1998), among other scholars, has also contributed to dismantling Nicaragua's "myth of *mestizaje*" by documenting the ongoing struggles of Indigenous peoples in western and central Nicaragua. My work builds on theirs to argue for an LGBTQ+ history of western Nicaragua that centers Indigenous survivance, particularly in relation to long-standing communities of trans market women.

The work of Pablo Antonio Cuadra (1912–2002) and José Coronel Urtecho (1906–1994) exemplified the racism of the *vanguardista* literary/ideological movement of the early 20th century and to a great extent the racism of almost their entire generation of Nicaraguan writers. It also established the economic and cultural importance of the Indigenous open-air markets before and after the Spanish conquest of Nicaragua's Pacific coast. Moreover, Cuadra's essay "The market woman" ("*La vivandera*") found in his collection of essays titled *The Nicaraguan*, and Coronel Urtecho's writing on "The tiangue economy" ("*La economía tiánguica*)", published in *Reflections*, both emphasized the crucial role of Indigenous women in the *tiangues*, a role I argue – in *Diversidad Sexual* (González-Rivera/Kampwirth 2021) – is fundamental to understanding western Nicaragua's LGBTQ+ history.

Indeed, I have argued (González-Rivera/Kampwirth 2021) that some contemporary communities of market women with members who today might identify as trans women have historical antecedents in the pre-conquest period. Moreover, since most Indigenous women before the 1520s were expected to work in the local *tiangues*, and because local men were not allowed to even enter the *tiangues*, a strong relationship between local commerce and femininity developed in that region of Nicaragua. This helps explain the vast number of women (cis and trans) engaged in local commerce in and around open-air markets today on Nicaragua's Pacific coast. It also helps explain the *relative* tolerance and acceptance expressed towards trans women by cis Nicaraguans today in those spaces. Although *tiangues* after the conquest had to incorporate men and people of all racial backgrounds, Indigenous women continued to work in the *tiangues* and these markets remained Indigenous (and working-class) spaces in the national imaginary. I contend that this sheds light on why the discrimination against trans women **that does exist** in Nicaragua today is deeply sexist, classist, and anti-Indigenous, and not only homophobic and transphobic.

Mestizaje and Vanguardismo

Mestizaje is the term used in those areas of Latin America colonized by the Spanish to describe the process by which a nation or a region becomes racially "mixed". It refers to the "mixing" (whether "biological" or cultural) of Indigenous peoples and Europeans, specifically the Spanish. In the case of many Latin American countries, nation-building endeavors in the nineteenth century post-independence or "modern" period often had *mestizaje* at its core. Elites considered *mestizos* superior to all other non-Europeans due to their proximity to whiteness. The ideology of *mestizaje* however, was frequently aspirational. And it has always necessitated the disappearance of Indigenous peoples *as such*. Moreover, the concept only works if the European enslavement of millions of peoples from Africa is ignored. In other words, *mestizaje* is not a neutral or descriptive term, it is about who holds and retains power. As Juliet Hooker has noted, "in Nicaragua official nationalisms have legitimated exclusive *mestizo* political power through the erasure of Blacks and Indians as citizens" (2005:18).

In the twentieth century, there were numerous individuals of *mestizo* backgrounds throughout the Americas who celebrated their own *mestizaje* and that of their followers to counter anti-miscegenation and racial purity ideologies. They were specifically contesting those ideologies that elevated the racial background of Protestant Europeans in the United States over those of mixed-race peoples everywhere. In the U.S., for instance, *mestizaje* became central to the development of the Chicano Movement of the 1960s and 1970s. Another important example is the movement led by Augusto Cesar Sandino (1895–1934) against the U.S. Marine occupation of Nicaragua in the 1920s. Sandino referred frequently to the Indo Hispanic race in opposition to U.S. Anglo-imperialism in Latin America. These celebratory versions of *mestizaje* however, were problematic because they tended to center and privilege *mestizos* at the expense of their contemporaries who were Indigenous and/or of African ancestry (cf. Hooker 2005; Gould 1998; Blandón 2003).

Juliet Hooker (2005) has documented what she notes are the three main strains of official *mestizo* nationalist ideologies in Nicaragua: "*vanguardismo*, Sandinismo[3], and [...] '*mestizo* multiculturalism,' [which] emerged in the 1930s, 1960s, and 1990s respectively in Nicaragua" (ibid: 15). In this chapter I focus exclusively on the *mestizo* nationalist ideology of the *vanguardistas*, as expressed in the writings of Pablo Antonio Cuadra and José Coronel Urtecho, two of the most important members of this intellectual and ideological movement.

The importance of the *vanguardistas* cannot be overstated. They were prominent in their day and their impact on Nicaraguan politics and culture can still be felt today. What is most relevant to this discussion is that "[f]or the *vanguardistas* the colonial era was [...] not a time of conquest and subjugation of the Indigenous population by their Spanish conquerors; it was an idyllic era of peace and harmonious coexistence, where everyone knew and followed their 'natural' place in the social and political order" (ibid: 25). This false representation of the past, while largely debunked by the 1979 leftist Sandinista revolution and *their* version of *mestizo* nationalism (which acknowledged Indigenous resistance against the Spanish conquest but still embraced the myth of complete and ineludible *mestizaje*), made it difficult to locate western Nicaragua's LGBTQ+ history and find any historical LGBTQ+ continuities from Nicaragua's pre-colonial period.

According to Hooker, "harmonious mestizaje, Indigenous passivity, and colonial peace [...] were central elements of *vanguardismo*" (ibid: 26). Coronel Urtecho **did** see Indigenous peoples during the colonial period as agents, but of *mestizaje*, which led him to view the colonial *tiangue* (an Indigenous institution) as the epicenter of *mestizaje* on the Pacific coast of Nicaragua:

> It was totally at the service of the people, contributing to unify its diverse racial and cultural elements in one organic everything with deep roots in Nicaraguan soil, and due to that, had an unmistakable Nicaraguan seal [...] Although of Indigenous origin, more than Spanish, the tiangue economy of the colonial city was eminently mestiza and mestizante [actively promoting mestizaje]. The same, of course, must be said regarding the life that developed around the tiangue [...] That is where, it can be affirmed, the Indians of Nicaragua became Nicaraguans [...] and where they themselves

---

3   Sandinismo is a political movement and ideology that arose in the 1960s in opposition to the U.S.-supported right-wing Somoza dictatorship in Nicaragua. It built on the legacy of the anti-imperialist Augusto Cesar Sandino.

> Nicaraguanized, so to speak, criollos [Spaniards born in the Americas] and mestizos of different varieties.
> At the same time [...] they [Indigenous peoples] were not completely absorbed by racial mestizaje... (Coronel Urtecho 2001:131-133).[4]

In these writings, Coronel Urtecho (2001) fetishized *mestizaje* as an active process of *becoming* (non-Indigenous) Nicaraguan. And in the process of becoming *mestizo*-Nicaraguans, Indigenous peoples stopped being Indigenous but did not necessarily become **racial** *mestizos*: "The *tiangue* became a communal manifestation of daily life, of the popular culture and of the colonial economy. The [cultural] *mestizaje* that came out of there or which was circulating there, was more important than the racial one, since it was nothing less than the *mestizaje* of life" (ibid: 135).

While Coronel Urtecho idealized the *tiangue* as the center of colonial economic and cultural life on Nicaragua's Pacific coast, he ignored the punitive regulations that sought to curtail Indigenous women's economic participation in the *tiangues* in the post-independence modernizing period, some of which I have documented in my earlier work (González-Rivera/Kampwirth 2021). Moreover, Coronel Urtecho failed to address the impact that colonialism had on women's livelihood in the *tiangues* after the conquest, reducing a multilayered and complex set of experiences to one that simply brought people together towards one inescapable and desirable end: *mestizaje* and "Nicaraguanization." In this vein, Coronel Urtecho wrote:

> The *tiangue* signified, in this sense, a synthesis of the countryside and the city. It was also a point of intersection between Indians, Blacks, and Spaniards *(intersección del indio, el negro y el español)*. That is where the following would meet: the Indian market women, the woman with the *batea* [selling items from a wooden tray], the woman who owned a small store, the woman servant, the woman who did not work outside the home *(ama de casa)*, the woman beggar, the male merchant, the businessman, the male beggar [...] the soldier [...] the male servant [...] the male laborer, the craftsman, the male settler, the male landowner, the clergyman, and the government official" (Coronel Urtecho 2001: 135).

---

4   All translations from Spanish into English are my own. All the quotes from Cuadra, Coronel Urtecho, and Belli were originally in Spanish.

Not surprisingly, trans women and others who did not uphold or embrace Spanish colonial gender norms were not mentioned on this list, given the heteronormative nature of *vanguardista* texts.

Unlike Coronel Urtecho, Pablo Antonio Cuadra choose to write not about the *tiangue*, but about "the market woman":

> As far as I know no one has studied that ancestral inheritance – that thread in the fabric of our history – that comes to us from the pre-Hispanic Nahua: the market woman [...] The percentage of women in small businesses is still immense [...] [as is their presence] in Nicaragua's markets [...] The history of women engaged in commerce (*la mujer comerciante*) has – as I have stated – yet to be written. José Coronel Urtecho, in his "Reflections on the History of Nicaraguan" surprises us by demonstrating the importance of the *tiangue* or market – with Indigenous roots – in the social, economic, and even cultural formation of our people (*de nuestro pueblo*). And the *tiangue* is a feminine product (*obra femenina*). Just as the small store in someone's home, selling[5], the market, and the popular economy also are feminine (*Como femenina es la pulpería, la venta, el mercado y la economía popular*) (Cuadra 1987 [1967]:116-118).

Cuadra (1987 [1967]) even called the Indigenous tradition of women market vendors a "strange [Indigenous] feminist legislation" and ultimately a mystery he could not decipher: "Why did this merchant people have this strange feminist legislation in their trade? It is a mystery, that custom has always been a mystery to me" (ibid: 116–117). Cuadra then went on to objectify market women in a story he told, comparing them unfavorably to *mestiza* women:

> She was a stout woman, with a powerful back, strong arms and legs and that wide and resistant neck produced by the exercise of carrying [a basket with products to sell] on the head; many times I have seen that feminine architecture in our people – a body where work has defeated her sex, a short body like the Church of Subtiava, Indian temple, a sexless body (not like the Church of Xalteva which shoots up, with her crinoline which is the *mestiza* body swaying her "turris aburnea" [ivory tower]), a businesswoman's body – (ibid: 115).

---

5 I have translated the word "venta" as "selling" but there are other potential translations such as "sales" and "store".

Cuadra continued to portray Indigenous market women as admirable but also frightening:

> The market woman, the businesswoman, the woman owner of a small store in her home [...] that entire hidden cult of marketing – to be feared and so thorough – where the most implacable usury is often practiced – the almost cannibalistic usury of the widows and the women without husbands (ibid: 115–116).

To describe market women's lending practices as "almost cannibalistic" is to revive a colonial lens in order to make Indigenous women legible to the cultural heirs of the Spanish conquest. To assign this characteristic to women without male partners is particularly misogynistic and heteronormative. It is also disingenuous, given the impact that the conquest and colonization themselves (as well as post-independence economic and social policies) had on disrupting heterosexual Indigenous families.

Cuadra went a step further in describing his supposed encounter with an Indigenous market vendor in the *tiangue*, comparing her to an animal who transported him to Nicaragua's Indigenous past:

> I went back five or six centuries, and I felt how that market woman was there bringing in her gestures, in her commercial acumen, in her insightful countenance, a potent and ancient tradition, a relic that I was losing at the bottom of time or at the bottom of her vigilant and almost aggressive eyes like those of a bird of prey (ibid: 116).

Cuadra's descriptions of Indigenous women who were his contemporaries demonstrated the triumphant *mestizo* logic of twentieth century western Nicaragua. The words "defeated," "sexless," "cannibalistic," "bird of prey," "hidden cult," and "to be feared" used to describe Indigenous market women prevented the presumably *mestizo* reader from recognizing themselves in her. In fact, at the end of his short essay, Cuadra juxtaposed his wife (presumably with a body that "shoots up," "a mestiza body swaying her ivory tower"), with the Indigenous market woman to point out that the latter supposedly swindled him by charging him a bit more than usual for a handful of fruit (ibid: 118). While this final juxtaposition was necessary for Cuadra to make his final point – that he now understood why men were not allowed to enter pre-colonial *tiangues* – it also underscored a point that is rarely mentioned in histories of Nicaragua: the complicity (and sometimes the full participation) of many *mestiza* women in the formation and propagation of racist elite ideologies.

Indigenous market women and their labor in *tiangues* on the Pacific coast was a central theme in the history of Nicaragua as told by José Coronel Urtecho and Pablo Antonio Cuadra in their search for the essence of what made someone "Nicaraguan"[6]. But theirs was an incomplete and distorted version of the past, and as such it could not account for the full diversity of market women.

More Recent Histories of Nicaragua

In 2019, Humberto Belli (1945-), the Catholic Minister of Education under Violeta Barrios de Chamorro, Nicaragua's first woman president (in power from 1990 to 1996), published a history of Nicaragua titled *Searching for the Promised Land. History of Nicaragua 1492–2019*. Belli's book, published before he fled from Daniel Ortega's government and went into exile in 2021, was highly influenced by the writings of José Coronel Urtecho and Pablo Antonio Cuadra. Works such as Belli's are important to analyze because they allow us to understand how racism, classism, and sexism (and not only homophobia and transphobia) have prevented a full account of Nicaragua's LGBTQ+ history from being told.

Like the *vanguardistas*, Belli deemphasized conflict in the conquest and colonization of Nicaragua. On this subject, he wrote:

> Authors like [the Sandinista] Jaime Wheelock and Francisco Barbosa Miranda have tried to emphasize the magnitude of Indigenous resistance, more due to the ideological imperative to present history as conflict between oppressors and oppressed than due to strong evidence. The instances of documented Indigenous rebellions are few (Belli 2019: 45).

Belli, a conservative, acknowledged that *vanguardistas* such as Coronel Urtecho did "exaggerate and simplify certain characteristics" and that they put forth "literary and non-scientific" descriptions. Nonetheless, Belli contended that the Nicaraguan culture that grew out of the colonial period was "morally opaque, with a propensity towards lying" (ibid: 72).

---

6   Hooker addresses the *vanguardista* search for "the essence of Nicaraguan-ness" in her work (2005: 21).

Specifically with regards to Indigenous peoples and *mestizaje* on the Pacific coast, Belli wrote:

> The Indian population was not only shrinking in proportion to the *mestizos*, but in its own racial identity. Their cultural inferiority complexes caused many to assimilate, without being *mestizos*, into the *mestizo* population. This was facilitated by the physical similarity between them and *mestizos*. By the beginning of the 19th century, the Pacific coast of Nicaragua was essentially Hispanicized. The still significant Indigenous remnants would rapidly lose their original language and clothing, making it difficult to differentiate between the two groups (ibid: 93).

Like the *vanguardistas*, Belli assumed his readers would identify with the colonial authorities who could not differentiate among the masses of *mestizos* and Indigenous peoples, colonizers who only saw profound deficits in Indigenous peoples and cultures. It makes sense that Belli's book is not only racist, sexist, and classist, but also heteronormative and homophobic.

Conclusion

When the history of western Nicaragua is told through the lens of colonial zoomorphism[7] (such as the comparison between Indigenous women and birds of prey) and other racist, sexist, and classist tropes, the nuanced histories of Indigenous market women are replaced by the longings and aspirations of **ideological** *mestizo* elites, (i.e. individuals who promote the official *mestizo* nationalisms studied by Juliet Hooker regardless of their own ethnic/racial backgrounds). The LGBTQ+ history of western Nicaragua however, by necessity, has to be one that centers the experiences of Indigenous trans market women, alongside those of other Indigenous peoples. This region's LGBTQ+ history is a profoundly Indigenous history, one which is deeply tied to femininity and local commerce, although other traditions – such as those of Afro Nicaraguans in the region – remain to be documented.

Against a backdrop of anti-Indigenous hegemonic elite writings such as the ones discussed in this chapter, I argue that the concept of "Indigenous survivance" is useful when discussing the continued/continuous presence of trans

---

7   For more on colonial zoomorphism in the Americas see Tumbaga (2020: 762).

and cis women vendors in the main open-air markets of western Nicaragua, markets such as the Roberto Huembes, Ivan Montenegro, *El Mayoreo*, Israel Lewites, and *El Oriental*.[8] The concept of survivance is useful because it refers to "Native survivance ...[as] an active sense of presence over absence, deracination, and oblivion in history; survivance is the obvious continuance of stories, not a mere reaction [...] Survivance stories are renunciations of state dominance" (Vizenor 2009:138). Documenting Indigenous survivance as we slowly piece together western Nicaraguan's LGBTQ+ histories means rethinking not only what constitutes Indigenous and LGBTQ+ histories of that region, but also what constitutes the broader history of Nicaragua such that it eventually includes all of us.

References

Belli, Humberto (2019): Buscando la tierra prometida. Historia de Nicaragua 1492–2019, Managua: Impresión comercial La Prensa.
Blandón, Erick (2003): Barroco descalzo: Colonialidad, sexualidad, género y raza en la construcción de la hegemonía cultural en Nicaragua, Managua: Uraccan.
Coronel Urtecho, José (2001 [1962, 1967]). "Reflexiones sobre la historia de Nicaragua. De la colonia a la independencia. Colección cultural de Centro América." In: Serie histórica 13, Managua: Fundación Vida.
Cuadra, Pablo Antonio (1987 [1967]): El nicaragüense, San José: Libro Libre.
González-Rivera, Victoria/Kampwirth, Karen (2021): Diversidad sexual en el pacífico y centro de Nicaragua. 500 años de historia, San Diego: No press.
Gould, Jeffrey L. (1998): To Die in this Way. Nicaraguan Indians and the Myth of Mestizaje, 1880–1965, Durham: Duke University Press.
Hooker, Juliet (2005): "'Beloved Enemies': Race and Official Mestizo Nationalism in Nicaragua." In: Latin American Research Review 40/3.
Montgomery Ramírez, Paul Edward (2021): "The Deer and the Donkey: Indigenous Ritual and Survivance in Nicaragua's El Güegüense." In: Latin American Research Review 56/4.

---

8 This is not the first time that Indigenous survivance is used in the context of western Nicaragua's Indigenous history. The Nicaraguan scholar Paul Edward Montgomery Ramírez (2021) has used it in his argument for Indigenous authorship of western Nicaragua's world-famous play, *El Güegüense*.

Tumbaga, Ariel Zatarain (2020): "Indios y Burros: Rethinking 'La India María' as Ethnographic Cinema." In: Latin American Research Review 55/4.

Vizenor, Gerald (2009): Native Liberty. Natural Reason and Cultural Survivance, Lincoln, Nebraska: University of Nebraska Press.

Conceptual Tensions within a *Cuir* [Queer]-Feminist Sociological Approach to Sexuality in Mexico[1]

César Torres-Cruz and Hortensia Moreno-Esparza

Introduction: From Queer Theory to *Cuir* Theory

The appearance in 1976 of Michel Foucault's *The History of Sexuality* represents a milestone in the sociological inquiry about the body and corporeal practices. The characterization of a disciplinary device for control of the body and sexual behavior that brands non-reproductive practices as "perverse" constituted a breakthrough in the field. A decade later, and inspired by Foucault's theoretical contribution, both the queer movement and queer theory would emerge in the United States as a result of the mobilization by nonconformist and AIDS groups, as well as the call by Teresa de Lauretis to "build another discursive horizon, another way of thinking about the sexual" (2010: 23).[2]

Although no consensus has been reached on queer theory, we agree with Arlene Stein and Kenneth Plummer when they say that its main contributions have been:

> 1) A conceptualization of sexuality which sees sexual power embodied in different levels of social life, expressed discursively and enforced through boundaries and binary divides; 2) the problematization of sexual and gender categories, and of identities in general; 3) a rejection of civil rights strategies in favor of a politics of carnival, transgression, and parody which leads to antiassimilationist politics; 4) a willingness to interrogate areas

---

1   Translated from Spanish by Luis Lorenzo Esparza Serra.
2   Years later, this author would renounce some of the uses of this theoretical approach which, in her opinion, had turned into an advertising strategy (Jagose 1996: 129).

which normally would not be seen as the terrain of sexuality, and to conduct queer "readings" of ostensibly heterosexual or nonsexualized texts (1994: 181–182).

As early as the first decade of the twenty-first century, queer theory began to reach academic as well as activism spaces in Latin America, and *"cuir* theory" began to be discussed to address issues of non-hegemonic sexualities thanks to the 'devious' epistemological twist derived from its translation – which both researchers and activists found very useful to challenge the status quo.

This article purports to analyze the conceptual tenets of some of the sociological studies on sexuality in Mexico, including *cuir* theory. Our proposal is that sociological *cuir* feminism can, through a situated and *tense* dialogue, account for the various power mechanisms that define sexuality in Mexico, as well as the possibilities that open up for re-signifying heteronormative mandates.

Translations, Debates and Displacements of Queer Theory Through the Global South

In the early days of the year 2000, many people in Mexico and other Latin American countries (mostly postgraduate students and young researchers) observed, in awe, the incursion of queer theory in feminist and gender studies. This novel perspective – not free from snobbism – opened up the possibility of doing away with the binary frameworks of sexuality and gender and applying the sophisticated concepts of post-structuralism in its English-language reinterpretations. In order to position oneself in a queer (or *cuir*) perspective, one had to have a certain cultural capital and have read Judith Butler and Michel Foucault. In the world of activism, too, new ideas emerged but the fact was that those who didn't belong to academia were left behind.

However, in these contexts, the term queer/*cuir* and its possible translations (*raro* [odd], *extraño* [strange], *torcido* [devious], *anómalo* [abnormal]) did not evoke aspects of everyday life. Some texts (cf. Moreno-Esparza 1997; Córdoba 2005; Viteri 2008; Epps 2008; Viteri/Serrano/Vidal-Ortiz 2011; Arboleda 2011; Rivas 2011) agree that the term has no easy translation into Spanish, and that its enunciation is in itself a de-contextualizing act in which the *performative context* (Rivas 2011) is lost. For Epps (2008), its complexity goes beyond finding an "apt" translation, for we run the risk of silencing stories in which the term in question alludes to personal experiences.

This is partly why in Latin American academic circles the queer approach has polarized opinion and triggered a controversy between those who cultivate its use (cf. Moreno-Esparza 1997, 2016; Núñez 2007; Fonseca/Quintero 2009; Viteri/Serrano/Vidal-Ortiz 2011; Parrini/Brito 2014; Valencia 2015; List 2016), and those who see in the adoption of this term a concession to the imposition of hegemonic US academic theory (cf. Viteri 2008; Rivas 2011; Gargallo n.d.; Mogrovejo 2012; Falconí 2014; Espinosa-Miñoso 2014).

Though we share these concerns with such imperialistic practices, we mustn't overlook the fact that queer theory and queer culture have their roots in political freedom movements (Chinn 2010) and place themselves at the intersection and on common ground between various identities and social positionings to produce "a strategy that often defies the established order" (Sáez 2004: 31). These are women collectives of lesbians, Chicanas, Latinas, Black, and unemployed individuals – i.e., people who have been directly affected by colonization processes. Theirs is a struggle for visibility, not only of their diverse sexual positionings, but also a gender, race/ethnicity, social class, and physical ableness issue that should be acknowledged at the centers of power of both the feminist movement (dominated by White, heterosexual women) and the gay movement (dominated by White men).

We likewise concur with Paco Vidarte when he says that:

> when addressing the problematic re-translation of the queer term in geopolitical spaces outside the US, it is important to keep in mind that this term is, to a certain extent, a product of the re-translation to the North American context of French post-structuralism (2005: 83).

It would be naïve to think that the concept has the ability to lodge itself in the theoretical reflections of Latin American academia without critical assessment. It is therefore more appropriate to "talk about the multiple ways in which such a proposal has been read [...] and develop a critique among us" (Figari 2014: 72–73), which would add to the long history of studies on sexualities and gender identities outside the heterosexual norm that applies in Latin America.

In this order of things, we embrace the proposal by several authors (Valencia 2015; Lanuza/Carrasco 2015) of using the term *cuir* (an unorthodox rendering of the word queer) to distance ourselves from the queer theory produced in the United States, while enriching it and questioning its achievements and limitations. We understand *cuir* theory as a possibility of critically confronting queer theory from the Global South. If anything can be rescued from the early contributions of queer theory, it is its flexible quality and its ability to resist academic normalization and standardization (Butler 1990, 2004; Warner 1993; Halperin 1995; Jagose 1996).

The queer/*cuir* approach is neither the first nor the only theoretical effort to deal with sexuality in the region. Before its appearance, the social sciences and humanities already had a wide agenda on the subject (notably feminist gender studies). As a scientific discipline, sociology had already made inroads into the social dimension of sexuality.

The Sociology of Sexuality

For all the contributions by several forms of feminism, gender and sexuality were not considered relevant topics for sociology before the second half of the twentieth century. Even in our time, sexuality remains at the margins of the discipline (Stein/Plummer 1994). According to Steven Seidman, the earliest sociological works that dealt with sexuality – among them those of Ira Reis (1960, 1964) – "approached sex as a specialty area like organizations, crime, or demography. Sex was imagined as a property of the individual, whose personal expression was shaped by social norms and attitudes" (1994: 169).

In the heyday of pragmatism and symbolic interactionism, a few works on homosexual males saw the light. Some of them used the 'labeling' approach to analyze the complex ways in which 'deviation' is built in social interactions marked by a hierarchy of practices that impose cultural parameters related to the notion of 'normality' (Goffman 1963; Becker 1963).

As a pioneer on the subject, Kenneth Plummer (1975, 1989) analyzed how one learns to live as a homosexual in the UK, where the discrimination and segregation resulting from the stigma attributed to certain sexual practices contribute to the formation of a social identity. The effervescence created by this topic in English-language sociology would last several years (Adam 1996/Weeks 1996).

The breaking of social movements around LGBTQ+ pride in the 1960s and 1970s, and the consolidation of Gay and Lesbian Studies departments at anglophone universities influenced the sociology of urban gay and lesbian experiences in public spaces (Plummer 1989; Stein/Plummer 1994). Laud Humphreys (2008) analyzed the configuration of sexual practices among men in public restrooms in the US, while in the UK Jeffrey Weeks (1985) treated sexuality as a cultural construct resulting from the political and historical tensions that define what we understand as sexual.

In the 1990s, Spanish sociologist Óscar Guasch pointed out the need to have a field within sociology devoted to the study of sexuality, "with sex, a social activity, as its subject matter" (1993: 106). In France, Michel Bozon (2002) called for the inception of a "sociology of sexuality," but its basic assumptions were anchored in the heterosexual norm, treating non-heterosexual practices and identities as "minorities". Unlike the sociology of the body and the sociology of emotions, the sociology of sexuality has failed to establish itself in the institutional curriculum. This is the case in Mexico, where it is hard to find a course on the subject in a university program.

One of the most thought-provoking recent proposals on the sociology of sexuality is Adam Isaiah Green's theory of sexual fields (2013). A combination of Pierre Bourdieu's ideas about practice and the role of interaction in structured contexts studied by Erving Goffman, this theory looks at the distribution of erotic socialization and entertainment within the gay communities of New York and Toronto.

Notwithstanding their relevance, these contributions continue to be biased, since most of them have been produced by White men in the gay scene of the Global North and are anchored in urban homosexuality.

In Mexico, in 1994, the now canonic work of Guillermo Núñez Noriega *Sexo entre varones. Poder y resistencia en el campo sexual* (Sex Among Men. Power and Resistance in the Sexual Field) was published. Based on an ethnography of homoeroticism in the state of Sonora, Núñez addresses the complexities of representing sexuality and the social conditions under which sexual and gender norms are resisted and re-signified. Núñez applies Bourdieu's ideas to analyze the way in which the *sexual field* is conformed, as well as its implications in terms of *habitus*, that is, social and bodily practices.

In 2003, César González – under Kenneth Plummer's supervision – published his doctoral dissertation *Travestidos al desnudo. Homosexualidad, identidades y luchas territoriales en Colima* (Naked Transvestisms. Homosexuality, Identities, and Territorial Struggles in Colima), where he analyzes how notions of deviance and "abnormality" are produced in that state and the traces of agency that can be found among those affected.

In 2014, an analysis of the homoerotic interaction that takes place in a Mexico City cinema was published by Andrés Álvarez, who applied Goffman's and Simmel's notions of frameworks of meaning, order of interaction, and physical contact. In 2018, Galindo and Torres-Cruz presented their research on the social configuration of *"metreo"*, or "sexual practices in the subway" found in Mexico City's underground system lines. Their theoretical approach to tackle the social reduction of contingency in such practices combines notions coming from Goffman, Luhmann, Elias, Bourdieu, and Latour, and for a detailed analysis of the construction of such practices, the authors resort to feminist notions such as the *heterosexualization* of public space and *the heterosexual matrix*.

As in the countries of the Global North, research on sexuality in Mexico tends to concentrate on the homoerotic practices of *cisgender* men. We have found only two works that deal with the experience of transgender males in Mexico City, one by Eleonora Garosi (2004) and the other one by Ana Carvajal (2019). These two authors analyze transition processes of body and identity, how these processes redefine sexuality, and the social disputes for the recognition and the enactment of masculinity.

Sociology continues to face important challenges to account for the social dimension of sexuality. The social readings of the various brands of feminism and *cuir* studies are central to the analysis of the complexities of sexuality, as determined by factors such as ethnic affiliation, social class, and age.

Cuir Sociology? Concluding Remarks from a Conceptual-Tension Viewpoint

Our conceptual proposal stems from a social understanding of sexuality: *i)* at the macro level, from the ways in which heteronormativity performatively produces subjects within binary frameworks; *ii)* at the intermediate level and from a relational perspective, the mechanisms through which certain institutions discursively generate processes of subjectivation based on ethnicity, social-class, age, and physical-ableness strata; and *iii)* at the micro level, from the dynamics of resignification of heterocentric mandates by bodies in social interaction, and the subjects' construction of new interpretations of practices and pleasures.

Though the *cuir* notion offers an interesting theoretical framework, we must make sure it doesn't lose its gender and feminist dimensions. In adding other intersections, feminism must be maintained as the starting point for the understanding of sexualities and for emphasizing the roles of gender and (hetero)patriarchy.

As Eve Kosofsky Sedgwick (1999, 2003) argues, any analysis of modern Western culture calls for an understanding of the excluding and regulatory binary identity categories. This approach allows to uncover the power mechanisms that impact the lives and practices of all people, including those who consider themselves as *cis* and heterosexual, for they too suffer under the normative requirements of hegemonic femininity and masculinity.

We propose a *cuir*-feminist sociology of sexuality that, in its macro dimension, takes into account its relationship with gender and the body as a productive element of sociocultural analysis, in tune with Judith Butler's queer feminism to *cuir* theory, her analysis of heterosexuality as a normative matrix of body control through a binary framework, and of the performative dimension of the production of subjectivities and sexualized and gendered bodies embedded in social structures (Butler 1990, 1993, 2004, 2009).

Though queer theory and sociology share the same vision of sexuality "as a social and historical construct" (Miskolci 2009: 151), their theoretical corpora are in constant tension over the understanding of the subject and the self. While queer (*cuir*) theory is focused on deconstructing the subject by proposing fluid ways to position sexuality and gender, sociology tries to understand the social construction of subjects to focus on identity as a fixed process. At the same time, both theoretical approaches understand sexuality as an historical process embedded in power.

It is for this reason that we adopt the critique of biological essentialism from the *cuir* approach and its rejection of universal classifications. At the intermediate level, it is essential to describe the discursive practices of institutions and the subjectivation processes permeated by, among other factors, ethnicity, social class, age, and physical ableness. We understand sociology more as "a way of thinking than a finite body of theories and data; it entails questioning existing social arrangements, an awareness that they are a product of history, an understanding of the social shaping of personal life and experience" (Jackson 1999: 49).

We refer to a sociological feminism with a *cuir* approach to emphasize a tense dialogue among these schools of thought. Such conceptual conversation exercise allows us to understand, at the micro level, not only the performative dimension of sexuality, within agency processes, but also the social dimension of social interaction in the process of making sense of sexuality, gender, and the body (Moreno-Esparza/Torres-Cruz 2018, 2019). This gives us an opportunity to think of the complexities of sexuality and gender. In our conceptual proposal, we highlight the relevance of incorporating both the discursive and social complex dimensions of bodies and pleasures, informed by empirical insights.

Finally, the *cuir*-feminist sociology we propose must take into account the complexities derived from the intersection of sexuality with gender, nationality, social class, ethnicity, physical ableness, etc. as overlapping dimensions of inequality (Viveros 2016).

References

Adam, Barry D. (1996): "Structural Foundations of the Gay World." In: Steven Seidman (ed.), Queer Theory/Sociology, Cambridge: Blackwell Publishers, pp. 111–126.

Álvarez, Andrés (2014): El marco de la interacción homoerótica en el cine nacional de la Ciudad de México. Master's Thesis, Mexico City: Universidad Nacional Autónoma de México, December 11, 2021 (http://132.248.67.65/F/?func=find-b&local_base=TES01&find_code=WRD&request=El+marco+de+la+interaccion+homoerotica+en+el+cine+&adjacent=N).

Arboleda, Paola (2011): "¿Ser o estar 'queer' en Latinoamérica? El devenir emancipador en Lemebel, Perlongher y Arenas." In: Íconos. Revista de Ciencias Sociales 39, pp. 111–122, DOI: https://doi.org/10.17141/iconos.39.2011.1219.

Becker, Howard (1963): Outsiders. Studies in the Sociology of Deviance, New York: Free Press.

Bozon, Michel (2002): Sociologie de la sexualité, Paris: Nathan.

Butler, Judith (1990): Gender Trouble. Feminism and the Subversion of Identity, New York and London: Routledge.

Butler, Judith (1993): Bodies that Matter. On the Discursive Limits of Sex, New York and London: Routledge.

Butler, Judith (2004): Undoing Gender, New York and London: Routledge.

Butler, Judith (2009): "Performatividad, precariedad y políticas sexuales". In: AIBR. Revista de Antropología Iberoamericana 4/3, pp. 321–336.

Carvajal, Ana (2019): La configuración social de transmasculinidades en la Ciudad de México: entre la reiteración y la disputa de la masculinidad hegemónica. Master's thesis, Mexico City: Universidad Iberoamericana.

Chinn, Sarah (2010): "Performative Identities: From Identity Politics to Queer Theory." In: Margaret Wetherell/Chandra Tapalde Mohanty (eds.), The Sage Handbook of Identities, London: Sage Publications, pp. 104–124.

Córdoba, David (2005): "Teoría queer: reflexiones sobre sexo, sexualidad e identidad. Hacia una politización de la sexualidad." In: David Córdoba/Javier Sáez/Paco Vidarte (eds.), Teoría queer. Políticas bolleras, maricas, trans, mestizas, Barcelona: Egales, pp. 21–67.

De Lauretis, Teresa (2010): "Teoría queer: sexualidades lesbiana y gay." In Mauricio List/Alberto Teutle (eds.), Florilegio de deseos. Nuevos enfoques, estudios y escenarios de la disidencia sexual y genérica, Puebla: Benemérita Universidad Autónoma de Puebla and Ediciones Eón, pp. 21–47.

Epps, Brad (2008). "Retos, riesgos, pautas y promesas de la teoría queer." In: Revista Iberoamericana LXXIV/225, pp. 897–920.

Espinosa-Miñoso, Yuderkys (2014): "Una crítica decolonial a la epistemología feminista crítica." In: El cotidiano 184, pp. 7–12.

Falconí, Diego (2014): "La leyenda negra marica: una crítica comparatista desde el sur a la teoría *queer* hispana." In Diego Falconí/Santiago Castellanos/María Amelia Viteri (eds.), Resentir lo queer en América Latina. Diálogos desde/con el Sur, Barcelona: Egales, pp. 81–127.

Figari, Carlos. (2014): "Fagocitando lo *queer* en el cono sur." In Diego Falconí/Santiago Castellanos/María Amelia Viteri (eds.), Resentir lo queer en América Latina. Diálogos desde/con el Sur, Barcelona: Egales, pp. 63–78.

Fonseca, Carlos/Quintero, María (2009): "La teoría *queer*: La de-construcción de las sexualidades periféricas." In: Sociológica 24/69, pp. 43–61.

Foucault, Michel (1980[1976]): The History of Sexuality. Volume I: An Introduction, New York: Vintage.

Galindo, Jorge/Torres-Cruz, César (2018): "Diálogo de miradas. Un acercamiento al 'metreo' como orden interactivo." In: Sociológica 33/93, pp. 319–353.

Gargallo, Francesca (n.d.): ¿Existe, se expresa de algún modo el pensamiento queer en América Latina?, December 13, 2021 (https://francescagargallo.wordpress.com/ensayos/feminismo/feminismo-genero/a-proposito-de-lo-queer-en-america-latina/).

Garosi, Leonora (2004): "¡Son cosas de la vida! Trans-masculinidades en la Ciudad de México." In: Rodrigo Parrini/Alejandro Brito (eds.), La memoria y el deseo. Estudios gay y queer en México, Mexico City: Programa Universitario de Estudios de Género de la UNAM, pp. 177–222.

Goffman, Erving (1963): Stigma. Notes on the Management of Spoiled Identity, New York: Prentice-Hall.

González, César (2003): Travestidos al desnudo. Homosexualidad, identidades y luchas territoriales en Colima, Mexico City: Centro de Investigaciones y

Estudios Superiores en Antropología Social (CIESAS) and Miguel Ángel Porrúa.

Green, Adam Isaiah (2013): "The Sexual Fields Framework." In: Adam Isaiah Green (ed.), Sexual Fields. Towards a Sociology of Collective Sexual Life, Chicago: Chicago University Press, pp. 25–56.

Guasch, Óscar (1993): "Para una sociología de la sexualidad." In: Reis, Revista Española de Investigaciones Sociológicas 64, pp. 105–122.

Halperin, David (1995): Saint Foucault. Towards a Gay Hagiography, New York: Oxford University Press.

Humphreys, Laud (2008): Tearoom Trade. Impersonal Sex in Public Places, New York: Aldine Transaction.

Jackson, Stevi (1999): "Feminist Sociology and Sociological Feminism: Recovering the Social in Feminist Thought." In: Sociological Research Online 4/3, pp. 43–56.

Jagose, Annamarie (1996): Queer Theory. An Introduction, New York: New York University Press.

Lanuza, Fernando R./Carrasco, Raúl M. (2015): Queer & Cuir. Políticas de lo irreal, Querétaro: Universidad Autónoma de Querétaro and Fontamara, pp. 19–37.

List, Mauricio (2016): "Teoría queer." In: Hortensia Moreno-Esparza/Eva Alcántara (eds.), Conceptos clave en los estudios de género, volumen 1, Mexico City: Centro de Investigaciones y Estudios de Género de la UNAM, pp. 289–305.

Miskolci, Richard (2009): "A Teoria Queer e a Sociologia: o desafio de uma analítica da normalização." In: Sociologias 11/21, pp. 150–182.

Mogrovejo, Norma (2012): Lo queer en América Latina, November 5, 2020 (http://normamogrovejo.blogspot.com/2012/11/lo-queer-en-america-latina.html)

Moreno-Esparza, Hortensia/Torres-Cruz, César (2018): "Performatividad." In: Hortensia Moreno-Esparza/Eva Alcántara (eds.), Conceptos clave en los estudios de género, volumen 2, Mexico City: Centro de Investigaciones y Estudios de Género de la UNAM, pp. 233–250.

Moreno-Esparza, Hortensia/Torres-Cruz, César. (2019): "La noción de performatividad de género para el análisis del discurso fílmico." In: Cadernos Pagu [online] 56, pp. 1–36, http://dx.doi.org/10.1590/18094449201900560010

Moreno-Esparza, Hortensia (1997): "Editorial." In: Debate feminista. Raras rarezas 8/16, pp. IX-XIV.

Moreno-Esparza, Hortensia (2016): "La sexualidad reproductiva como paradigma epistemológico." In: Revista de estudios de antropología sexual 1/6, pp. 24–45.

Núñez, Guillermo. (1994): Sexo entre varones. Poder y resistencia en el campo sexual, Hermosillo: El Colegio de Sonora.

Núñez, Guillermo (2007): Masculinidad e intimidad: identidad, sexualidad y sida, Mexico City: Programa Universitario de Estudios de Género de la UNAM, El Colegio de Sonora and Miguel Ángel Porrúa.

Parrini, Rodrigo/Brito, Alejandro (2014): La memoria y el deseo. Estudios gay y queer en México, Mexico City: Programa Universitario de Estudios de Género de la UNAM.

Plummer, Kenneth (1975): Sexual Stigma: An Interactionist Account, London: Routledge and Kegan Paul.

Plummer, Kenneth (1989): "Lesbian and Gay Youth in England." In: Journal of Homosexuality 17/3-4, pp. 195–224.

Reis, Ira (1960): "Toward a Sociology of the Heterosexual Love Relationship." In: Marriage and Family Living 22/2, pp. 139–145.

Reis, Ira (1964): "The Scaling of Premarital Sexual Permissiveness." In: Marriage and Family 26/2, pp. 188–198.

Rivas, Felipe (2011): "Diga 'queer' con la lengua afuera: Sobre las confusiones del debate latinoamericano." In: Coordinadora Universitaria por la Disidencia Sexual/CUDS (eds.), Por un feminismo sin mujeres, Santiago: Alfabeta Artes Gráficas, pp. 59–77.

Sáez, Javier (2004): Teoría queer y psicoanálisis, Madrid: Síntesis.

Sedgwick, Eve Kosofsky (1999): "Performatividad queer: *The Art of the Novel* de Henry James." In: Nómadas 10, pp. 198–214.

Sedgwick, Eve Kosofsky (2003). Touching Feeling: Affect, Pedagogy, Performativity, Durham and London: Duke University Press.

Seidman, Steven (1994): "Queer-Ing Sociology, Sociologizing Queer Theory: An Introduction." In: Sociological Theory 12/2, pp. 166–177.

Stein, Arlene/Plummer, Kenneth (1994): "'I Can't Even Think Straight'/ 'Queer' Theory and the Missing Sexual Revolution in Sociology." In: Sociological Theory 12/2, pp. 178–187.

Valencia, Sayak (2015): "Del queer al cuir: ostranénie geopolítica y epistémica desde el sur glocal." In: Fernando R. Lanuza/Raúl M. Carrasco (eds.), Queer & Cuir. Políticas de lo irreal, Querétaro: Universidad Autónoma de Querétaro and Fontamara, pp. 19–37.

Vidarte, Paco (2005): "El banquete uniqueersitario: disquisiciones sobre el s(ab)er queer." In: David Córdoba/Javier Sáez/Paco Vidarte (eds.), Teoría queer. Políticas bolleras, maricas, trans, mestizas, Barcelona: Egales, pp. 77–111.

Viteri, María Amelia/Serano, Fernando/Vidal-Ortiz, Salvador (2011): "¿Cómo se piensa lo "queer" en América Latina?" In: Íconos. Revista de Ciencias Sociales 39, pp. 47–60.

Viteri, María Amelia (2008). "'Queer no me da': traduciendo fronteras sexuales y raciales en San Salvador y Washington D.C." In: Kathya Araujo/Mercedes Prieto (eds.), Estudios sobre sexualidades en América Latina. Quito: Facultad Latinoamericana de Ciencias Sociales (FLACSO-Ecuador), pp. 91–108.

Viveros, Mara (2016): "La interseccionalidad: una aproximación situada a la dominación." In: Debate feminista 52, pp. 1–17.

Warner, Michael (1993): Fear of a Queer Planet. Queer Politics and Social Theory, Minneapolis: Minnesota University Press.

Weeks, Jeffrey (1985): Sexuality and its Discontents. Meanings, Myths & Modern Sexualities, London and New York: Routledge.

Weeks, Jeffrey (1996): "The Construction of Homosexuality." In: Steven Seidman (ed.), Queer Theory/Sociology, Cambridge: Blackwell Publishers, pp. 129–144.

"May Our Voice Echo"
Housemaids' Narratives in *Eu, Empregada Doméstica*

Larissa Satico Ribeiro Higa

Brazil's first Covid-19-related death occurred on 17 March 2020. The deceased person was a housemaid whose employers had traveled to Italy. During the coronavirus pandemic, this sector of the Brazilian labor market was greatly affected. In 2020, more than two million women lost their jobs (Pereira 2021), and others had their incomes reduced or risked their lives reporting to work so as not to be dismissed. The vulnerability of housemaids is not new, but has a long history of invisibility, stigmatization, wage devaluation, precarious working conditions, and deprivation of rights. In fact, domestic work is devalued because it constitutes a heritage of colonial relations and of slavery in the country.

Brazil has the world's largest contingent of housemaids. There are 6.2 million people performing this job, of which 92 per cent are women. It is the sector with the largest female workforce in the country, occupied by 14.6 per cent of all employed women (Pinheiro et al. 2019). In addition, 3.9 million of these women are Black and a total of 70.1 per cent still work informally, without guaranteed labor rights (Pinheiro et al. 2020). Their job encompasses a myriad of tasks, from cleaning the house and often also cooking, to taking care of children and the elderly.

The fight against overexploitation of these women intensified with union struggles in the last decades of the 20th century. Its main demand was the institutionalization of domestic work. In 1943, Brazil had its first Consolidation of Labor Laws, but this category of work was excluded from it. Only in 1972 did employees obtain the right to sign a work card, take paid leave, and have access to social security. The 1988 Brazilian Constitution also guaranteed nine labor rights (Teixeira 2021: 65), yet it was only in 2015, with the passage of the Housemaids Proposal for Constitutional Amendment (*PEC das Domésticas*), that domestic work was legally equated to other labor categories.

Despite legislative isonomy, housemaids are still in a vulnerable condition. Lélia Gonzalez states that "gender and ethnicity are manipulated so that, in the Brazilian case, the lowest levels of participation in the workforce, 'coincidentally' are occupied by women and the Black population" (2020: 27).[1] Housemaids suffer from the structural racism and sexism that are a legacy of Brazilian colonial and slave past. For Gonzalez, "the maid is not much different from yesterday's 'mucama'" (ibid: 217). *Mucama* was the enslaved Black woman responsible for the chores in the farmhouse, subjected to the landowners' brutalities that resemble the treatment received by housemaids.

By articulating the structures of class, race, and gender for the analysis of paid domestic work in the 1980s, Gonzalez adopts an intersectional perspective.[2] According to Carla Akotirene, intersectionality, as a methodological and analytical tool, is an ancestral and epistemological legacy of Black women, which "allows feminists political criticality to understand imposed subaltern identities" (2019: 37). This article employs an intersectional approach to analyze the book *Eu, empregada doméstica – a senzala moderna é o quartinho da empregada*[3] (2019), highlighting how structures of oppression operate in current housemaids' lives.

The book *Eu, empregada doméstica* is an anthology of 286 stories selected by historian, rapper, and former housemaid Joyce Fernandes, better known as Preta-Rara. In 2016, she launched a Facebook fan page[4] to expose abusive employment advertisements and stories lived by housemaids. The activist herself published the statements on the Internet, preserving the respondents' identities and form of expression. The narratives selected for the book were written mainly by housemaids – valuing, therefore, the "lugar de fala"[5] (Ribeiro 2017)

---

[1] All the quotes in this article – including the long ones from *Eu, empregada doméstica* – were originally in Portuguese. All translations from Portuguese into English are my own.

[2] Gonzalez pioneered the connections among race, class, and gender. According to Angela Davis, "[s]he was already talking about the links between Blacks and indigenous peoples in the struggle for rights. That's one of the lessons America can learn from Black feminism here" (Alves 2017).

[3] The book's title can be translated as *I, housemaid – the modern slave quarter is the maid's little bedroom*. The *little bedroom* refers to a very common room in Brazilian employers' house where the maid sleeps.

[4] The page can be accessed at the address https://www.facebook.com/euempregadadomestica.

[5] "Lugar de fala" is an expression that is related to the positionality of the speaker. According to Djamila Ribeiro (2017), "lugar de fala" is a category of analysis that consid-

of poor and mostly Black women – but also by family members, friends, and conscious employers. By grouping these narratives, Rara engages in a feminist practice, since her book helps composing the history and testimony of a collectivity[6] that has historically been silenced.

It is not only Rara who adopts an important feminist posture by creating the Facebook page and publishing *Eu, empregada doméstica*. According to Ribeiro, "speaking is not restricted to the act of uttering words, but of being able to exist" (2017: 37). Therefore, the speaking subjects of the book are vocalizing their feminist point of view about being a housemaid. In doing so, they are affirming their right to exist as human beings whose positionality enables them to question official Brazilian history and challenges the hierarchy of discursive power.

In the book, housemaids show awareness of the historical roots of their jobs. The connections between domestic and slave labor appear in many workers' narratives. There are references to the women employer as *sinhá*[7], to the mistreatment as *whipping*, to the workplace as *master's house* and countless allusions to the times of *slavery*. Such slave logic and the dehumanization that mark domestic work can also be inferred from three recurring topics in the narratives selected for this analysis: the disregard of maids' autonomy; restrictions related to food, and the psychological impact caused by the treatment they receive.

1. "She Fired Me, Calling Me a Little Black Slum Girl"

One of the narratives by a maid's daughter shows that her mother's employer seemed to want to have "sovereignty over her body and will" (Rara 2019: 94). In another one, a daughter states that the employer thought she had "power over my mother, controlling the free time that, by law (and as a matter of humanity, empathy), is the right of any worker" (ibid: 46). These aspects – regarding

---

ers the position that the speaking subject occupies in a socially determined hierarchy of power. This position enables the subject to talk about experiences historically shared by the specific group to which they belong.

6   Books of testimonial content by four maids – Lenira Carvalho, Francisca Souza da Silva, Rosalina Ferreira Basseti, and Zeli de Oliveira Barbosa – , written between the 1980s and 1990s, are analyzed by Sonia Roncador, in *A doméstica imaginária* (2008).

7   "Sinhá" was the noun used by enslaved Black people in reference to the landowner's wife.

the control of workers' bodies, desires, and time – refer to servitude conditions according to which the maid is treated not as a subject, but as an object considered to be the employers' private property.

For Sonia Roncador, the disrespect for workers' autonomy is linked to a "bourgeois ideal of servitude" (2008: 213) that leads to their "affective and social alienation" (ibid: 217). In the book, there are examples of employers discouraging their maids from studying, having partners, and forming a family. In one of the cases, the maid had a high-risk pregnancy and needed to be careful and take it slow. According to a friend's statement:

> One day, the employer came arguing a lot, asking why she was not cleaning on top of the wardrobe or the windows. She said that she had already talked about it and that the doctor recommended it due to the risk of falling and losing the baby.
> The employer's answer: *"Who cares? It will be just one less poor person in the world!"* She got sick and had the baby prematurely (Rara 2019: 74, my emphasis).

The employer's answer disregards the maid's pregnancy and her desire to have a child. The statement also devalues the life of this woman. There are other examples in which employers think the maid's life is worth less. One worker cut herself badly with a broken bathroom box and the employer seemed more concerned about the repair costs than with the employee's injury. In another narrative, a maid was threatened by her employer with a firearm because she refused to redo a chore.

The contempt for the maids' lives falls under class and racial motivations. In some reports, the employers feel "disgusted" by the workers, forcing them to do degrading activities, such as washing feces-soiled towels and menstruation-stained panties, while throwing away objects the maids touched. For one of the employers, "[a]fter Benedita da Silva,[8] that 'colored' Congresswoman (rubbing her finger on her arm), entered Congress, we could no longer find anyone in 'decent conditions'" (ibid: 51), lamenting that the guarantee of legal rights was getting in the way of her ability to abuse her power.

---

8   Benedicta da Silva (PT-RJ) is a Black politician who was Governor of Rio de Janeiro (2002–2003) and, as a Federal Deputy, served as rapporteur of the Housemaids Proposal for Constitutional Amendment in 2012.

The contemporary objectification of workers is connected not only to the treatment received by enslaved Black women, but also by Black women in the post-abolition era, when, according to Teixeira, they "were not treated as *subjects*, but as servants available to satisfy all their employers' wills" (2021: 32, original emphasis). There are other, subtler ways in which class, race, and gender oppressions are manifested in the employers' houses, such as disputes over meals and food consumption.

2. "I Used to Feel Almost Like an Animal Eating the Remains of the 'Royal' Table"

Many narratives denounce restrictions on food consumption in the workplace. In Brazil, it is common for a housemaid to eat only after serving the meal to the employer's family. But the book shows a more cruel and complex reality. In addition to eating at separate times and places, some housemaids reveal that they must eat with inappropriate kitchen utensils or use separate tableware.

Such separation is also evident in relation to types of food. Employers consider certain foods inadequate for employees' consumption. For instance, housemaids are not allowed to eat meat, fish, and special types of sausage and are offered cheaper products of lower nutritional quality, such as nuggets, hotdogs, and rice. Some workers list quality foods or delicacies that are off limits to them, such as olive oil; black pepper; chocolate; cheese; juice; Coke; "sweets, milk, soda, everything light, chestnuts, salads, fruits" (Rara 2019: 130), and bottled water.

Maids are often accused of stealing groceries. The notion of ownership extends all the way to the employers' garbage: A worker was accused of theft for picking "cookies" out of the trash at her workplace. There are also employers who offer spoiled food and give the maids expired food products. The most shocking cases of food-related humiliation occur when workers must eat the leftovers from their employers' meals, as in the following report:

> I was 14. I had to have lunch after them, because I had to serve everyone, and by the time they finished, I sat at the table, but the employer told me to go wash my hands. I told her I'd already washed them. She insisted a lot and I went to wash. When I got back, my dish was already done, but it looked like the food was scrambled. I was surprised, but because I was very hungry, I ate it. I saw it wasn't hot. It went on like this for 1, 2, 3 days. On the

fourth day, I pretended to go wash my hands and came back right away. And I saw the employer putting the leftover food from the other dishes in mine. Son, I ran away and *cried a lot* (ibid: 155, my emphasis).

Eating leftovers is cruel and demeaning, especially for a child. As shocking as it may sound, it is common for employees to eat leftovers rejected by their employers. A worker reports eating scraps left by a tuberculous man. There are also countless stories of maids going hungry during working hours. Many housemaids claim that if there was nothing left of the employers' meals, they simply would not eat all day. Some of them had just water to drink and the employers did not bother to guarantee them a meal, especially when they were not at home.

Dehumanization reaches an extreme when employers prioritize the quality and quantity of their pets' food. Dogs eat expensive snacks, which the maids cannot afford, and maids must share leftovers with the animal, or even serve the pet first and eat after them. In one narrative, the housemaid and the family dog are served the same meal, "cooked corn meal and guts," while employers "eat rice, beans, and meat" (ibid: 43). Certainly, these workers "had no right to food worthy of a human being" (ibid: 97).

Finally, in the quoted passage, the maid reveals how much the oppressive situation upset her. Many maids who experience humiliation and contempt cry as they report their abuses. Dehumanized treatment has devastating effects on housemaids' mental health, which deserves attention and reflection.

3. "I Just Felt the Chills, Wanted to Throw Up and Cry"

Eu, empregada doméstica enables contact with maids' feelings and afflictions. They express sadness, anger, and embarrassment, which leave them traumatized, "marked forever" (ibid: 106), with negative effects on their mental health. The book also reveals crises of anxiety and depression that have persisted throughout the workers' lives.

In one case, a former maid's daughter discovered that her mother "never liked Christmas, New Year's, or Easter" (ibid: 169) because these festivities aroused memories of the meals she served her employers and did not get to eat herself. In another situation, a daughter states that her "mother is terrified of celebrating her birthday" (ibid: 143) because, at the age of 12, she worked in the house of a family whose daughter's birthday was on the same day as hers, so she was forced to serve the employers at the girl's party and then was locked in a room while they were celebrating.

Another consequence of workers' mistreatment is low self-esteem. Invisibility of paid reproductive work and dehumanization affect the way housemaids build their self-image. This problem is evident in the following passages:

> *She has an inferiority complex.* She doesn't eat with guests. She doesn't like to leave the house. She doesn't like to get dressed. She's depressive. She takes controlled medicine. It is the result of a very unsuccessful maid-employer relationship (ibid: 36, my emphasis).
>
> The trauma was so bad that it took years of therapy for her to get over it. She once said that it was the psychologist who made her *realize she was a person, that her feelings mattered, too, and that no one could treat her like someone inferior* (ibid: 85, my emphasis).

These excerpts are paradigmatic of Gonzalez' statement that "Black women have undergone a process of reinforcement regarding the internalization of difference, 'inferiority', subordination" (2020: 42). The maids quoted had psychological and psychiatric support to elaborate on situations of violence and affirm their subjectivity. This opportunity, however, is unusual in Brazil, because there are no effective public policies aimed at ensuring mental health for low-income people.

Anxiety, depression, and low self-esteem are mental health conditions that can have serious consequences if left untreated. One worker states that humiliation made her think about suicide. Another former employee claims that if she had to work as a housemaid again, she would kill herself. According to Carneiro, there is a lack of "study in the country on one of the most perverse aspects of racism and racial discrimination: psychological harm and, above all, the blow to self-esteem that discriminatory mechanisms produce in victims of racism" (2011: 79). Thus, although distressing, knowledge of the houseworker's plight is important for raising awareness on this invisible problem.

Despite the pain caused by remembering traumatic experiences, employees affirm the need to speak, so that their perspectives are documented and published. Their narratives enable an elaboration of these oppressive experiences and a denunciation of the perpetuated slave logic. When housemaids name their pain and suffering, they engage in a collective healing process once they make the system of oppression and exploitation visible, which is an important step for social and cultural changes. Moreover, the reports not only expose violence: They also present resistance and confrontation, highlighting these workers' agency. Housemaids question their employers' conduct; they quit their jobs; they are proud that their daughters go to university, disrupting the "matriarchy of misery" (Carneiro 2011: 127); they view their work with dignity; they support Preta-Rara's Facebook page.

Consciousness and insubordination are part of the workers' daily political struggle, and the publication of narratives confronts housemaids' stigmatizations – as "potentially criminal, unfaithful, incompetent, and morally corrupt" (Roncador 2008:190) – which still subsist throughout Brazilian hegemonic cultural imaginary. In fact, the book's narratives shock and give rise to reflection. Knowing the maids' perspectives is important for cultural changes and for the collective fight against class, race, and gender oppressions. Intersectional Black feminism teaches us that women's emancipation depends on the emancipation of the most vulnerable sector among us, which reaffirms the centrality of the struggle for better paid domestic work conditions in the country.

Brazil's pandemic and governmental situation in 2022 is not favorable to housemaids. Preta-Rara reminds us that "[t]he current President of Brazil[9] was the only one who did not sign the Housemaids Proposal for Constitutional Amendment" (Rara 2019: 8). This adverse context emphasizes the importance of Rara's feminist action. The publication of *Eu, empregada doméstica* is a successful collective effort to make the production of knowledge of Black poor women evident. It exposes the epistemology of women with dissident voices, disputing the narrative about housemaids and Brazilian History. Therefore, Rara's work is part of a broader social and cultural fight for better working conditions, and against racism and sexism in Brazil. In conclusion, Rara's book is a huge feminist contribution to spread Brazilian housemaids' words, supporting their shared desire: "May our voice echo" (ibid: 89).

References

Alves, Alê (2017): "Angela Davis: 'Quando a mulher negra se movimenta, toda a estrutura da sociedade se movimenta com ela'." In: El país, December 15, 2021 (https://brasil.elpais.com/brasil/2017/07/27/politica/1501114503_610956.html).

---

[9] During the Housemaids Proposal for Constitutional Amendment voting period, Jair Bolsonaro was a Federal Deputy.

Akotirene, Carla (2019): Interseccionalidade, São Paulo: Sueli Carneiro and Polén.
Carneiro, Sueli (2011): Racismo, sexismo e desigualdade no Brasil, São Paulo: Selo Negro.
Gonzalez, Lélia (2020): Por um feminismo afro-latino-americano, Rio de Janeiro: Zahar.
Pereira, Gabriela (2021): "ONU Mulheres: 2 milhões de trabalhadoras domésticas perderam o emprego em 2020", June 22, 2021 (https://brasil.un.org/pt-br/132608-onu-mulheres-2-milhoes-de-trabalhadoras-domesticas-perderam-o-emprego-em-2020).
Pinheiro, Luana et al. (2019): Os Desafios do Passado no Trabalho Doméstico do Século XXI: reflexões para o caso brasileiro a partir dos dados da PNAD Contínua, Brasília; Rio de Janeiro: IPEA, December 9, 2021(http://repositorio.ipea.gov.br/bitstream/11058/9538/1/td_2528.pdf)
Pinheiro, Luana et al. (2020): Vulnerabilidades das trabalhadoras domésticas no contexto da pandemia de covid-19 no Brasil, Brasília; Rio de Janeiro: IPEA, December 9, 2021 (https://www.onumulheres.org.br/wp-content/uploads/2020/06/213247_NT_Disoc-N_75_web.pdf).
Rara, Preta (2019): Eu, empregada doméstica: a senzala moderna é o quartinho de empregada, Belo Horizonte: Letramento.
Ribeiro, Djamila (2017): O que é lugar de fala?, Belo Horizonte: Letramento and Justificando.
Roncador, Sonia (2008): A doméstica imaginária: literatura, testemunhos e a invenção da empregada doméstica no Brasil (1889–1999), Brasília: Editora da Universidade de Brasília.
Teixeira, Juliana (2021): Trabalho doméstico, São Paulo: Jandaíra.

Indigenous Literature and Ecofeminism in Brazil

Anna-Lena Glesinski

> Woman! Come, sister
> drink from this fountain that awaits you
> my sweet tender words.
> (Potiguara 2004: 76)[1]

This essay examines two different perspectives on the relationship between women and nature, both of which are deeply rooted within the Latin American continent and especially in the Brazilian rainforest. The movement of contemporary indigenous literature of Brazil makes visible how indigenous literature has always existed and explains the importance and strength of its narratives. From the 2000s until the present, female voices are particularly strong within this movement and often reflect the position of women in history, society and nature. Another aspect presented in this essay is the ecofeminist movement, which had its starting point in the 1980s as part of feminist theology.

Contemporary indigenous literature embodies experiences of trauma of 500 years of colonialism at the same time as 500 years of indigenous resistance and resilience. Its texts witness production processes of knowledge of culture and a change in historical views on indigenous subjects, whereas the early Brazilian ecofeminists' intentions were to deconstruct colonial and patriarchal power structures and create a different view on female bodies and identities on the theological stage. The ecofeminist and indigenous movements are tied to constant change. The ecofeminist movement and the use of the term *ecofeminism* has come a long way and changed during the last 40 years.

---

1   All translations made by the author.

Both movements function as developers of theories and practitioners of change. The female writers create a collective voice of indigenous women and at the same time prompt a metatextual literary criticism of indigenous authorship. This short investigation marks similarities, differences and convergences of the two perspectives and defines crucial points of the discourse on women and nature. It provides insights into processes of theorizing, action-taking and changing dominant discourse and examines how feminist, ecological and decolonial theories are always bound and interconnected with concrete practices.

Strong Female Voices of the Movement of Contemporary Literature and Literary Criticism of Brazil

As Julie Dorrico highlights, the movement of contemporary indigenous literature from Brazil arose and consolidated in the 1990s and positions itself in a supporting role within the sociopolitical indigenous movement that was originally strengthened in the 1980s and associates directly with it (Dorrico 2018: 165). Julie Dorrico herself is an author and literary critic with a PhD on indigenous literature, publishes poetry and belongs to the Macuxi. In recent years, she has published important articles and co-edited various anthologies on the movement (Dorrico 2017; Dorrico 2018; Dorrico et al. 2018; Dorrico et al. 2020). She highlights different aspects in which indigenous literature integrates into and complements the indigenous movement, namely politicization, activism, militancy and engagement (Dorrico 2018: 267). The indigenous movement's aims can be described as follows:

> Since its beginning, therefore, the politicization and publicization of the indigenous movement represented, correlatively, a gesture of self-affirmation and ethnic-identitarian self-expression and a praxis of resistance and political-cultural struggle against exclusion, marginalization, and violence experienced and suffered by indigenous peoples as a political minority in the dual sense of the term: as a negative political-normative construction on the part of our peripheral modernization and its epistemological-political and sociocultural baseline subjects – such as the engenho lord, the bandeirante, the slave owner, the military, the missionary, the landowner, the professional politician and the state bureaucrat -, and as the result of a political process of material violence in which the domestication and, even more so, the destruction of the indigenous were the central goal (Dorrico 2018: 167).

Indigenous literature in Brazil aligns with the idea of constructing oneself as a voice-praxis activist (voz-práxis ativista), militant and engaged in the indigenous cause (Dorrico 2018: 172). Indigenous leaders and intellectuals keep emphasizing that the indigenous people need to be and remain protagonists of their own cause, create and stabilize autonomy, auto-affirmation, and auto-expression without any mediation when it comes to the narration of anthropological-ontological as well as sociocultural and epistemological singularity and the narration of exclusion, marginalization, violence, and they will always have to assume themselves as subjects and political actors (Dorrico 2018: 170). Theoretical and literary texts of indigenous authorship often refer to shamanism, which reflects life as an interwoven whole where nature, culture and metaphysical or religious perspectives are imbricated and interdependent (Dorrico 2018: 170). Dorrico states that intellectuals have to publish to influence public and political discourse about modernity and the urge to protect nature for indigenous as well as non-indigenous people:

> protection of nature – she who constitutes this vital and normative whole in which we are inserted, this whole that is the condition of human life itself and its development over time – is conditio sine qua non for human well-being they write to whites, in the sense of dialoguing and interacting with them (Dorrico 2018: 178).

Graça Graúna is another important voice in creative writing and academia. In 2013 she published a monography on indigenous literature in Brazil where she explains the main counterpoints of contemporary indigenous literature between a life in the large cities and roots in small villages. In addition, she asks the question of what role literature and literary critics play in decolonizing processes and the extent to which they can influence understandings of reality and the world (Graúna 2013: 11).

> Contemporary indigenous literature is a utopian place (of survival), a variant of the epic through orality; a place of confluence woven of voices silenced and exiled (written) throughout more than 500 years of colonization. Rooted in its origins, contemporary indigenous literature has been preserved in the self-history of its authors and in the reception of a differentiated reading public, that is, a minority that sows other possible readings in the universe of autochthonous poems and prose. In this process of reflection, the voice of the text shows that the rights of indigenous peoples to express their love of the land, to live their customs, their social organiza-

tion, their languages, and to manifest their beliefs have never really been considered (Graúna 2013: 15).

In her poem *Escrevivência* (2020), Graça Graúna expresses the same complementarity: "In writing, I make sense of my ancestry; of my way back, of my place in the world" (Dorrico et al. 2020: 19). These few lines show how words and writing open possibilities to reflect one's own social and personal position, while simultaneously being an important part of life itself. Indigenous literature must be seen as an embodiment of the indigenous experience, which at the same time (re)creates knowledge and works as a medium to transfer knowledge.

Although not always in written letters, indigenous forms of expression have always existed. As Graúna highlights, in various indigenous cultures the word is a holy element with a soul and is not only spoken by human beings but every entity of the world: "words filled with water, words coming out of the earth, words heated with fire, words so necessary as the air one breaths; words that cross the time" (2013: 173). Highlighting that the word comes from the world (*terra*), she refers to the earth as female – as many different cultures do – which indicates a deep-rooted belief in female power in the world and an urge to listen to these words, like the Chiapas people from Mexico who are always striving to strengthen the connection to mother earth in search of democracy, equality and justice (2013: 173).

Not all writers of the movement have an academic background, although a significant part of the female writers do. Their words not only spread in a creative sense, but they challenge the dominant literary field as well as the field of literary criticism. The literary field is also an imbalanced ecosystem. The indigenous perspective of the academic texts adds a very important perspective to the scientific discourse about indigenous literature and is crucial in processes of decolonizing academia. The authors themselves play an active role in the discussion process and reception of indigenous texts. They have strengthened their own voice and appropriated the theoretical[2] discourse on indigenous literature.

---

[2] Since the 1980s and especially the 1990s, various theoretical texts have existed on social, political and educational questions written by indigenous authors in Brazil, such as Davi Kopenawa, Daniel Munduruku, and Ailton Krenak.

The most well-known authors of indigenous literature in Brazil might be Daniel Munduruku[3] and Eliane Potiguara. Thinking of the literary work of Eliane Potiguara in isolation from her social and political activism does not make any sense. She was born in 1950 in Río de Janeiro as child of a family of displaced Potiguara people (Da Costa 2020: 98). At a very young age, she started her activism and founded the women's network GRUMIN, which shows how she has always acted on different levels: *A terra é a mãe do índio* [The earth is the mother of indigenous the people] (1989, financed by Unesco) was a publication intended to inform and fight analphabetism (Potiguara 2004: 140). The narrative is a connection between literary and social levels of activism.

Eliane Potiguara's groundbreaking book *Metade cara, metade mascara* [Half face, half mask] (2004) might be the most read and analyzed narrative publication of the movement. It is a text of different structures and narrators. It shows fictional as well as factual elements and alludes to biographical content as well as mythical stories. It has been translated into English and analyzed in various dissertations about Ecocriticism and Ecofeminism in the United States, because it reflects the fights of Potiguara women (Graúna 2013: 97). Graça Graúna describes *Metade Cara Metade Máscara* [Half face, half mask] (2004) as a space of multi-signification and an ensemble of different voices (2013: 98). One of these voices is the narrator of the first chapter: "Invasão às terras indígenas e a migração" [Invasion of indigenous lands and migration] (Potiguara 2004: 23). This part introduces the life of dislocated and separated families and the ways in which women built intergenerational resilience and connects female bodies to territories of mother earth:

---

3 Daniel Munduruku publishes novels and children's books and has been invited to international book fairs (for example, the German Buchmesse in Frankfurt, 2013). His works are dedicated to the question of belonging, indigenous identity, a change of perspective and indigenous consciousness (Todas as coisas são pequenas (2013), among others). Munduruku has a doctorate in education and connects the creative and the academic worlds in his educational seminars and workshops for the indigenous community as well as non-indigenous public to create consciousness about indigenous history and present. He has also published different essays on indigenous literature. Like many writers of the movement of contemporary indigenous literature, he acts on different levels, in literary, academic and social activism. Other important male figures are Yaguarê Yamã, Olivio Jecupé, Cristino Wapichana, and Renê Kithãulu, among others.

With the exception of one Aunt Evanilda, all of them married and, some time later, their husbands left or died, leaving them alone with their children to raise and facing the racism and intolerance of society. The girl to whom we refer, had this story as her life scenario and became a very observant, quiet, sensitive, and spiritualized person, an inheritance from these indigenous women who, even outside their original lands and violated by the historical, political, and cultural process, have maintained their culture and traditional habits, especially their ties with their ancestors, their cosmology, and their spiritual heritage (Potiguara 2004: 26).

The narrator also clarifies that the word of the grandmother saved the character (*a menina*) when she tells her real stories that took her into a magic and literary world (Potiguara 2004: 26) and describes how indigenous women have always been sources of energy and as well as savage and resilient, resisting to the dominant culture and using their intuition and forces of nature spirits to guarantee the survival of their family (Potiguara 2004: 46). This heritage allows contemporary authors and activists to be strong in wider social contexts when it comes to human rights, the demarcation of indigenous lands as well as the recovery and recuperation of cultural and literary space. Various poems of the book specify and demand women leadership and sorority and use metaphors of nature or direct references to the relation between women and nature:

> "*Woman! Come, sister*
> *drink from this fountain that awaits you*
> *my sweet tender words.*
> *Shout to the world*
> *your story*
> *go ahead and don't be despaired*
> *[...]*
> *Come sister*
> *wash your pain by the riverbank*
> *call for the little birds*
> *and sing like them, even alone*
> *and see your strong body flourish*
> (Potiguara 2004: 76f.).

Humans are part of nature and people should be able to grow with it and find mental awareness and physical strength when acknowledging this fact. The moment of realization is the moment when ties are built. This development opens possibilities and cultural and political space to strike back against patriarchy and colonialism in a collective and intergenerational way. There are two axes of female power – the sorority between women in a synchronic moment and the diachronic bond between mothers, grandmothers and female ancestors – both of which are directly connected to Potiguara's ecological and feminist criticism. The analyzed literary texts can show this collectivity as a whole. In *Metade cara metade máscara* [Half face, half mask] (2004), female complicity and ancestry are not merely a topic, but an element that determines the narrative discourse itself.

The idea of a strong bond between mothers and daughters as a textual structuring element leads directly to Julie Dorrico's literary creation. Her book *Eu sou macuxi e outras historias* [I am Macuxi and other stories] (2019) includes a chapter called "Contos de minha avó" [Tales of my grandmother]. This text combines passages of a female narrator remembering her grandmother and her daily occupations in a very natural and fluid way – giving a vivid impression of life in an indigenous countryside household – with mythical stories. Many of the passages refer to the crucial role of mothers and grandmothers in the daily production of food and home for families. The whole text integrates an inherent criticism of patriarchy and domination while presenting a dynamic and equal world system between male and female human characters as well as non-human characters and entities. The following excerpt demonstrates the interwoven structure of references that the text makes. On various occasions, passages imply a certain direct or indirect complicity between women, like the grandmother's paxiúba trees that the homodiegetic narrator grandmother planted near the river and that serves as a hiding place and medium for the seduction of a man.

> She hid behind the paxiúba my grandmother had planted on the riverbank. Seduced, the man dropped his bananas and swam into the river trying to get closer, but every time it seemed he would be able to embrace the woman, the man saw her image further away [...] The man followed the current without bothering about the danger of the deep water. He didn't know, the woman was the daughter of the waters, she was the daughter of Makunaima. When at last he could reach her, the woman, in an abrupt gesture, took him to the depths of the river. The woman was a mermaid. The mermaid was an enchanted being (Dorrico 2019: 50).

The whole passage describes how a man falls in love with the daughter of the river who lures him into the deep waters. In the water, the man becomes part of the enchanted world of non-human beings of the water. Attributions like male/female or human/non-human exist in complementarity rather than competition or domination, lines and between them tend to be fluid and reflect transformation between states of natural existence.

> Under the water, the man came across the mermaid's father, the shaman of the waters, the sisters, the sisters-in-law, the grandmother, the great-grandmother, the curumins. And they all turned into fish, stones, wells, of all kinds, always choosing the form they liked best. He realized that he was in the non-human world of the waters (Dorrico 2019: 51).

Apart from the literal sense of the story, it tells about the dynamic relationship between humans and nature, explains how traditions and knowledge pass from one generation to the other and how family strings and interpersonal (not necessarily interhuman) strings are tied. Relations must not always be neither harmonic nor always peaceful but display balanced movement systems and power structures between different entities. The siren has seductive power over the man, female characters share power in complicity, the man engages in a teacher/learner relationship with the water community, and finally, the former stranger becomes an important member of the community.

> There he learned the ritual of the young girl, the time of planting manioc, how to find the piranha wells, the seasons that favored the cultivation of pumpkin, dar, ingá, bananas, hunting, fishing and gathering, and all the things that the water enchanted cared for. Many, many moons have passed and man has not forgotten his family. Even though he did not forget his sister-in-law and his children of the earth, the man married the daughter of the waters, had children, and became an important member of the community of the encantados (Dorrico 2019: 51).

This section is accompanied by drawings of figures that cannot be clearly identified as humans or plants. The text by Julie Dorrico (re)constructs female intergenerational memory, which is neither limited to place nor time and includes mother earth as the creator of life:

> In the times of creation, Mother Earth looked at Makunaima and the brothers playing in the fields and wanted to create another son, because she

liked to see the backyard full of people. [...] the mother is the trees, rivers and hills. Everything that is beyond inside the earth and beyond the sky (Dorrico 2019: 35f.).

The female writers of the movement of contemporary indigenous literature in Brazil act on many different levels when it comes to conceptualizing and reconstructing the awareness of the earth relations, the relationship between all living beings on earth, which includes human and non-human life. The first mentioned level is the conceptualization on an intra-textual level as part of the narrational process and content of prose and lyric texts. On a second level, indigenous literature challenges the dominant literary canon. The third level is the metatext of these publications and the creation of valuable theory on indigenous literature, which discusses indigenous texts as well as those written by indigenous academics. For example, Julie Dorrico fulfils the two roles within this movement, namely as a writer and a literary critic. On a broader level, indigenous literature, and theory form possibilities to create new standpoints and voices regarding the history about indigenous people and with it the opportunity to make their official version of history visible (Dorrico 2018: 242) to a large audience that will also have an influence on political discourse. The social and political activism of the writers reaches another level during public workshops and lectures at cultural centers, institutions and the annual reunion of indigenous writers and artists at the fair of the Fundação Nacional do Livro Infantil e Juvenil. Since 2020, the number of online talks and courses has increased, and a true culture of online communication has emerged within the literary movement and towards the world.

As mentioned, literary and critical strategies of the movement deeply connect to the political movement and combine various decolonial practices to challenge dominant literary, social, historical and political fields and discourses, especially in terms of female resistance and feminist cultural recovery. In conclusion, it changes the understanding of western ideas of democracy and modernization: "And, by doing this, it brings new ontologies, ethics, aesthetics and utopias to the center of democratic life. We believe that indigenous thought can be the base for a new theoretical-practical perspective of criticism and reconstruction of modernization" (Dorrico et al 2020: 10). The natural world (which includes human and non-human beings) and its resilience are generally essential in indigenous literature and female characters have strong voices in it. Literature and indigenous authorship incorporate the autonomous and sometimes militant voice of marginalized subjects based on their own singularity (Dorrico et al 2020: 10).

Ecofeminism

Another movement that is deeply rooted in Brazil has come a long way during the last 40 years. It has emerged from a theological movement in liberal theology and spread out to become many different movements with different political, social or literary anchors. One main concept is the idea that there are structural parallels between patriarchal and colonial oppression and the exploitation of natural resources. Brazilian Ecofeminism is a theological and philosophical way of thinking and a social movement that sees the ideological connection of exploitation of nature and exploitation of women within the patriarchal system. Ecofeminism intends to reinforce nature and women who have been oppressed and dominated by the patriarchal system thinking of modernity and reduced to being entities of reproduction for the growth of capital (Gebara 2000: 18).

An essay of the collective of investigation and action called *LaDanta LasCanta* from Venezuela mentions the most important voices of theological ecofeminism: Ivone Gebara in Brazil, Coca Trillini in Argentina, Fanny Geymonat Pantelís and Aleira Agreda in Bolivia, Agamedilza Sales de Oliveira, Sandra Duarte and Sandra Raquew in Brazil, Mareia Moya in Ecuador, Rosa Dominga Trapasso in Peru, Mary Judith Ress in Chile, Graciela Pujol in Uruguay, and Gladys Parentelli and Rosa Trujillo in Venezuela (LasCanta 2017: 36). The most important international ecofeminist collective and magazine (1992–2009) called Con-spirando was founded in 1991 and – for example – offered a historical perspective of indigenous peoples in Latin America (LasCanta 2017: 37). The first wave of ecofeminism has been criticized as essentialist, spiritualist and new age, although these interpretations did not take the complexity of the Latin American reality into account (LasCanta 2017: 35, 38). Some northern ecofeminists even ignored Brazilian ecofeminist theory due to their religious roots and do not mention Gebara's important role in current retrospectives. Ivone Gebara explained the original cause of her ecofeminist work as follows:

> I try to be an ecologist in a feminist perspective and a feminist in an ecological perspective. I try to explain ecology as one of the deepest concerns

of feminism and ecology as having a deep resonance or a political and anthropological consequence from a feminist perspective. Both feminism and ecology want to understand human beings as female and male living in a complex web of different cultures and ecosystems (Gebara 2003: 94).

While in contemporary indigenous literature the lines between human and natural lives are erased, the definition of Gebara's quote shows that lines exist but everything is connected. Elaine Nogueira-Godsey(2013) argues that Brazilian theological ecofeminism by Ivone Gebara has always been "on the move" because it was "grounded in the changing needs of the marginalized in her own environment, and by her engagement and dialogues with global realities that intersect with local concerns" (90). Ecofeminism never stopped being on the move and it is always changing depending on the social and ecological context of its theorists. One of the most important ideas of ecofeminist thinkers is the connection between theory and practice. Even Ivone Gebara highlighted that while theorists are arguing about theory details, human and non-human beings are dying due to a capitalist-caused ecological crisis (Gebara 2003: 94f.). She essentially argues that ecofeminist action is not purely theoretical but that rather it must be combined with concrete social actions. This is where the indigenous and ecofeminist movements come together.

In recent years, extractive industries and projects have demanded that depatriarchalizing, decolonizing struggles and fights for collective rights have found their way onto the agenda of worldwide ecofeminist concerns, especially in Latin America. Therefore collectives like the Colectivo Miradas Críticas del Territorio desde el Feminismo develop new methodologies of fieldwork and participative investigation action-taking within and outside of academia with a strong protagonism of indigenous women's organizations (LasCanta 2017: 39f.).

Climate change, extractivism, forced displacement and many other factors are producing a new wave of transdisciplinary ecofeminism in cultural and literary studies worldwide and demand a change of perspective and academic culture. This ecological and ecofeminist turn in scientific work directly depends on the force of social movements from the so-called global south, which are increasingly represented by strong female voices who at all times reflect the interlocking dimensions of different axes of oppression and inequality in their daily political activism. The postcolonial challenge for hegemonic literary and cultural studies in the 21st century is to delink criticism and discourse from the colonial matrix of power and internalize the knowledge and strategies of the ecofeminist and indigenous movements described in this essay without falling into the trap of theoretical appropriation.

References

Da Costa, Heliene Rosa (2020): Identidades e ancestralidades das mulheres indígenas na poética de Eliane Potiguara, Uberlândia: Universidade Federal de Uberlândia.

Dorrico, Julie (2019): Eu sou macuxi e outras histórias, Nova Lima: Editora Caos & Letras.

Dorrico, Julie (2018): "Uma literatura militante: sobre a correlação de movimento indígena e literatura indígena brasileira contemporânea." In: Aletria 28/3, pp. 163–181.

Dorrico, Julie (2017): "Literatura indígena e seus intelectuais no Brasil: da autoafirmação e da autoexpressão como minoria à resistência e à luta políticoculturais." In: Revista de Estudos e Pesquisas sobre as Américas 11/3, pp. 114–136.

Dorrico, Julie/Danner, Fernando/Danner, Leno Francisco (eds.) (2020): Literatura indígena brasileira contemporânea: autoria, autonomia, ativismo, Porto Alegre: Editora Fi.

Dorrico, Julie/Danner, Leno Francisco/Correia, Heloisa/Danner, Fernando (eds.) (2018): Literatura indígena brasileira contemporânea: criação, crítica e recepção, Porto Alegre: Editora Fi.

Gebara, Ivone (2003): "Ecofeminism: A Latin American Perspective." In: Cross-Currents 53/1, pp. 93–103.

Gebara, Ivone (2000): Intuiciones ecofeministas. Ensayo para repensar el conocimiento y la religión, Madrid: Trotta.

Graúna, Graça (2013): Contrapontos da literatura indígena contemporânea no Brasil, Belo Horizonte: Maza Edições.

LasCanta, LaDanta (2017): "De la teología al antiextractivismo: Ecofeminismos en Abya Yala." In: Ecología Política: Cuadernos de debate internacional, 54, p. 35.

Nogueira-Godsey, Elaine (2013): "A History of Resistance: Ivone Gebara's Transformative Feminist Liberation Theology." In: Journal for the Study of Religion 26/2, pp. 89–106.

Potiguara, Eliane (1989): A terra é a mãe do índio, Rio de Janeiro: GRUMIN.

Potiguara, Eliane (2004): Metade cara, metade máscara, São Paulo: Global.

Environmental Knowledges in Resistance
Mobilization, (Re)Production, and the Politics of Place. The Case of the Cooperativa Mujeres Ecologistas de la Huizachera, Jalisco (Mexico)

Daniela Gloss Nuñez and Itxaso García Chapinal

Abstract: *The modern/colonial-gender system has imposed a hierarchy on gender, knowledges, nature, and humans. The consequences of this pattern are interwoven in a crisis of civilization; one of its greatest symptoms is the socio-environmental crisis that multiple vulnerable groups have been resisting, such as women in Latin American urban peripheries. In this chapter, we will assume a qualitative, decolonial, and feminist perspective to analyze the case of the Cooperativa Mujeres Ecologistas de la Huizachera in El Salto (Jalisco, Mexico), whose members have mobilized different types of knowledges to confront gender and environmental inequalities in their families and community.*

1. Introduction

From the outset, social, political, and economic inequalities produced by the modern/colonial-gender system (cf. Quijano/Wallerstein 1992; Lugones 2007) have been met with resistance by socially marginalized groups, such as women, peasants, and indigenous and afro-descendant groups. These resistances have mobilized, produced, and reproduced knowledges usually ignored and disregarded by colonial epistemology.

Regarding environmental conflicts and the defense of place[1], such as struggles against deforestation or water pollution, the high level of social mobilization of women stands out, often combined with demands for women's rights. These demands vary in their levels of need, such as basic means to ensure menstrual health and hygiene, food safety, easy and safe access to clean water, among others; issues that are frequently linked with access to education, safe transit, public participation, and spaces that are free of violence against women. In this chapter, we will analyze, from a decolonial gender perspective, the mobilization of knowledges and the process of change driven by women of the Cooperativa Mujeres Ecologistas de la Huizachera (Ecologist Women of La Huizachera Cooperative), short COMEH, in Jalisco (Mexico). The members of the COMEH are an example of how environmental conflicts are interlaced with several gender-based vulnerabilities that women face daily, especially from lower socioeconomic sectors of less privileged geographies. This way, their defense of place is also a defense of their own right to produce and inhabit spaces safely while ensuring their families' survival.

2. Modernity/Coloniality, Gender, and Environment

Since the Europeans' arrival in the Americas in the 14th century, European colonization has imposed a global pattern that Lugones has termed the modern/colonial-gender system. This term was coined by Lugones applying a feminist perspective to the world system and a decolonial analysis by Wallerstein (1974) and Mignolo (2000). In this chapter, we will use the concept of the colonial/modern-gender system, since it links gender, modernity, and coloniality under capitalism. The modern/colonial-gender system is based on the hierarchical distinction between supposed races, human and nature, as well as hierarchical gender relations between woman and man (Lugones 2011). The

---

1 We understand environmental conflicts to be multifactorial, thus they are not only understood as distributive conflicts but as one of the most evident symptoms of a larger social and environmental crisis, linked to a generalized crisis of civilization, based upon three main ideological axes: 1) civilization as a synonym of economic development and moral superiority, linked to the conception of the labor force and of land as merchandises; 2) Occidental science as the only and morally superior form of knowledge, related to mechanization, colonization, and disciplining of the bodies, passions, and the Other and 3) gendered and racial division of work and societies (Gloss 2021).

gender system it imposed is based on the subjugation of women in all spheres of life. Women are defined by their relation to men, and are thus considered inferior in economic, political, social, and epistemological terms (Lugones 2007). In the Americas, this imposition resulted in different gender patterns derived from a blending with local societies and particular transformations (ibid), thereby creating different gender positions, experiences, practices, and knowledges for the colonized and the colonizing men and women, as Lugones explains:

> Colonialism did not impose precolonial, European gender arrangements on the colonized. It imposed a new gender system that created very different arrangements for colonized males and females than for White bourgeois colonizers. Thus, it introduced many genders and gender itself as a colonial concept and mode of organization of relations, of production, property relations, of cosmologies and ways of knowing (Lugones 2007: 186).

The domination of the native population has implied a feminization of the native population as part of the symbolic domination and humiliation, allowing their exploitation and sexual abuse (Lugones 2011; Maldonado/Torres 2007). However, native men collaborated with European colonizers to establish the colonial gender system within their communities (Lugones 2007) and became representatives as well as part of the reproductive system of the modern/colonial-gender system (Segato 2011). Men assumed positions of power within their communities and took on the role of mediators with the colonial administration; while women were excluded from leadership structures and subordinated to their male counterparts (Oyěwùmí 2001; Segato 2011). The modern/colonial-gender system and its hierarchies continue today transformed and adapted to the current socio-economic necessities of the world system (Quijano/Wallerstein 1992).

From the perspective of the modern/colonial-gender system, the environment is characterized by the dichotomy of human/nature and the exploitation of the latter by the former (De Sousa Santos 2014). Economic growth is the main objective, which is achieved by extracting natural resources at a large scale, ignoring the social and ecological consequences of this exploitation (Svampa 2019). In the last two decades, this pattern of extractivism has been pushed again and updated in the Americas. Regions with natural resources have been considered "socially empty" and thus suitable to be extracted regardless of the people living there, their opinion, culture, or well-being (ibid). One example is

La Huizachera, an industrialized peripheral community in the metropolitan area of Guadalajara (Mexico).

In environmental conflicts, women are subject to a double dispute; on the one hand, the distributive conflict of natural resources; and on the other hand, the existing gender inequalities in the distribution of resources and the use of space in the affected communities (Martinez Alier 2005). Due to the different types of oppression that women suffer through their bodies (disregard, violence, economic dependence, unwanted pregnancies...), the defense of their own bodies is usually the starting point and the reason for their political involvement. As a consequence, their primary demands are gender-related, such as autonomy, reproductive rights, sexual emancipation, or a life without violence (Harcourt/Escobar 2002).

Due to the socially constructed role of women in the family, they are usually, and especially in communities with economies of self-subsistence, the first to react to conditions of privatization, scarcity, or contamination of fundamental resources that threaten the survival of their families (Bryant/Bailey 2005; Martínez Alier 2005). The same women (and bodies) who claim gender rights simultaneously defend their territory, its meaning, and value to ensure their families' survival (Harcourt/Escobar 2002). In this way, feminist demands, and environmental struggles are often entangled.

These practices of resistance have (re)produced epistemologies that are different from Western science, based on previous knowledges of communities, methods of organization, and experiences (De Sousa Santos 2018: 2). For example, these epistemologies propose different alternatives in defense of nature through an integrative and holistic perspective (Harcourt/Escobar 2002). The variety of knowledges, acquired through different practices and social bonds, some of them maintained throughout generations of women, are often underestimated or ignored within the capitalist modern/colonial-gender system. The epistemology of the modern/colonial-gender system is based on scientific knowledge, that is to say, on "systematic observation and controlled experimentation" (De Sousa Santos 2018: 5.) Knowledge produced following these principles is considered universal as well as objective, the only valid way of understanding the world and change it. This epistemic system has not only underestimated other knowledges, and in the Mexican context specifically those mobilized by women and indigenous communities, but also contributed to the reproduction of the modern/colonial-gender system (De Sousa Santos 2018).

Given this situation, the ecologies of knowledges defend a non-hierarchical dialogue and co-existence of diverse epistemologies. The promotion of this dialogue would require identifying other knowledges, their values, and methods (De Sousa Santos 2014). For this purpose, we must question the universality and objectivity of colonial epistemology. However, challenging Occidental universality and acknowledging epistemic diversity does not mean cultural or epistemic relativism. Such an endeavor implies a more complex analysis of different world views and the entanglements between them (De Sousa Santos/Meneses 2014). Moreover, from a gender perspective, it is necessary to consider gender inequalities in the access, production, and legitimacy of knowledge production. Women of the COMEH put this dialogue into practice by combining different knowledges – scientific knowledges, local knowledges, and new knowledges acquired by their collective experience – in the field, as we will show in the following analysis. Experiences and struggles such as those led by the women of the COMEH evidence the multiple levels on which the coloniality of gender operates and remains present, increasing women's multiple vulnerabilities, in this case, those of poor peripheral communities in Latin America. Following Lugones (2011), we argue that the analysis of their struggles for survival and their rights as women at the margins of privilege can contribute to feminist decolonial studies, as their political action is centered around different needs and priorities than those of middle and upper class Mexican mainstream feminist women.

3. Knowledge Mobilization and Production: Towards a Politics of the Ordinary

The following qualitative analysis is based on ethnographic fieldwork consisting mainly of interviews, group discussions, and participant observation carried out from 2013 to 2014 and between 2019 and 2021, involving members of the COMEH in La Huizachera, El Salto, (Jalisco, Mexico). We will introduce this section with a short contextualization to situate the women of the COMEH and illustrate the everyday socio-environmental problems they face and the scope and relevance of their political action.

The women of the COMEH live in La Huizachera, a small peripheral community in the municipality of El Salto, part of the metropolitan area of Guadalajara, Mexico. They are mainly women between the ages of 35 to 70, and their families face constant economical and health difficulties. The socio-environmental conflict that the cooperative COMEH is confronted with is multidimensional. One of its most urgent challenges is the alarming water pollution of the Santiago River, the most polluted river in Mexico. The Santiago River flows through El Salto and El Ahogado canal, one of the most densely contaminated bodies of water that crosses La Huizachera. Additionally, the air in this area is highly contaminated due to several national and transnational industrial activities[2]. Other vulnerabilities the communities there are facing are a lack of basic services, such as access to clean water, proper sewage maintenance, and trash collection. Among other social problems, people in La Huizachera face unemployment, poverty, corrupt authorities, political manipulation, and criminal networks (Gloss 2015).

Due to the high level of air and water pollution, many inhabitants of La Huizachera and El Salto suffer pollution-related diseases like cancer, renal failure, and respiratory and dermatological illnesses (Tribunal Interamericano del Agua 2007; Universidad Autónoma de San Luis Potosí/Comisión Estatal del Agua de Jalisco 2010; Greenpeace 2012). The correlation between pollution and chronic diseases in this area has been consistently denied by the state of Jalisco's government. Through a state confidentiality clause that was in effect from 2011 to 2021, official evidence of heavy metals in children's blood was hidden for ten years (Arístegui Noticias 2020).

The knowledges that the COMEH mobilizes and generates are linked to several sources and contexts (Gloss 2021; Corona 2021): community knowledge, indigenous cultures, ecofeminism, agroecology, the Zapatistas (EZLN), specifically regarding the role of women and the construction of autonomies, popular education, and ecological building techniques.

Their practice of incorporating diverse knowledges into their daily lives and group activities has defied cultural community guidelines on several occasions. Through agroecology and its practice, women of the COMEH started to signify nature as a living entity. As they worked the soil at their community and domestic orchards, which was infertile because of the multiple sources of pollution surrounding their community, they developed parallel strategies linking the healing of the earth and of themselves. This process implied learning about natural cycles and their relation with the phases of the moon, which usually guide traditional farming in Mexico. Specifically, the analogies made between the phases of the moon, women's cycles and natural cycles generated conflicts with the knowledge promoted by the Catholic Church and validated by the community. The cluster of knowledges that the COMEH constructed

---

2   These industries are focused on the production of metal-mechanics, car components, pharmaceuticals, chemicals, and food and drinks.

through their defense of place[3], in combination with their biographical and family knowledge, led them to recognize themselves as experts in agroecology and eco-technologies in their community, as well as in other communities they visited. This action had a strong political impact inside their families and community because it implied being "visible" in the public space, as women who acted differently from the rest; it also implied being "seen" and judged as crazy, lazy, negligent with their care labors, rebels, or libertines (Gloss 2015).

This self-recognition process, as women who "know", had two main functions. The first one relates to the fact that these knowledges have led the women to understand nature, and themselves, through – and as a part of – nature. As Carla, the community educator that has accompanied the COMEH from the beginning, points out:

> The patriarchy somehow has naturalized our body. Based on that, it has exploited it [...] seeing it as merchandise, as an object, and it has feminized nature, considered it a woman he has to exploit [...] When I speak about feminizing earth, it's not in this capitalist sense of exploitation, but in a loving sense that women have as this caregiver's role that has been given to us, I speak about caring, protecting. Esperanza [her friend] expressed it very well 'I am a mother of people, trees, plants, and animals' (Personal communication, 5 May 2018).

Relating themselves to nature and soil as mothers and as caretakers and guardians of life through their socially constructed roles led them to recognize their own captivities and violences to which they are ordinarily exposed in the streets, jobs, and homes. Building a safe space for expressing and validating their feelings and needs also led them to build places for contemplating both the past and the future. Remembering their past experiences, as hard as they could be, drove them to recognize, celebrate, value, and admire their power,

---

[3] We consider it important to vindicate the notion of place, as a dynamic set of relations, practices and meanings that frequently, yet not necessarily, are rooted in a physical or even real space (Escobar 2010; Gloss 2015, 2021). Throughout Mexico and Latin America, the defense of territory is the most commonly used term to express struggles related to socio-environmental or land dispute conflicts. In this case, the use of place is important because of its analytical scope, specially concerning women's struggles. This way, we can understand the defense of place in its multiple social and spatial dimensions – body, family, group, community, public space, glocal meshworks and nature – on the basis of the analytical approaches and framework relating to "women and the politics of place" (Harcourt/Escobar 2007, 2012; Gloss, 2015, 2017, 2021).

resilience, and the set of knowledges they have produced and mobilized to survive and confront multiple adverse conditions. As the women of the COMEH gained knowledge about nature and learned different techniques to live in harmony with it, they simultaneously gained knowledge about themselves (individually), about each other, and the community (collectively), and ways of self-care and collective, sisterly care, and love. These practices also became projects, such as opening special moments to speak of their feelings and internal conflicts or participating in larger women networks.

The second function of recognizing knowledges which the COMEH produced, gained, and mobilized has to do with self-esteem; this implied overcoming the fear of speaking up, being seen, and recognizing themselves as capable of learning from different sources. This way, recognizing and valuing their diverse stocks of knowledges built trust in their own abilities, their power to take control over spaces in their homes and claim their place in the decision-making processes in the public and private spheres.

The women of the COMEH recognized that neither public nor private spheres had been properly theirs until they were able to use them, transit, and occupy them. This process entailed a defense of their bodies, as the first place that is inhabited and socially produced, and their right to have spaces of their own. For them, this discussion goes beyond notions of "legal property" of their households, typically or traditionally owned by men[4]. Home is a place of care, production and reproduction of life, a place that the women of the cooperative consciously intervene in through their political action, and which they use for the common good. The COMEH also defies the private property or government property logic that is part of the modern/colonial-gender system, as they understand nature as a shared living system that transcends individuals or human beings in general.

The dominant economic-production and gender system is also challenged as the women of the COMEH evidence and vindicate their active role, skills, knowledges, and experiences as caregivers and in the preservation and reproduction of life. Simultaneously, they also point out their capabilities to reach several autonomies through agroecological practices, political, and eco-technological knowledges. Ana, a member of the COMEH, recalls when she claimed a space in her household to set up her domestic orchard:

---

4   In most of Latin America, in families dedicated to agriculture, culturally and traditionally, women could not, and in some cases still cannot, own land, because only men are socially legitimated to be landowners and farmers.

> This was formerly my sons' garage [...] When I planted here, they told me: 'Mom, you invaded our plot.' I told them: 'No, you are crazy, how is it I invaded your plot? Well, this is my house and you have not respected it, and from here to there, I don't want you to step on anything.' (Ana, personal communication, 17 October 2014).

The first response most of the women in the COMEH received to their involvement in the cooperative's activities were anger, judgment, and/or rejection from their families. Gradually, as members of their families benefited from the domestic orchards and the implementation of eco-technologies, they started to contribute and get involved in the COMEH's projects; with daughters, grandchildren, and daughters-in-law being the most receptive, and husbands and sons the most reluctant.

The knowledges women of the COMEH have acquired, but also valued and vindicated retrospectively, represent opportunities of economic autonomy and food sovereignty for them, their families, and other women of their community. Put into practice, these knowledges have been used to build productive and reproductive places, like their domestic or community orchards, which represent an autonomous and/or alternative food source. To produce and consume through processes that respect nature is actively resisting the dominant agro-industrial production system. Producing and consuming homegrown fruits and vegetables means taking an important political stand on health and nutrition. Such practices are especially relevant in the socio-environmentally devastated immediate context of the COMEH – an increasingly generalized reality in Mexican rural, suburban, and urban areas.

Through ecological technologies they built at their homes and the community orchard, members of the COMEH have to spend less on natural gas and potable water from private waterpipes – given the lack of potable water from public pipelines. This also enhances their autonomy from the traditional assistance and manipulative politics of the local government and the dominant political parties in the community. By putting into practice these alternative forms of knowledge, granddaughters, grandsons, daughters, sons, daughters-in-law, and even husbands – the most reluctant family members, followed by sons – started to explicitly value and become engaged with the activities of the cooperative.

As Zibechi (2012) points out, "societies in movement" in Latin America have strong territorial bonds and are led by women, especially in peripheral areas, taking a stand to highlight the dimensions of rootedness and important micro-politics, or politics of the ordinary, that are inherent in these struggles and movements. The small groups that form these societies in movement frequently resemble a family organization and are grounded in specific families as the nucleus of the group, as we can observe as a relevant and potent quality of the COMEH's struggle, among other groups facing similar problems (Zibechi 2012; Gravante/Poma 2018; Gloss 2017, 2020).

The central and constant learning experiences have resulted in the COMEH's members recognizing the repression and domination mechanisms inside their homes and community. At the same time, this process led them to recognize the reach of their political actions, which is centrally, but not exclusively, based on daily life. For communities who are facing and resisting socio-environmental conflicts like La Huizachera and El Salto, their form of applying their own knowledge is a form of "everyday resistance" (Sofia Enciso, Personal communication, April 2021), or a politics of the ordinary.

4. Final Thoughts

Thinking and learning collectively, through self-reflective processes, has enabled groups such as the COMEH to map, understand, and critically analyze their specific contexts and the related social and environmental problems. As a result, the members of the group have become political, learning, and knowledge-producing subjects. At the margins of the modern/colonial-gender system and its epistemology, groups like the COMEH are able to name, abstract, and conceptualize their realities following a practical and contextualized, or place-grounded, logic. A logic that defies hegemonic, colonial, and patriarchal hierarchies in knowledge production processes, that values and vindicates diverse sources, as well as knowledges produced by individual and collective direct experiences.

Regarding research such as the one discussed in this chapter, research related to groups of people who defend their place, and specifically women, one of the most persistent questions is which concepts these groups have appropriated from the researchers' intervention in their realities. In the case of women's groups, and specifically the COMEH, one could ask if they, for example, consider themselves feminists. Feminism is within their scope, but not necessarily central, even though their political practice could be considered and labeled as such. When health and basic conditions of survival are disputed, every day turns into a fight for survival or for not living in fear of premature death and disease. In this light, concepts that are deemed important according to dominant epistemology do not have the same relevance for resisting communities. One could ask, for instance, whether feminism, in this case, is not better considered as a continuously nurtured practice or an individual and collective process in constant movement, as part of a politics of the ordinary that is simultaneously a politics of place, care, and knowledge.

References

Bryant, Raymond L./ Bailey, Sinéad (2005): Third World Political Ecology, London: Routledge.
Corona, Isabel Yoloxóchitl (2021): Movilización del conocimiento y sus efectos en la configuración de lo político: La cuenca alta del Río Santiago en Jalisco. Social Sciences Ph.d. Thesis, Mexico City: Facultad Latinoamericana de Ciencias Sociales México.
De Sousa Santos, Boaventura (2014): Epistemologies of the South. Justice against Epistemicide, London: Paradigm Publishers.
De Sousa Santos, Boaventura (2018): The End of the Cognitive Empire: The Coming of Age of Epistemologies of the South, Durham and London: Duke University Press.
De Sousa Santos, Boaventura/Meneses, Maria Paula (2014): Epistemologías del sur (perspectivas), Madrid: Ediciones Akal.
Domínguez Cortinas, Gabriela (2011): Propuesta metodológica para la implantación de una batería de indicadores de salud que favorezcan el establecimiento de programas de diagnóstico, intervención y vigilancia epidemiológica en las poblaciones ubicadas en la zona de influencia del proyecto de la presa Arcediano en el Estado de Jalisco, Guadalajara: Universidad Autónoma de San Luis Potosí-Comisión Estatal del Agua de Jalisco.
Escobar, Arturo (2010): Territorios de diferencia: Lugar, movimientos, vida, redes, Popayán: Envión Editores.
Gloss, Daniela Mabel (2015): Las formas de apropiación del espacio en la defensa del lugar: El caso de la Cooperativa Mujeres Ecologistas de la Huizachera, Communication of Science and Culture Master Thesis, Guadalajara: ITESO-Universidad Jesuita de Guadalajara.
Gloss, Daniela Mabel (2017): "Reclaiming the Right to Become Other-Women in Other-Places: The Politics of Place of the Ecologist Women of La Huizachera Cooperative, Mexico." In: Wendy Harcourt (ed.), Bodies in Re-

sistance. Gender Politics in The Age of Neoliberalism, London: Palgrave Macmillan, pp. 57–78.

Gloss, Daniela Mabel (2021): Del corazón a la organización: El apego al lugar en experiencias de defensa del territorio en Jalisco. Social Sciences Ph.d. Thesis, Guadalajara: Universidad de Guadalajara.

Gravante, Tommaso/Poma, Alice (2018): "Manejo emocional y acción colectiva: Las emociones en la arena de la lucha política." In: Estudios sociológicos, 108/36, pp. 595–618.

Greenpeace (2012): Estudio de la contaminación en la cuenca del Río Santiago y la salud pública en la región. Greenpeace. November 14, 2022 (http://www.greenpeace.org/mexico/global/mexico/report/2012/9/informe_toxicos_rio_santiago .pdf).

Harcourt, Wendy/Escobar, Arturo (2002): "Women and the Politics of Place." In: Development 45/1, pp. 7–14.

Lugones, María (2007): "Heterosexualism and the Colonial / Modern Gender System." In: Hypatia 22/1, pp. 86–209.

Lugones, María (2011): "Hacia un feminismo descolonial." In: Revista La Manzana de La Discordia 6/2, pp. 105–117.

Maldonado Torres, Nelson (2007): "Sobre la colonialidad del ser: contribuciones al desarrollo de un concepto." In: Santiago Castro-Gómez/Ramón Grosfoguel (eds.), El giro decolonial: reflexiones para una diversidad epistémica más allá del capitalismo global, Bogotá: Siglo del Hombre Editores, pp. 127–168.

Martínez Alier, Joan (2005): El ecologismo de los pobres: Conflictos ambientales y lenguajes de valoración, Barcelona: Icaria Editorial.

Mignolo, Walter (2000): Local Histories/Global Designs: Coloniality, Subaltern Knowledges and Border Thinking, New Jersey: Princeton University Press.

Oyěwùmí, Oyèrónkẹ (2001): The Invention of Women: Making an African Sense of Western Gender Discourses, Minneapolis: University of Minnesota Press.

Quijano, Aníbal/Wallerstein, Immanuel (1992): "Americanity as a Concept, or the Americas in the Modern World-System." In: International Social Science Journal 44/4, pp. 549–557.

Redacción Aristegui Noticias (2020): "Jalisco ocultó por 10 años estudio sobre contaminación del Río Santiago; las muertes, una constante en la zona." In: Aristegui Noticias, November 14, 2022 (https://aristeguinoticias.com/3001/mexico/jalisco-oculto-por-10-anos-estudio-sobre-contaminacion-del-rio-santiago-las-muertes-una-constante-en-la-zona/).

Segato, Rita (2011): "Género y colonialidad: en busca de claves de lectura y de un vocabulario estratégico descolonial." In: Karina Bidaseca/Vanesa Vázquez Laba (eds.), Feminismos y poscolonialidad. Descolonizando el feminismo desde y en América Latina, Buenos Aires: Godot, pp. 17–48.

Svampa, Maristella (2019): Las fronteras del neoextractivismo en América Latina. Conflictos socioambientales, giro ecoterritorial y nuevas dependencias, Guadalajara: CALAS.

Tribunal Interamericano del Agua (2007): Caso: Deterioro y contaminación del río Santiago. municipios de El Salto y Juanacatlán, estado de Jalisco, República Mexicana Tribunal Interamericano del Agua. November 14, 2022 (http://tragua.com/wp-content/uploads/2012/04/caso_rio_santiago_mexico.pdf).

Universidad Autónoma de San Luis Potosí/Comisión Estatal del Agua de Jalisco (2010): Propuesta metodológica para la implantación de una batería de indicadores de salud que favorezcan el establecimiento de programas de diagnóstico, intervención y vigilancia epidemiológica en las poblaciones ubicadas en la zona de influencia del proyecto de la presa arcediano en el estado de Jalisco, San Luis Potosí: UASLP-CEA. November 14, 2022 (https://transparencia.info.jalisco.gob.mx/sites/default/files/u531/INFORME%20FINAL%20ARCEDIANO_CEA_UEAS_JALISCO_2011_1%20-%20copia_0pt.pdf).

Wallerstein, Immanuel (1974): The Modern World-System: Capitalist Agriculture and the Origins of the European World-Economy in the Sixteenth Century, New York: Academic Press.

Zibechi, Raúl (2012): Territories in Resistance: A Cartography of Latin American Social Movements, Oakland and Edinburg: AK Press.

Part III
Feminist Conversations

Set Fear on Fire!
A Conversation with the Collective LASTESIS on Aesthetic, Performance and Feminist Resistant Practices

Edith Otero Quezada and Lívia de Souza Lima[1]

LASTESIS is an interdisciplinary feminist collective from Valparaíso, Chile, founded by Sibila Sotomayor, Daffne Valdés, Lea Cáceres, and Paula Cometa. During the political uprising in Chile in 2019, the collective created the performance "Un violador en tu camino" [A rapist in your path], where they denounced the sexual violence experienced by women and people from de LGBTQIA+ community in this political context. This performance was later replicated worldwide by other women and people from de LGBTQIA+ community who wanted to denounce the systematic violence, especially sexual violence, experienced in their local contexts, through their bodies and voices. The practice initiated by LASTESIS thus helped build a new form of global feminist protest.

In this interview, we talked with LASTESIS about the relationship between performance, feminist aesthetics, and politics as well as their 2021 feminist manifesto "Quemar el miedo" [Set fear on fire] (Verso 2023).

In what sense can performance be a tool for emancipation?

Sibila: Why a tool of emancipation? For us, the fundamental element of performance is something concrete; it is the body that is a characteristic of performance in general, not only the artistic performance but any manifestation that comes from the body. That is also linked to this idea of action, which is

---

[1] The interview was conducted on 29 September 2021. Translation by Edith Otero Quezada.

closely related to this concept of the performative, which is not the same as the performatic, but that does not matter.

The point here is that the basis is the body and what happens with the body according to what we have been reflecting on and reading over the years. This is how we have been working. Our first work addresses this issue, for example, how the oppression of women's bodies sustains the capitalist system, as Silvia Federici states. Being a Marxist herself, she makes this important critique of how Marx specifically did not consider the reproductive sphere that sustains capitalism.

Hence, it is crucial to understand, structurally and systematically, how the bodies of women and people with the capacity to conceive a life, whether they are women or not, ultimately sustain the capitalist system, the capitalist production. Moreover, the unpaid work of childrearing, raising new workers, new women workers, etc. Then we add other dimensions, such as the body as an object; we see that the body is understood as space and territory of oppression, a territory of extractivism. We can consider it as a Cuerpo-Territorio [Body-Territory], which is part of this extractivism that keeps the capitalist machine transforming itself.

So, what happens with the performance that sustains those bodies? The body is the protagonist, and there we see a major change of focus that shifts from being a territory of oppression, which of course continues to be so, but it also becomes a weapon of struggle, of resistance; it becomes the territory, the materiality, the place from which you enunciate, activate, and fight against these oppressions.

This exercise of re-appropriation generated by the body's performance is fundamental because sometimes it is taken for granted, as if "yes, the performance makes the body, it does not matter". But we must consider the significance of these bodies, their vulnerability, and what it means for women's bodies and dissident corporealities of the sexual-gender system, for example, to occupy the public space to manifest themselves. Those vulnerabilities that we have in the public space, that sometimes other bodies do not have, are not insignificant.

This political exercise is very important. Hence, our decision to work with performance, even though we are an interdisciplinary collective that expresses its opinion using different languages, the basis of our work is always the performance; it is our bodies.

We as performers are constantly activating [our bodies], whether on a stage with our work, in the street, at a concert, or a demonstration in a public space.

This is always present because we also believe in the transformative potential of performance, of how a body activates the political in a way that generates changes for the better, disturbances, and changes at the level of institutional politics, for example, regardless of whether we are militants in that sphere.

If you consider there is such a difference – what might be the effects of the performances on the audience?

Lea: I think we do not worry about the effects. Yes, one does consider and work on some functions related to art, and from art to the performatic, that hopefully mobilizes and raises awareness in the observers. Then, when you are part of it, it may change some ways of perceiving the body itself. But as an implicit intention of the creative process, like "this is going to happen, this is going to be," no. That happens more naturally.

Daffne: Perhaps we mainly consider that we usually summarize some other author's thesis and our concern is how to transmit this thesis. This synthesis should be given in the best way and using different languages, whether we share this thesis through the body of the performance, projection, music, a flyer, and whatever elements we consider necessary for communicating these ideas.

We hope that our ideas reach as many people as possible, keeping in mind that people have different ages, backgrounds, forms of understanding information, and of relating to each other, among other things. Perhaps this is what we consider the most.

Sibila: It is not that we are not concerned about the effect on the person. On the contrary, there is a concern, as Dafne says, to reach that person from different stimuli, languages, and that means looking for an active role in that person. We do not want passivity, we do not want them just to sit and watch something, and nothing happens. We want people who watch, and something happens.

But it also affects the audience, meaning that everyone is touched or connected by it from different perspectives. It is in the sound for some, and for others, it is more on the body. Some people reflect more on the idea itself, but our intention is always to mobilize, which means there is a place for action, not passivity.

Lea: There is an aesthetic concern that there is a continuous line between the performances and how they communicate with each other aesthetically. There is a visuality. But we have no control over the rest, like the emotional part of it.

What do you consider feminist aesthetics, and how is it framed in creating your performances?

Lea: For example, a very common, symbolical element when we do workshops is usually the *capuchas* [masks]. The *capuchas* are an aesthetic and iconic symbolism connected to the history of women's public demonstrations in the public space. So, there are some elements that one clearly takes back because it enables others to identify with this image, but we also try to create our own visual identity.

One that we call our own but probably is not. Instead, it is something more closely connected to our visual resources of the territories, of our background of references. It is like a mixture of many elements generated in the context, although it has a language, and references and evokes many other feminist manifestations. It also seeks to be something that is refreshing in feminism: brevity. That says a lot about our time, memes, quick information, and the minute that the reel allows you.

Sibila: The other aspect is our goal with the collage methodology, where there is no hierarchy of one element over another, but this idea of viewing the work as a kind of landscape and being able to see all the elements simultaneously and choose what you relate to, a search for non-hierarchies. Also, horizontality at a structural level that is neither linear nor ascending. We feel this is a feminist way of approaching performance in terms of content and form.

The way the performance is structured and how we also organize ourselves as a collective, to position ourselves as a horizontal collective. Not to say this person does this and that, if you ask us, of course we will say it, but it is a very different logic from the traditional one of the great dramaturgic adviser, the great director, the great artist with a name and surname, the genius artist. We have a feminist way of approaching creation and how we organize ourselves to create.

In your book "Set Fear on Fire" you refer to Judith Butler and Silvia Federici to talk about bodies, but you also analyze the collective dimension of care. What does it imply to think about care on a collective level?

Sibila: Well, as we said before in reference to Silvia Federici, care and the reproductive dimension are not included in the capitalist production system. So, there is also this critique of why care is always left to "mothers".

It is also related to aspects that we mentioned in the book regarding family structures. Silvia Federici talks about the nuclear family in which there is a mother, a father, and children. How the family model is created and how society, in general, is designed for it, from public policies, taxes, and many other things. Everything is conceived for that model because it sustains the capitalist system and now the neoliberal one.

Then, the question we ask ourselves and those around us is that many times family configurations are not like that, instead, they are different. Familiar bonds are also diverse, they are configured in different ways, and not necessarily by sexual-affective or biological aspects. This is when we begin to think of the family in another way and how care work could be conceived differently. For example, with a communitarian approach. These are not models that we came up with but models that have existed historically. Besides, in countries like ours, the same-sex parent or single-parent, for example, of a mother, grandmother, or aunt, are very common.

In sum, we think of family and familiar bonds differently and, therefore, we have a different perspective about care.

Your book is titled "Set Fear on Fire" and contains several references to the idea of burning, burning the patriarchy. What does this mean more concretely? What does it mean to burn the patriarchy, or how should we burn it?

Daffne: The reference to burning or fire actually has to do with transmuting, how to transform something so deeply rooted that constitutes the foundations of our entire society as a patriarchy. You cannot reform it. The only way is to transmute it all, burn it, and then start again.

That is the idea. It doesn't work [...] I mean, there are changes, advances, and laws. For example, the law against street harassment. Indeed, it is an advance, a debate that congress would never have carried forward many years ago. Still, it does not solve the fundamental problem of ongoing violence against women or sexual dissidents. It is like we would have to start all over again to build a society without a patriarchal base, and fire has to do with that. It is related to the ritual aspect.

Lea: Burning fear because it has kept us silenced, because it has created intellectual obscurity in human evolution of not having the same historical relevance that masculinities have had. I believe that fear is something that we all usually live with. Some of us control it better, some don't. Still, I think this is an invitation to burn the fear in communities, collectives, learning and researching our ancient ways of seeing society.

Daffne: Yes, to see fear as something that paralyzes and immobilizes. Then it is about doing the opposite.

What do you think about the critics within the left itself who consider that performances and other repertoires of street protests are not very effective instruments for a political practice of emancipation?

Sibila: In fact, we have a very clear and concrete position on this issue, and our perspective is that the class struggle and the feminist struggle are not two different things. We think the feminist struggle is as subversive as other social and political struggles. Feminism is also mobilizing this from the grassroots and it is through feminism that we are going to be able to find solutions to these problems. This insistence on saying that the feminist struggle disunites is basically the expression of misogyny.

To say that it undermines class struggles, changes the focus, etc., relegates us eternally to a second, third, fourth, or last category. To say indeed that feminist struggles are not as important as the class struggle is a perspective that for us is obsolete because they are not, they cannot be separated, they go together.

We state in the book that the enemies of feminism or feminisms are everywhere, they are not only among right-wing conservatives but also in other political spheres, and we hope, of course, that this will change.

Lea: I also think that we should communicate to these people that they do not seek freedom. Their quests are archaic and precarious. Their sense of collectivity is quite null.

If they continue to disintegrate feminisms and actions for freedom in the streets without understanding them, considering them as something that divides, they should go home and sign a resignation paper because they do not know what is happening. They are in a situation so alienated from *realidades comunes* [common realities] that, hopefully they will withdraw from *lo común* [the common].

Marielle Presente!
Defending the Memory and Legacy of Marielle Franco in Brazil. An Interview with Anielle Franco

Lívia de Souza Lima, Julia Roth and Edith Otero Quezada[1]

Anielle Franco is a teacher, journalist, and activist for Black women's rights in Brazil, born and raised in the Favela da Maré in Rio de Janeiro. In 2023, she was appointed Minister of Racial Equality in the newly elected Lula government. After the brutal assassination of her sister Marielle Franco on 14 March 2018, Anielle and her family founded the Marielle Franco Institute, which is dedicated to fighting gender, racial, and political violence in the country, in particular, as well as supporting Black women politicians and candidates. Its endeavors also include demands for justice, as this yet unresolved crime hangs like a shadow over the family and other Black women, especially those who are active in politics. In this conversation, Anielle talks with us about her trajectory and her continuous efforts to fight and defend the memory and legacy of Marielle Franco in Brazil. In the context of the systematic erasure of Black women's memory and history, preserving Marielle Franco's legacy is a strategic part of the Afro-Brazilian feminist struggle.

Tell us about the process of creating and constituting the Marielle Franco Institute.

After they killed my sister in 2018, I was thinking about creating a space dedicated to her name and memory where I could teach English, Portuguese, and Math to teenagers and young people. And when I started thinking and asking people about that, many Black women activists who already worked at NGOs approached me to say that I could do that and other things, as well. They

---

1   The interview was conducted on 17 September 2021.

advised me to create something bigger and more expansive because Marielle Franco, my sister, is the definition of a global leader. So those Black women who approached me before assisted us in this process, and together with my family, we sat down for a few months, working extensively on creating a concept, an idea of how we would like the Institute to be. Besides the educational front, we as a family wanted to incorporate everything that we used to do into the Institute. For example, our family was always asked to go to the police, and talk about the investigation, so we included that. There was much fake news about Marielle, and we were always talking about it, denying the false rumors, and fighting against that, as such, defending her memory. So currently, everything we do in the Institute serves the mission of spreading Marielle's legacy. For example, when we give an interview, we spread the legacy; when we deny fake news, we defend her memory, which is how the Institute was built and structured. We are also thinking collectively and structuring an advisory political council with names such as Bianca Santanna, Lucia Xavier, and Sueli Carneiro, women active in the Black women's movement, to help us out in this endeavor.

We see that the idea of memory is central for the Institute. Why do you think it is essential to defend the memory and legacy of Marielle Franco, not only for Brazil, but also from a global perspective?

I think that we, and I particularly, did not expect my sister to become known worldwide the way she did after the assassination. That made us very proud, but at the same time very sad, thinking and seeing how much more she could have done, you know? But at the same time, I understood the importance and value that Marielle had and still has for us and the mission that we now have to speak about her, not only here, but also outside of Brazil.

Defending Marielle's memory and constantly remembering her assassination goes beyond the intersection of human rights and politics, you know, I think it extends to every Black woman who works hard, every LGBTQIA+ who looks at her and wonders why they killed her. We still don't know why they killed her, and we still don't know who ordered the killing, and I think the task of finding out is going to be with us for decades to come. Perhaps I will no longer be here when they do because things like that take time in Brazil. And my family has been building this Institute, this organization, for future generations to understand how important it is for us to continue to speak about her. I think it is not only to keep her memory alive, but also to inspire other people. These other women will follow in her footsteps, especially and specifically maybe women who believe that it is possible to be in politics and be a politician. In any country, at the same time, it is important to be alive.

You mention that your sister's case is not about just one person, that it actually represents a global phenomenon, highlighting how it can be very difficult for women to enter politics. That is why we need to start insisting on and finding justice in this case. How do you see the role of the Institute and how does the Institute help Brazil to think of an alternative political project?

We live in a time in Brazil that is very delicate; people do not respect each other's opinions right now. Our current President [Jair Bolsonaro] legitimizes this type of behavior, so I see the Institute as a place where we are going to fight for democracy, where we are going to inspire other women to continue and to follow their dreams, since many women are interested in entering politics after Marielle's murder. But at the same time, it is not only about that. I think that after her assassination, we started a movement that tried to bring back women who did not want to discuss politics or be in a social movement, which is very important. And I think the Institute has the right to do it; it is a legitimate action to think about who Marielle is and what our family represents in this context. At the same time, I think people look at us and see a possibility within civil society to inspire, discuss, and fight for rights and things they were not interested in before.

What are your visions and the Institute's vision for the role and importance of the potential of Black women for Brazilian politics? Especially reflecting on the fact that numerous Black women started to claim a position within the political institutions following Marielle's assassination.

It is huge, but some things worry me about Black women as political candidates. First, because Black women in Brazil are seen, I will use a strong word, as "nothing"! Because we are not allowed to be protagonists when we want to, and we know we can. Second, Black women do not receive any support and investment when they wish to be candidates. Third, when we talk about politics in Brazil, we only see White men on top, you know?

We have a few women who are just now entering institutional politics. I think their role is vast, but at the same time, we do not receive the instruments necessary for us to be in the place where we should be or we have to be. For example, Marielle wanted to be a Senator, and many people said no, that was not the time for her to do this. I don't know if it was the time or not; maybe she could have been one. At the same time, we understand that it is essential to have Black women in those spaces of power, where they can represent us; we know that it is tough for us to get there. So I think that is the kind of role that we have to work together, with women who offer their bodies with much courage and say: "Hey, I am going to be a candidate". On the other hand, the Institute has to help them and speak about security, financial resources, and protagonism, and not silence Black people.

We also understand that the Institute's mission is to inspire and empower women and the LGBTQIA+ community. What does this mean in practice? What activities and projects are you promoting to work with this mission?

We have many projects going on. In 2021, it was the first municipal elections after Marielle's assassination; we created a campaign called: Plataforma antiracista nas eleições (PANE- Anti-racist electoral platform), an anti-racist action where the candidates could access and sign an endorsement to express a public commitment with Marielle's ideas. Many people who wanted to vote in those elections would consult our website to check if their candidates were committed to Marielle's ideas.

We were working on building this kind of influence. Another example of action: the Institute posted and shared the names of the candidates that people could vote for. We were not doing publicity for candidates, but provided a space where people could identify what political projects we endorsed.

And we are doing another project similar to this for the 2022 elections, which we are still working on. Because this time, we will vote for the President, and governments, so it is going to be a little different, but we will do something.

We are also committed to fighting against political violence, doing research about it, speaking about the topic, holding events, meeting with politicians who have already suffered political violence, and generally discussing this topic extensively. We are working on a project called Marielle Franco schools where we would like to bring in intellectual Black women to speak to teenagers, and we are currently constructing a Memorial Center. And in everything we do, we try to specifically bring Black women to join our efforts.

How are your projects received? And what are the challenges or impediments you have been facing as you are making things happen and working with your missions?

The reception by like-minded people and supporters of the Institute has been excellent. But [...] as I said before, we are facing a time in Brazil where there is much hatred because of the President [Bolsonaro (2021)]. Sometimes we get threats, we get cursed, well [...] once when I was walking in the streets with my daughter by my side, someone spit in my face, just because, you know, I am Marielle Franco's sister. They think they get to be very rude to us. It is not easy and we don't always get full support for our launch projects. It is challenging.

Are you finding support within the political community?

No, no law in Brazil can give us support because we are an NGO. Maybe if we were politicians, it would be easier. Sometimes they share what we post, sometimes they ask to speak about it, but that is it.

Do you have support from entities outside institutional politics or social movements?

Yes, social movements are always with us because we are part of them. So besides sharing, we are also discussing, writing for newspapers, sometimes we hold events together. Sometimes when we need financial support, they might know how to help us and tell us where to go.

Does your Institute collaborate with other feminist groups outside Brazil? Are you in dialog with them?

Yes, we do. We have met with three or four groups these past months. With Brazilian women who are living in the USA or in Europe. There are at least four collectives that we have been speaking to and with whom we have considered projects for the next year or so.

Do you have other forms of exchange with Black Lives Matter or Ni Una a Menos, or any other of these movements?

Yes, we do. We had a couple of trips scheduled for this year and the past year, but we could not do them because of the COVID-19 pandemic. But we do have plans to resume these trips and maybe open up more significant and global avenues for the Institute.

Do you consider it necessary for the Institute's work to be more visible?

Yes, definitely, because every time we do things in Brazil, and even if we go out of the country and share this in the news, we gain more visibility. Once, we went to France and Paris to meet and speak with the French President, which was all over Brazil's news. So we already understood that the more visibility we get outside the country, the better we do inside Brazil.

Looking back to Brazil and maybe other places, how do you relate your work and your struggle and practices to the history of feminism in Brazil and maybe in the Americas more broadly? I know there is a long tradition of Black feminisms in Brazil.

I think there are many ways we connect and see the movement in general, but especially for Black women, since this life is a struggle from day one. Many decades ago, we had so many Black women feminists who wrote extensively and inspired us. I think Marielle and my family are just one more example of what feminism and feminists, and Black women have faced for so long. When you have Angela Davis come to Brazil and compare what she used to do with what our family is doing, this is very important; this is big. When you have Angela Davis saying: You are looking out at me, but you have to pay attention to Lélia Gonzalez, who is so vital for us. I think we all have connections. We use a term in Brazil, which is "dororidade," coined by Brazilian Black feminist Vilma Piedade. She says that Black women are connected by their pain, losses, and struggles. On the other side, you have bell hooks, who is not Brazilian, saying that we also connect by love and seeing each others' pains, solidarity, compassion, etc. I think it is essential to be able to have these connections because, yes, we do have feminism for White women and all the others, but we also have Black feminism. I don't believe we can construct a better world if we don't come together collectively.

But there is also a solid indigenous women's movement in Brazil.

Yes, of course, quilombolas and indigenous. And this is what I always say: We do have to come together; otherwise, we will have only struggles and no results.

What message would you like to pass on to the international feminist community?

I think I would repeat what I have just said. Because it is tough to understand what people go through without putting yourself in that position. So I believe that even if you are US-American, English, or Brazilian, it is essential for us to come together and always have empathy for what is happening to many different women in other parts of the world. If I could say something to the international feminist community, I think that would be it. We are doing – we can do – whatever we want, and we can go even further if we come together and construct things together, if we fight together.

Feminist Activism and Constitutional Change in Chile
A Conversation with María José Oyarzún Solís

Nicole Schwabe[1]

María José Oyarzún Solís is a Professor of Philosophy at the University of Valparaiso in Chile and has been an elected representative of the Valparaiso Region since April 2021. Oyarzún Solís was born during the military dictatorship of Augusto Pinochet, in a time when the government tried to gain some political legitimacy and within this context, ratified the 1980 Constitution that, although having its validity questioned, marked a new institutional step for the authoritarian government. María José Oyarzún Solís's personal path crossed with the Chilean Constitution again as she participated in the Marca AC movement, a citizens' organization that proposed establishing, and called on citizens to demand, a Constituent Assembly to replace the 1980 Constitution. Driven by massive citizen demonstrations in 2019, a new constituent process was opened in Chile. Oyarzún Solís is part of the new Constituent Assembly and defines herself as a feminist activist.

In this interview, Nicole Schwabe talks to María José Oyarzún Solís about her activism, feminist mobilization, and the condition of women in Chile, taking into account the country's authoritarian past. Moreover, Oyarzún Solís also reflects on the present and the future of feminist mobilizations in Chile and the possible implications of this new Constitutional process for gender equality.

I would like to know more about the motivation behind your activism. How did you come to do what you are doing today? What has been your motivation on the path that brought you to the Constituent Assembly? What has driven your feminist activism?

---

1   The interview was conducted on 12 January 2022. Translation by Lívia de Souza Lima.

I believe this is a process that has involved a whole generation. It is not just about me, but about a generation that went out to look for its own path. A path that was predetermined and riddled with mostly unjustified restrictions. I'm talking about the inequality between men and women. Because I could not do certain things. The definitions of gender roles in Chile were very marked back then. Until 1990, women could not even request a loan. We also had restrictions, from how to dress to what career to study. Although it had changed a little in the transition of the 1990s to the 2000s, these distinctions were very strong and prevented the necessary development, not to mention all the material inequalities that were maximized over the years. The crisis of 2019 was precisely related to this difference between rich and poor. The difference that exists between workers and wealthy people, who might also be workers, but who have a very substantial material difference compared to others.

I believe that all these things converged: the need to be able to develop without limits, without gender limits, without economic limits, without moral limits and, of course, the ability to seek material equality. I think these were the reasons that drove the revolt in Chile, the constitutional change, and the activism of many people.

The Chilean Historical Memory has been built from its social movements. In the struggle for truth and justice, the Mapuche movement and the student mobilizations, to name just a few emblematic examples. What did you learn from the historical feminist movements? What connects and divides the recent feminist movement in Chile from previous women's movements?

Look, the truth is that I have known the movement since the 1800s. From the search for truth to the struggles for citizenship, since we were not citizens for a long time. And, of course, the idea of equality connects us. To think of the equality of equals, as Carole Pateman said, to counter this idea of equality only between men who have a certain degree of property. This connects us today with the feminist movement, and I believe this has not changed much. We do have citizenship rights, and we can certainly not ignore this fact. But it has been a constant struggle to have equal rights between men and women, which is still part of a struggle that has continued over the centuries. I do not see the feminist movement as divided into different historical sections; I think it has been mutating, a constantly evolving continuum, because there are always new things that are unravelling. Currently, the most urgent demand is for our bodies. This claim for our bodies as truly ours [...].

And what divides us? I think that, in some way, there are certain generational differences, for example, regarding sexual freedom. We have gone from having less to having more rights. But I don't know if there is a concrete division. There are very different women, and the feminist movement has been mutating; it has grown, and more feminisms have been born. I don't see that many divisions. Maybe I am an optimist. Maybe there are different ways of standing up in the feminist struggle 40 years ago and 100 years ago than the ones we have today.

To return to the present challenges, I would like to know a little more about your feminist agenda. You are part of the Democratic Revolution Party. In April 2021, you were elected to be part of the Constituent Assembly as a candidate who showed up with a raised fist and a green handkerchief with the demand: "Never again without us". Can you tell us a little more about the pillars of your feminist agenda for the Constitutional Process? How do you write a constitution in a feminist way?

Well, the first thing is to incorporate women into the Constitution, since the 1980 Constitution mentions women only once. The new one intends to mention women in a transversal way across all its sections and simultaneously determine equality between men and women through constitutional norms. On the other hand, we are thinking of a caring Constitution that understands and incorporates care issues within the body. And by this, I do not mean "women are the ones who take care", but to highlight that women are the majority of caregivers in our country. And well, the recognition of domestic work has never existed and is a fundamental part of the economy, as 20% of the BIP is generated by domestic work. In our country, 90% of domestic work is done by women, which is still unrecognized and unpaid work. And this must be acknowledged.

And another point is the family. The family is an institution that has roles. And these roles are very clearly determined between men and women – the roles of the father and the mother. The description of the family in the current Constitution of Chile is incredible to read. And that is something that should change now. To talk about families in terms of the roles that have been changing and reflecting the diversity of our current population. Besides that, parity will also be incorporated into the new Constitution.

To conclude, I would like to discuss the political landscape beyond the constituent process and the possibilities and challenges of implementing gen-

der equality. How can gender equality become a principle for politics? Fundamental principles can be secured in the Constitution. But what does the perspective for achieving gender equality look like in the current political scenario?

The first thing is that gender parity – in my opinion – is here to stay. We are the first Constitutional Convention in the world that applies gender parity. And I believe that this will not only be installed in the Convention, but in Congress, at the governmental level and in the administrative regions. We must incorporate it in all the state entities and, hopefully, in all private entities. I believe that it is essential that we gradually achieve this balance between men and women.

Another pendulum that allows gender equality, and which we hope will be included in the new Constitution, is the recognition of domestic work. This will also generate a substantive change for women. They will be entitled to a salary because they are dedicated all day long to the home. And they are also in a situation of subordination to their partners, especially male partners. This is something that must change. As Simone de Beauvoir said, without a salary, it is tough to achieve the emancipation necessary to construct a subject. I think recognizing domestic work will generate an essential change in Chilean families and women because they will understand their work is needed. And that they will have monetary compensation that will allow them to get around more freely.

And another point is sexual and reproductive rights. The right to your sexual health. The right to acquire knowledge. To tell women that their sexuality is not something terrible. In Chile, for a long time, women had sex thinking that they were doing something wrong. Their body depended first on their parents, then on their husbands. They had to get pregnant. We recently had a presidential candidate who would not allow his partner to take birth control pills. I think these things are relevant and more importantly, they must be incorporated into our educational centers so that girls and boys can be educated on sexual and reproductive rights.

And on the other hand, there is the issue of recognizing care. Undoubtedly, we must stop thinking of women as the only ones who should take care of children, the elderly, and the sick. I believe this is a worrying situation. And I hope that the Constitutional Convention will consider these issues because it is tough to go backwards when we have achieved so much regarding rights.

"Rap is Our Best Feminist Tool"
Interview with the Cuban Hip Hop Duo La Reyna y La Real

Julia Roth[1]

The hip hop movement of the late 1990s and early 2000s in Cuba had a decisive impact on the creation of an afro-descendant, ant-racist feminist discourse on the island. After the Cuban revolution of 1959, the discourse of alleged equality had made any form of feminist and anti-racist debate difficult. The end of the Cold War and the partial opening of the island led to a very vivid music scene, particularly during the years the Festival Cubano de Rap took place. From the beginning, women artists have claimed this format as a space for discussion panels on gender issues, creating a public space that did not exist before.[2] Today (as of 2022), the rap duo "La Reyna y La Real" who belong to the second generation of Cuban hip hop artists, have become one of the most audible voices of the second generation of the Cuban underground afro-descendant feminist music scene. Reyna Mercedes Hernandez Sandoval (La Reyna) and Yadira Pintado Lazcano (La Real) formed the Havana-based duo "La Reyna y la Real" to represent a voice of women's empowerment and the fight against pre-established gender roles in Cuban (hip hop/rap) music. La Reyna (born 1986) studied Industrial Chemistry and practiced this profession for five years before she joined an all-women group/project called "Alzar la voz," [Raise your voice]. La

---

1   The interview was conducted on 2 and 4 September 2022. Translated from Spanish by Julia Roth.
2   On the Cuban Hip Hop movement, see Alejandro Zamora Montes (2009): Rapear una Cuba utópica:testimonios del movimiento hiphopero, Sevilla: Guantanamera; on the creation of a feminist public sphere, see Tanya L. Saunders (2016): Cuban Underground Hip Hop: Black Thoughts, Black Revolution, Black Modernity, Austin. University of Texas Press, and Julia Roth (2017): "Rapear el feminismo de otra manera: Hip-Hop y modos alternativos de producir conocimiento." In: Cuba Posible, January 23, 2017 (https://cubaposible.com/rapear-feminismo-otra-manera-hip-hop-modos-alternativos-producir-conocimiento/).

Real (born 1986) graduated as a social worker and simultaneously began to rap and to perform with several neighborhood rappers.[3] After occasional collaborations since 2010, La Reyna and La Real came together as a duo in 2012.[4] They have been performing regularly in Cuba since 2013, e.g. at the Second Women's Hip Hop Festival "Mar-genes" [Mar-gins], in the province of Holguin as well as at the Hip Hop Symposium at the Palacio de La Rumba in Havana. In the summer of 2022, they toured Europe, performing in Berlin, Germany, and various locations in Sweden. Since 2015, La Reyna y la Real have been listed in the catalog of the Cuban Rap Agency. So far, the duo has published the albums *Beef con Kriño* (2015), *Miky y Repa* (2017, TumiMusic) *Mírame* (2020), and *Dale Despacio* (2021). La Reyna y la Real fuse rap and hip hop with jazz, R&B, and other elements, often combining vocalists with piano, guitar, drums, trumpet, trombone, and saxophone, and sometimes also choirs and percussion.[5] Their musical style reflects their identification as strong afro-descendant women, often identifying as "cimarrona(s)"[6] and celebrating Afro-Cuban religious rituals in their self-designed outfits and jewelry. The dialogic notion and the strong and empowering feminist message of their music come out even more strongly in their live performances, in which they directly address the audience and ask them to dance, sing along, and breakdance.

How did you get involved in hip hop? How and when did you start?

La Reyna: In my case, I became familiar with the hip hop movement in the early 2000s. I didn't know, I had no knowledge that rap existed in Cuba, let alone that it was so powerful at that time. By the year 2004, 2005, in my neighborhood, Luyano, a fan club of the group Orishas was created. At that time, Orishas were very popular in both Cuba and Europe. There, I became aware that an entire, and very powerful, rap movement existed in Cuba. I came to know groups that we now call "old school", such as Obsesión, Krudas Cubensi, Anónimo Consejo, and Explosión Suprema etc. Once I got to know everything about this existing rap movement, I took an interest in writing lyrics, expressing what I thought,

---

3   See: http://www.tumimusic.com/La-Reyna-y-La-Real/812/artists/music/; https://festivalcervantino.gob.mx/artista/152/la-reyna-y-la-real.
4   See: https://suenacubano.com/lareyna-y-lareal/.
5   See: https://revistamaces.com/la-reyna-y-la-real-yo-tambien-soy-ellas/
6   *Cimarrona*: female maroon (runaway enslaved person). *Cimarronaje* (marronage) also refers to resistance against enslavement in general.

and I wrote it, and showed it to the people in the club, so they knew I was writing. Then, in 2009, Carmen González, a Cuban writer and poet started a project called "Alzar la voz" [Raise your voice], a women's project, where I also met [spoken word artist] Afibloa [Sinufola], and she asked me to join her project if I dared to rap and write. And it was there, in 2009, that I started to make a name for myself in the rap world as La Reyna.

As for La Real, she started in her neighborhood Jesús María around the same time. She had been in the rap movement for a little longer, she started rapping with a group of men, and now she is the only one who is still rapping. She's been around a few years longer than me.

What role does the hip hop movement of the early 2000s play? Who were and are the artists that inspired you the most (in and outside of hip hop)?

La Reyna: In the early 2000s, hip hop in Cuba was a very powerful movement. It was one of the strongest movements in Latin America, one can say. We didn't rap at that time, but this movement became a strong influence on our work. And nowadays, when we talk about references, we can't stop talking about the strong rap movement that existed at the beginning of the 2000s in Cuba. A very strong movement that boosted and raised the voice of Cuban rap, nationally and internationally.

Well, there were a great many artists that inspired us. In the beginning, we listened to a lot of music from the United States that came to us thanks to the sailors who brought their cassettes. So we didn't even know which artists we listened to, or who they were. But we did know that we liked them. In terms of national rap, we were very inspired by Krudas Cubensi, the first female rappers in Cuba, by Obsesión, Anónimo Consejo, Explosión Suprema. Internationally, we listened a lot to Missy Elliot, Erykah Badu, Lauryn Hill. And all this mix of rap, both national and international, inspired us, and led us to what we do today.

What does hip hop mean to you?

La Reyna: To us, hip hop is life, it is part of our culture and a way of expression [...] Hip hop is a very strong, a very powerful tool for communication. It harnesses the power of the word, the power of the message, the power of the experience. And, of course, for us to be able to master this tool is a great step, a great power that makes us the artists that we are and makes us great. To have the power to bring this message to all the people who can listen to us, to the people who can see themselves reflected in us, to the people who can identify with us and for whom we can serve as an example, as an inspiration, for us, it is a great blessing to have this tool. Really, to have this tool, this gift of the word, this strength, this power that allows us to have rap, the rap that we defend, and the hip hop that we live.

Where do you see the particularities of Cuban hip hop? Do you see a decolonial dimension? Which international ties do you have through hip hop?

La Real: [...] [T]alking about rap, well, we think that each place has its own way of doing it because of its own history, its own culture. And what makes Cuban rap Cuban is that it has our warmth, it has our charisma. And what sometimes differentiates it from rap from other places [is] our idiosyncrasy. We could say that the ties that we have today internationally, we practically owe all of that to rap, to hip hop, because of our music. That is, for having gone to other countries, or someone who discovered our music and wrote to us from Mexico, from Peru, from Chile, from Argentina. From many places they have written to us, and they have told us that they identify with our music. And to me, that is one more link that we have created internationally. And all this thanks to rap.

In how far do you see hip hop as a tool for communicating and presenting feminist topics (and feminist knowledge)?

La Real: La Reyna and La Real speak from a position of womanhood, as women, and for women, based on our experiences, on our lives, and serving our message to identify, to represent, to reflect the reality that all women live in Cuba, as well as in Latin America, as well as in the whole world. Our message is a feminist message that places women where they should always be. Where in many occasions we are placed. Where many people do not recognize our worth.

Rap is the strongest weapon we have because it is a very big communication media, which we can expand. And we can achieve great reach because many women listen to the messages that we want to convey. For many women, uh, see our experiences, feel our experiences, many women can identify with us and see other solutions, see other realities, see that everything is possible. Of course, rap is our best tool. And it is the basis on which we rely for this discourse, make it extensive and try to take it to every corner of our world. Or as far as we can.

Which other inequalities (beyond gender) do you think are important to address?

La Real: More than talking about inequalities, we like to highlight the equality that we do have, to get people to see every day that even though they are Black – because there is still a little bit of racism in some minds, in some types of people – to tell them that we are equal, that we can do the same things that other people can do because we are people. We are not from another planet. We're obviously human beings, who think, live, and whose hearts beat just like everybody else's. And speaking of rap, well, we think that each place has its own way of doing things because of its own history, its own culture.

Memory, Re-Imagination and Commemoration
Bridging Academia and Activism. An Interview with Afua Cooper

Safa Al-Dilaimi[1]

Jamaican-born Canadian scholar, poet and performer Afua Cooper is currently the James R. Johnston Professor of Black Canadian Studies at Dalhousie University, Halifax (Canada), co-founder of the Black Canadian Studies Association and a founding member of the Toronto Dub Poets Collective (2002). Her work as a performing artist and speaker facilitates a critical and global reflection on the current socio-political and socio-environmental challenges of feminisms and the remembrance of historical female figures. The interview focuses on Afua Cooper's (feminist) experience as a performing artist, activist and educator; and the difficulties she has faced in the process. As a professor who works in an academic institution and creates a direct link to the community, Afua Cooper shares her perspective on memory and feminisms in Canada, the bridges to the U.S. and transregional connections.

In how far would you describe your work as feminist? Which other dimensions do you consider central to it?

Yes, I would describe my work as feminist and I grew up in that atmosphere of the idea of feminism. Well, not just the idea, but also in practice, growing up with my aunts, my mother's sisters. And seeing my mother's experience was formative for me because I saw women being able, having the ability and having the capacity. But also more than that, having the belief that they could do things. My mother herself was not in the workforce. She was a housewife, she had nine children. But she also had this vision of making sure that we got

---

[1] The interview was conducted on 9 July 2022.

a good education, making sure that we had good food, as a mother and as a housewife. She also sewed our clothes when we were kids. But she was also involved in community development. So, she taught at the local community center. She taught things like nutrition and how to prepare certain dishes and recipes. These are things that we nowadays would not consider feminist studies, but it meant that she left her home. She interacted with other people, with other women. She developed her own intellectual capacity. And then some of my aunts actually went away to the United States and England to work, made their own money. And they also got married and they came back to Jamaica. They bought houses, they bought land, they bought property. It was really nice to see. When you're ten years old or eight years old, you're not thinking "oh, this is a feminist gesture", but just the example of it enters your subconscious mind. And then I also grew up in a society where people felt girls as well as boys or boys as well as girls should have access to and the opportunity for an education. And so, I was lucky in that sense. But I also came of age at a time, in the seventies, where in my own country – this was Jamaica – and the world at large, women faced a particular disadvantage. You look around and you see that the people who are in politics, people who control the economy and the political structure, are mainly men and then they use the resources of the state to do whatever they want. And usually, these are not things that are benefiting women and children. I was watching a documentary about some women in Nigeria who created an after-school program. They said the Nigerian government puts 22 percent of the national budget in the military and only six percent into education. Six percent! And they're saying: What if we could flip that 22 percent into six percent for the military? They said that Nigeria is now within a foreign power, so why is the military so strong? Why does it have all these armaments? So, [men typically, or] the patriarchal thinking put money into things or structures that rarely benefit women and should really benefit society as a whole, men, too, right? So, my work came out of that sensibility to address, or look at, or give voice to these inequalities in the world, especially those that empower women and girls and children in general. Well, I would also say it's a humanistic way. It's a humanistic perspective on practice, because one of the things that we always see is that women are human beings, too and women's rights are human rights. So, those ideas, those sensibilities have informed my work from a young person, whether it's activism, or poetry, or academia.

How do you relate your work and specifically, the Canadian case, with the work of other (Black) feminist writers?

You know, coming from the Caribbean, the Caribbean countries are really new societies. These societies emerged out of slavery and colonization in their present manifestation. So, there's a newness to them. But then you also feel that you have this opportunity where you could recreate yourself in a way, to a certain degree. But because these societies come out of slavery and colonization, it means that they evolved via an experience or a trajectory of illusion which was rooted in immense brutality. I was thinking about that this morning for the interview. We experienced immense brutality then and still are now. So, those experiences are going to shape who you are and they're going to shape your thoughts. They're going to shape the way you think about yourself, about our position in the world, our position as a place, as a geographic territory, where other powers and other people of big powers can say, "this is how you should behave", "this is how you should think", "we are going to set the terms of trade", "we will tell you how much we will pay for your bananas", "you should know you don't have a voice", or "we will tell you how much we're going to pay you for that". So, we have always been at the receiving end of imperialism and imperialist thinking. And that means that we are influenced also by a lot of patriarchal thinking that's coming from the metropolises, so to speak. They impose their ideas of gender, what women should be, how far women should go. Even within slavery, there was this kind of what I'm going to call a brutal equality, because women had to do the same kind of work men did, and the additional burden of having to perform reproductive work. But throughout that, I think after slavery ended, for example, we had this sense that women, – that we – could do things, because sometimes we were the only ones who were there to do things for ourselves. Sometimes we were the only ones who were there to defend ourselves and to defend our lives. So, I think for Caribbean women and Black women in general, within the Americas, we have a kind of capacity that I don't see anywhere else. And it's not something I'm valorizing. I'm not saying "hey, hey, hey, you know, we're big and strong", but just saying because of the fact of our history and also the previous history before the Caribbean or in Africa, coming from certain spaces where women were also held in high regard and high esteem and have certain positions in life and a certain kind of power. That also the memory of that and some living memory of that – will give us that kind of capacity that other people don't have. And the same goes for Black women within South America or Latin America or North

America. So, we kind of go through life knowing and thinking we have this capacity for a change, for transformation, for making our lives better than the lives we were born into. Canada is/was once a colonized space, but at the same time, the dominant ideology, the Eurocentric ideology, is a European/North American ideology in which White people are on top. So, the kind of feminism or the dominant feminism is that of White Eurocentric feminism. And White women generally had different sorts of interests than Black women in terms of a feminist agenda or what it is that they think women want. So there always has to be a different kind of articulation from Black and racialized women. So, you know, liberal feminism is about women getting jobs, being in the workplace, the right to abortion, all of those things. Whereas Black women are saying "well, we have been in the workforce for so long, maybe we need to get a break. Maybe we need the right to stay home with our children. Maybe what we want is the right to have children and not to have those children taken away from us by the state. And if we're in the workforce, getting a decent salary for what we do, good benefits, a good vacation package", all of those things. So, White women's articulation always seems to be about work, about their sexuality, you know that sort of thing. I'm not saying Black women aren't concerned about that. Those definitely both are concerns, too. But we also have other concerns which sometimes are diametrically opposed to what White women want. And then we have to think about Black women working in the homes of some White women who are themselves feminists, who are arguing for women's rights and so on. But then you have a Black woman in your home cleaning, cooking your food, looking after your children. How are you treating her? Are you paying her a decent salary? Those are some of the issues I find with liberal feminism.

Many of your works, whether poetry, fiction/literature or performance, have a strong sense of history, place, memory, and experience. In which ways can literature, or any expression of art, serve as a tool to transform the highly dominant, androcentric, and colonial narrative (e.g. in *The Hanging of Angélique: The Untold Story of Canadian Slavery and the Burning of Old Montréal* (2006), where you break the androcentric, male-centered perspective)?

Well, I think art can do that to some degree, to a certain degree, but not fully 100 percent, because with whatever art we do, poetry, the activism component, the change won't happen unless you're engaging bodily and materially. And that is where the activist work is important. I can perform a poem, write a book, and be on YouTube, and people will see it and hopefully get inspired. But I'm under no illusion that that's going to transform the world. Many things need to come together for that transformation happen. In transformation, many things have to be going on simultaneously, or maybe not even simultaneously, but many things have to be happening. Because art is kind of a fragile thing. It's also very strong, but it's fragile. Look at some poets like the Turkish poet Nazim Hikmet, for example, who was constantly being imprisoned because of his poetry and his political leanings. One time, he spent twelve years in prison. So, that's a fragile thing. You know, you write some poems, write some books, you publish in a magazine and then you end up in prison. Also Antonio Gramsci, the Italian philosopher who died in jail because of his writings. He was anti-fascist, he opposed Mussolini, and then he died in jail. So, if there is not another movement of struggle going on simultaneously, then art might not count for anything. But art can also inspire people, whatever art it is, e.g. graffiti. We know art has inspired movements that have led to positive change. So, within liberal democracies, or maybe I should say bourgeois democracy, like Canada or Germany, there's always the desire on the part of the state or people in power to co-opt art. They will put it in a museum. "We'll make this art fabulous. We'll give them a number one book and make it a bestseller". And then the art becomes redefined. You just go, you sign your book, you win a big prize and you pose, and that's fine, because the artist has to reproduce her material life. You have to make a living. But the tendency in bourgeois societies is to just co-opt art and make it harmless. You know, take a thing, e.g. put Che Guevara on a t-shirt or have multiple poses of Che Guevara at the Guggenheim Museum or wherever. And people say: "Oh, isn't that great?". You know, Che Guevara turns over in his grave because he was a revolutionary. So, that's a tendency in democracies. And because the state is so strong, they always have a way of killing things or neutralizing. So, I'm not under any illusion at all. We see how bourgeois societies deal with art. You know, when Van Gogh was alive, he couldn't even sell one of his paintings. People thought it was ugly. The guy died in poverty. And fortunately, he had a nice brother who helped him and at least bought one of his paintings. And now one of his paintings is sold for $200 million and he's not around to enjoy it. So, one minute they say, "oh, your work is ugly. You're not a good painter", a hundred years later it's "wow, you're all the rage". So, that's what they do with art. They kill the revolutionary potential of art. So, I'm not under any illusion. I mean, I do my work because I'm driven to do it. And hopefully it will inspire some people.

You mentioned that transformation cannot happen unless there are many things going on simultaneously. What are those additional things that you consider helpful to drive transformation?

First of all, there has to be a commitment. And you see it on the right, you see it in conservative circles. They have that commitment. You know, Roe v. Wade was in 1973 and everybody thought, "hey, victory, we have won this battle". 50 years later, they overturned it, which meant that they never slept. That's why they kept chipping away. And that's the problem with people on the left. It's that you win a victory today, then they think, "oh, we got it all", and they kind of stop. Conservatives don't stop. They keep going until they achieve what they want. So, first, there has to be that commitment because we are living in a society, in a global society, in which certain forces feel that the majority of people should be slaves and serfs straight up. We shouldn't have any aspirations, they should be on top and tell us what to do. That thinking hasn't changed from the Middle Ages until present times. It's the same mentality we're experiencing, just in different forms. When you look at the people who compose the G7 nations, who are they? These are former slave owners. These are the big powers who were the slave powers and who are the colonizing powers. It's the same people and they have the same attitude. They're telling us how much they're going to pay us for our resources. They're telling us "you don't have all the resources". France is saying to Nigeria "we only need uranium in Nigeria. Don't even bother to think that's yours. We're going to tell you how much money we'll give, if we give you anything". Now, the G7 are the same people who were colonizing the world a hundred years ago. So, that's their attitude towards us. If we don't know that this struggle is multipronged, then we have lost the fight even before we begin to fight. So, there has to be activism inside and outside the academy on the streets. We see a lot that we have gained. You know, we started talking about feminism earlier on and, you know, feminism as a movement, as a practice, was a street thing. It was on the street with people marching. [It was because of that.] Then you had it in the university. It inspired feminist studies in the university. So, the academic feminism came out of street feminism. Now what I see is that feminism is becoming like an academic exercise. It has lost its trade. The street power isn't there anymore. [And that is part of the reason with feminism, because now it's gone. Everybody is theorizing and theorization is killing us. Now it becomes more and more sophisticated.] But we have these real-life material issues that we're dealing with, that people who are teaching feminist studies in the university, in graduate school, have no idea about because they are members of the bourgeoisie. So, my point is that we have to be back on the streets. We see some of that with the whole Black Lives Matter movement. We have to have activism on the street, we have to work in certain spaces like in the universities and in trade unions. So, it has to be multi-pronged. The writers, the artists, they're all very important to this. And then finally, the upcoming generations, the generation that comes behind us must be inspired to carry on the work. You know, no one generation can say, "this is the end. We have covered it. We've got it done". So, that intergenerational practice has to happen, too. These are some of the ways.

What are the possibilities and key challenges about re-imagination through literature? And how can memory and re-imagination help to commemorate past women's legacies, which are crucial to today's understanding of different layers/axes of inequalities, e.g. gender inequality, social class, race/ ethnicity and other social markers?

Yes, I am going to begin with imagination and reimagination. It is absolutely crucial that we imagine or reimagine a possibility, the kind of possibility that we want for ourselves, for our own lives and for the world. Because when you see the world as it is in its material manifestation and its three-dimensional manifestations, you might think, "okay, this is now really cruel", but how do you want it to be? Do you want gardens to be a park or a garden at every intersection or in the main square of the town? How do you see your world? What is it you want in your own personal world? And that is where the imagination comes in, because we have to imagine a way out of this. So, in terms of struggle, in terms of Black women's work, how do we get all of this? There's a term being used nowadays called withering, which is basically about something being eroded by constant brutality, so to speak. And I think it was in *Beloved* by Toni Morrison, where there was a woman in the woods. She's a speaker, an orator and she's talking about your hands, "look at your hands. Love your hands!". And I said, well, why should we love our hands? Why our hands? Are hands important? And then you have to begin to imagine our hands within the context of the time that the woman spoke and worked for other people. Now, they didn't really work for us. You're cooking for other people, you're washing other people's clothes, bathing other people's children, you're raising other people's children, you're taking care of other people's crops. And what you're using to do this is your hands, right? Also your mental capacity, but what's physically manifesting in it is the hands as the tools. And so, you know, this woman, this orator, and thus also the writer Toni Morrison, is asking people to imagine a new possibility for your life. So, I always think of grasping a new vision. And so someone like Phillis Wheatley[2] used her imagination. She created another possibility. And some people say, "oh, well, you know, she died when she was 34 and she died in poverty". Yeah, we all know that. But in a way, she's like this kind of mythical hero. She died when she was 33 or 34, but look at the legacy that she left behind. And maybe she knew that would be her task in life. That would be her purpose in life.

Now to the point of memory. We have to remember her as she remembered all the education that she got from the Wheatleys in Boston and then all her memory, the memory of her past, because she has a poem called *memory* in which she invoked this as her education. We can't fault her for this. She invoked the Greek goddess of memory, one of the nine muses. You know, here she's talking about memory. She's remembering her past in Senegal or Gambia. She was something like nine years old when she came to the Americas. But we also now have the task of remembering her and of trying to remember what she remembered and how she came out of that brutality. Or maybe she didn't come out of it and it was the brutality that also ushered in her demise.

In which ways do these legacies that form a central part of your work contribute to broadening hegemonic archives and to thinking new forms of the social?

Okay, so back to imagination, because of what we know about Phillis Wheatley and then I'm going to come to Henry Bibb. We have these scraps of information about Phillis. We know a lot more about her owners, the Wheatleys, because they were rich, White and literate. And you know, they left an archive behind on their own ships. So, we have these bits of information about her, which all the people who have worked on her put together to hopefully get a rounder picture of her. And maybe a century later, or not quite a century, but several decades

---

2 Phillis Wheatley, born free in 1753, was captured at the age of seven by slave traders from West Africa, Senegambia (modern-day Gambia/ Senegal) to Boston (Massachusetts) and became the first African American female poet of the 18th century, under the status of an enslaved person. With her work *Poems on Various Subjects, Religious and Moral* (1773), Wheatley led to a reconsideration of enslaved African Americans' inferiority on both sides of the Atlantic. Though subtly veiled through Christianity, her works persistently incorporated her individual enslavement experiences through themes of freedom and redemption. Footnote added by the interviewer.

later, you have Henry Bibb[3] with lots more archives, because he wrote his autobiography and he published a newspaper and lots more was written about him. And so we have these things and we really have to reinterpret them. These are not just people who were resisting White supremacy. Yes, for sure. But they were also creating a narrative of their own internal life, of their own personal life, which sort of goes against the Eurocentric form of thinking. So, if we come to Marie-Josèphe Angélique[4], she's also an 18th-century figure like Phillis. So, there's this fire and there are the archives that are created by the colonial powers. So, the governor has to write a report, the court documents are written by the judges. They have to write up the narrative and so on. But they have this perspective of the White male, White elite male, who think Black people are inferior, for one, and using the natural condition of Black people of enslavement. And the same archives we look at, we look at them differently. We try to look at them as much as possible through the eyes of Marie-Josèphe Angélique, wondering, "what was she thinking?". So, to your question, we are not necessarily expanding the archives, but expanding the interpretation of the archives, expanding the perspective of these archives to say, "okay, what did Black people think? What were their motivations?". You know, the intendant of New France at that time was a man, who said "Marie-Josèphe Angélique is a wicked negress. She set fire to the city". He had no sympathy for her. And [that] she was a slave and was unhappy. She made White people uncomfortable. She made them distressed. Because of her they couldn't sleep, couldn't work. And it is completely okay for him to have that. But that's his perspective. He's a ruler, he's an elitist and a White supremacist. Fine. That's your perspective. We come and we reinterpret. We offer a different interpretation. What was this woman feeling and

---

3 Henry Bibb, born 1815 into slavery in Shelby County (Kentucky), became renown as an anti-slavery lecturer, civil rights advocate, abolitionist, author, and editor in both the United States and Canada. After multiple escapes, he found his way to Upper Canada (nowadays Ontario) and published his slave narrative *Narrative of the Life and Adventures of Henry Bibb: An American Slave* (1849). In 1851, he established the first African Canadian newspaper *The Voice of the Fugitive*. Footnote added by the interviewer.

4 Marie-Josèphe Angélique, born 1705 in Portugal, was sold to Montreal in her late twenties. She was officially charged with the arson of Old Montreal in 1734. Despite a lack of evidence, she was hanged and burned by French colonial officials. Cooper challenges this dominant Canadian historical narrative and the Black enslaved female's subaltern identity in early Canada in her work *The Hanging of Angelique: The Untold Story of Canadian Slavery and the Burning of Old Montreal* (2006). Footnote added by the interviewer.

what was she thinking? As you were saying earlier, people have childhoods and because they're human, they need certain comforts. They have certain desires, they have lost a lot in their lives because they have suffered. What were their needs? It is our task to ask those questions.

You have done excessive work outside of the "ivory tower of academia", as you like to call it. Can you tell us how your personal background has informed your activism? And in this context, how can academia and activism work together?

I always felt when I went to university that everybody should know this knowledge, that everybody should have access to what I'm doing. I should share it with people. I couldn't understand that it was supposed to be this secret thing that's just kind of kept in a bubble. That I just didn't understand. And so I felt that, if I'm writing about whatever it is, or I'm studying, I can't go and give a lecture on it, but maybe I could present knowledge in another format. And through activism, it was usually through poetry or music, I could. You know, at the beginning I couldn't understand why knowledge was so encased in the academia. Sure, you could put it in a journal that nobody reads, or you could write a book. That is why to me, open access is great, because when you have a published journal, you have subscriptions, you have people who subscribe to you, you have libraries who buy it. But by and large, it still remains secret knowledge. How many people are going to read it? And a lot of good work has been researched, produced, and written. Nobody sees it. So, that's the legacy of the medieval university. It was a cloistered space. The scholars were monks and priests. They were very erudite people who knew a lot. But it was for that specific circle and that context. And that's how it evolved. Certain people or children of the elite will come to university and get this knowledge, and they learn Latin and whatever it is, and philosophy, and Greek history, and it stays there. Then they go and they become rulers, and ministers, and diplomats. It was always something for the elite. So, when people like me, the great unwashed, get sent to university, one thing that could happen is that you feel so alienated that you leave, you don't stick around. Well, if you stick around, it's a constant fight. And I did stick around and it was a constant fight for me. And so I needed another outlet. I needed another way of being. And that was in the community, that was through the arts, that was through activism. That was what sort of gave me a purpose to say, you know what, I can transfer or reinterpret some of what I'm doing here into this space. And the academy is changing quite a bit. I mean, I see people doing all kinds of things that I was thinking about, or I used to do as an undergraduate. I see people writing pieces on certain things that thirty years ago or even twenty years ago, they wouldn't get the support to do. So, it's changing quite a bit, or it has changed. But for me, not fast enough. Because the hypocrisy still remains in academia. You know, I just don't want to be a part of it. I don't want to be a part of that hypocrisy.

As a founding figure of the Toronto Dub Poets Collective (2002), you helped in situating the dub poetry movement in Canada and organized the International Dub Poetry Festival and Conference throughout the years. How would you describe the inherently different experience of an embodied performance in the art (of dub poetry) and the experience of writing about real-life female legacies (such as Phillis Wheatley, Marie-Josèphe Angélique, or Chloe Cooley)?

I like performing, and it doesn't necessarily mean I'm running all over the stage. For me it means having the words flowing through me. What do I do with my arms, my hands, my knees, or my feet? I could be running across the stage. Performance for me means making the words live in my body, making my body express them. That's what it means to me. And also what songs want to come out? Because I may read the same poem and if I read it sometime, it's going to be different because there might be a sound that wants to be expressed in a particular time when I'm reading that. Or there could be an image that comes in my mind because sometimes as I'm reading, images will come in my mind that perhaps have nothing to do with the poem that I'm reading. Although I'm sure it has to do with it, you know, to be on stage with a poem and then my imagination is actually somewhere else. I could see myself flying through the sky or I could see Harriet Tubman walking in the room. I'm thinking, "oh my God, is that Harriet Tubman who just walked in?". At this point, it has nothing to do with Harriet Tubman. Or does it? I don't know. So, that's what reading does for me. Sitting down to write a piece, a book or an article is a reflective experience. It's also one – obviously – of the imagination, because I have to think "how is this going to be? What's the purpose of this character? What does this character want to say?". Well, it is a time of reflection and just really for everything, it is the imagination and getting into the body, getting into the spirit. And I feel like everything we do, academic writing, everything, has a spiritual dimension to it because we are calling. We are calling in new worlds, we are creating new worlds. You're the creator, because what we do, whatever writing we do, we are creating something. And through this act of creation, we are ushering in something new. We also tend to think of scientific writing or academic writing as something without creativity. It's an extremely creative endeavor. Even the way you structure the work as "this is going to go first as a section. What am I going to talk about here?". It is an act of the imagination. Comparing writing and performing, writing for me could take weeks, months, or years. If I'm willing to write something, I have to think about it first. It's like a mental exercise. I'm writing a poem now. Someone asked me to write a poem as a kind of praise for somebody else. And so mentally, I'm constructing in my head what it is I want to say and how I'm going to bring in all these ideas. I haven't written anything down yet on paper, I think I will do that next week. But once I sit down, sketch up my ideas on paper, I know new things are going to emerge before I write this poem. So, the writing for me, it's in several stages. It could be spontaneous, it could be something that happens like that. But it's also a very reflective kind of thing, too. So, if I now take that same piece of writing and I'm going to do a performance of the poem, it's going to be a different experience.

Intuitive Feminism[1]

María Galindo

It is powerful because it is inappropriate
It is powerful because it is the personal reading of your mother's tits.
Because it is the personal reading of your sister's market bag and pregnancy.
It is powerful because it is not an acquired rational instruction like behavioral instructions are acquired.
Nobody taught it to you, you didn't learn it on a Monday, you made it yourself, like when you cook, like when you bake bread.
It is not only useful to understand your friend, your grandmother, or your neighbor.
It serves for an infinity of things in life.
It is like a key,
like a key,
like a yeast
like a pinch of salt.
It is potent because it is an infallible vomitive to purge the feminine duty to be and expel it by heaving through the mouth, anus, or both simultaneously.
It serves to deflate egos, block violences, demystify bosses and loves, disconnect discourses, disarm traps, set traps, weave complicities, break undesirable bonds.
Intuitive feminism could be called a thousand other ways, the name is the least, the important thing is to know it, to understand it, to enjoy it, to locate it, and to feel its thunderous historical force.
The name is the least important thing, the interesting thing is to be able to perceive its passionate palpitation in the beds and in the classrooms, in the markets, and in the courts.
It could really be called something else.

---

1 Translated from Spanish by Julia Roth.

What is important is to feel its capacity to inhabit an underworld and to move there, removing family, social, neighborhood, and affective structures, unsettling the very foundations of its place and destabilizing soils from the subsoil.

Intuitive feminism is invisible to the eyes of the media, invisible to the eyes of academia, invisible to the microscope, unnoticed by borders and other forms of control.

The media needs to say that we lack self-esteem, ideas, or location in the world and that is why they killed us. We know that we were killed for rebellion on the day we decided to enjoy life. That certainty is given to us by intuitive feminism. It is not a feminism of banner, it is a feminism of look, of gesture in the mouth, it is a feminism of distance or corporal proximity. It is a way of standing before life and death. It is a way of standing before others, them and her, it is a way of embracing and understanding the facts.

Intuitive feminism is massive and comes from below and not from above. It is therefore plebeian, bastard, without legitimacy, without academic title, without bombastic doctoral credentials. Without an author to sustain it, although its sustenance is dense, deep, and historical.

Intuitive feminism could argue with Spivak's thesis of the subaltern's muteness.

It would tell her, for example, that one speaks with the body.

That one refutes with one's ass.

That history is made with the tits.

And that there is a politics that is the politics of touch.

Its contents are not derived from a stupid workshop on empowerment and self-esteem paid for by the *oenegé* [NGO] of the day with funding from the World Bank.

Intuitive feminism is inappropriate. It does not fit into the policies of states, of UN Women-type organizations, nor of those who need to qualify us as driven by their useless act of salvation.

Its contents are not in a book neither by Butler, nor by Segato, nor by any other author because it is not constituted by philosophical, historical, or psychoanalytical theories. It is constituted by the consistency of rebellion made flesh of ordinary women.

It is constituted by the rebelliousness when the high-street trans woman takes to the street.

It not only embodies women's bodies, but also understands that down here it circulates through women, girls, children, trans, *maricas*, and other monsters.
It comes crushing police stations and justice apparatuses in every state.
It comes demanding a billion hours to declare one by one the bruises and say that we are not willing to take one more punch, not one more kick.
It looks like a woman with a baby in her arms, without a job and without housing, who seed capital in life is a lot of desire to live and a lot of anger.
It looks like the whore on the corner who knows everything and can give you lessons in masculinity that would put all androcentrism in crisis.
It looks like the peasant woman who knows that all sovereignty begins and ends on the land.

Intuitive feminisms could be infinite, or at least difficult to enumerate, they escape any attempt at classification. Counting them becomes unnecessary. How many women/*maricas*/trans in rebellion there are in a room, that's how many intuitive feminisms you will have to deal with as a teacher, as a boss, or as a judge.

It's handmade, personal, manual.
It is a collage that glues ideas with feelings and darns feelings with experiences, images with sensations making a deformed chaotic composition that does not admit rigidity, nor unique forms.
It is powerful because it does not require consensus, but connection. Emotional connection, capacity to identify with the other through rebellion.
A connection that passes through the solidarity of staying with them or her when they or she is threatened, when they or she aborts, when they or she rebels. Their rebellion ignites yours as when you share a lighter or a cigarette. You don't even know how you decide to share a path and action without a second thought.

Intuitive feminism is massive. It circulates in the neighborhoods, in the markets, in the parties, and in all kinds of spaces in an underground way without a letter of introduction, or a sign on the chest. Intuitive feminism is not ideological, but that does not mean it is not political. It is very political but from a form of politics of tact. That form of politics makes us sisters when we take each others' hands to cross the border of what is allowed.
Intuitive feminism is the huge disobedience that inhabits us women and others today and that comes out through our eyes and the posture of our hips.

I know that it is invisible to you and that you think I am hallucinating.
Of course, I am hallucinating, because I see it, I touch it, I smell it and I name it.
I get on the boat that sails against the current.
I cross the bridge in the opposite direction
I defy one thing and another and go towards what seems to be a route that heads nowhere in a journey of no return.
I feel like I'm on the border of Mexico and the U.S. being Honduran,
I seem to be on a boat in the Mediterranean about to sink.
I seem to be where there is no place to be
Where it is forbidden to be.
Where it is dangerous to be.
It seems as if I were in the anteroom of death when it is the anteroom of life.
That is precisely where intuitive feminism is; where it seems that there is no place to be and at the same time the only place worth being.

Feminismo Intuitivo

Es potente porque es inapropiable
Es potente porque es la lectura personal de las tetas de tu madre.
Porque es la lectura personal de la bolsa del mercado y del embarazo de tu hermana.
Es potente porque no es una instrucción racional adquirida como se adquieren las instrucciones de comportamiento.
Nadie te lo enseño, no lo aprendiste un lunes, lo fabricaste tu misme, como cuando cocinas, como cuando haces pan.
No solo sirve para entender a tu amiga, tu abuela o tu vecina.
Sirve para una infinidad de cosas en la vida.
Es como una clave,
como una llave,
como una levadura
como una pisca de sal.
Es potente porque es un vomitivo infalible para purgar el deber ser femenino y expulsarlo con arcadas por la boca, el ano o ambos simultáneamente.
Sirve para desinflar egos, bloquear violencias, desmitificar jefes y amores, desconectar discursos, desarmar trampas, armar trampas, tejer complicidades, romper vínculos indeseables.

El feminismo intuitivo podría llamarse de mil otras maneras, el nombre es lo de menos lo importante es saberlo, entenderlo, disfrutarlo, ubicarlo y sentir su estruendosa fuerza histórica.
El nombre es lo de menos, lo interesante es poder percibir su palpitar apasionado en las camas y en las aulas, en los mercados y en los juzgados.
Podría realmente llamarse de otra manera.
Lo importante es sentir su capacidad de habitar un submundo y moverse ahí removiendo estructuras familiares, sociales, barriales, y afectivas descolocando los cimientos mismos de su lugar y desestabilizando suelos desde el subsuelo.
El feminismo intuitivo es invisible a los ojos de los medios de comunicación, es invisible a los ojos de la academia, es invisible al microscopio, pasa inadvertido por fronteras y otras formas de control.
Los medios necesitan decir que carecemos de autoestima, de ideas o de ubicación en el mundo y que por eso nos mataron. Nosotres sabemos que nos mataron por rebeldía en el día en el que habíamos decidido disfrutar de la vida. Esa certeza nos la da el feminismo intuitivo.
No es un feminismo de pancarta, es un feminismo de mirada, de gesto en la boca, es un feminismo de distancia o proximidad corporal. Es una forma de pararse ante la vida y la muerte. Es una forma de pararse ante el otre y la otra, es una forma de abrazar y de entender los hechos.

El feminismo intuitivo es masivo y viene de abajo y no de arriba. Es pues plebeyo, bastardo, sin legitimidad, sin título académico, sin credencial doctoral rimbombante. Sin autora que lo sustente, aunque su sustento sea denso, profundo e histórico.
El feminismo intuitivo le podría discutir a la Spivak su tesis de la mudes del subalterno.
Le diría por ejemplo que se habla con el cuerpo.
Que se rebate con el poto
Que se hace historia con las tetas.
Y que hay una política que es la política del tacto.

Sus contenidos no son derivados de un estúpido taller de empoderamiento y autoestima pagado por la oenegé de turno con financiamiento del Banco Mundial.
El feminismo intuitivo es inapropiable. No encaja en las políticas de los estados, de los organismos tipo ONU Mujeres, ni de quienes necesitan calificarnos

como urgidas de su inservible acto de salvación.

Sus contenidos no están en un libro ni de Butler, ni de Segato, ni de autora alguna porque no está constituido por teorías filosóficas, históricas o psicoanalíticas. Está constituido por la consistencia que tiene la rebeldía hecha carne de mujer de a pie.

Está constituido por la rebeldía que fabrica la trans de a pie con su pie.

No solo encarna cuerpos de mujeres, sino que comprende que aquí abajo circula por mujeres, niñas, niñes, trans, maricas y otros monstruos.

Viene colapsando las comisarías de policía y los aparatos de justicia de todos los estados.

Viene exigiendo mil millones de horas para declarar uno a uno los moretones y decir que no estamos diespuestes a recibir ni un solo golpe más, ni una patada más.

Su pinta es la de una mujer con bebe en brazos sin trabajo y sin vivienda que tiene como capital para empezar la vida muchas ganas de vivir y mucha bronca.

Su pinta es la de la puta de la esquina que se las sabe todas y puede darte lecciones de masculinidad que pondrían en crisis todo androcentrismo.

Su pinta es la de la campesina que sabe que toda soberanía empieza y termina en la tierra.

Los feminismos intuitivos podrían ser infinitos, o por lo menos de difícil enumeración, escapan a todo intento de clasificación. Contarlos se hace innecesario. Cuantas mujeres/maricas/trans en rebelión haya en una sala, esa es la cantidad de feminismos intuitivos con las que tendrás que lidiar como maestro, como jefe o como juez.

Es artesanal, personal, manual.

Es un collage que pega ideas con sentimientos y zurce sentimientos con experiencias, imágenes con sensaciones haciendo una composición caótica deforme que no admite rigidez, ni formas únicas.

Es potente porque no requiere consenso, sino conexión. Conexión emocional, capacidad de identificarse con la y le otre a través de la rebeldía.

Una conexión que pasa por la solidaridad de quedarte con elle o ella cuando la amenazan, cuando aborta, cuando se rebela. Su rebeldía enciende la tuya como cuando se comparte un encendedor o un cigarro.

No sabes ni como decides compartir camino y acción sin pensártelo dos veces.

El feminismo intuitivo es masivo. Circula en los barrios, en los mercados, en las fiestas, y en todo tipo de espacios de forma subterránea sin carta de presentación, ni letrero en el pecho. El feminismo intuitivo no es ideológico, pero no por eso no es político. Es muy político pero desde una forma de política del tacto. Esa forma de política que nos hermana cuando nos damos la mano para cruzar la frontera de lo permitido.

El feminismo intuitivo es la descomunal desobediencia que nos habita hoy a las mujeres y les otres y que se nos sale por los ojos y la postura de las caderas.

Yo se que les resulta invisible y que piensan que estoy alucinando.

Claro que estoy alucinando, porque lo veo, lo toco, lo huelo y lo nombro.

Me subo al barco que navega a contracorriente.

Atravieso el puente en sentido contrario

Desafío una y otra cosa y voy hacia lo que parece ser una ruta que se dirige hacia ninguna parte en un viaje sin retorno.

Parece que estuviera en la frontera de México con EEUU siendo hondureña,

Parece que estuviera en una patera en el mediterráneo a punto de hundirme

Parece que estuviera donde no hay que estar

Donde está prohibido estar.

Donde es peligroso estar.

Parece que estuviera en la antesala de la muerte, cuando es la antesala de la vida

Ahí es donde justamente está el feminismo intuitivo; donde parece que no hay que estar y al mismo tiempo en el único lugar que vale la pena estar.

Contributors

Afua Cooper is a poet, spoken word artist, author, scholar, and historian. Her many books range across genres such as poetry, history, fiction, and children's literature. She served as the Poet Laureate of Halifax Regional Municipality for the 2018–2020 term. She is a founder of the Canadian Dub Poetry Movement and recipient of numerous prizes and awards, including the Portia White Prize, the J.M. Abraham Atlantic Poetry prize, the Bob Marley Award, the Royal Society of Canada's J.B. Tyrrell Historical Medal for Outstanding Contributions to Canadian history and was a finalist for the Governor General's Literary Prize. Her poems have been included in numerous literary anthologies and recorded on four CDs. Afua Cooper holds a PhD in history and is expert on Black Canadian history. She is a full professor at Dalhousie University where she holds a Killam Research Chair. Further, she is the principal investigator for *A Black People's History of Canada*, a project that engages in new research on Black history, accompanied by a new Black history curriculum. Her latest book of poetry, *The Halifax Explosion*, is set to be released in 2023.

Anielle Franco is an educator, journalist, writer, feminist, mother, and activist from Brazil. In 2023, she was appointed Minister of Racial Equality in the newly elected Lula government. With her family, Anielle Franco founded the Marielle Franco Institute, an organization created to honor the legacy of her sister Marielle Franco, and acted as its Executive Director until the end of 2022. She talks and writes about Black feminism, gender and racial equality, and political violence of gender and race, and she holds an MA in Ethno-racial relations from the Federal Center of Technological Education Celso Suckow da Fonseca in Rio de Janeiro.

Anna-Lena Glesinski is a doctoral student at the University of Hamburg, Germany. Her dissertation project was financed by the Heinrich Böll Foundation and the equality fund of the University of Hamburg. Her research focuses on ecocriticism, indigenous literature, and Latin American feminisms. She was co-founder of the social association CIEL e.V. as well as the feminist collective Miradas Feministas, and currently volunteers as co-coordinator for Mexico and Central America at Amnesty International Germany.

Audes Jiménez González is an Afro-descendant activist, human rights defender, and scholar aligned with Black and decolonial feminisms. She holds a Master in Caribbean Studies from the Universidad Nacional de Colombia and served as coordinator of the Colombian Truth Commission's territorial offices in Atlántico, Norte de Bolívar, and San Andrés.

César Torres-Cruz is associate researcher at the Centro de Investigaciones y Estudios de Género (CIEG) at the Universidad Nacional Autónoma de México (UNAM). He is a cuir-feminist-sociologist scholar interested in gender, health, and sexuality studies. He takes part in The National System of Researchers in Mexico's Science Secretariat (SNI-CONACyT).

Daniela Gloss Nuñez holds a PhD in Social Sciences at the University of Guadalajara and is an associate professor and researcher at the Interdisciplinary Center for Social Formation and Vinculation at ITESO, Guadalajara. Her research interests are focused on emotions and the defense of place in socio environmental conflicts in Mexico.

Edith Otero Quezada is a PhD candidate in Interamerican Studies and a member of the research training group "Experiencing Gender" at the Interdisciplinary Center for Gender Studies at Universität Bielefeld. She was a scholarship holder of the German Foundation Rosa Luxemburg Stiftung (2017–2020). Her research interests are postcolonial and decolonial feminist epistemologies, political subjectivity, (post)memory, guerrillas, and social movements, especially in Latin America and Central America.

Fátima Elizondo Rodríguez holds a BA in Humanities and Philosophy from Universidad Centroamericana in Nicaragua as well as a double-degree MA in Interamerican Studies from the Universität Bielefeld and Interamerican Literatures from the Universidad de Guadalajara. She is an autonomous researcher whose current interests are language and literature, social movements, indigenous knowledge, and intercultural and intermedia topics, especially in the peripheries.

Hortensia Moreno-Esparza is editor of the journal Debate Feminista at the Centro de Investigaciones y Estudios de Género (CIEG) at the Universidad Nacional Autónoma de México (UNAM). She is interested in gender, sexuality, sports, and education studies. She takes part in The National System of Researchers in Mexico's Science Secretariat (SNI-CONACyT).

India S. Lenear is a third-year PhD student at the department of Political Science at Rutgers University. Her work broadly studies Women and Politics, Black Politics, and American Politics. More specifically, her work focuses on Black Women's studies, Body Politics, and Black Feminism(s). Her research examines Black women's political behavior, ideology, and participation through Black feminist theoretical lenses. She holds a BA in Political Science from North Carolina Central University. Email: India.S.Lenear@rutgers.edu

Itxaso García Chapinal holds an MA in Interamerican Studies from the Bielefeld University and is currently a PhD candidate at the Bielefeld Graduate School in History and Sociology. She focuses on indigenous knowledges, environmental topics, and intercultural projects, especially in Mexico.

Julia Roth is a professor of American studies with a focus on gender studies and director of the Center for InterAmerican Studies (CIAS) at Universität Bielefeld, where she is also PI of the graduate school "Experiencing Gender". She was PI of the ZiF research group "Global Contestations of Women's and Gender Rights". Her research interests are gender approaches, intersectionality theorizing, gender and citizenship, right-wing populism and gender, migrant knowledges, and new feminist movements. Alongside her academic work, she organizes cultural-political events.

Juliana González Villamizar is researcher and doctoral candidate at Justus-Liebig-Universität Gießen in Germany, and she collaborates with the Instituto Colombo-Alemán para la Paz — CAPAZ. Her research focuses on the mainstreaming of intersectionality in the Colombian Truth Commission. Her work incorporates participative-action methodologies, aiming to build ethical solidarity among activist and knowledge-production networks.

Julieta Paredes Carvajal is an indigenous woman from the Aymara people of Bolivia, activist, creator of communitarian feminism, and author of books on poetry, sexuality, politics, feminist education, and communitarian feminism. She is a doctoral student at the Psychology Institute at the Universidade de São Paulo (Brazil) in the area of "Problemas Teóricos e Metodológicos da Pesquisa Psicológica". She was also co-founder of *Mujeres Creando*. She is currently a member of *Comunidad Mujeres Creando Comunidad*. Representing the movement and social organization Abya Yala Communitarian Feminism, she has published several texts on the issue, among them: "Hilando fino desde el feminismo comunitario" (2009), "El desafío de la despatriarcalización" (2016), and "Para descolonizar el feminismo" (2020). She is a singer-songwriter and graffiti artist who turns "her fears and pain into an inexhaustible force that does not give up".

Larissa Satico Ribeiro Higa is an autonomous researcher. She has a PhD in Brazilian Literature (2019, University of São Paulo) focused on sexual violence in contemporary Brazilian author Sérgio Sant'Anna's literature. For nine months (2015–2016), she was a visiting scholar at the University of Minnesota (USA). Her MA in Literary Theory and History (2011, State University of Campinas) is focused on the politics and aesthetics of Patrícia Galvão's literature. Her current interests are decolonial and intersectional feminism as well as contemporary Brazilian literature written by women.

LASTESIS is a Chilean interdisciplinary women's collective consisting of Daffne Valdés Vargas, Paula Cometa Stange, Lea Cáceres Diaz, and Sibila Sotomayor Van Rysseghem. The collective is focused on disseminating feminist theory and thought by means of performances. These artistic interventions leverage different approaches in the performing arts, employing sounds, choreography, graphics, and textile design. The performance "Un Violador en tu Camino," created by LASTESIS, was reproduced by women all over the world as a form to performatively respond to and resist gender-based sexual violence.

La Reyna y La Real are: **La Real** (Yadira Pintado Lazcano) was born in the neighborhood of Jesus Maria in Havana and studied psychology. Before she decided to dedicate herself to music, she trained as a social worker. **La Reyna** (Reyna Hernández Sandoval) was born in the Havana neighborhood of Luyanó. She is a technician in Industrial Chemistry and a mother of one. The two artists met at the rap club Club Karachi led by DJ Neuris. After collaborating on several songs and stage performances, they decided to join as a duo in 2012, making the group official in 2013. So far, the duo has published the albums *Beef con Kriño* (2015), *Miky y Repa* (2017, TumiMusic) *Mírame* (2020), and *Dale Despacio* (2021). They are considered the most well-known feminist rap group of the second generation, performing e.g. at the gala of the Jornada of the Plataforma Afrofeminista Cubana. In 2022 and 2023, La Reyna y La Real toured Europe and gave concerts in Berlin and at several Swedish venues.

Ligia Fabris is a professor at the Rio de Janeiro Law School of the Getulio Vargas Foundation and coordinator of the Diversity and Inclusion Program. She is a PhD candidate at the Humboldt Universität zu Berlin and holds a Master of Law from PUC-Rio. She is also a co-founder of the Rio de Janeiro State Forum for More Women in Politics. Currently, she is a member of the National Observatory of Women in Politics, which is operated by the Brazilian Chamber of Deputies. Her main research and teaching focus are Gender and Law, Feminist Legal Theory, Women's Political Representation, Gender-Based Political Violence, and Rights of LGBTQ+ persons.

Lívia de Souza Lima is a PhD Candidate at the Faculty of Linguistics and Literary Studies at the University of Bielefeld and a doctoral fellow of the Rosa Luxemburg Foundation. Her work is centered around the interconnection between the topics of political representation, Black feminism, intersectionality, and radical democracy. Her current research examines the exercise of political representation by Black women in Brazil and the (re)imagination of institutional politics. She is also a co-founder of the Hamburg-based feminist collective Miradas Feministas, a group that seeks to integrate activism and academia by employing the idea that Latin American feminist activist strategies are a source of knowledge.

Mara Viveros Vigoya holds a PhD in Anthropology (EHESS, Paris) and is a professor at the Faculty of Human Sciences of the Universidad Nacional de Colombia at the School of Gender Studies, of which she has been director on three occasions and is the current director. Her career as a researcher and teacher has been guided by a critical feminist project, both in its theoretical, political, and ethical dimensions. She has been a member of the School of Social Science at the Institute for Advanced Study, Princeton (2014–2015) and President of the Latin American Studies Association, LASA (2019–2020). Her current areas of interest are the "Black" middle classes in Colombia, anti-racist ideologies and practices, and the intersections between class, gender, sexuality, and race in Latin American social dynamics. She is the author of *El oxímoron de las clases medias negras. Movilidad social e Interseccionalidad* (Editorial Universidad de Guadalajara, 2021), *Les Couleurs de la masculinité* (Paris: La découverte, 2018), *As cores da Masculinidade* (Rio de Janeiro: Papéis Selvagens Edições, 2018) and editor of *Black Feminism: Critical Theory, Violence, and Racism. Conversations between Angela Davis and Gina Dent* (Bogotá: UNAL, 2019).

María Lugones was an Argentine feminist philosopher, activist, and a professor of Comparative Literature and of Women's Studies at Carleton College in Northfield and at Binghamton University in New York State. Lugones was part of the Latin American Subaltern Studies Group and advanced Latino philosophy in theorizing various forms of resistance against multiple oppressions. She is known for her work on decolonial feminism and for developing the concept of the "coloniality of gender," departing from Aníbal Quijano's concept of the coloniality of power to elaborate, from an intersectional feminist lens, on the very diverse gender positions coloniality has created, and emphasize the fundamental role of gender for colonial-racial hierarchies. Among her most influential publications are: (2007) "Heterosexualism and the Colonial/Modern Gender System." In: Hypatia 22/1, (2008) "Colonialidad y género." In: Tabula Rasa 9 (2010) "Toward a Decolonial Feminism." In: Hypatia, (2020) "Gender and Universality in Colonial Methodology." In: Critical Philosophy of Race 8/1–2.

María José Oyarzún Solís is a philosophy teacher, a graduate of the University of Valparaiso (Chile), and a politician of the party *Revolución Democrática*. She has worked as a university professor of Feminism and Sexual Diversity, established the first Feminist Library, and co-founded the Interdisciplinary Gender Network of the University of Valparaíso. She was also part of the national board of the political movement *Marca AC* and spokesperson of the network *Bancada por la Asamblea Constituyente*. In 2021, she was elected a member of the Chilean Constitutional Convention representing the Valparaíso Region.

María Galindo is a Bolivian activist, radical feminist, writer and communicator, as well as co-founder and member of the *Mujeres Creando* collective. Some of her publications: *No se puede descolonizar sin despatriarcalizar* (2013), *Espejito mágico* (2015, with María Renne and Galindo Neder), and with Sonia Sánchez: *Nin-*

guna mujer nace para puta (2007). Her book *Feminismo bastardo* (2021) was published in six countries.

Nadia E. Brown is a professor of Government, chair of the Women's and Gender Studies Program, and affiliate in the African American Studies program at Georgetown University, USA. Dr. Brown is a founding board member of Women Also Know Stuff. She is also one of the American politics editors at The Monkey Cage. Dr. Brown's research interests lie broadly in identity politics, legislative studies, and Black women's studies. She is the author of *Sisters in the Statehouse: Black Women & Legislative Decision Making* (2014) and co-author of *Sister Style: The Politics of Appearance for Black Women Political Elites* (2021)

Nicole Schwabe is a historian at Bielefeld University (Germany) and has worked on the history of social movements and the history of education in Chile. She is currently writing her PhD thesis on the history of education in the FRG and the GDR (1949–1990) and deals with global imagination in discourses on educational policy.

Rita Laura Segato is an Argentine anthropologist, feminist activist, Senior Researcher of the Brazilian Council of Sciences and professor emerita of anthropology and the graduate programs in Bioethics and Human Rights at the University of Brasilia. Her work focuses on gender issues in indigenous, African American and Latin American communities, gender violence, and the relationship between gender, racism and coloniality. In 2018, she received the Latin American and Caribbean Social Science Prize CLACSO 50 years and in 2020 the Fanon Prize from the Caribbean Association of Philosophers. She has served as Aníbal Quijano Chair at the Museo Reina Sofía of Madrid since 2018. Some of her publications include *Santos e Daimones* (1995), *Las estructuras elementales de la violencia* (2003), *La nación y sus otros: raza, etnicidad y diversidad religiosa en tiempos de políticas de la identidad* (2007), *La escritura en el cuerpo de las mujeres asesinadas en Ciudad Juárez* (2013), *Las nuevas formas de la guerra y el cuerpo de las mujeres* (2014), *La guerra contra las mujeres* (2017 and forthcoming the English edition by Polity), *Contrapedagogías de la crueldad* (2018), *La crítica de la colonialidad en ocho ensayos* (2018 and 2022 the English edition by Routledge), *Escenas de un pensamiento incómodo* (2022) y *Expuesta a la muerte* (2023).

Safa Al-Dilaimi holds an MA in British and American Studies and is a member of the transdisciplinary Black Americas Network at the Center for InterAmerican Studies at Bielefeld University. Throughout her MA program, she specialized in the works of Afua Cooper. Her research interests comprise the link between the atrocities of the past (in the African American context) and their inherent aftermath in the presence, memory politics, activism in commemoration, and autobiographic re-imaginations of translocal legacies. In particular, the eye-witness mode (of enslaved children) in the transmission of agency, female subjectivity, and community empowerment.

Sandra Heidl (she, they) is a psychologist, journalist, editor of gender issues, and researcher. Sandra holds a BA in Psychology from the University of Havana (1996), a Diploma in Gender and Communication from José Martí International Institute of Journalism (2005), and an MA in Gender Studies from the University of Havana (2008). Sandra is the author of *Negra cubana tenía que ser* (Ediciones Wanafrica, 2020) as well as the founder of *Afrocubanas* afrocubanas.com and of the online dictionary and archive *Directorio de Afrocubanas* directoriodeafrocubanas.com.

Saskia Bante holds a BA in British and American Studies and Sociology and an MA in British and American Studies, Social Sciences, and Educational Studies. She studied at Bielefeld University and at the Pontifícia Universidade Católica do Rio de Janeiro (PUC-Rio) in Brazil. She currently works as a teacher at a comprehensive school in Germany.

Victoria González-Rivera grew up in Matagalpa, Nicaragua, in the 1970s and early 1980s. She holds a PhD in Latin American History from Indiana University. In 2001, she co-edited the book *Radical Women in Latin America. Left and Right*. Her second book, *Before the Revolution. Women's Rights and Right-Wing Politics in Nicaragua, 1821–1979*, was published by Penn State University Press in 2011. With the support of an American Council of Learned Societies (ACLS) Fellowship, she is completing a third book titled *500 Years of Western Nicaraguan LGBTQIA+ History*. She is also the author of the 2020 essay "Why My Nicaraguan Father Did Not 'See' His Blackness and How Latinx Anti-Black Racism Feeds on Racial Silence[1]". She is an associate professor at the Department of Chicana and Chicano Studies at San Diego State University.

Yuderkys Espinosa-Miñoso is an Afro-Caribbean anti-racist and decolonial theorist, teacher, researcher, and popular educator. She is one of the forerunners and main exponents of anti-racist and decolonial feminism in Latin America and the Caribbean. She is a founding member of the Grupo Latinoamericano de Estudios, Formación y Acción Feminista (GLEFAS) and the director of the Caribbean Institute of Decolonial Thought and Research del GLEFAS. Her main contributions consist in advancements towards a criticism of the coloniality of feminist reason. She is a frequent guest speaker at universities, organizations, and social movements in Latin America, the US, and Europe. In 2021, she obtained a scholarship from the Käte Hamburger Center for Apocalyptic and Postapocalyptic Studies for a research stay at the University of Heidelberg. Her texts have been translated into English, German, Portuguese, French, and Italian.

---

1   https://medium.com/@victoriagonzalezrivera/why-my-nicaraguan-father-did-not-see-his-blackness-and-how-latinx-anti-black-racism-feeds-on-738249ddd100

[transcript]

PUBLISHING.
KNOWLEDGE. TOGETHER.

transcript publishing stands for a multilingual transdisciplinary programme in the social sciences and humanities. Showcasing the latest academic research in various fields and providing cutting-edge diagnoses on current affairs and future perspectives, we pride ourselves in the promotion of modern educational media beyond traditional print and e-publishing. We facilitate digital and open publication formats that can be tailored to the specific needs of our publication partners.

OUR SERVICES INCLUDE

- partnership-based publishing models
- Open Access publishing
- innovative digital formats: HTML, Living Handbooks, and more
- sustainable digital publishing with XML
- digital educational media
- diverse social media linking of all our publications

Visit us online: www.transcript-publishing.com

Find our latest catalogue at www.transcript-publishing.com/newbookspdf